AF446329

DISCOVERING BIBLICAL TREASURES

UNDERSTANDING MARK

A COMMENTARY ON THE GOSPEL OF MARK
USING ANCIENT BIBLE STUDY METHODS

Michael Harvey Koplitz

This edition 2022 copyright © by Michael H. Koplitz

All rights reserved. No part of this publication may be reproduced or transmitted in any form or by any means without the permission of the publisher.

All Scripture quotations, unless otherwise noted, are taken from the *New American Standard Bible®*, Copyright © 1960, 1962, 1963, 1968, 1971, 1972, 1973, 1975, 1977, 1995 by the Lockman Foundation. Used by permission (www.Lockman.org)

The NASB uses italic to indicate words that have been added for clarification. Citations are shown with large capital letters.

Published by Michael H. Koplitz

Table of Contents

INTRODUCTION

While I was attending Seminary earning my M. Div. degree, I started to question what the instructors and reference books were saying about the Scriptures. One of the ideas being offered then was that the Bible was full of errors and not factual. I found that attitude disturbing for Seminary instructors to be teaching. After all, the Seminary experience is to train pastors to go out into God's world and preach the Bible. How can you preach the Bible if you believe what these instructors are teaching? The methods that were being taught to examine the Bible just seemed inaccurate to me.

After graduating from Seminary, I spent much time reading different views about the Bible. I eventually read the Zohar. According to Kabbalists, this collection of Midrashim is considered the secret work of the Torah. Also, I learned quite a bit about Messianic Judaism. Their view of the Bible is quite different from the Seminary view.

I decided that the biblical interpretation that was being taught in the Seminary was not the biblical interpretation the people heard when Jesus Christ (whose Hebraic name is Yeshua) preached. I went on a quest to learn what the people of Yeshua's day thought about Scripture and what they thought when the Scriptures were read. This quest led me to Dr. Anne Davis and The Bible Learning University. Dr. Davis was in search of the same thing I was searching for. She had made many discoveries that helped me in my quest. I earned the Ph. D. degree from The Bible Learning University in Hebraic Studies in Christianity, concentrating on ancient Bible Studies methods.

Finally, I found someone who believed that the Church had placed almost 1900 years of theological ideas about the Scriptures and, in many places, possibly distorting its original meaning. What is also vital to hear is that the basic tenants of Yeshua as God's Messiah, my Lord, and Savior are in the Bible. My faith in Yeshua is more vital now that I have learned from Dr. Davis how to study the Scriptures in the same manner that the people did in Yeshua's day.

I have included an article that describes the differences between Greek learning methods and Hebraic learning methods. Please do not skip this chapter unless you are familiar with ancient Bible study methods. If you do, then the analysis and commentary that follows may become difficult for you to understand.

Our God is vast and infinite, and so is His Word. May God bless you in your discovery of what God's Word is about.

THE MAIN DIFFERENCES BETWEEN THE GREEK METHOD AND THE HEBRAIC METHOD OF TEACHING

Once a student becomes aware of these two teaching styles, the student will determine if the class attended or if a book was read, whether the teaching method is either a Greek or Hebraic method. In the Greek manner, the instructor is always right because of advanced knowledge. In the college situation, it is because the Professor has his/her Ph.D. in some area of study, so one assumes that he or she knows everything about the topic. For example, Rodney Dangerfield played the role of a middle-aged man going to college. His English midterm was to write about Kurt Vonnegut Jr. Since he did not understand any of Vonnegut's books, he hired Vonnegut himself to write the midterm. When he received the paper from the English Professor told Dangerfield that whoever wrote the paper knew nothing about Vonnegut. The Professor's words are an example of the Greek method of teaching. Did the Ph.D. English Professor think that she knew more about Vonnegut's writings than Vonnegut did? [1]

In the Greek teaching method, the Professor or the instructor claims to be the authority. If one attends a Bible study class and the class leader says, "I will teach you the only way to understand this biblical book," you may want to consider the implications. This method is standard since most Seminaries and Bible colleges teach a Greek mode of learning, which is the same method the Church has been utilizing for centuries.

Hebraic teaching methods are different. The teacher wants the students to challenge what they hear. It is through questioning that a student can learn. The teacher also wants his/her students to excel to a point where the student becomes the teacher.

If two rabbis come together to discuss a Scripture passage, the result will be at least ten different opinions. All points of view are acceptable if each is supported by biblical evidence. It is permissible

---

[1] *Back to School*. Performed by Rodney Dangerfield. Hollywood: CA: Paper Clip Productions, 1986. DVD.

and encouraged that students develop many ideas. There is a depth to God's Word, and God wants us to find all His messages contained in the Scripture.

Seeking out the meaning of the Scriptures beyond the literal meaning is essential to understand God's Word fully.[2] The Greek method of learning the Scriptures has prevailed over the centuries. One problem is that only the literal interpretation of Scripture was often viewed as valid, as prompted by Martin Luther's "sola literalis," meaning that just the literal translation of Scripture was accurate. The Fundamentalist movements of today base their beliefs on the literal interpretation of the Scripture. Therefore, they do not believe that God placed more profound, hidden, or secret meanings in the Word.

The students of the Scriptures who learn through Hebraic training and understanding have drawn a different conclusion. The Hebrew language itself leads to different possible interpretations because of the construction of the language. The Hebraic method of Bible study opens avenues of thought about God's revelations in the Scripture never considered. Not all questions about the Scripture studied will have an immediate answer. If so, it becomes the responsibility of the learners to uncover the meaning. Also, remember that many opinions about the meaning of Scripture are also acceptable.

---

[2] Davis, Anne Kimball. *The Synoptic Gospels*. MP3. Albuquerque: NM: BibleInteract, 2012.

METHODOLOGY

The methodology employed is to use First Century Scripture study methods integrated with Yeshua's day's customs and culture to examine the Hebrew and Christian Scriptures, thus gathering a more in-depth understanding by learning the Scriptures in the way the people of Yeshua's day did.

I have titled the methodology of analyzing a passage of Scripture in a Hebraic manner the "Process of Discovery." The author developed this methodology, which brings together various areas of linguistic and cultural understanding. There are several sections to the process, and not all the parts apply to every passage of Scripture. The overall result of developing this process is to give the reader a framework for studying the Word in more depth.

The "Process of Discovery" starts with a Scripture passage. An examination of the linguistic structure of the passage is next. The linguistic structure includes parallelism, chiastic structures, and repetition. Formatting the passage in its linguistic form allows the reader to visualize what the first century CE listener was hearing. Their corresponding sections label the chiasms, for example, A, B, C, B', A.' Not all passages of the Scriptures have a poetic form.

The next step is to "question the narrative." The questioning of the narrative process, assuming the reader knows nothing about the passage. Therefore, the questions go from the simple to the complex. The next task is to identify any linguistic patterns. Linguistic patterns include, but are not limited to, irony, simile, metaphor, symbolism, idioms, hyperbole, figurative language, personification, and allegory.

A review of any translation inconsistencies discovered between the English NAU version and either the Hebrew or Greek versions is done. There are times when a Hebrew or Greek word is translated in more than one way. Inconsistencies also can be created by the translation committee, which may have decided to use traditional language instead of the actual translation. The decision of the translation committee is in the Preface or Introduction to the Bible. Perhaps some of the inconsistencies were intentionally added to convey some deeper meaning. An examination for every discrepancy is done.

The passage is analyzed for any echoes of the Hebrew Scriptures in the Christian Scriptures. Using a passage from the Hebrew Scriptures in the Christian Scriptures, an echo occurs.[3] Also, echoes are found when Torah (Genesis through Deuteronomy) passages are used in other Hebrew Bible books. Cross-references in the Scripture are references from one verse to another verse, which can help the reader understand the verse.

The names of persons mentioned in the passage are listed. Many of the Hebrew names have meaning and may be associated with places or actions. Jewish parents used to name their children based on what they felt God had in store for their child. An example of this is Abraham, whose original name was Abram and was changed to mean eternal father (God changed Abram's name to Abraham, indicating a function he was to perform). When the Hebrew Bible gives names, many of the occurrences mean something unique. The same importance can occur for the names of places. The time it takes to travel between locations can supply insight into the event.

Keyphrases are identified in verses when they are essential to an understanding of that passage. There are no rules for selecting the keywords. Searching for other occurrences of the keywords in Scripture in a concordance is necessary to understand the Word's usage; this must be done in either Hebrew or Greek, not in English. A classic Hebraic approach is to find the usage of a word in the Scripture by finding other verses that contain the Word. The usage of a word in its original language is discovered by searching the Scripture in the language of the Word. Verses that contain the Word are identified, and a pattern for the usage of the Word is discovered. Each verse is examined to see what the usage of the Word is which, may reveal a model for the Word's usage. For Hebrew words, the first usage of the Word in the Scripture, primarily if used in the Torah, is essential. For the Greek words, the Christian Scriptures are used to determine the Word usage in the Scripture. Sometimes finding the equivalent Greek Word in the Septuagint then analyzing its Hebrew usage can be very helpful.

The Rules of Hillel are used when applicable. Hillel was a Torah scholar who lived shortly before Yeshua's day. Hillel developed several rules for Torah students to interpret the Scriptures, which refer to halachic Midrash. In several cases, these rules are helpful in the analysis of the Scripture.

---

[3] Mitzvot are the 613 commandments found in the Torah that please God. There are positive and negative commandments. The list was first development by Maimonides. The full list can be found at: ttp://www.jewfaq.org/613.htm.

The cultural implications from the period of the writing are done after the linguistic analysis is completed. The culture is crucial because it is not explicitly referenced in the biblical narratives, as indicated earlier.

From the linguistic analysis and the cultural understanding, it is possible to obtain a deeper meaning of the Scripture beyond the plain text's literal meaning. That is what the listeners of Yeshua's time were doing. They put linguistics and culture together without even having to contemplate it.

The analysis will lead to a set of findings explaining what the passage meant in Yeshua's day. Most of the time, the Hebraic analysis leads to the desire for more in-depth analysis to fully understand what Yeshua was talking about or what was happening to Him. Whatever the result, a new, more in-depth understanding of the Scripture is obtained.

The components of the Process of Discovery are:

Language

Process of Discovery

Linguistics Section

Linguistic Structure

Discussion

Questioning the Passage

Verse Comparison of citations or proof text

Translation Inconsistencies

Biblical Personalities

Biblical Locations

Phrase Study

Scripture cross-references

Linguistic Echoes

Rules of Hillel

Culture Section

Discussion

Questioning the passage

Cultural Echoes

Culture and Linguistics Section

Discussion

Thoughts

Reflections

Only the applicable sections are included in this document.

MARK 1:1-8

Language

New American Standard 1995	Koine Greek
[1] The beginning of the gospel of Jesus Christ, the Son of God.	Ἀρχὴ τοῦ εὐαγγελίου Ἰησοῦ χριστοῦ, υἱοῦ τοῦ θεοῦ.
[2] As it is written in Isaiah the prophet, "Behold, I send My messenger before Your face, Who will prepare Your way;	[2] Ὡς γέγραπται ἐν τοῖς προφήταις, Ἰδού, ἐγὼ ἀποστέλλω τὸν ἄγγελόν μου πρὸ προσώπου σου, ὃς κατασκευάσει τὴν ὁδόν σου ἔμπροσθέν σου.
[3] The voice of one crying in the wilderness, 'Make ready the way of the Lord, Make His paths straight.'"	[3] Φωνὴ βοῶντος ἐν τῇ ἐρήμῳ, Ἑτοιμάσατε τὴν ὁδὸν κυρίου· εὐθείας ποιεῖτε τὰς τρίβους αὐτοῦ.
[4] John the Baptist appeared in the wilderness preaching a baptism of repentance for the forgiveness of sins.	[4] Ἐγένετο Ἰωάννης βαπτίζων ἐν τῇ ἐρήμῳ, καὶ κηρύσσων βάπτισμα μετανοίας εἰς ἄφεσιν ἁμαρτιῶν.
[5] And all the country of Judea was going out to him, and all the people of Jerusalem; and they were being baptized by him in the Jordan River, confessing their sins.	[5] Καὶ ἐξεπορεύετο πρὸς αὐτὸν πᾶσα ἡ Ἰουδαία χώρα, καὶ οἱ Ἱεροσολυμῖται, καὶ ἐβαπτίζοντο πάντες ἐν τῷ Ἰορδάνῃ ποταμῷ ὑπ' αὐτοῦ, ἐξομολογούμενοι τὰς ἁμαρτίας αὐτῶν.
[6] And John was clothed with camel's hair and *wore* a leather belt around his waist, and his diet was locusts and wild honey.	[6] Ἦν δὲ ὁ Ἰωάννης ἐνδεδυμένος τρίχας καμήλου, καὶ ζώνην δερματίνην περὶ τὴν ὀσφὺν αὐτοῦ, καὶ ἐσθίων ἀκρίδας καὶ μέλι ἄγριον.
[7] And he was preaching, and saying, "After me One is coming who is mightier than I, and I am not fit to stoop down and untie the thong of His sandals.	[7] Καὶ ἐκήρυσσεν, λέγων, Ἔρχεται ὁ ἰσχυρότερός μου ὀπίσω μου, οὗ οὐκ εἰμὶ ἱκανὸς κύψας λῦσαι τὸν ἱμάντα τῶν ὑποδημάτων αὐτοῦ.
[8] "I baptized you with water; but He will baptize you with the Holy Spirit."	[8] Ἐγὼ μὲν ἐβάπτισα ὑμᾶς ἐν ὕδατι· αὐτὸς δὲ βαπτίσει ὑμᾶς ἐν πνεύματι ἁγίῳ.

Process of Discovery

Linguistics Section

Linguistic Structure

[Opening statements] [1] The beginning of the gospel of Jesus Christ, the Son of God.

[Prophesy] [2] As it is written in Isaiah the prophet, "Behold, I send My messenger before Your face, Who will prepare Your way;

[Prophesy] [3] The voice of one crying in the wilderness, 'Make ready the way of the Lord, Make His paths straight.'"

A [4] John the Baptist appeared in the wilderness preaching a baptism of repentance for the forgiveness of sins.

> **B** [5] And all the country of Judea was going out to him, and all the people of Jerusalem; and they were being baptized by him in the Jordan River, confessing their sins.

> **B'** [6] And John was clothed with camel's hair and *wore* a leather belt around his waist, and his diet was locusts and wild honey. [7] And he was preaching, and saying, "After me One is coming who is mightier than I, and I am not fit to stoop down and untie the thong of His sandals.

A' [8] "I baptized you with water; but He will baptize you with the Holy Spirit."

Discussion

Mark's Gospel commences with two citations from the Hebrew Scripture about Yeshua and John's involvement in the narrative. In verses four to eight, the small chiasm describes John and what he was doing in the wilderness.

Questioning the Passage

1. Why does the Gospel of Mark start with John the Baptist?

   The author of Mark's Gospel believed that Yeshua's Good News commenced with His introduction to the world. Verse one starts with the words "The beginning," which is almost the same as Genesis's beginning, which starts "In the beginning." The creation of Heaven and Earth commenced in the beginning. The creation of the Kingdom of Heaven commenced with the beginning of Yeshua's work on the Earth. The beginning of Yeshua's ministry, according to Mark, is His baptism in the Jordan River by John the Baptist. This marks a new era that the LORD brought through Yeshua's ministry and the beginning of the Kingdom of Heaven.

2. Where was the wilderness? (v. 4)

The wilderness in this verse refers to any uninhabitable area used for religious purposes only.

3. What is a baptism of repentance? (v. 4)

The word repentance is derived from the Hebrew word *shuwu*. It means to "turn" or "return." The baptism of repentance refers to the action of turning or returning to the LORD. It means to leave any sin and evil ways behind and live by the Laws of the LORD through His Torah. The mitzvah performed after repentance brings forgiveness of sin and salvation.[4]

4. What is the significance of John's clothing? (v. 6)

John's clothing was what was worn by the prophets of Israel. His diet was also one that was followed by the prophets. Mark's author is clearly saying that John the Baptist was a prophet from the LORD, just like the prophets Isaiah, Ezekiel, and the rest.

5. What did the people know about the Holy Spirit? (v. 8)

The Holy Spirit was the Ruach of the LORD, also known as the Shekinah. Ruach from the Hebrew means spirit. In Genesis, the Ruach of the LORD passed over the chaos and created the Heavens and the Earth. The Shekinah is considered the feminine attributes of the LORD. A list of these attributes are:[5]

- God comforts his people like a mother comforts her child (Isaiah 66:13)

- Like a woman would never forget her nursing child, God will not forget his children (Isaiah 49:15)
- God is like a mother eagle hovering over her young (Deuteronomy 32:11)

---

[4] Rocco A. Errico, George M. Lamsa, *Aramaic Light on the Gospels of Mark and Luke: a Commentary on the Teachings of Jesus from the Aramaic and Unchanged Near Eastern Customs* (Smyrna, GA: Noohra Foundation, 2001).

[5] "God's Feminine Attributes," The Moody Church, accessed October 7, 2020, https://www.moodychurch.org/gods-feminine-attributes/.

- God seeks the lost like a housekeeper, trying to find her lost coin (Luke 15:8-10)
- God cares for his people like a midwife that cares for the child she just delivered (Ps 22:9-10, Ps 71:6, Isa 66:9)
- God experiences the fury of a mother bear robbed of her cubs (Hosea 13:8)
- Jesus longed for the people of Jerusalem like a mother hen longs to gather her chicks under her wings (Luke 13:34)

The Shekinah is the glory of the LORD, which appeared to the Israelites as the tower of fire, which saved them from the Egyptians when they crossed the Red Sea. It was the cloud that led the people through the Sinai. The Shekinah resided in the Temple in Jerusalem. When the Temple was about to be destroyed, Ezekiel described the Shekinah as a green mist that left the Holy of Holies.

The Shekinah is the essence of the LORD, which people on Earth can feel and see its actions. One Kabbalistic view of the world's creation is that the Ein Sof (God) created ten vessels to hold His power. However, when the Light of Ein Sof entered the vessels, they all broke. The light of Ein Sof that arrived at the tenth vessel, Malkhut, is the Shekinah. The Shekinah cannot leave Malkhut because of the broken vessel.

The Holy Spirit (Shekinah, Ruach of the LORD) guides and directs those who wish to live by the mitzvot of the Torah. In Christianity, the Holy Spirit is a part of the Trinity. This understanding will not exist until Bishop Origen presents his Trinity doctrine around 180 CE.

6. Why does John say that Yeshua will baptize with the Holy Spirit when Yeshua does no baptisms in this Gospel?

Yeshua performing baptisms is quite problematic. Why would John say that Yeshua was going to baptize with the Holy Spirit when He did not do any baptisms? An explanation is that the Mithras churches converted into Yeshua churches maintained baptism's initiation ritual and are included here. The initiation ritual for Mithras was baptism. It was a baptism in the name of Mithras, which initiated new members into the Mithras church. The proto-orthodox Church, which originated from Paul's conversion of Mithras churches, believed that Mithras' baptism, now Yeshua, was necessary to join the faith. The modern Church uses baptism today as an initiation rite. This comment about baptism by John can be viewed as a church add-on.

Verse Comparison of citations or proof text

1. Behold, I send my messenger ahead of you, who will prepare your way; (v. 2)
    This is from the book of Malachi.

Malachi 3:1 (NAS95S) "[a]Behold, I am going to send [b]My [1]messenger, and he will [2c]clear the way before Me.

Sanitation departments did not exist in the Near East in Yeshua's time. The governments did not build new bridges or roads when they deteriorated. Neither did governments fix roads that were constructed in the past. There were obstacles to go around when on the road. Piles of refuse on the roads were usually sold to farmers, and they moved the piles when they were ready.

The people cleaned up the city and roads when they expected a king or prince's official visit. Rivalry arose in the city as people tried to outdo each other with their decorations and cleaning so that the special visit might give them a great honor.[6]

The symbolism is that John was calling on the nation of Israel to clean its house. He wanted the removal of sin through repentance and the return to good works. The New Era that was ushered in by Yeshua, the Messiah, was a better interpretation of the Torah, allowing the people to serve the LORD better. The elders' false teachings and burdensome

---

[6] Rocco A. Errico, George M. Lamsa, *Aramaic Light on the Gospels of Mark and Luke: a Commentary on the Teachings of Jesus from the Aramaic and Unchanged Near Eastern Customs* (Smyrna, GA: Noohra Foundation, 2001).

traditions placed upon the people had to be removed. Only then could the Kingdom of Heaven be established.

2. "The voice of one crying in the wilderness, 'Make ready the way of the Lord, make his paths straight.'" (v. 3)
This is from the book of Isaiah.

Isaiah 40:3 (NAS95S) A voice [1]is calling, "Clear the way for the LORD in the wilderness; Make smooth in the desert a highway for our God."

The voice in the wilderness is symbolic, meaning John and Yeshua's words were clear and direct. The wilderness is a barren and silent region without habitation. "Wilderness" does not mean that it is a desert. An oasis can be a wilderness if life does not inhabit it. The human voice carries best when the land is flat and there are no manufactured objects to block the sound. Hills and mountains create echoes, which make voices hard to hear.

John's voice was like a shepherd attempting to call the people back to righteousness. John did not expound on any doctrine or theological positions. He did not want to confuse people with much God-language. His message was that the people needed to return to genuine piety, integrity, and justice. This change was to be accomplished by the people repenting for their sins.

Repenting means being sorrowful for a sin committed but, more importantly, turning back to the LORD and not committing the sin again.

Biblical Personalities
1. St. John the Baptist, "(born 1st decade BCE, Judaea, Palestine, near Jerusalem—died 28–36 CE; feast day June 24), Jewish prophet of priestly origin who preached the imminence of God's Final Judgment and baptized those who repented in self-preparation for it; he is revered in the Christian church as the forerunner of Jesus Christ. After a period of desert

solitude, John the Baptist emerged as a prophet in the region of the lower Jordan River valley. He had a circle of disciples, and Jesus was among the recipients of his rite of baptism."[7]

Thoughts

In Mark's Gospel, the beginning of Yeshua's ministry is when John baptizes him. What happened to Mary, Joseph, and the trip to Bethlehem? For Mark's author, it is not essential how and where Yeshua is born. His lineage at this point is also not significant. What is essential is that Yeshua came to Earth to usher in a new era of peace, grace, and love. Scholars believe that Mark's Gospel was written first. Without the birth narrative, Mark's author may not have been influenced by the Mithras cult. Since Paul had been converting Mithras house churches into Yeshua house churches, Mithras' full influence should have been here. Mithras was born of a virgin mother, which corresponds to today's belief about Yeshua. Mark's Gospel may prove to have less Mithras influence than the other Gospels.

Reflections

The Holy Spirit is introduced to the reader, along with John the Baptist. The Holy Spirit was known as the Shekinah or the Spirit of the LORD in the Hebrew Scriptures. The concept that the Holy Spirit is received when a person is baptized probably developed from these narratives and similar ones in the other Gospels. The Shekinah led the Hebrew people through the wilderness of Sinai during their forty-year experience. The Shekinah was viewed as helping the community. With Yeshua's baptism, the Shekinah would now guide the individual. The difficulty with this concept is that Yeshua never baptized anyone. Baptism was a Mithras initiation ritual. Paul may have inserted the Shekinah into the baptism ritual to give it less of a pagan feel.

---

[7] John Strugnell, "St. John the Baptist," Encyclopædia Britannica (Encyclopædia Britannica, inc., May 8, 2020), accessed October 7, 2020, https://www.britannica.com/biography/Saint-John-the-Baptist.

MARK 1:9-13

Language

New American Standard 1995	Koine Greek
[9] And it came about in those days that Jesus came from Nazareth in Galilee, and was baptized by John in the Jordan. [10] And immediately coming up out of the water, He saw the heavens opening, and the Spirit like a dove descending upon Him; [11] and a voice came out of the heavens: "Thou art My beloved Son, in Thee I am well-pleased." [12] And immediately the Spirit impelled Him *to go* out into the wilderness. [13] And He was in the wilderness forty days being tempted by Satan; and He was with the wild beasts, and the angels were ministering to Him.	[9] Καὶ ἐγένετο ἐν ἐκείναις ταῖς ἡμέραις, ἦλθεν Ἰησοῦς ἀπὸ Ναζαρὲτ τῆς Γαλιλαίας, καὶ ἐβαπτίσθη ὑπὸ Ἰωάννου εἰς τὸν Ἰορδάνην. [10] Καὶ εὐθέως ἀναβαίνων ἀπὸ τοῦ ὕδατος, εἶδεν σχιζομένους τοὺς οὐρανούς, καὶ τὸ πνεῦμα ὡσεὶ περιστερὰν καταβαῖνον ἐπ᾽ αὐτόν· [11] καὶ φωνὴ ἐγένετο ἐκ τῶν οὐρανῶν, Σὺ εἶ ὁ υἱός μου ὁ ἀγαπητός, ἐν ᾧ εὐδόκησα. [12] Καὶ εὐθὺς τὸ πνεῦμα αὐτὸν ἐκβάλλει εἰς τὴν ἔρημον. [13] Καὶ ἦν ἐκεῖ ἐν τῇ ἐρήμῳ ἡμέρας τεσσαράκοντα πειραζόμενος ὑπὸ τοῦ Σατανᾶ, καὶ ἦν μετὰ τῶν θηρίων, καὶ οἱ ἄγγελοι διηκόνουν αὐτῷ.

Process of Discovery

Linguistics Section

Linguistic Structure

[Transition] [9] And it came about in those days that Jesus came from Nazareth in Galilee, and was baptized by John in the Jordan.

[Jesus' baptism] [10] And immediately coming up out of the water, He saw the heavens opening, and the Spirit like a dove descending upon Him; [11] and a voice came out of the heavens: "Thou art My beloved Son, in Thee I am well-pleased."

[The purification ritual] [12] And immediately the Spirit impelled Him *to go* out into the wilderness. [13] And He was in the wilderness forty days being tempted by Satan; and He was with the wild beasts, and the angels were ministering to Him.

Discussion

This narrative has two actions. The first action is that a peasant from Nazareth named Yeshua came to the Jordan River to be baptized by John. The second action is Yeshua going into the Wilderness to be purified for His work.

Questioning the Passage

1. Why is it essential that Yeshua is from Nazareth? (v. 9)

   In the Gospel of Matthew and Luke, it was important for the author to say that Yeshua was a descendant of a royal line that started with King David. Mark's author decided to offer an obscure lineage for Yeshua. Saying that Yeshua came from the Galilee (Nazareth was located in the Galilee) is equivalent to saying that Yeshua came from "nowheresville." It is somewhat anticlimactic that the Savior of the world came from such a place where peasants and Gentiles lived. Southern Jews living in Judea regarded anyone from Nazareth with contempt. The people from the Galilee were Gentiles, poor, and geopolitically cut off from Judea and Samaria. They were considered backward people. According to Mark's Gospel, Yeshua came from the lowest class of people of His day.[8]

2. Who was Satan? (v. 13)

Satan is a Christian theological entry. The Kabbalist's understanding of evil is called Evil Inclination. A person can be attacked by Evil Inclination, which makes every attempt to pull the person away from the LORD. The Christian view of evil is the personification of Evil Inclination. The negative forces of the Universe are necessary. When they accumulate in a person, it can become overwhelming and drive the person toward pure evil. The Klippot forms around the person, and they cannot absorb positive energy. The person will turn away from the LORD. Christianity needs a personification of evil, named Satan (from the Hebrew word, which means evil) to explain "who" the person turns toward when turning away from the LORD.

3. Why was Yeshua impelled to go into the Wilderness? (v. 12)

The Wilderness is where a profit is sanctified and purified for the LORD's work. Moses was sent into the Wilderness for forty years until he was ready to do the LORD's work. Yeshua needed forty days in order to prepare Himself for the LORD's work. Reading this as a Semitic story, it is not crucial if Yeshua factually spent forty days in the Wilderness. The message that is being conveyed is that Yeshua was prepared for His ministry. Every prophet went through some preparation and initiation into the LORD's work.

4. What does the reference to wild animals and angels mean? (v. 13)

The reference to wild animals is because wild animals are dangerous to humans because of the Fall of Adam from the Garden of Eden. Adam was able to control the wild animals before the Fall. When he and Chava were removed from the Garden of Eden, he lost that control. Yeshua was different from Adam. Mark's author is saying that Yeshua was no ordinary man. Therefore, the wild animals did not see Yeshua as a man but as something else. The angels' reference is from the Midrash that Heaven's angels

---

[8] Ched Myers, *Binding the Strong Man a Political Reading of Mark's Story of Jesus* (Maryknoll, NY: Orbis Books, 1988).

carried Adam's dead body from the Earth back into Heaven. In this case, the angels did not have to take Yeshua's body back to Heaven, indicating that He was more than just a human.[9]

Linguistic Echoes

1. [10] Immediately coming up out of the water, He saw the heavens opening, and the Spirit like a dove descending upon Him;

Isaiah 64:1 (NAS95S) Oh, that You would rend the heavens *and* come down, that the mountains might quake at Your presence — [2] As fire kindles the brushwood, *as* fire causes water to boil — To make Your name known to Your adversaries, *that* the nations may tremble at Your presence!

The echo is that there was a request for the LORD to come down and help His people in Isaiah. Mark's author is inferring that Yeshua was the answer to that request. Therefore, Mark is saying that Yeshua is the Messiah that people were waiting for. He did this with an Isaiah passage. Did the heavens tear open? The way Semitic storytellers write it probably did not happen. Semitic stories are not based on facts but rather on symbols, metaphors, and allegories. The author is making a strong statement that readers usually get overlooked because they concentrate on Heaven's actual tearing instead of the symbolism of the statement. Mark is asking the question: "could this unknown Nazarene villager be the fulfillment of Isaiah's longing? "[10]

This reference is an apocalyptic symbol. It is the first of three distinct moments in Mark's Gospel. Therefore, Mark's author views Yeshua as the one to bring the apocalypse.

---

[9] *The New Interpreter's Bible: General Articles & Introduction, Commentary, & Reflections for Each Book of the Bible, Including the Apocryphal/Deuterocanonical Books* (Nashville: Abingdon Press, 1994).
[10] IBID.

2. [11] and a voice came out of the heavens: "You are My beloved Son, in You I am well-pleased."

Isaiah 42:1 (NAS95S) "Behold, My Servant, whom I uphold; My chosen one *in whom* My soul delights. I have put My Spirit upon Him; He will bring forth justice to the nations.

"The servant songs (also called the servant poems or the Songs of the Suffering Servant) are four songs in the Book of Isaiah in the Hebrew Bible, which include Isaiah 42:1–4; Isaiah 49:1–6; Isaiah 50:4–7; and Isaiah 52:13–53:12. The songs are four poems written about a certain "servant of YHWH" (Hebrew: עבד יהוה, *'ebed Yahweh*). God calls the servant to lead the nations, but the servant is horribly abused among them. In the end, he is rewarded. Some scholars regard Isaiah 61:1–3 as a fifth servant song, although the word "servant" (Hebrew: עבד, *'ebed*) is not mentioned in the passage. It is claimed that they were first identified by Bernhard Duhm in his 1892 commentary on Isaiah."[11]

3. [11] and a voice came out of the heavens: "You are My beloved Son, in You I am well-pleased."

Psalms 2:7 (NAS95S) "I will surely tell of the [1]decree of the LORD: He said to Me, 'You are My Son, today I have begotten You.

This verse's meaning is that David was to be the spiritual light by being the righteous person of his generation. The Zohar says that there is at least one righteous person in every generation. King David was the righteous person of his generation. It was through the righteous that the LORD could send His Light to the people of the world.

---

[11] "Servant Songs," Wikipedia (Wikimedia Foundation, April 27, 2022), https://en.wikipedia.org/wiki/Servant_songs.

"You are my son" means that David became the King because of the LORD's actions, not by the election of men. The LORD chose David because he desired to serve the LORD.

Mark is saying that Yeshua was selected by the LORD to be the messenger for His period. "Son of God" does not mean that Yeshua is divine. It means that the LORD selected him for a particular purpose. The misinterpretation of this phrase has led the church to a misunderstanding of who Yeshua from Nazareth was.

David's selection as a spiritual leader was something new that the LORD had done.

Thoughts

The introduction of Yeshua appears at the literary level; it is not impressive. However, the echoes and other references to the Hebrew Scripture indicate that this man was something special. He was not just a regular poor man from Nazareth. He was poor in materialism, but he was full of spiritualism. Mark's author will continue to build a case that Yeshua is the Messiah that the LORD had promised. He starts the process very subtly with the baptism from John.

Reflections

Perhaps this short narrative is a reminder that we should never judge a person on first impressions. For the modern reader, this narrative is unimpressive. It is rather dull because there is not much action. It seems an anticlimactic way to introduce the Savior to the world. However, when the reader learns about Semitic writings, it is clear that Mark has opened up the idea that Yeshua is the Messiah the world has been waiting for. How many times have you met a person and judged them on first impressions? A lesson here is not to do that. Do not judge other people before you get to know them.

MARK 1:14-20

Language

New American Standard 1995	Koine Greek
[14] Now after John had been taken into custody, Jesus came into Galilee, preaching the gospel of God, [15] and saying, "The time is fulfilled, and the kingdom of God is at hand; repent and believe in the gospel." [16] As He was going along by the Sea of Galilee, He saw Simon and Andrew, the brother of Simon, casting a net in the sea; for they were fishermen. [17] And Jesus said to them, "Follow Me, and I will make you become fishers of men." [18] Immediately they left their nets and followed Him. [19] Going on a little farther, He saw James the son of Zebedee, and John his brother, who were also in the boat mending the nets. [20] Immediately He called them; and they left their father Zebedee in the boat with the hired servants, and went away to follow Him.	[14] Μετὰ δὲ τὸ παραδοθῆναι τὸν Ἰωάννην, ἦλθεν ὁ Ἰησοῦς εἰς τὴν Γαλιλαίαν, κηρύσσων τὸ εὐαγγέλιον τῆς βασιλείας τοῦ θεοῦ, [15] καὶ λέγων ὅτι Πεπλήρωται ὁ καιρός, καὶ ἤγγικεν ἡ βασιλεία τοῦ θεοῦ· μετανοεῖτε, καὶ πιστεύετε ἐν τῷ εὐαγγελίῳ. [16] Περιπατῶν δὲ παρὰ τὴν θάλασσαν τῆς Γαλιλαίας εἶδεν Σίμωνα καὶ Ἀνδρέαν τὸν ἀδελφὸν αὐτοῦ τοῦ Σίμωνος βάλλοντας ἀμφίβληστρον ἐν τῇ θαλάσσῃ· ἦσαν γὰρ ἁλιεῖς. [17] Καὶ εἶπεν αὐτοῖς ὁ Ἰησοῦς, Δεῦτε ὀπίσω μου, καὶ ποιήσω ὑμᾶς γενέσθαι ἁλιεῖς ἀνθρώπων. [18] Καὶ εὐθέως ἀφέντες τὰ δίκτυα αὐτῶν, ἠκολούθησαν αὐτῷ. [19] Καὶ προβὰς ἐκεῖθεν ὀλίγον, εἶδεν Ἰάκωβον τὸν τοῦ Ζεβεδαίου, καὶ Ἰωάννην τὸν ἀδελφὸν αὐτοῦ, καὶ αὐτοὺς ἐν τῷ πλοίῳ καταρτίζοντας τὰ δίκτυα. [20] Καὶ εὐθέως ἐκάλεσεν αὐτούς· καὶ ἀφέντες τὸν πατέρα αὐτῶν Ζεβεδαῖον ἐν τῷ πλοίῳ μετὰ τῶν μισθωτῶν ἀπῆλθον ὀπίσω αὐτοῦ.

Process of Discovery

Linguistics Section

Linguistic Structure

[**Transition**] [14] Now after John had been taken into custody, Jesus came into Galilee, preaching the gospel of God, [15] and saying, "The time is fulfilled, and the kingdom of God is at hand; repent and believe in the gospel."

[**Calling the first disciples**][16] As He was going along by the Sea of Galilee, He saw Simon and Andrew, the brother of Simon, casting a net in the sea; for they were fishermen. [17] And Jesus said to them, "Follow Me, and I will make you become fishers of men." [18] Immediately they left their nets and followed Him.

[**Calling James and John**] [19] Going on a little farther, He saw James the son of Zebedee, and John his brother, who were also in the boat mending the nets. [20] Immediately He called them; and they left their father Zebedee in the boat with the hired servants, and went away to follow Him.

Discussion

The first calling of Yeshua's disciples does not offer what words were said that caused the fishermen to drop their occupations. Yeshua said that the Kingdom of the LORD was to be initiated by persuasion and not through force. Yeshua's words call the first disciples. Yeshua walked the walked and talked the talk.

Questioning the Passage

1. Why was it necessary to have John arrested before Yeshua started His work? (v. 14)

   Mark's author wanted to be clear that John came before Yeshua. Therefore, he got John off the scene so that Yeshua could begin His work.

2. What does the word "Gospel" mean in Yeshua's day? (v. 14)

   The Gospel authors used three distinct words that are translated as "Gospel" in English — *swarta, evangalion, and karozuta.*

Swarta comes from the root *swr,* which means to "hope, trust, declare, announce, tell, bring news and publish abroad." A fair translation is a joyful "message, hope, or expectation."

Evangalion came from the Greek language. Aramaic nouns that end in "ion" are loaned words from Greek. The Greeks came to the Near East around 250 BCE. Some of their language and culture infiltrated Semitic culture. An example is the idea of the separation of body and spirit upon death. This word means "good news." It has a secondary meaning in Greek – one of absolution when a king ascends to the throne.

Karozuta is derived from the root word *krz,* which means to "preach, declare, make known, announce, and publicly celebrate." Yeshua said that the joyful announcement of the LORD's reigning presence was about to come.[12]

3. What does the "kingdom" mean? (v 15)

    Malkuta is derived from the root *mlkh* which means to "advise, counsel, reign, and rule." A king was also considered a counselor. Yeshua's message was a call to recognize the LORD's presence in the world. Yeshua said that the LORD would start working among the people in their daily lives. The LORD was to come to help the people and relieve their poverty, fears, and suffering.[13]

4. What does it mean to be fishers of men? (v. 17)

    The Aramaic word for fishers is *sayadeh.* This word means "hunters." Aramaic-speaking people in Yeshua's day used this same word for "fishermen" and bird hunters. "I will make you fishers of men" is a metaphorical expression that means "you will catch and persuade men by your speech." It has nothing to do with the fishing trade. The church today likes to use the symbolism of catching people like fish and reeling them into the church because the first four disciples in Mark's Gospel were fishermen.[14]

---

[12] Rocco A. Errico, George M. Lamsa, and George M. Lamsa, *Aramaic Light on the Gospels of Mark and Luke: a Commentary on the Teachings of Jesus from the Aramaic and Unchanged Near Eastern Customs* (Smyrna, GA: Noohra Foundation, 2001).

[13] IBID.

[14] IBID.

In Yeshua's day, winning people over to your ideas was done through debates. That is why there are so many debates recorded in the Gospels. What Yeshua meant by "fishers of men" is that He trained His disciples so well and they were so versed in Scripture that by their words, they would convince people to join the kingdom. They could also stand before the High Priests and silence him with their words. The disciples learned how to take the new teachings about the Kingdom of the LORD and convince people to change their ways.

Biblical Personalities

1. "Saint James, also called James, son of Zebedee, or James the Greater, (born, Galilee, Palestine—died 44 CE, Jerusalem; feast day July 25), one of the Twelve Apostles, distinguished as being in Jesus' innermost circle and the only apostle whose martyrdom is recorded in the New Testament (Acts 12:2)."[15]

2. John son of Zebedee – "To learn the history of John, the disciple of Jesus, we begin with his life before he met Jesus. John, his brother James, Peter, and Andrew were all partners in the fishing business before they became disciples of Jesus. John was the son of Zebedee who was also a fisherman in Galilee. John's mother's name was Salome and some say that Salome was the sister of Jesus' mother, Mary. John owned a home in Jerusalem. Shortly before the destruction of Jerusalem by the Romans in 70 AD, John moved to Ephesus. John pastored a church in Ephesus. He communicated with other churches in the area as stated in the book of Revelation. He advised and counseled many people who would later become believers in Jesus Christ as the Son of God."[16]

---

[15] "Saint James," Encyclopædia Britannica (Encyclopædia Britannica, inc.), accessed Apri 27, 2022, https://www.britannica.com/biography/Saint-James-son-of-Zebedee.
[16] Toni, "History of John the Disciple of Jesus," AllAboutJesusChrist.org (All About Jesus Christ, June 20, 2005), Accessed April 27, 2022, https://www.allaboutjesuschrist.org/history-of-john-the-disciple-of-jesus-faq.htm.

3.   Simon – "The holy apostle Simon is called "the Zealot," (Luke 6:15; Acts of the Apostles 1:13), possibly to differentiate him from Simon/Peter. But there is a hypothesis that Simon, along with James the Younger, Jude Thaddaeus, and Judas Iscariot, formerly belonged to the Zealots, a religious sect of "freedom fighters" severely opposed to Roman control over Judea. Some scholars maintain that Jesus made certain announcements recorded in the Bible of a groundbreaking nature that affiliated him with members of the Zealot movement. Still others presume that the word "zealot" when discussing to Simon only suggested that he was a zealous advocate of the faith."[17]

4.   Andrew – "According to the Christian Bible, Jesus Christ had 12 principal followers. One of them, however, had to be first. That person was Andrew, known in ecclesiastic traditions as the *Protocletus*, or the first called. Disciple, apostle, and saint, Andrew holds a special place in Christian cultures. After all, it's a big deal to be first."[18]

Biblical Locations

1.   "Galilee (Hebrew: הַגָּלִיל, *HaGalil*; Arabic: الجليل, romanized: *al-Jalīl*) is a region mainly located in northern Israel. Galilee traditionally refers to the mountainous part, divided into Upper Galilee (Hebrew: גליל עליון, romanized: *Galil Elyon*) and Lower Galilee (Hebrew: גליל תחתון, romanized: *Galil Tahton*)."[19]

---

[17] Maria Nerushenko, "Get to Know the 12 Disciples of Jesus Christ: Apostle #9: Simon, the Zealot," The Talkative Man, August 31, 2017, accessed April 27, 2022, https://www.talkativeman.com/apostle-simon-the-zealot/.

[18] Study.com, accessed April 27, 2022, https://study.com/academy/lesson/andrew-the-apostle-biography-facts-death.html.

[19] "Galilee," Wikipedia (Wikimedia Foundation, September 23, 2020), accessed April 27, 2022, https://en.wikipedia.org/wiki/Galilee.

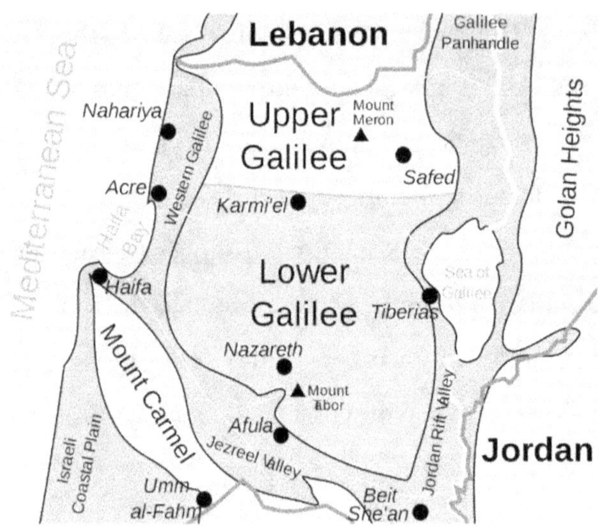

Culture Section

Discussion

The message that John started and Yeshua was to fulfill was that the current age of humankind had to end, and the age of the LORD's sovereign presence had arrived. Repent meant to return to the LORD and have confidence in the positive message that the LORD sent through Yeshua. Semitic people dreamed of a better government and laws that would benefit everyone whenever they were being oppressed. When the human justice system did not work, they looked to the LORD as the only true and fair sovereign. The people in Yeshua's day wanted genuine justice, happiness, and prosperity. A Semitic person believed that the LORD was a house of refuge during a time of trouble and a shelter amid persecution and war. They fully and unconditionally trusted in the LORD. They prayed continually and waited patiently for the coming of the LORD's sovereign presence.[20]

Judea, Samaria, and Galilee were the middle of the known world in Yeshua's day. The crossroads between the great empires of the north and Egypt in the south went through these lands. Many wars between the north and south occurred in this country. A war would devastate everything

---

[20] Rocco A. Errico, George M. Lamsa, and George M. Lamsa, *Aramaic Light on the Gospels of Mark and Luke: a Commentary on the Teachings of Jesus from the Aramaic and Unchanged Near Eastern Customs* (Smyrna, GA: Noohra Foundation, 2001).

and kill a multitude of people. Eventually, the great empires of Egypt and Persia fell. Unfortunately for the Semitic peoples, the Greeks came into their lands and annexed them. The Romans followed the Greeks. The people longed to be free and to be rid of these invaders.

During Yeshua's time, the Romans ruled. The people were burdened with three significant forms of taxation. There was a tax that went to Caesar in Rome. A second tax was collected for the Jewish state, which was for Herod's sons. A third tax was placed on the people to support the Temple in Jerusalem. In David's day, there was only one tax on the people. The people were being taxed to death. Everyone had to pay a minor tax called the head tax.[21]

The people longed for the Messianic kingdom on earth. The pagans would be overthrown, and Israel would be restored to its former power, glory, and prosperity. It was believed that the Messianic kingdom would transform into the kingdom of the LORD. A spiritual and moral character would prevail in this kingdom regardless of racial differences. The Galileans were overjoyed to hear Yeshua announcing that the LORD's kingdom was about to come.

Questioning the passage

1. Why does it mean that Yeshua's ministry starts in Galilee?

   The author of Mark's Gospel had to understand that the tremendous apocalyptic upheaval was to occur when the LORD returned to earth. The author is not saying that this will not happen but rather implies that this event is not yet going to happen. Why? Because Yeshua starts His work on the periphery of society. Galilee was not the center of the Jewish faith. If Yeshua went first to the Temple in Jerusalem and made His proclamation, then the people would expect the minor prophets' apocalypse. So, Yeshua went to Galilee and decided to work from the fringes of society and eventually did make His way to the center of Judaism.

---

[21] IBID.

2. What is Mark announcing when Yeshua said, "the time is fulfilled?"

The people had been waiting for the arrival of the new order, where the oppressors would be overthrown. The story starts with John the Baptist, whom the author believes to be the reincarnation of Elijah. John said a stronger prophet than he was about to arrive. Messianic tradition said that Elijah would return before the Messiah. Yeshua said, "the time is fulfilled," and meant that it was time for the Kingdom of the LORD to occur. As explained by the minor prophets, the quick pace of the Day of the LORD was to be a slow process, not quick at all. Perhaps the process is continuing through us today?[22]

Cultural Echoes

1. [17] And Jesus said to them, "Follow Me, and I will make you become fishers of men." (Mark 1:17)

Jeremiah 16:16 (NAS95S) "Behold, I am going to send for many ᵃfishermen," declares the LORD, "and they will fish for them; and afterwards I will send for many hunters, and they will ᵇhunt them ᶜfrom every mountain and every hill and from the clefts of the rocks.

The echo demonstrates that the metaphor "fishers of men" is echoed in Jeremiah 16:16.

Thoughts

Fishers of men have become a metaphor that the church likes to use as real fishing of people. Of course, it is metaphorical. Every disciple of Yeshua must learn His words and the Scripture that supports His words so that they can discuss the Kingdom of the LORD. It is the responsibility of the disciples of Yeshua to spread the word of joy, love, peace, and grace. In today's world, that is a

---

[22] Ched Myers, *Binding the Strong Man a Political Reading of Mark's Story of Jesus* (Maryknoll, NY: Orbis Books, 1988).

problem, especially in North America and western Europe. Religion is on the decline. Why? There are many answers, but one is that most Christians do not live up to the moral and ethical standards that the Gospels set. Perhaps the faith needs to stop evangelizing for a moment and clean up its own house. Then the faith will be prepared to go out and spread the Word.

Reflections

The LORD's word and Yeshua, our Messiah, need to be understood in its original form. The filters of the church must be removed. The blinders that prevent Yeshua's disciples from understanding the truth of the Gospels and from sharing it must be dissolved. It is difficult to near impossible to converse with a non-believer and convince them to join the Kingdom of the LORD when filters of the church blur things. Learn the original meaning of what it means to be a "fisher of men," and you will learn the true essence of the LORD's Word and the ways of Yeshua the Messiah.

MARK 1:21-28

Language

New American Standard 1995	Koine Greek
²¹ And they went into Capernaum; and immediately on the Sabbath He entered the synagogue and *began* to teach. ²² And they were amazed at His teaching; for He was teaching them as *one* having authority, and not as the scribes. ²³ And just then there was in their synagogue a man with an unclean spirit; and he cried out, ²⁴ saying, "What do we have to do with You, Jesus of Nazareth? Have You come to destroy us? I know who You are-- the Holy One of God!" ²⁵ And Jesus rebuked him, saying, "Be quiet, and come out of him!" ²⁶ And throwing him into convulsions, the unclean spirit cried out with a loud voice, and came out of him. ²⁷ And they were all amazed, so that they debated among themselves, saying, "What is this? A new teaching with authority! He commands even the unclean spirits, and they obey Him." ²⁸ And immediately the news about Him went out everywhere into all the surrounding district of Galilee.	²¹ Καὶ εἰσπορεύονται εἰς Καπερναούμ· καὶ εὐθέως τοῖς σάββασιν εἰσελθὼν εἰς τὴν συναγωγήν, ἐδίδασκεν. ²² Καὶ ἐξεπλήσσοντο ἐπὶ τῇ διδαχῇ αὐτοῦ· ἦν γὰρ διδάσκων αὐτοὺς ὡς ἐξουσίαν ἔχων, καὶ οὐχ ὡς οἱ γραμματεῖς. ²³ Καὶ ἦν ἐν τῇ συναγωγῇ αὐτῶν ἄνθρωπος ἐν πνεύματι ἀκαθάρτῳ, καὶ ἀνέκραξεν, ²⁴ λέγων, Ἔα, τί ἡμῖν καὶ σοί, Ἰησοῦ Ναζαρηνέ; Ἦλθες ἀπολέσαι ἡμᾶς; Οἶδά σε τίς εἶ, ὁ ἅγιος τοῦ θεοῦ. ²⁵ Καὶ ἐπετίμησεν αὐτῷ ὁ Ἰησοῦς, λέγων, Φιμώθητι, καὶ ἔξελθε ἐξ αὐτοῦ. ²⁶ Καὶ σπαράξαν αὐτὸν τὸ πνεῦμα τὸ ἀκάθαρτον καὶ κράξαν φωνῇ μεγάλῃ, ἐξῆλθεν ἐξ αὐτοῦ. ²⁷ Καὶ ἐθαμβήθησαν πάντες, ὥστε συζητεῖν πρὸς ἑαυτούς, λέγοντας, Τί ἐστιν τοῦτο; Τίς ἡ διδαχὴ ἡ καινὴ αὕτη, ὅτι κατ' ἐξουσίαν καὶ τοῖς πνεύμασιν τοῖς ἀκαθάρτοις ἐπιτάσσει, καὶ ὑπακούουσιν αὐτῷ; ²⁸ Ἐξῆλθεν δὲ ἡ ἀκοὴ αὐτοῦ εὐθὺς εἰς ὅλην τὴν περίχωρον τῆς Γαλιλαίας.

Process of Discovery

Linguistics Section

Linguistic Structure

A [21] And they went into Capernaum; and immediately on the Sabbath He entered the synagogue and *began* to teach. [22] And they were amazed at His teaching; for He was teaching them as *one* having authority, and not as the scribes.

> **B** [23] And just then there was in their synagogue a man with an unclean spirit; and he cried out,

> > **C** [24] saying, "What do we have to do with You, Jesus of Nazareth? Have You come to destroy us? I know who You are-- the Holy One of God!"

> **B'** [25] And Jesus rebuked him, saying, "Be quiet, and come out of him!" [26] And throwing him into convulsions, the unclean spirit cried out with a loud voice, and came out of him.

A' [27] And they were all amazed, so that they debated among themselves, saying, "What is this? A new teaching with authority! He commands even the unclean spirits, and they obey Him." [28] And immediately the news about Him went out everywhere into all the surrounding district of Galilee.

Discussion

This narrative forms an A-B-C chiasm. The chiasm is asking the question about the mission of Yeshua.

Questioning the Passage

1. What is the significance that Yeshua went into the synagogue at Capernaum on the Shabbat? (v. 21)

   This event is the first public event that Yeshua participated in, according to Mark's Gospel. Through verse twenty-one, Yeshua moved from society's symbolic margins into the heart of the provincial Jewish social order. The synagogue was considered sacred, and the Shabbat was a sacred time.[23]

---

[23] Ched Myers, *Binding the Strong Man a Political Reading of Mark's Story of Jesus* (Maryknoll, NY: Orbis Books, 1988).

While in the synagogue, Yeshua taught about the LORD and the Torah. A common practice in the synagogue was to have open, healthy debates about the Scriptures' interpretations and meanings. The Sage Hillel introduced this process about seventy years before Yeshua's birth.

2. Where was the teaching of the scribes? (v. 22)

Yeshua started teaching in the synagogue, which was reserved for the scribes. He broke into their sacred place.

3. Why did the man with the unclean spirit yell at Yeshua? (v. 24)

When the man with the unclean spirit saw Yeshua, he could not hold back his anger toward him. Undoubtedly, this man heard from other men that Yeshua was a threat and that His teachings were demonic. Therefore, the man with the unclean spirit yelled out at Yeshua in an attempt to get rid of Him. Men who disagreed with Yeshua's words called Him a dangerous prophet. They did not trust Him and always looked for a way to stop him. However, they were cowards because they did not directly address Yeshua. Instead, they sent other people to raise accusations.

4. Did Yeshua have the power of demons?

Rabbi Yochanann Ben-Zakkai convened the Yavneh Council around 90 CE to develop the structure and Bible of the post-Temple rabbinic Judaism. He studied the speech of demonic spirits. No demonic spirits obeyed Rabbi Ben-Zakkai. However, the demonic-spirited listened to Yeshua. This is why the men at the synagogue that day were amazed at what had happened.[24]

Linguistic Echoes

1. "The Holy One of God!"

[9] She said to her husband, "Behold now, I perceive that this is a holy man of God passing by us continually. 2 Kings 4:9

---

[24] IBID

The Holy One of God is a term used to describe the LORD's power with Elisha, the prophet. It is a Semitic title. Mark's Gospel is saying that Yeshua was recognized as a powerful prophet of the LORD in the same way that people recognized Elisha as a strong prophet of the LORD. Mark sets up Yeshua to do some great things and perhaps even exceed what the powerful prophet Elisha could do.[25]

Culture Section

Questioning the passage

1. Did healers always receive such criticism as Yeshua did?

   Healers and magicians were plentiful in Yeshua's day. They practiced freely because the Hellenistic culture accepted them openly.[26] Yeshua ran into what appears to be much resistance. The resistance debates between Yeshua and adversaries were not over His healing but rather over his theology about the LORD and the Jewish people's religious ways. In this passage, the scribes wanted to discover who Yeshua was and to which group of Judaism he belonged.

2. What is an unclean spirit? (v. 23)

   A person with an unclean spirit was unruly, mentally ill, or hot-tempered. An individual who had bad intentions or who was inclined to do evil was considered an unclean spirit. A person who was suffering from mental illness was considered possessed by an unclean spirit.

3. Were the screams of an insane person taken seriously?

   In the Near East in Yeshua's day, when an insane person rebuked a king or prince, the king or prince did not take offense to it. The royal person would not punish the insane person.[27] In the same way, Yeshua did not punish the man for yelling at Him. Instead, Yeshua accepted the man's mental illness and cured him. Yeshua was not affected by the insane man's words and actions toward Him.

---

[25] IBID.

[26] IBID.

[27] Rocco A. Errico, George M. Lamsa, and George M. Lamsa, *Aramaic Light on the Gospels of Mark and Luke: a Commentary on the Teachings of Jesus from the Aramaic and Unchanged Near Eastern Customs* (Smyrna, GA: Noohra Foundation, 2001).

4. What was "authority" to teach the Torah? (v. 27)

    Scribes were not ordained as rabbis. Therefore, they were not permitted to offer any new interpretation of the Scripture or any new laws pertaining to Scripture. Yeshua came into the synagogue without an ordination. Thus, he was viewed as a scribe, yet he offered new interpretations and laws about the Scripture. Yeshua's actions shocked the people because they did not expect Him to act as a rabbi.[28]

Cultural Echoes

1. Daniel 7:14 "And to Him was given dominion, Glory and a kingdom, That all the peoples, nations and *men of every* language Might serve Him. His dominion is an everlasting dominion which will not pass away, *a*nd His kingdom is one which will not be destroyed.

    Yeshua was echoing this verse in Daniel. He told the people that His authority to preach and create law was given to Him by the LORD Himself. Yeshua did not need earthly rabbinical teachings.

Thoughts

The question for today is the same question that people asked in Yeshua's day. What is your authority to talk about the LORD? When a new pastor comes to a church, the people want to know how educated they are. In Yeshua's time, ordination was done by a person's rabbi (teacher). When the rabbi believed a student was ready to go into the world as a rabbi, the person was ordained. Therefore, all who listened to the new rabbi could rest assured that the new rabbi knew what he was talking about. The idea of formal education is fading away in many churches, especially independent churches. As trained, ordained clergy continues to drop, the church has no choice but to make untrained people clergy.

---

[28] David H. Stern, *Jewish New Testament Commentary: a Companion Volume to the Jewish New Testament* (Clarksville, MD: Jewish New Testament Publications, 1999).

Reflections

Being educated about the ways of the LORD is crucial to the health and well-being of the church. Many churches are not using formally educated people to run their education classes. With education costs of college and Seminary skyrocketing, there are fewer and fewer candidates for ordained ministry. It is difficult to convince a person to spend over $100,000 for a low paying job. So, the church has to raise the salary packages they offer their pastor. The church desperately needs educated leaders and especially pastors.

MARK 1:29-45

Language

New American Standard 1995	Koine Greek
²⁹ And immediately after they had come out of the synagogue, they came into the house of Simon and Andrew, with James and John.	¹⁹ Καὶ προβὰς ἐκεῖθεν ὀλίγον, εἶδεν Ἰάκωβον τὸν τοῦ Ζεβεδαίου, καὶ Ἰωάννην τὸν ἀδελφὸν αὐτοῦ, καὶ αὐτοὺς ἐν τῷ πλοίῳ καταρτίζοντας τὰ δίκτυα.
³⁰ Now Simon's mother-in-law was lying sick with a fever; and immediately they spoke to Him about her.	²⁰ Καὶ εὐθέως ἐκάλεσεν αὐτούς· καὶ ἀφέντες τὸν πατέρα αὐτῶν Ζεβεδαῖον ἐν τῷ πλοίῳ μετὰ τῶν μισθωτῶν ἀπῆλθον ὀπίσω αὐτοῦ.
³¹ And He came to her and raised her up, taking her by the hand, and the fever left her, and she waited on them.	²¹ Καὶ εἰσπορεύονται εἰς Καπερναούμ· καὶ εὐθέως τοῖς σάββασιν εἰσελθὼν εἰς τὴν συναγωγήν, ἐδίδασκεν.
³² And when evening had come, after the sun had set, they *began* bringing to Him all who were ill and those who were demon-possessed.	²² Καὶ ἐξεπλήσσοντο ἐπὶ τῇ διδαχῇ αὐτοῦ· ἦν γὰρ διδάσκων αὐτοὺς ὡς ἐξουσίαν ἔχων, καὶ οὐχ ὡς οἱ γραμματεῖς.
³³ And the whole city had gathered at the door.	²³ Καὶ ἦν ἐν τῇ συναγωγῇ αὐτῶν ἄνθρωπος ἐν πνεύματι ἀκαθάρτῳ, καὶ ἀνέκραξεν,
³⁴ And He healed many who were ill with various diseases, and cast out many demons; and He was not permitting the demons to speak, because they knew who He was.	²⁴ λέγων, Ἔα, τί ἡμῖν καὶ σοί, Ἰησοῦ Ναζαρηνέ; Ἦλθες ἀπολέσαι ἡμᾶς; Οἶδά σε τίς εἶ, ὁ ἅγιος τοῦ θεοῦ.
³⁵ And in the early morning, while it was still dark, He arose and went out and departed to a lonely place, and was praying there.	²⁵ Καὶ ἐπετίμησεν αὐτῷ ὁ Ἰησοῦς, λέγων, Φιμώθητι, καὶ ἔξελθε ἐξ αὐτοῦ.
³⁶ And Simon and his companions hunted for Him;	²⁶ Καὶ σπαράξαν αὐτὸν τὸ πνεῦμα τὸ ἀκάθαρτον καὶ κράξαν φωνῇ μεγάλῃ, ἐξῆλθεν ἐξ αὐτοῦ.
³⁷ and they found Him, and said to Him, "Everyone is looking for You."	²⁷ Καὶ ἐθαμβήθησαν πάντες, ὥστε συζητεῖν πρὸς ἑαυτούς, λέγοντας, Τί ἐστιν τοῦτο; Τίς ἡ διδαχὴ ἡ καινὴ αὕτη, ὅτι κατ' ἐξουσίαν καὶ τοῖς πνεύμασιν τοῖς ἀκαθάρτοις ἐπιτάσσει, καὶ ὑπακούουσιν αὐτῷ;
³⁸ And He said to them, "Let us go somewhere else to the towns nearby, in order that I may preach there also; for that is what I came out for."	²⁸ Ἐξῆλθεν δὲ ἡ ἀκοὴ αὐτοῦ εὐθὺς εἰς ὅλην τὴν περίχωρον τῆς Γαλιλαίας.
³⁹ And He went into their synagogues throughout all Galilee, preaching and casting out the demons.	²⁹ Καὶ εὐθέως ἐκ τῆς συναγωγῆς ἐξελθόντες, ἦλθον εἰς τὴν οἰκίαν Σίμωνος καὶ Ἀνδρέου, μετὰ Ἰακώβου καὶ Ἰωάννου.
⁴⁰ And a leper came to Him, beseeching Him and falling on his knees before Him, and saying to Him, "If You are willing, You can make me clean."	³⁰ Ἡ δὲ πενθερὰ Σίμωνος κατέκειτο πυρέσσουσα, καὶ εὐθέως λέγουσιν αὐτῷ περὶ αὐτῆς·
⁴¹ And moved with compassion, He stretched out His hand, and touched him, and said to him, "I am willing; be cleansed."	³¹ καὶ προσελθὼν ἤγειρεν αὐτήν, κρατήσας τῆς χειρὸς αὐτῆς· καὶ ἀφῆκεν αὐτὴν ὁ πυρετὸς εὐθέως, καὶ διηκόνει αὐτοῖς.
⁴² And immediately the leprosy left him and he was cleansed.	

⁴³ And He sternly warned him and immediately sent him away,

⁴⁴ and He said to him, "See that you say nothing to anyone; but go, show yourself to the priest and offer for your cleansing what Moses commanded, for a testimony to them."

⁴⁵ But he went out and began to proclaim it freely and to spread the news about, to such an extent that Jesus could no longer publicly enter a city, but stayed out in unpopulated areas; and they were coming to Him from everywhere.

³² Ὀψίας δὲ γενομένης, ὅτε ἔδυ ὁ ἥλιος, ἔφερον πρὸς αὐτὸν πάντας τοὺς κακῶς ἔχοντας καὶ τοὺς δαιμονιζομένους·

³³ καὶ ἡ πόλις ὅλη ἐπισυνηγμένη ἦν πρὸς τὴν θύραν.

³⁴ Καὶ ἐθεράπευσεν πολλοὺς κακῶς ἔχοντας ποικίλαις νόσοις, καὶ δαιμόνια πολλὰ ἐξέβαλεν, καὶ οὐκ ἤφιεν λαλεῖν τὰ δαιμόνια, ὅτι ᾔδεισαν αὐτόν.

³⁵ Καὶ πρωῒ ἔννυχον λίαν ἀναστὰς ἐξῆλθεν, καὶ ἀπῆλθεν εἰς ἔρημον τόπον, κἀκεῖ προσηύχετο.

³⁶ Καὶ κατεδίωξαν αὐτὸν ὁ Σίμων καὶ οἱ μετ' αὐτοῦ·

³⁷ καὶ εὑρόντες αὐτὸν λέγουσιν αὐτῷ ὅτι Πάντες σε ζητοῦσιν.

³⁸ Καὶ λέγει αὐτοῖς, Ἄγωμεν εἰς τὰς ἐχομένας κωμοπόλεις, ἵνα καὶ ἐκεῖ κηρύξω· εἰς τοῦτο γὰρ ἐξελήλυθα.

³⁹ Καὶ ἦν κηρύσσων ἐν ταῖς συναγωγαῖς αὐτῶν εἰς ὅλην τὴν Γαλιλαίαν, καὶ τὰ δαιμόνια ἐκβάλλων.

⁴⁰ Καὶ ἔρχεται πρὸς αὐτὸν λεπρός, παρακαλῶν αὐτὸν καὶ γονυπετῶν αὐτόν, καὶ λέγων αὐτῷ ὅτι Ἐὰν θέλῃς, δύνασαί με καθαρίσαι.

⁴¹ Ὁ δὲ Ἰησοῦς σπλαγχνισθείς, ἐκτείνας τὴν χεῖρα, ἥψατο αὐτοῦ, καὶ λέγει αὐτῷ, Θέλω, καθαρίσθητι.

⁴² Καὶ εἰπόντος αὐτοῦ εὐθέως ἀπῆλθεν ἀπ' αὐτοῦ ἡ λέπρα, καὶ ἐκαθαρίσθη.

⁴³ Καὶ ἐμβριμησάμενος αὐτῷ, εὐθέως ἐξέβαλεν αὐτόν,

⁴⁴ καὶ λέγει αὐτῷ, Ὅρα, μηδενὶ μηδὲν εἴπῃς· ἀλλ' ὕπαγε, σεαυτὸν δεῖξον τῷ ἱερεῖ, καὶ προσένεγκε περὶ τοῦ καθαρισμοῦ σου ἃ προσέταξεν Μωσῆς, εἰς μαρτύριον αὐτοῖς.

⁴⁵ Ὁ δὲ ἐξελθὼν ἤρξατο κηρύσσειν πολλὰ καὶ διαφημίζειν τὸν λόγον, ὥστε μηκέτι αὐτὸν δύνασθαι φανερῶς εἰς πόλιν εἰσελθεῖν, ἀλλ' ἔξω ἐν ἐρήμοις τόποις ἦν· καὶ ἤρχοντο πρὸς αὐτὸν πανταχόθεν.

Process of Discovery

Linguistics Section

Linguistic Structure

[Simon's Home] [29] And immediately after they had come out of the synagogue, they came into the house of Simon and Andrew, with James and John. [30] Now Simon's mother-in-law was lying sick with a fever; and immediately they spoke to Him about her. [31] And He came to her and raised her up, taking her by the hand, and the fever left her, and she waited on them.

[Day after Shabbat] [32] And when evening had come, after the sun had set, they *began* bringing to Him all who were ill and those who were demon-possessed.

[Semitic hyperbole] [33] And the whole city had gathered at the door.

[More healings] [34] And He healed many who were ill with various diseases, and cast out many demons; and He was not permitting the demons to speak, because they knew who He was.

[Break between healings] [35] And in the early morning, while it was still dark, He arose and went out and departed to a lonely place, and was praying there. [36] And Simon and his companions hunted for Him; [37] and they found Him, and said to Him, "Everyone is looking for You." [38] And He said to them, "Let us go somewhere else to the towns nearby, in order that I may preach there also; for that is what I came out for."

[Transition] [39] And He went into their synagogues throughout all Galilee, preaching and casting out the demons.

[Another healing] [40] And a leper came to Him, beseeching Him and falling on his knees before Him, and saying to Him, "If You are willing, You can make me clean." [41] And moved with compassion, He stretched out His hand, and touched him, and said to him, "I am willing; be cleansed." [42] And immediately the leprosy left him and he was cleansed.

[Warning to be quiet] [43] And He sternly warned him and immediately sent him away, [44] and He said to him, "See that you say nothing to anyone; but go, show yourself to the priest and offer for your cleansing what Moses commanded, for a testimony to them." [45] But he went out and began to proclaim it freely and to spread the news about, to such an extent that Jesus could no longer publicly enter a city, but stayed out in unpopulated areas; and they were coming to Him from everywhere.

Discussion

This narrative has three different healing stories. Each one has something different, making them unique. The first one is curing Simon's mother-in-law, who was suffering from a fever. There is a transition to the second set of healings, which includes exorcisms. Then another transition to the leper healing. This last healing has Yeshua telling the healed person not to talk about it.

Questioning the Passage

1. Why was Yeshua's first healing done in private? (v. 29)
    Mark's author started Yeshua's disease healing in a private mode because it was still the Shabbat. Mark will have Yeshua healing on the Shabbat, focusing on whether healing could occur on Shabbat. The first healing focuses on Yeshua's healing power.

2. How do we know that the second healing was done after the Shabbat? (v. 32)
    Verse thirty-two says that evening came, and Yeshua started to heal. The day begins at sunset in the Hebraic calendar. Therefore, the Shabbat was over. The controversy about healing on the Shabbat was not a problem at this time. The healing power of Yeshua was being demonstrated.

3. Is there a pattern to the healings?
    The healing narratives in Mark follow a pattern.[29]
    a. The person requiring healing is brought to Yeshua often with the help of friends or family.
    b. Yeshua encounters the person sometimes with dialogue.

---

[29] Ched Myers, *Binding the Strong Man a Political Reading of Mark's Story of Jesus* (Maryknoll, NY: Orbis Books, 1988).

    c. Yeshua responds to the request for healing with a touch or words.

    d. The healing is reported as Yeshua instructs the person.

4. Did the entire town come out to see the healings? (v. 33)

This statement is an example of Semitic hyperbole. It is an exaggeration to emphasize the work that Yeshua was doing.

5. Can Yeshua's healing narratives be a metaphor for societal changes?

The belief in healing miracles could be viewed as a metaphor for social changes. Yeshua's mission was to go to the poor and disenfranchised people of his society. These people were shunned from worshiping the LORD by the culture of the day. People who had leprosy were shunned and placed outside of their community. They had no chance to worship the LORD nor participate in any of the rituals of the religion. They were usually forgotten except for the kind relatives that brought them food and water. Disease, hunger, and danger were part of the lives of Galilee and Judea's peasants. The life of a poor person was not valued as much as a rich person. Society did not value these persons, so they were placed outside the community when they acquired a disease. Yeshua's healing work brought these people back into society. He was trying to teach the people that all lives are essential to the LORD. Society should be taking care of the infirmed rather than casting them off to exile. Yeshua's healing was an attempt to bring the oppressed and marginalized people of Galilee and Judea back into society and to give them value.

6. Why did Yeshua touch the leper? (v. 41)

In this narrative, Mark's author demonstrated the courage of Yeshua by breaking with cultural traditions. Yeshua touched the untouchable person. He was not concerned about getting the disease. Either He knew that skin diseases were not transmitted by touch, or He was so determined to help this helpless person that He was bold. Yeshua had tremendous courage to break out of the norms of His culture.

7. Why did Yeshua tell the person cured of leprosy to see the local priest? (v. 44)

Leviticus 14:1 (NAS95S) Then the LORD spoke to Moses, saying, [2] "This shall be the law of the leper in the day of his cleansing. Now he shall be brought to the priest, [3] and the priest shall go out to the outside of the camp. Thus the priest shall look, and if the infection of leprosy has been healed in the leper

These verses are examples of how Yeshua did not come to destroy the Torah but instead fulfilled the Torah and the Prophets. The person cured of leprosy was excited to be cured. Yeshua acknowledged the person's joy but reminded him that he had an obligation under the Torah law to go to the priest and be declared clean. Yeshua always sought to strengthen the Torah.

8. Why did Yeshua tell the man with leprosy not to tell anyone? (v. 44)

Yeshua was concerned that if the people discovered that He was the Messiah, they would attempt to make him King of Israel immediately. The traditional messianic view was that the Messiah was going to overthrow Rome and Herod's oppressive government, thus restoring Israel's nation, and the Messiah would be the King. Yeshua knew that this was not the way the LORD wanted Him to proceed. Therefore, it tried to keep things quiet about the messiahship.

Culture Section

Discussion

In the summer, the heat in Galilee was unbearable during the day. Laborers did very little work in the heat of the day. Farmers took a rest and waited for harvest time. Most people stay indoors during the day to avoid the heat. They gathered on their housetops or under trees to discuss town affairs or debate religious subjects in the evening.

People who were sick or infirmed remained in the house until sunset. If a person had a fever, they would rise in the evening to perform as much of their daily task that they could. Near

Eastern people believed that the sun was harmful to sick people. So, in the evening most people were outside. This time was perfect for Yeshua to preach and heal the sick.[30]

Questioning the passage

1. Who suffered the most from disease and physical disabilities?

    Generally speaking, poor people suffered the most from disease and physical ailments. Day laborers who became ill, meant unemployment and instant impoverishment.[31]

2. What was leprosy? (v. 40)

    Any skin disease was considered leprosy in Yeshua's day. When a person was declared unclean because of a skin disease, it became unlawful to touch them. People believed that skin diseases were transmitted by touch. They did not know that hygiene conditions caused leprosy. The leper was put outside the community, usually near the garbage dump of the town.

3. How did Semites regard healers and holy men about diseases?

    Semitic people believed that healers and holy men were immune from diseases. They believed that these people were special messengers from the LORD. With the LORD's protection, they would not be able to pick up a disease when healing.

4. What is an unclean spirit?

    An unclean spirit was also known as a demon in Jesus's day. The demons were believed to be the spirits of the 199 angels, called the Watchers. In Genesis chapter six, there is a short overview of what happened. The story is expanded in the Book of the Watchers, which is the first thirty-six chapters of 1 Enoch. The Ethiopian Orthodox church has Enoch's books as a part of their Canonical (Bible) books.[32]

---

[30] Rocco A. Errico, George M. Lamsa, and George M. Lamsa, *Aramaic Light on the Gospels of Mark and Luke: a Commentary on the Teachings of Jesus from the Aramaic and Unchanged Near Eastern Customs* (Smyrna, GA: Noohra Foundation, 2001).

[31] Ched Myers, *Binding the Strong Man a Political Reading of Mark's Story of Jesus* (Maryknoll, NY: Orbis Books, 1988).

[32] http://www.ethiopianorthodox.org/english/canonical/books.html. Accessed on April 27, 2022

There are several possible reasons why the proto-orthodox Church (which becomes the catholic, orthodox and protestant churches) rejected Enoch's books. There are theological thoughts in Enoch that did not fit the Church's beliefs about God, angels, and humans. Paul did not seem to be a fan of Enoch and infers that Enoch and other such writings are false teachings. Paul was a student who studied Scripture and would have been familiar with Enoch, along with several other extra-Biblical writings. It appears that if a writer did not comply with Paul's view of Christ, he labeled it false teaching. If Paul's theory that he used the Mithras cult as a basis for his view of Jesus is correct, then Enoch would not fit the narrative.

The Gospel of Mark contains several encounters between Jesus and the demons. Examining Genesis chapter six and the Watchers' Book, it can be seen how the demons came into being. There is a midrash about Azazel and Shemihazah (they were angels) coming before God's throne and asking if they could have permission to visit the humans on the Earth. The LORD warned them against doing this because the humans' evil would influence the two angels. Azazel and Shemihazah decided to visit the Earth anyway. While in human form, the two angels experienced the evil of the world. The Midrash stops there. It is possible to continue the Midrash using the events in Genesis, chapter six, and Watchers' Book of Watchers. When the two angels return to Heaven, the LORD made them part of a group of angels called the Watchers. Their job can be described as being guardian angels. Since Azazel and Shemihazah lived on the Earth, they would know what humans did and how they thought. It is stated in Genesis six that the Watchers saw how beautiful the daughters of men were. Why would the angels be concerned about this? Speculation is that when Azazel and Shemihazah were on the Earth, they could have experienced the joys of knowing the women on the Earth. They could have desired to have that union with women again and convinced 198 other Watchers to join them. It is unclear in the Book of the Watchers why the 198 Watchers joined them.

The 200 Watchers came to Earth and took human male form. Genesis six says that the Watchers took wives for themselves. This tells us that they had sex with the women who got pregnant and gave birth to children who were the Giants. The Scripture calls them the Nephilim. According to the Book of the Watchers, Genesis chapter six is a very sketchy overview of what happened. That book says that the offspring of the Watchers' union and the women were called the Giants. The Giants had offspring called the Nephilim, and their offspring were called the Elioud. It was the actions of the Elioud that caused all the problems.

The Elioud and the humans of that day entered into a war against each other. The Elioud were physically large in comparison to the humans, and they were killing humans. The Elioud committed the one sin that inflamed the LORD more than any other sin. They drank the human blood.

[26] 'You are not to eat any blood, either of bird or animal, in any of your dwellings. [27] 'Any person who eats any blood, even that person shall be cut off from his people.'" (Lev. 7:26-27 NAU)

Azazel and Shemihazah knew that they had brought sin upon their fellow Watchers and the Earth. They attempted to repair the problem. The angels were divided into groups of ten with a lead angel. Each leader of the group of ten offered a secret of Heaven to the humans. Azazel offered humans the knowledge of metallurgy. This enabled humans to create weapons that would help them to destroy the Elioud. This secret and several others were given to humans against the wishes of the LORD. If the LORD wanted the humans to know these secrets, He would have dispatched angels to transmit the information. Instead, the Watchers decided to offer the information.

The LORD was angered by what the Watchers did and the evil that was growing on upon the Earth. Unfortunately, by giving a free choice to the humans, the LORD enabled them to create their sin. Humans do not need help from anyone to sin. However, with Heaven's secrets that the Watchers gave the humans, sin and evil spread rapidly. The Flood that the LORD brought upon the Earth was to cleanse the Earth of this sin. Perhaps the flood was also necessary to kill the Elioud and their descendants. The Flood could have served this dual purpose.

The court of the LORD was held, and the indictment about the Watchers was read before the LORD. The Watchers were found guilty of sin, and the LORD pronounced punishment. Azazel was thrown into the Pit (which becomes Hell). He was the fallen angel that became Satan. The other 199 Watchers were punished by being condemned to live in the foundations of the Earth. Ancient people believed that pillars of rock held up the land of the Earth. They also believed that there was a river of water that flowed under the Earth. They believed this because when they dug into the ground, they hit a rock, and in other cases they hit the water. The 199 Watchers were believed to have been placed inside the rock, the foundation of the Earth.

Therefore, when the LORD brought the Flood upon the Earth, the Watchers were not destroyed. Since they were forced to live in the Earth's foundation, they were not affected by the Flood. The evil and sinful people, Giants, Nephilim, and Elioud of the Earth, were killed by the Flood. Noah and his family were righteous people, so God spared them. There are various midrashim about the Flood because the following verse can be found in Numbers.

[33] "There also we saw the Nephilim (the sons of Anak are part of the Nephilim); and we became like grasshoppers in our own sight, and so we were in their sight." (Num. 13:33 NAU)

There is a legend that the King of the Nephilim begged Noah to save him. The King was told that he could ride on the Ark. Several beams stuck out of the Ark, and the King sat on one. Noah cut a special window into the Ark, which allowed him to give the King food and water. Since the Nephilim seemed to survive the flood according to Numbers, the King's mate must have also survived. The Midrash does not tell us about her. Perhaps she was on a beam on the opposite side of the Ark. If only the King was on a beam, the Ark certainly would have tipped over because of the King's weight. Therefore, logically speaking, there had to be a counterweight on the opposite side. The easiest counterweight would have been the queen of the Nephilim. It is believed that Goliath was a descendant of the Nephilim, thus giving rise to this type of legend.

So, the 199 Watchers survived the Flood. Chronologically there is nothing written about their activities until Jesus's time. The purpose of the Flood was to eliminate evil and sin from the Earth, then how come evil and sin continued after the Flood? A reason is that the earthly bound Watchers took revenge against humans because of their punishment from the LORD. The influence of the Watchers could account for history's horrific events of people killing each other before Jesus's arrival.

How could the LORD remove the Watchers' evil influence on the Earth? In Jesus's day, the Watchers were known as demons. From Mark 1:21-28 and several other encounters with demons, Jesus, the Son of God, exorcised the demons out of humans and condemned them to the Pit to join Azazel. The Book of the Watchers was well-read in Jesus's day. The Hebrew people believed that the demons were those spirits of the condemned Watchers. From the narratives, in the Gospels, the demons knew who Jesus was.

In the book of the Watchers, the Watchers are called unclean spirits. The Watchers became unclean spirits, which prohibited them from returning to Heaven. Only the perfect, the pure, and the clean spirits are permitted into Heaven. Instead of destroying the Watchers' spirits, the LORD had them condemned into the Foundations of the Earth. The Christian Scripture references to the unclean spirits is another linguistic connection between the Book of the Watchers and the Gospel exorcism narratives.

In several places in the letters of the Christian Scripture, there are words about the unclean spirits. The Watchers, who become the demons from the time of Noah, are spoken about. In addition to the Gospels, these references demonstrate that the people of Jesus's time understood who the demons and the unclean spirits were.

[18] For Christ also died for sins once for all, *the* just for *the* unjust, so that He might bring us to God, having been put to death in the flesh, but made alive in the spirit;[19] in which also He went and made proclamation to the spirits *now* in prison, [20] who once were

disobedient, when the patience of God kept waiting in the days of Noah, during the construction of the ark, in which a few, that is, eight persons, were brought safely through *the* water. (1 Pet. 3:18-20 NAU)

[6] And angels who did not keep their own domain, but abandoned their proper abode, He has kept in eternal bonds under darkness for the judgment of the great day, (Jude 1:6 NAU)

[9] And the great dragon was thrown down, the serpent of old who is called the devil and Satan, who deceives the whole world; he was thrown down to the earth, and his angels were thrown down with him. (Rev. 12:9 NAU)

[4] For if God did not spare angels when they sinned, but cast them into hell and committed them to pits of darkness, reserved for judgment; [5] and did not spare the ancient world, but preserved Noah, a preacher of righteousness, with seven others, when He brought a flood upon the world of the ungodly; (2 Pet. 2:4-5 NAU)

The Peter letters and Jude might have been written for a mainly Jewish community of believers in Jesus because of the references to the Watchers of Noah's time. The Book of the Watchers was well-read in Jesus's day. So, Jesus reversed the damage the Watchers created by exorcising them out of humans.

However, where did the demons go? In Mark 5:1-20, the narrative speaks about a man who was possessed by several demons. Jesus was about to do his exorcism when the demons asked Jesus to send them into a herd of pigs. Jesus allowed them to do this. Then the narrative takes an exciting twist and says that the pigs jumped into the sea and are killed. Why would the pigs do this? Even the unclean pigs did not like being possessed by the demons. The middle of the Sea of Galilee was also known as the Abyss, which was another name for the Pit, which was another name for Hell. It was believed that if your boat sank in the middle of the Sea of Galilee that your spirit would be condemned to the Hell. Therefore, the reference to the pigs jumping into the sea and dying tells us that the demons were sent to the Pit, to Hell, to join Azazel, who was known as Satan. Therefore, Jesus reversed the damage that was caused by the Watchers and rid the world of the demons.

The exorcism narratives of the Gospel all have this backdrop. Each of the narratives gives us other spiritual messages from Jesus about combatting evils and demons. If the Watchers were sent to Hell, they could have become the angels of Satan. The angels of Satan could still roam the Earth, trying to influence us to perform acts of evil. The difference is that Satan's angel cannot possess a human in the same way the demons could. Therefore, we must not let down our guard against the forces of Satan and evil. Besides this, we must remember to be aware that human free will can cause us to sin against the LORD. Jesus saved us from the forces of evil brought upon us by the Watchers. Following Jesus's words can keep us safe from ourselves.

Thoughts

The disenfranchised people of society were Yeshua's primary concern. How could He help them? He had to teach people that being sick or riddled with a disease was not a reason to place a person outside the community. Everyone has a right to find the LORD, worship Him, and to receive blessings from Him. This idea not only included sick people but all people. There were rules and regulations about who could come into the Temple at Jerusalem, and even entry into the local synagogues could be blocked. That is not the way of the LORD. The LORD and Yeshua value all people of all races and nations.

Reflections

Church politics tend to disenfranchise people. A church I was assigned to had two types of members. The first I call the "elite." These families controlled every aspect of the Church, especially finances. The second type was the "2nd class members." They were expected to perform the Church's work and be silent. During my years there, I elevated the 2nd class members showing them that they were equal to the elite in the same way Yeshua demonstrated that there are no 2nd class citizens in the Kingdom of Heaven. The elite became so obsessed that I did this that they worked overtime to get me moved to a different church. The elite won after three years. Sadly the 2nd class membership was reinstated by the elite, and those true disciples of Yeshua stayed at the Church. The 2nd class members showed loyalty to a church that did not respect them. It is NOT supposed to be this way. Do not let this happen in your Church. Every disciple is an elite member of Yeshua's Church.

Additional Thoughts

Yeshua desired to bring unity to a fractured Jewish community. The Hebraic people of Galilee and Judea had been under oppressive rule for centuries. This pressure caused their society to break apart. Groups of people followed Roman rule because they wanted to obtain financial and materialistic gains. Another group of persons opposed the Roman occupation with all their might. Most of the common people were from the peasant class. They were concerned about daily life. The Pharisees, Sadducees, Essene, and Zealots formed during this period of oppression. Each group had a different agenda and sometimes fought with each other. Even though their ideal situation was to work together to overthrow the oppressors, they had different ideas on how to do this and how to protect themselves. Thus, their division allowed Roman rule to continue.

The divisions that started almost immediately in the Church is an example of what was happening in Judaism. Yeshua was interested in unity. The healing narratives are examples where Yeshua teaches us that unity is an essential feature of the Kingdom of Heaven. It must start on Earth. The man with leprosy was separated from the community. Thus, the community was divided. Some people in the community were allowed access to the LORD, while others were not. Yeshua spoke about charity. He wanted people with excess resources to help people with little.

During Yeshua's day, the differences in the philosophy of the Jewish groups kept them separated. Again, Yeshua wanted unity. He demonstrated this concept throughout the Gospel of Mark. The intolerance of the groups in Yeshua's day prevented them from being one nation. People today can learn from Yeshua's lesson about unity.

In the United States, it can be generally defined that two groups are competing with each other. The two groups are Modernists and Post-Modernists. Over the past twenty years, it has become clear that age is no longer a determining factor as to which group a person aligns with. When Post-Modernism was introduced in the late 1900s, it was based on age. Young people were being taught Post-Modernism. Unfortunately, the teachers of Post-Modernism, and the founders of the movement, taught their disciples not to be very tolerant of Modernists.

Modern and Post-Modern thinking does have things in common. A new way of human thinking is always based on existing thinking. History has proven this. The problem today seems to be that the Modernists and Post-Modernists have gone to war. In the late 1900s, the two groups coexisted and worked together. Clashes always occurred because there are some substantial differences between the two philosophies. However, the two sides showed respect for each other. A compromise was occurring between the two groups, and society grew and learned to adapt to a new way of thinking.

When the new century began, the war started. It does not matter which side started the war, and perhaps it was a mutual thing. In 2020 the two sides were incredibly intolerant of each other. Both sides work toward destroying the other. It does not matter which side controls the U.S. government because the side out of power will fight instead of compromising. Also, the side in power now pushes the other side out of the picture whenever possible. This move is occurring whether Modernists or Post-Modernists are in power. Compromise has almost become a dead issue. When does comprise occur? When the thinking of Modernists and Post-Modernists intersect. That does happen from time to time. It is happening less often, which is sad.

This phenomenon is also occurring in Yeshua's churches. The division among denominations that have stood for centuries is occurring. The Modernists and the Post-Modernists in the Church are fighting with each other. Each side has been obstinate in listening to the other side. Most of the large denominations have already been divided. The United Methodist Church will probably divide into Moderns and Post-Moderns in 2021.

Yeshua wanted unity for His people. Every time there is a division in Yeshua's Church, He must be weeping. How can people say they are disciples of Yeshua and are good with divisions in the Church?

The Church is not united, and since 48 CE it never has been. Society's war of Modernists and Post-Modernists is in the Church. Therefore, the divisions of the Church will probably continue.

How can both groups come together? In November 2020, after the Presidential election, it was apparent that something drastic had to happen to bring Modernists and Post-Modernists together. Yeshua stands for unity. He also demonstrated the courage to tell His people that their fracturing was allowing the oppression to occur.

A man approached Yeshua with leprosy. The law of the day says that one does not touch a person with leprosy. What did Yeshua do? He touched the man and healed him. Yeshua demonstrates courage! People in that day believed that touching a person with leprosy would transmit the disease. Did that stop Yeshua? No, He had courage. The allegorical meaning of the narrative is that Yeshua demonstrated that courage was needed to reunite the Hebrew people. Once united, they could stand up to their oppressors.

The Church has numerous oppressors today, both inside and outside. The Church is dying because of oppression. The Church needs people of courage to come forward and reunite it to defend itself from oppression. The people of the Church need to take Yeshua's example of courage. Touch the untouchable! The untouchable subject of compromise must be reinstated as the norm of how the Church works. Modernists and Post-Modernists in the Church need to have the courage to live the way Yeshua wants us to live. We are supposed to live in harmony and unity.

Who will have the courage to stand up and unite the factions of the Church? Perhaps that person is you. The greatest thing that could be done for Yeshua's Church is to bring all of its factions together! The LORD is calling for someone to come forward. Isaiah answered the call of the LORD when no one else would. Yeshua is calling for all His disciples to come forward. Let us answer the call together.

MARK 2:1-12

Language

New American Standard 1995	Koine Greek
[1] When He had come back to Capernaum several days afterward, it was heard that He was at home. [2] And many were gathered together, so that there was no longer room, not even near the door; and He was speaking the word to them. [3] And they came, bringing to Him a paralytic, carried by four men. [4] Being unable to get to Him because of the crowd, they removed the roof above Him; and when they had dug an opening, they let down the pallet on which the paralytic was lying. [5] And Jesus seeing their faith said to the paralytic, "Son, your sins are forgiven." [6] But some of the scribes were sitting there and reasoning in their hearts, [7] "Why does this man speak that way? He is blaspheming; who can forgive sins but God alone?" [8] Immediately Jesus, aware in His spirit that they were reasoning that way within themselves, said to them, "Why are you reasoning about these things in your hearts? [9] "Which is easier, to say to the paralytic, 'Your sins are forgiven'; or to say, 'Get up, and pick up your pallet and walk '? [10] "But so that you may know that the Son of Man has authority on earth to forgive sins "-- He said to the paralytic, [11] "I say to you, get up, pick up your pallet and go home." [12] And he got up and immediately picked up the pallet and went out in the sight of everyone, so that they were all amazed and were glorifying God, saying, "We have never seen anything like this."	[1] Καὶ εἰσῆλθεν πάλιν εἰς Καπερναοὺμ δι' ἡμερῶν· καὶ ἠκούσθη ὅτι εἰς οἶκόν ἐστιν. [2] Καὶ εὐθέως συνήχθησαν πολλοί, ὥστε μηκέτι χωρεῖν μηδὲ τὰ πρὸς τὴν θύραν· καὶ ἐλάλει αὐτοῖς τὸν λόγον. [3] Καὶ ἔρχονται πρὸς αὐτόν, παραλυτικὸν φέροντες, αἰρόμενον ὑπὸ τεσσάρων. [4] Καὶ μὴ δυνάμενοι προσεγγίσαι αὐτῷ διὰ τὸν ὄχλον, ἀπεστέγασαν τὴν στέγην ὅπου ἦν, καὶ ἐξορύξαντες χαλῶσιν τὸν κράββατον ἐφ' ᾧ ὁ παραλυτικὸς κατέκειτο. [5] Ἰδὼν δὲ ὁ Ἰησοῦς τὴν πίστιν αὐτῶν λέγει τῷ παραλυτικῷ, Τέκνον, ἀφέωνταί σοι αἱ ἁμαρτίαι σου. [6] Ἦσαν δέ τινες τῶν γραμματέων ἐκεῖ καθήμενοι, καὶ διαλογιζόμενοι ἐν ταῖς καρδίαις αὐτῶν, [7] Τί οὗτος οὕτως λαλεῖ βλασφημίας; Τίς δύναται ἀφιέναι ἁμαρτίας εἰ μὴ εἷς, ὁ θεός; [8] Καὶ εὐθέως ἐπιγνοὺς ὁ Ἰησοῦς τῷ πνεύματι αὐτοῦ ὅτι οὕτως αὐτοὶ διαλογίζονται ἐν ἑαυτοῖς, εἶπεν αὐτοῖς, Τί ταῦτα διαλογίζεσθε ἐν ταῖς καρδίαις ὑμῶν; [9] Τί ἐστιν εὐκοπώτερον, εἰπεῖν τῷ παραλυτικῷ, Ἀφέωνταί σου αἱ ἁμαρτίαι, ἢ εἰπεῖν, Ἔγειραι, καὶ ἆρόν σου τὸν κράββατον, καὶ περιπάτει; [10] Ἵνα δὲ εἰδῆτε ὅτι ἐξουσίαν ἔχει ὁ υἱὸς τοῦ ἀνθρώπου ἀφιέναι ἐπὶ τῆς γῆς ἁμαρτίας- λέγει τῷ παραλυτικῷ- [11] Σοί λέγω, ἔγειραι καὶ ἆρον τὸν κράββατόν σου, καὶ ὕπαγε εἰς τὸν οἶκόν σου. [12] Καὶ ἠγέρθη εὐθέως, καὶ ἄρας τὸν κράββατον, ἐξῆλθεν ἐναντίον πάντων· ὥστε ἐξίστασθαι πάντας, καὶ δοξάζειν τὸν θεόν, λέγοντας ὅτι Οὐδέποτε οὕτως εἴδομεν.

Process of Discovery

Linguistics Section

Linguistic Structure

[Transition] [1] When He had come back to Capernaum several days afterward, it was heard that He was at home. [2] And many were gathered together, so that there was no longer room, not even near the door; and He was speaking the word to them.

A [3] And they came, bringing to Him a paralytic, carried by four men.

> **B** [4] Being unable to get to Him because of the crowd, they removed the roof above Him; and when they had dug an opening, they let down the pallet on which the paralytic was lying. [5] And Jesus seeing their faith said to the paralytic, "Son, your sins are forgiven."

> > **C** [6] But some of the scribes were sitting there and reasoning in their hearts, [7] "Why does this man speak that way? He is blaspheming; who can forgive sins but God alone?" [8] Immediately Jesus, aware in His spirit that they were reasoning that way within themselves, said to them, "Why are you reasoning about these things in your hearts?

> **B'** [9] "Which is easier, to say to the paralytic, 'Your sins are forgiven'; or to say, 'Get up, and pick up your pallet and walk '? [10] "But so that you may know that the Son of Man has authority on earth to forgive sins "-- He said to the paralytic, [11] "I say to you, get up, pick up your pallet and go home."

A' [12] And he got up and immediately picked up the pallet and went out in the sight of everyone, so that they were all amazed and were glorifying God, saying, "We have never seen anything like this."

Discussion

The center of the chiasm is the attack of the scribe. The attack is because they believed that only the LORD could forgive sin. If this was true, then Yeshua could not do it. Yeshua also questioned the Debt code that sin creates some debt to the LORD.

Questioning the Passage

1. Why were the scribes angry? (v. 7)

Did the scribes honestly believe that the LORD was the only one to forgive sins? Most historians indicate that they were concerned about their livelihood. After all, people came to Jerusalem to have a sacrifice made for them to forgive their sins. If Yeshua could forgive sins for the LORD, why could not other people do the same thing? If sins were forgiven without a sacrifice, then the scribes and priests would have starved.

2. How are poor people described in Mark's Gospel?

The poor people are referred to as the people of the land. The Greek term used is *ochlos*.[33] The main characteristics of the people of the land are:

a. They form the omnipresent background of Yeshua's ministry.

b. They are identified as sinners and social outcasts.

c. Though differentiated from the disciples, they are accepted as a part of Yeshua's community.

d. Unlike the disciples, they are never directly criticized or given special instructions.

e. They are alienated from the Hebraic leadership and thus largely supportive of Yeshua in his struggle against them.

f. They are feared by the ruling class, which in the end, can manipulate them against Yeshua.

Verse Comparison of citations or proof text

1. [10] "But so that you may know that the Son of Man has authority on earth to forgive sins" — He *said to the paralytic

Daniel 7:13 (NAS95S) "I kept looking in the night visions, and behold, with the clouds of heaven One like a Son of Man was coming, And He came up to the Ancient of Days and was presented before Him.

---

[33] Ched Myers, *Binding the Strong Man a Political Reading of Mark's Story of Jesus* (Maryknoll, NY: Orbis Books, 1988).

"This is an angel that Daniel saw who was in human form. This messenger came from the LORD to announce the glorious reign of the Messiah. The angel stood in front of the Messiah when the announcement was proclaimed. A differing view is that the one like a son of man is the Messiah. The Messiah comes from the clouds as opposed to the sea, which the beasts came from, to distinguish the difference in the creation of the kingdom they come from. The beast kingdom was created by war and force. The Messiah's kingdom is to be created by peace and good deeds."[34]

Culture Section

Discussion

The house that Yeshua visited was constructed of rough stones, unbaked bricks, and mud. Homes were built in the shape of a squared boxes without windows. There would have been an air chimney in the center of the home. The roof was flat. It would have been made of beams and branches of trees. A layer of straw and earth was the composition of the roof. If possible, the home was built with the back wall on a hilly slope. The homes were one story high. Houses were built adjacent to each other so that the roofs could serve as a playground for children.

Business and social conversation passed between the people on the roof and those inside the home. Homes for the peasants were not very large.[35]

Questioning the passage

1. What does this narrative say about poverty in Galilee?

    The house having an earthen roof was a sign of poverty. Rich people had concrete roofs. The one described in this narrative is the roof of a low-income family. When the rains came, the roof leaked. The word used for "mat" or "pallet" is κράβαττος. This

---

[34] Michael Harvey Koplitz, *Understanding Daniel* (York, PA: Independently Published, 2019).

[35] Rocco A. Errico, George M. Lamsa, and George M. Lamsa, *Aramaic Light on the Gospels of Mark and Luke: a Commentary on the Teachings of Jesus from the Aramaic and Unchanged Near Eastern Customs* (Smyrna, GA: Noohra Foundation, 2001).

Greek word describes a poor man's bed or mattress. The word was also used to describe a bedroll that soldiers used.[36]

2. What is the "debt code?"

   The Debt Code believes that a person has a debt that is payable to the LORD because of their sin or inherited sin. The belief was that the LORD could only forgive the debt to the LORD. Jesus demonstrated that the debt could be repaid in other ways. When He told the paralyzed man that He was cured, he asserted that the man owed to the LORD was paid. Since the debt caused by sin was gone, the man was cured.

3. Why did people believe that sin caused illness and infirmities?

   People in Yeshua's day did not understand what caused disease and infirmities. Therefore, the idea that the LORD caused these events can come into existence. Sin, which was not forgiven, was blamed for all diseases, illnesses, and infirmities. It was believed that the sins of the parents caused congenital disabilities.

Thoughts

The forgiveness of sin through words had to be established after the destruction of the Temple in Jerusalem. Interestingly, in this narrative, Yeshua tells the paralyzed man that his sins were forgiven. Should he have taken an animal to the Temple in Jerusalem and make the necessary sacrifice? Yeshua said that his sins are forgiven definitely would cause concern by the religious ruling elite. Is it against the Torah? Or is Yeshua telling the people that sin does not cause diseases or infirmities?

Reflections

In Yeshua's day, He healed people. That is something that everyone agrees with. Could Yeshua's healing be the cure for sin after 70 CE when the Temple was destroyed? We will never know since we do not have the original Mark Gospel. It is possible that the forgiveness of sin was added to the

---

[36] Ched Myers, *Binding the Strong Man a Political Reading of Mark's Story of Jesus* (Maryknoll, NY: Orbis Books, 1988).

narratives when the Gospel was copied and changed over the decades after 70 CE. That would account for Yeshua's apparent blasphemy. It was blasphemy in His day, but after 70 CE, it became an accepted understanding of the Jewish and Christian faith. A conclusion is that Yeshua did not say, "your sins are forgiven." These words were added later.

Afterthoughts

Suppose Yeshua canceled the Debt Code with the three healings from chapter one and chapter two. Why does the church preach that you need to be a disciple of Yeshua to receive salvation? Let us expand that just a bit. The church says that only through faith in Yeshua can a person's sins be forgiven. The church says that Yeshua died for all past, present, and future sins. However, Yeshua canceled the Debt Code for sin! If He canceled the Debt Code, then forgiveness has been given to everyone. This occurred before His death. Therefore, His death does not answer the question of forgiveness of sin. Yeshua said that the debt was paid before His death.

The Mithras cult believed that Mithras died for the sins of the people of the world. Therefore, if the theory that Paul converted Mithras churches holds true and Yeshua took Mithras's place, then it is clear why the church believes that Yeshua died as the price for sin. The problem is that Mark's Gospel contradicts that notion in a big way! Yeshua came to tell us that the Debt Code had been eliminated. If one lives a life according to the Word of the LORD, the forgiveness of sin was a part of the system.

The Zohar says that when the Torah came before the LORD to preach its case against humans, the LORD told the Torah that safeguards in the system would allow for the forgiveness of sin by humans. The LORD's blueprint to the Universe included a safeguard against sin. The LORD gave humans a free choice, and the LORD knew that this would lead to sin. If the Universe has atonement built it into it already, then Yeshua's death did not say people from sin. Instead, it is Yeshua's words and deeds that save humans from Sheol. It is asking for forgiveness and giving restitution, which saves people.

MARK 2:12–17

Language

New American Standard 1995	Koine Greek
[13] And He went out again by the seashore; and all the people were coming to Him, and He was teaching them. [14] As He passed by, He saw Levi the *son* of Alphaeus sitting in the tax booth, and He said to him, "Follow Me!" And he got up and followed Him. [15] And it happened that He was reclining *at the table* in his house, and many tax collectors and sinners were dining with Jesus and His disciples; for there were many of them, and they were following Him. [16] When the scribes of the Pharisees saw that He was eating with the sinners and tax collectors, they said to His disciples, "Why is He eating and drinking with tax collectors and sinners?" [17] And hearing *this*, Jesus said to them, "*It is* not those who are healthy who need a physician, but those who are sick; I did not come to call the righteous, but sinners."	[13] Καὶ ἐξῆλθεν πάλιν παρὰ τὴν θάλασσαν· καὶ πᾶς ὁ ὄχλος ἤρχετο πρὸς αὐτόν, καὶ ἐδίδασκεν αὐτούς. [14] Καὶ παράγων εἶδεν Λευῒ τὸν τοῦ Ἀλφαίου καθήμενον ἐπὶ τὸ τελώνιον, καὶ λέγει αὐτῷ, Ἀκολούθει μοι. Καὶ ἀναστὰς ἠκολούθησεν αὐτῷ. [15] Καὶ ἐγένετο ἐν τῷ κατακεῖσθαι αὐτὸν ἐν τῇ οἰκίᾳ αὐτοῦ, καὶ πολλοὶ τελῶναι καὶ ἁμαρτωλοὶ συνανέκειντο τῷ Ἰησοῦ καὶ τοῖς μαθηταῖς αὐτοῦ· ἦσαν γὰρ πολλοί, καὶ ἠκολούθησαν αὐτῷ. [16] Καὶ οἱ γραμματεῖς καὶ οἱ Φαρισαῖοι, ἰδόντες αὐτὸν ἐσθίοντα μετὰ τῶν τελωνῶν καὶ ἁμαρτωλῶν, ἔλεγον τοῖς μαθηταῖς αὐτοῦ, Τί ὅτι μετὰ τῶν τελωνῶν καὶ ἁμαρτωλῶν ἐσθίει καὶ πίνει; [17] Καὶ ἀκούσας ὁ Ἰησοῦς λέγει αὐτοῖς, Οὐ χρείαν ἔχουσιν οἱ ἰσχύοντες ἰατροῦ, ἀλλ' οἱ κακῶς ἔχοντες. Οὐκ ἦλθον καλέσαι δικαίους, ἀλλὰ ἁμαρτωλοὺς εἰς μετάνοιαν.

Process of Discovery

Linguistics Section

Linguistic Structure

A [13] And He went out again by the seashore; and all the people were coming to Him, and He was teaching them. [14] As He passed by, He saw Levi the *son* of Alphaeus sitting in the tax booth, and He said to him, "Follow Me!" And he got up and followed Him.

> **B** [15] And it happened that He was reclining *at the table* in his house, and many tax collectors and sinners were dining with Jesus and His disciples; for there were many of them, and they were following Him.

> **B'** [16] When the scribes of the Pharisees saw that He was eating with the sinners and tax collectors, they said to His disciples, "Why is He eating and drinking with tax collectors and sinners?"

A' [17] And hearing *this*, Jesus said to them, "*It is* not those who are healthy who need a physician, but those who are sick; I did not come to call the righteous, but sinners."

Discussion

This simple chiasm is formed from the narrative. The A block refers to Yeshua calling sinners to discipleship. The B block is Yeshua actually doing the calling of the sinners.

Questioning the Passage

1. Why did Yeshua sit with sinners? (v. 15)

   In the previous passage, Yeshua canceled the Debt Code. There was nothing owed to the LORD because of sin. If the Debt Code was removed, then everyone was a sinner before the LORD. There was no way to "pay" for forgiveness with material items. The way to receive forgiveness from sin was to repent, which involved a spiritual response, like a prayer. So, in Yeshua's mind, all people were sinners.[37] There was no distinction between tax collectors and Pharisees. The Pharisees did not see themselves as sinners. Yeshua tries to convince them that they were through the remainder of Mark's Gospel. There were only sinners on the road of discipleship.

---

[37] Ched Myers, *Binding the Strong Man a Political Reading of Mark's Story of Jesus* (Maryknoll, NY: Orbis Books, 1988).

2. What was Yeshua's mission? (v. 17)

Yeshua believed that everyone was a sinner. Therefore, His mission was to move the sinners to repentance on the road of discipleship for the LORD. His mission was for every person on Earth. According to the Zohar and the Kabbalah, there are only one or two righteous persons on Earth at the same time. That leaves the world full of sinners. The righteous persons would be people like Moses, Elijah, Isaiah, and Yeshua. The rest of humanity has to recognize that all people are sinners and require repentance.

3. Who are the "scribes of the Pharisees?" (v. 16)

Mark's author introduces a new group of antagonists. This group is a new group of people who have a relationship with the Pharisees. These people are not Pharisees. Mark's author introduces other groups of people with difficulties with Yeshua's ways in later chapters.[38]

4. Why are the scribes of the Pharisees concerned about whom Yeshua eats with? (v. 16)

This group of people followed the laws as defined by the Pharisees. Mark is demonstrating that they are more concerned about their laws than the welfare of the people. They should have been concerned about turning the tax collectors away from sin.

Biblical Personalities

1. Λευί, ὁ (לֵוִי)

    1. son of Jacob

    2. son of Melchi; in the genealogy of Jesus Lk 3:24.

    3. son of Symeon; in the genealogy of Jesus vs. 29.

    4. a disciple of Jesus; this disciple was a son of Alphaeus

---

[38] IBID.

5. name of a high priest, partly restored

In Mark's Gospel, this is the only place where Levi is mentioned. In some Christian traditions, Levi is equated to Matthew. This is done because verse fourteen says that Levi was sitting at a tax booth. In Matthew's Gospel, the author said that Matthew was sitting at a tax booth.

Culture Section

Discussion

In Yeshua's time, some guests at home would sit upright on the floor with their legs folded under them in the Near East. The more honored guests in the home would recline against bedding, clothing, rugs, or other objects to create a cushion effect. As soon as Yeshua entered a home, the women would rush to him, bringing a carpet or quilt to put under him as a token of a hearty welcome. Food and drink would be placed before him immediately, no matter what time of the day it was.[39] Therefore, the description given in verse fifteen does not indicate that a meal was being shared. It could be the simple form of welcoming a guest into the house. The host would have sat down with Yeshua wanting to listen to every Word Yeshua said.

Questioning the passage

1. What was a tax collector in Yeshua's day? (v. 15)

Tax collectors were also known as publicans. They were not necessarily government employees, nor was their only task to collect taxes. Many times tax collectors purchased from the government the privilege of collecting taxes from the people. The government levied a tax on salt, animals, land, and specific exported and imported articles. It was then the task of the publican to collect the tax.

The government often allowed a bidding war between persons who wanted the tax collecting job. The job would typically go to the highest bidder. The publican would

---

[39] Rocco A. Errico, George M. Lamsa, and George M. Lamsa, *Aramaic Light on the Gospels of Mark and Luke: a Commentary on the Teachings of Jesus from the Aramaic and Unchanged Near Eastern Customs* (Smyrna, GA: Noohra Foundation, 2001).

hire men to do the actual tax collecting. The hired men were shrewd and cruel in collecting the tax. It was vital for them to earn a profit from the taxes of the poor.

Publicans would survey crops, and count sheep so that they could levy a tax. The government was not concerned about how the taxes were collected, nor what the publican charged. As long as they received their required amount, they left the publicans alone. There was a lot of dishonesty and bribery that occurred.

Many times, violence and force were used in order to collect the taxes. Sheep, crops, and other valuables would be confiscated if a tax was not paid. Publicans were known to invade a home in search of money and goods that they could claim. These actions created panic among women and children. This situation is the reason the general population hated publicans so intensely and considered them sinners.

The general population considered tax collectors unforgivable. They also believed that the LORD would not forgive them in the world to come. They were considered traitors to their people. "Bread of blood" was the publican's bread, and many people would not share this bread. Pharisees did not eat with publicans because breaking bread was time for discussion and prayer. The Pharisee's adherence to strict ethical codes prevented much contact with tax collectors.[40]

2. Why did the tax collectors like Yeshua?

   Yeshua was not a friend of the Pharisees and priests. The tax collectors had the same attitude toward them. Therefore, the tax collectors were friendly to Yeshua. Priests and Pharisees would impose taxes on the people in the name of the LORD, i.e., the Temple Tax. Tax collectors did not impose any tax in the LORD's name.

Thoughts

---

[40] IBID.

The idea that Yeshua declares that everyone is a sinner is interesting. If the Debt Code is removed, then there is no payment for sin. Repentance is the way to receive forgiveness. What happens to this analysis if the idea that Yeshua died for sins is explored? It could be said that Yeshua died to bring us the secrets of Heaven that were lost over the centuries. Yeshua preached repentance. He did not declare himself God. He never said that He died to free people from sin. Instead, Yeshua said you free yourself by repentance and then follow the Torah the way He shows us. This methodology is a radically different way of understanding atonement than the church preaches.

Reflections

The Zohar says that there is at least one righteous person in every generation. Traditional Judaism says that the spirit of Moses is present in all generations. That leaves the rest of humanity as sinners. Yeshua came to help the sinners. We learn how to ask for and receive forgiveness for our sins through his words and actions. In his book The Soul, Adin Steinsaltz said that every soul passes to Genonim (Hell). This is not for punishment but rather a soul purification because of the Nefesh's sins (the body).[41] Then the soul travels to Heaven to be with the LORD. Yeshua shows us the path to righteousness so that our time in Genonim for purification is the shortest possible.

---

[41] Adin Steinsaltz, *The Soul* (New Milford, CT: Maggid Books, 2018).

MARK 2:18-22

Language

New American Standard 1995	Koine Greek
[18] John's disciples and the Pharisees were fasting; and they came and said to Him, "Why do John's disciples and the disciples of the Pharisees fast, but Your disciples do not fast?" [19] And Jesus said to them, "While the bridegroom is with them, the attendants of the bridegroom cannot fast, can they? So long as they have the bridegroom with them, they cannot fast. [20] "But the days will come when the bridegroom is taken away from them, and then they will fast in that day. [21] "No one sews a patch of unshrunk cloth on an old garment; otherwise the patch pulls away from it, the new from the old, and a worse tear results. [22] "No one puts new wine into old wineskins; otherwise the wine will burst the skins, and the wine is lost and the skins *as well*; but *one puts* new wine into fresh wineskins."	[18] Καὶ ἦσαν οἱ μαθηταὶ Ἰωάννου καὶ οἱ τῶν Φαρισαίων νηστεύοντες· καὶ ἔρχονται καὶ λέγουσιν αὐτῷ, Διὰ τί οἱ μαθηταὶ Ἰωάννου καὶ οἱ τῶν Φαρισαίων νηστεύουσιν, οἱ δὲ σοὶ μαθηταὶ οὐ νηστεύουσιν; [19] Καὶ εἶπεν αὐτοῖς ὁ Ἰησοῦς, Μὴ δύνανται οἱ υἱοὶ τοῦ νυμφῶνος, ἐν ᾧ ὁ νυμφίος μετ’ αὐτῶν ἐστιν, νηστεύειν; Ὅσον χρόνον μεθ’ ἑαυτῶν ἔχουσιν τὸν νυμφίον, οὐ δύνανται νηστεύειν· [20] ἐλεύσονται δὲ ἡμέραι ὅταν ἀπαρθῇ ἀπ’ αὐτῶν ὁ νυμφίος, καὶ τότε νηστεύσουσιν ἐν ἐκείναις ταῖς ἡμέραις. [21] Καὶ οὐδεὶς ἐπίβλημα ῥάκους ἀγνάφου ἐπιρράπτει ἐπὶ ἱματίῳ παλαιῷ· εἰ δὲ μή, αἴρει τὸ πλήρωμα αὐτοῦ τὸ καινὸν τοῦ παλαιοῦ, καὶ χεῖρον σχίσμα γίνεται. [22] Καὶ οὐδεὶς βάλλει οἶνον νέον εἰς ἀσκοὺς παλαιούς· εἰ δὲ μή, ῥήσσει ὁ οἶνος ὁ νέος τοὺς ἀσκούς, καὶ ὁ οἶνος ἐκχεῖται καὶ οἱ ἀσκοὶ ἀπολοῦνται· ἀλλὰ οἶνον νέον εἰς ἀσκοὺς καινοὺς βλητέον.

Process of Discovery

Linguistics Section

Linguistic Structure

[Question] [18] John's disciples and the Pharisees were fasting; and they came and said to Him, "Why do John's disciples and the disciples of the Pharisees fast, but Your disciples do not fast?"

[Answer – Parable #1] [19] And Jesus said to them, "While the bridegroom is with them, the attendants of the bridegroom cannot fast, can they? So long as they have the bridegroom with them, they cannot fast.[20] "But the days will come when the bridegroom is taken away from them, and then they will fast in that day.

[Parable – Parable #2] [20] "But the days will come when the bridegroom is taken away from them, and then they will fast in that day. [21] "No one sews a patch of unshrunk cloth on an old garment; otherwise the patch pulls away from it, the new from the old, and a worse tear results. [22] "No one puts new wine into old wineskins; otherwise the wine will burst the skins, and the wine is lost and the skins *as well*; but *one puts* new wine into fresh wineskins."

Discussion

This is a narrative about fasting. John's disciples confront Yeshua wanting to know what His belief in fasting was. The answer they received is in two parables.

Questioning the Passage

1. Why did not Yeshua's disciples fast? (v. 18)

    While Yeshua was with the disciples, they did not observe the traditions of the elders. There is an indication that they might have returned to fasting and other traditions after Yeshua's death. While Yeshua was with them, they did not follow the traditions of the elders. Instead, every day they rejoiced because they were with the Messiah. During a wedding feast, people did not follow their religious traditions. They rejoiced for the marriage. Yeshua uses this cultural backdrop to tell John's disciples that His disciples did not have to follow the elders' traditions while He was with them.

2. How does the patching of clothing relate to the question of fasting? (v. 21)

If one wants to receive a new teaching but insists on hanging onto the old teaching, then new teaching will often be rejected. In order to follow the new teachings that Yeshua brought, the old beliefs and ideas must be shattered. Yeshua did not teach a new Torah, but he taught a new way to interpret and live by the Torah. Yeshua's teaching contradicted the Elders and religious leaders of His day. New garments is a metaphor for new understandings, and they cannot be used to "patch" old traditions. The new understanding needed a "new garment."

3. How does the concept of wineskins relate to the question of fasting? (v. 17)

   The people of Yeshua's time needed a new understanding of the Kingdom of Heaven. They needed new teachers and leaders. The Elder's old traditions could not express the new interpretation and new understanding of the Scriptures that Yeshua was offering. In order to understand and accept Yeshua's understanding of the Scripture meant that they had to leave behind their old understandings and concepts of what the Scriptures meant. Once the people let go of the old ways, they could absorb and follow Yeshua's way to please the LORD.

Culture Section

Discussion

Yeshua's answer to John's disciples about why His disciples did not fast is offered in cultural terms. Without understanding the culture of the wedding feast and wineskins, the reader cannot move past the literal meaning of the text.

Questioning the passage

1. What is the culture of a wedding feast?

   Fasting is a tradition in the Near East. The Scripture calls for one mandatory fast each year (Leviticus 16:1-34). Wedding feasts were planned so that they would not coincide with a traditional fast. At a wedding feast, the guests would indulge in food and drink. Religious observations were placed on a temporary hold. The sadness of life in Yeshua's day would be replaced with joy, dance, and gladness. The rich and the poor would come together, and the divisions between people would disappear for this time. People were generous with their food and drank about would contribute to the feast. Even beggars and strangers would share in the abundance of food. Everybody at the feast was joyful. When the feast ended, a sudden gloom settled over the village. Everything went back to "normal."[42]

2. What was the custom of clothing? (v. 21)

Clothing was an expensive commodity in Judea during Yeshua's time. People wore clothing for its functionality rather than its beautification of the person. Clothing would be handed down through the generations. Old garments were usually repaired with a patch cut from a worn-out garment. If a patch from a new piece of clothing was sewed onto an old garment, it would come loose quickly. The new cloth was too heavy for the worn garment to hold, and after a few days, it would pull away and could leave a larger hole in the garment. Therefore, new clothing patches, which came from a new garment's sewing, were not used on old clothing.[43]

3. What was the relationship between wine and skins? (v. 22)

Goat skins were used as vessels for wine and water. A goat's insides would have been removed, its legs were tied together, and an opening was made in the neck. New wine was usually still fermenting. If new wine was placed in old skins, the fermentation process's gases would expand the skin, and an old skin could easily burst. Therefore, the new wine was placed in new skins because the new skins had the elasticity to handle the fermenting new wine.[44]

Thoughts

The wedding feast connection to the question of fasting raises some thoughts. Yeshua said that as long as He was with His disciples, they needed to discard the Elders' ways. The old ways were a stumbling block for them to realize what Yeshua's teachings were about. The old ways were never question anything, and it was time to do just that. The Sage Hillel put in place the idea of questioning the Scripture and interpreting the different depths of it. The idea of multiple interpretations of Scripture was new, maybe seventy years old. This passage tells the reader that the Scripture

---

[42] Errico, Rocco A., and George M. Lamsa. Aramaic Light on the Gospel of Matthew: A Commentary on the Teachings of Jesus from the Aramaic and Unchanged Near Eastern Customs. Santa Fe, NM: Noohra Foundation, 2000.
[43] IBID.
[44] IBID.

interpretation concept had not reached the traditional social interpretations that existed. The traditions needed to be questioned. Perhaps there are multiple ways of understanding what the religious responses to the Scripture should be. There needs to be room in religious responses to allow for new ideas. When the church moved to the west, it adopted Greek thinking. Once a "tradition" was established, it was never questioned. The Greek method of Bible interpretation does not allow room for new thoughts and new discoveries. For the most part, today's churches have stayed in that trap. The past's rules and regulations need to be evaluated to their value today. Yeshua said that there must be room to explore new interpretations and new expressions. Religion is our expression of following the LORD. As new insights are developed about the Scripture, there must be room for new expressions of understanding. The church becomes overly defensive when its traditions are questioned. Entrenched church people in the local churches react the same way. Try changing an event that the church has been doing for decades, thus modernizing it. The backlash is like a tsunami.

Reflections

Yeshua said that as long as He was with His disciples, they did not have to fast according to the Elders' traditions. Matthew's Gospel leaves the reader with the understanding that Yeshua is always with us. Disciples of Yeshua can call upon Him anytime. The actual presence is through the Holy Spirit, but since Christianity believes in a triune God, then if the Holy Spirit is with us, then Yeshua is with us. So, since Yeshua, in spirit, is always with us, why do we have to fast? The church adopted fasting as an integral part of worshiping God. How does fasting help one in prayer? Fasting generally makes one feel the pangs of hunger which can be distracting. Therefore, fasting as a mechanism to communicate with Yeshua does not seem to make sense. Yeshua is with us, and Matthew 9:14-17 says that we should always be rejoicing. So, where did the idea of fasting come from? Fasting was done in the Mithras cult. "Mithraism was a demanding religion, which its followers took very seriously. Devotees were held to rigorous moral and ethical standards. Fasting and continence were strongly encouraged."[45] It is clear that many, if not all, of the house churches that Paul established, were converted Mithras churches, then the practice of fasting would have continued. Yeshua says

---

[45] "INSTITUTE FOR HISTORICAL REVIEW." 'Schindler's List:' A review. Accessed April 27, 2022. http://www.ihr.org/jhr/v13/v13n2p34_weber.html.

that fasting is not necessary because He is with us. Therefore, the church practice of fasting for spiritual insight should be eliminated. Yeshua is with us today!

MARK 2:23-28

Language

New American Standard 1995	Koine Greek
[23] And it happened that He was passing through the grainfields on the Sabbath, and His disciples began to make their way along while picking the heads *of grain*. [24] The Pharisees were saying to Him, "Look, why are they doing what is not lawful on the Sabbath?" [25] And He said to them, "Have you never read what David did when he was in need and he and his companions became hungry; [26] how he entered the house of God in the time of Abiathar *the* high priest, and ate the consecrated bread, which is not lawful for *anyone* to eat except the priests, and he also gave it to those who were with him?" [27] Jesus said to them, "The Sabbath was made for man, and not man for the Sabbath. [28] "So the Son of Man is Lord even of the Sabbath."	[23] Καὶ ἐγένετο παραπορεύεσθαι αὐτὸν ἐν τοῖς σάββασιν διὰ τῶν σπορίμων, καὶ ἤρξαντο οἱ μαθηταὶ αὐτοῦ ὁδὸν ποιεῖν τίλλοντες τοὺς στάχυας. [24] Καὶ οἱ Φαρισαῖοι ἔλεγον αὐτῷ, Ἴδε, τί ποιοῦσιν ἐν τοῖς σάββασιν ὃ οὐκ ἔξεστιν; [25] Καὶ αὐτὸς ἔλεγεν αὐτοῖς, Οὐδέποτε ἀνέγνωτε τί ἐποίησεν Δαυίδ, ὅτε χρείαν ἔσχεν καὶ ἐπείνασεν αὐτὸς καὶ οἱ μετ᾽ αὐτοῦ; [26] Πῶς εἰσῆλθεν εἰς τὸν οἶκον τοῦ θεοῦ ἐπὶ Ἀβιάθαρ ἀρχιερέως, καὶ τοὺς ἄρτους τῆς προθέσεως ἔφαγεν, οὓς οὐκ ἔξεστιν φαγεῖν εἰ μὴ τοῖς ἱερεῦσιν, καὶ ἔδωκεν καὶ τοῖς σὺν αὐτῷ οὖσιν; [27] Καὶ ἔλεγεν αὐτοῖς, Τὸ σάββατον διὰ τὸν ἄνθρωπον ἐγένετο, οὐχ ὁ ἄνθρωπος διὰ τὸ σάββατον· [28] ὥστε κύριός ἐστιν ὁ υἱὸς τοῦ ἀνθρώπου καὶ τοῦ σαββάτου.

Process of Discovery

Linguistics Section

Linguistic Structure

A [23] And it happened that He was passing through the grainfields on the Sabbath, and His disciples began to make their way along while picking the heads *of grain*. [24] The Pharisees were saying to Him, "Look, why are they doing what is not lawful on the Sabbath?"

> **B** [25] And He said to them, "Have you never read what David did when he was in need and he and his companions became hungry; [26] how he entered the house of God in the time of Abiathar *the* high priest, and ate the consecrated bread, which is not lawful for *anyone* to eat except the priests, and he also gave it to those who were with him?"

A' [27] Jesus said to them, "The Sabbath was made for man, and not man for the Sabbath. [28] "So the Son of Man is Lord even of the Sabbath."

Discussion

The narrative is a simple chiasm that centers on Yeshua's interpretation of Scripture was different from the High Priest's at the Temple in Jerusalem.

Questioning the Passage

1. Why did the religious leaders question what Yeshua's disciples were doing on the Sabbath? (v. 23)

   The religious leaders wanted to know what Yeshua thought about the laws they created about the Sabbath. Was Yeshua a Pharisee or not? His answer clearly said that He believed in the original intent of the Sabbath as defined by Moses, and He disagreed with their additions.

2. What is the reference to King David? (v. 25)

   [NAU] 1 Samuel 21:1 Then David came to Nob to Ahimelech the priest; and Ahimelech came trembling to meet David and said to him, "Why are you alone and no one with you?" [2] David said to Ahimelech the priest, "The king has commissioned me with a matter and has said to me, 'Let no one know anything about the matter on which I am sending you and with which I have commissioned you; and I have directed the young men to a certain place.' 3 "Now therefore, what do you have on hand? Give me five loaves of bread, or whatever can be found." 4 The priest answered David and said, "There is no ordinary bread on hand, but there is consecrated bread; if only the young men have kept themselves from women." 5 David answered the priest and said to him, "Surely women have been kept from us as previously when I set out and the vessels of the young men were holy, though it was an ordinary journey; how much more then today will their vessels *be holy*?" 6 So the priest gave him consecrated *bread*; for there was no bread there but the bread of the Presence which was removed from before the LORD, in order to put hot bread *in its place* when it was taken away. (1 Sam. 21:1-6 NAU)

Rabbinical interpretation says that David's event occurred on the Sabbath because the consecrated bread was placed on the table on the Sabbath. David understood that the acts of mercy toward the poor and hungry were acts that pleased the LORD. Therefore, he received the consecrated bread from the priest as an offering of mercy. It was then lawful for David and his men to eat the bread.[46] Since Yeshua was the Son of David, it would be lawful for him to exercise the same act of mercy that His ancestor King David did.

3. What is the reference to the priests? (v. 26)
    9 'Then on the sabbath day two male lambs one year old without defect, and two-tenths *of an ephah* of fine flour mixed with oil as a grain offering, and its drink offering: 10 '*This is* the burnt offering of every sabbath in addition to the continual burnt offering and its drink offering. (Num. 28:9-10 NAU)

Matthew uses an example from Numbers. The priests were allowed to have a sacrifice on the Sabbath. Making a sacrifice is work. However, Sabbath is a day of rest. However, on the Sabbath, a sacrifice is permitted and was considered a holy thing to do. Yeshua reminds the religious leaders that sacrifice is greater than Sabbath observance.[47]

---

[46] *The New Interpreter's Bible. General Articles on the New Testament, the Gospel of Matthew, the Gospel of Mark* (Nashville, TN: Abingdon, 1995).

[47] IBID.

Biblical Personalities

1. "Abiathar, in the Old Testament, son of Ahimelech, priest of Nob. He was the sole survivor of a massacre carried out by Doeg. Fleeing to David, he remained with him throughout his wanderings and his reign. He was loyal through the rebellion of Absalom, but he supported Adonijah against Solomon. Abiathar probably represents an early rival house to that of Zadok, the official priestly family of Jerusalem down to the Exile (1 Samuel 22:20–23; 2 Samuel 15:24–37; and 1 Kings 2:26–27)."[48]

Abiathar is mentioned once in the New Testament. Historically Abiathar was not a High Priest. Mark's author is making a point by using the name Abiathar. He was a rival to the House of Zadok. The rivalry with the House of Zadok was not just about who had control of the Temple but also about power and control. The High Priest had a huge amount of power and influence over the people. The High Priest created the Temple tax, and there are no records to indicate what it was used for. The House of Zadok controlled the Temple. Abiathar, being called a high priest and Yeshua having dinner with him, tells us that Yeshua's Bible interpretation conflicted with the Bible's interpretation of the High Priest. Yeshua was a detractor of the High Priest.

Culture Section

Discussion

To fully appreciate this passage, it is necessary to understand what the customs and laws about the Sabbath were in Yeshua's day. Comprehensive writing on the Laws can be found in the Tractate Shabbat in the Babylonian Talmud. Feeding the hungry, taking care of one's animals, and healing on the Sabbath was legal during Yeshua's day. This was a generally accepted law of the Sabbath. If so, then why was Yeshua questioned about it? Matthew's author wanted to demonstrate that the Jewish leadership

---

[48] "Abiathar," Encyclopædia Britannica (Encyclopædia Britannica, inc.), accessed April 27, 2022, https://www.britannica.com/biography/Abiathar.

wanted Yeshua to be put to death. Therefore, he created situations where there would be a confrontation. Since Jewish people had learned from the Sage Hillel to debate Scripture and Halacha (the law), it was perfectly acceptable to have these debates. They were not confrontations but rather open debates. What is interesting about this debate is that all people agreed that what Yeshua and his disciples did was perfectly acceptable. As previously noted, it was a part of the plan to shift the blame for Yeshua's death from Rome to Jerusalem.

Questioning the passage

1. Why were Yeshua and His disciples walking through a wheat field? (v. 23)

   Wheat was the main product of Judea and Galilee. There were few roads in these areas to walk through wheat fields to get from place to place. The travelers would cut narrow passages through the fields. The farmers were not pleased with this practice, but they also knew no other way to travel. In the harvest season, farmers had to guard their fields from robbers. However, they would allow travelers to grab a handful of grain. This was a form of charity as instructed to do in the Torah. So, Yeshua and His disciples grabbed some grain to eat. It was lawful to do this on the Sabbath because a hungry person or child had to eat.[49]

2. What was the custom of the Sabbath in Yeshua's day?

   The LORD established the Sabbath through the fourth of the ten commandments. On the seventh day of creation, the LORD rested. He commanded us to observe a day of rest every week. Moses instituted the Sabbath. It was to be a day of rest and remember that Israel was held in bondage in Egypt, and the LORD brought them out of Egypt to freedom. The Sabbath is a holy day for the sake of the people. The Sabbath is a gift from the LORD. The religious leaders of Yeshua's day had created their interpretations of the Sabbath that had become a burden for the people. Yeshua restored the true meaning of the Sabbath in this passage. The religious leaders knew what Yeshua was saying was the

---

[49] Rocco A. Errico and George M. Lamsa, *Aramaic Light on the Gospel of Matthew: a Commentary on the Teachings of Jesus from the Aramaic and Unchanged Near Eastern Customs* (Santa Fe, NM: Noohra Foundation, 2000).

basic activities of the Sabbath. Their additions to the original intent of the Sabbath needed to be removed.[50]

Thoughts

Yeshua disagreed with the Temple leaders about the interpretation of the Scripture. In this narrative, Mark's author makes that extremely clear. He drew a line in the sand by saying that Yeshua had dinner with Abiathar, the High Priest. There was not a high priest named Abiathar during Yeshua's day. The name brings up the rivalry that existed against the House of Zadok. Zadok determined that he and his descendants were the true priestly lineage from Aaron. Once in power, Zadok created his interpretations of the Scripture. There was opposition to Zadok, and that came from Abiathar and his followers. So, by using that name, Mark's author says that Yeshua disagreed with the High Priest of His day. Mark's Gospel is telling us that it is all right to disagree with religious leaders.

Reflections

The church decided at its inception to keep the Word of the LORD from the followers of Yeshua. In 1964 at the Second Vatican Council, it was decided that Yeshua's Catholic followers were permitted to own and read the Bible. After the Reformation in the early 1500s, Protestants read the Bible in their vernacular language. A problem that arose was that even the local priests did not fully understand the Bible. Since the church has used Greek philosophy to interpret Hebraic philosophy, the church does not always interpret the Bible for the original meaning. Thus, rules and regulations were/are created that may not be biblically based. Yeshua believed that a lot of what was being imposed by the High Priest on the Hebrew people was not biblically based. He fought against a problem that still exists today. The difference being the leaders of Yeshua's day knew that their rules were not biblical. Some church doctrines are not based on the Bible because the wrong philosophy is being used to understand these Hebraic writings.

---

[50] IBID.

MARK 3:1-12

Language

New American Standard 1995	Koine Greek
[1] He entered again into a synagogue; and a man was there whose hand was withered.	[1] Καὶ εἰσῆλθεν πάλιν εἰς τὴν συναγωγήν. καὶ ἦν ἐκεῖ ἄνθρωπος ἐξηραμμένην ἔχων τὴν χεῖρα.
[2] They were watching Him *to see* if He would heal him on the Sabbath, so that they might accuse Him.	[2] καὶ παρετήρουν αὐτὸν εἰ τοῖς σάββασιν θεραπεύσει αὐτόν, ἵνα κατηγορήσωσιν αὐτοῦ.
[3] He said to the man with the withered hand, "Get up and come forward!"	[3] καὶ λέγει τῷ ἀνθρώπῳ τῷ τὴν ξηρὰν χεῖρα ἔχοντι· ἔγειρε εἰς τὸ μέσον.
[4] And He said to them, "Is it lawful to do good or to do harm on the Sabbath, to save a life or to kill?" But they kept silent.	[4] καὶ λέγει αὐτοῖς· ἔξεστιν τοῖς σάββασιν ἀγαθὸν ποιῆσαι ἢ κακοποιῆσαι, ψυχὴν σῶσαι ἢ ἀποκτεῖναι; οἱ δὲ ἐσιώπων.
[5] After looking around at them with anger, grieved at their hardness of heart, He said to the man, "Stretch out your hand." And he stretched it out, and his hand was restored.	[5] καὶ περιβλεψάμενος αὐτοὺς μετ᾽ ὀργῆς, συλλυπούμενος ἐπὶ τῇ πωρώσει τῆς καρδίας αὐτῶν λέγει τῷ ἀνθρώπῳ· ἔκτεινον τὴν χεῖρα. καὶ ἐξέτεινεν καὶ ἀπεκατεστάθη ἡ χεὶρ αὐτοῦ.
[6] The Pharisees went out and immediately *began* conspiring with the Herodians against Him, *as to* how they might destroy Him.	[6] Καὶ ἐξελθόντες οἱ Φαρισαῖοι εὐθὺς μετὰ τῶν Ἡρῳδιανῶν συμβούλιον ἐδίδουν κατ᾽ αὐτοῦ ὅπως αὐτὸν ἀπολέσωσιν.
[7] Jesus withdrew to the sea with His disciples; and a great multitude from Galilee followed; and *also* from Judea,	[7] Καὶ ὁ Ἰησοῦς μετὰ τῶν μαθητῶν αὐτοῦ ἀνεχώρησεν πρὸς τὴν θάλασσαν, καὶ πολὺ πλῆθος ἀπὸ τῆς Γαλιλαίας [ἠκολούθησεν], καὶ ἀπὸ τῆς Ἰουδαίας
[8] and from Jerusalem, and from Idumea, and beyond the Jordan, and the vicinity of Tyre and Sidon, a great number of people heard of all that He was doing and came to Him.	[8] καὶ ἀπὸ Ἱεροσολύμων καὶ ἀπὸ τῆς Ἰδουμαίας καὶ πέραν τοῦ Ἰορδάνου καὶ περὶ Τύρον καὶ Σιδῶνα πλῆθος πολὺ ἀκούοντες ὅσα ἐποίει ἦλθον πρὸς αὐτόν.
[9] And He told His disciples that a boat should stand ready for Him because of the crowd, so that they would not crowd Him;	[9] Καὶ εἶπεν τοῖς μαθηταῖς αὐτοῦ ἵνα πλοιάριον προσκαρτερῇ αὐτῷ διὰ τὸν ὄχλον ἵνα μὴ θλίβωσιν αὐτόν·
[10] for He had healed many, with the result that all those who had afflictions pressed around Him in order to touch Him.	[10] πολλοὺς γὰρ ἐθεράπευσεν, ὥστε ἐπιπίπτειν αὐτῷ ἵνα αὐτοῦ ἅψωνται ὅσοι εἶχον μάστιγας.
[11] Whenever the unclean spirits saw Him, they would fall down before Him and shout, "You are the Son of God!"	[11] καὶ τὰ πνεύματα τὰ ἀκάθαρτα, ὅταν αὐτὸν ἐθεώρουν, προσέπιπτον αὐτῷ καὶ ἔκραζον λέγοντες ὅτι σὺ εἶ ὁ υἱὸς τοῦ θεοῦ.
[12] And He earnestly warned them not to tell who He was.	[12] καὶ πολλὰ ἐπετίμα αὐτοῖς ἵνα μὴ αὐτὸν φανερὸν ποιήσωσιν.

Process of Discovery

Linguistics Section

Linguistic Structure

A [1] He entered again into a synagogue; and a man was there whose hand was withered. [2] They were watching Him *to see* if He would heal him on the Sabbath, so that they might accuse Him.

> **B** [3] He said to the man with the withered hand, "Get up and come forward!"

>> **C** [4] And He said to them, "Is it lawful to do good or to do harm on the Sabbath, to save a life or to kill?" But they kept silent.

> **B'** [5] After looking around at them with anger, grieved at their hardness of heart, He said to the man, "Stretch out your hand." And he stretched it out, and his hand was restored.

A' [6] The Pharisees went out and immediately *began* conspiring with the Herodians against Him, *as to* how they might destroy Him.

[Transition] [7] Jesus withdrew to the sea with His disciples; and a great multitude from Galilee followed; and *also* from Judea, [8] and from Jerusalem, and from Idumea, and beyond the Jordan, and the vicinity of Tyre and Sidon, a great number of people heard of all that He was doing and came to Him.

[Healing] [9] And He told His disciples that a boat should stand ready for Him because of the crowd, so that they would not crowd Him; [10] for He had healed many, with the result that all those who had afflictions pressed around Him in order to touch Him.

[Specific Healing] [11] Whenever the unclean spirits saw Him, they would fall down before Him and shout, "You are the Son of God!"

[Transition] [12] And He earnestly warned them not to tell who He was.

Discussion

Verses one to six form an A-B-C chiasm. The center of the chiasm is the question about what is legal to do on the Sabbath. The persons questioning Yeshua believed that even healing on the Sabbath was considered work. Verse seven is a transition from healing in one place and traveling to another place to do more healings. Verse eleven is the healing of insane people. Verse twelve is another transition verse.

Questioning the Passage

1. Why did Yeshua do Sabbath healing when He knew that would cause concern? (v. 2)

   Yeshua started His campaign of civil disobedience at this point in Mark's Gospel. Yeshua was not a fan of the culture, laws, and regulations that His day's religious leaders were imposing upon the people. By healing on the Sabbath, He said to the leaders that He was opposed to their interpretation of Scripture and authority. The campaign to reform the Temple leadership and the Sanhedrin had begun. Civil disobedience is the way of men and women of peace. Yeshua was a man of peace. Therefore, civil disobedience was the only way Yeshua could have gone. The debates with the religious leaders show that they were trying to figure out who Yeshua was and what sect of Judaism He belonged to. Eventually, the debates turn into pure civil disobedience. That is when the religious leaders took Yeshua seriously. A problem that developed was the religious leaders wanted to silence Yeshua. Instead of confronting Yeshua and discussing His views, the leaders did whatever they could to shutdown Yeshua.[51]

2. Who were the Herodians? (v. 6)

   The Herodians were an influential group in Yeshua's day. They believed in Herod the Great and his sons and supported their monarchy. They existed from 55 BCE to 93 CE. This group liked the status quo probably because they received financial support from the Herod family. They were displeased with the Messiah call because it threatened to undermine their political aspirations.

3. Why did Yeshua withdraw to the sea? (v. 7)

   This movement causes a transitional break between the actions of verses one to seven and eight through twelve.

4. Why did Yeshua tell the healed not to speak about Him? (v. 10)

   Yeshua did not want to embarrass other healers. The people who came to Him probably had seen other healers and were not healed. Yeshua wanted to protect the healers who could not have done what He did. Yeshua knew after His death, the other healers who had to take over His healing work

---

[51] Ched Myers, *Binding the Strong Man a Political Reading of Mark's Story of Jesus* (Maryknoll, NY: Orbis Books, 1988).

Biblical Locations

1. Idumea – "Idumea is the name given to the land controlled by the descendants of <u>Esau</u>, Jacob's brother, known as the Edomites (Genesis 25:30, 36:8). Throughout their history, they would have a troubled relationship with Israel."[52]

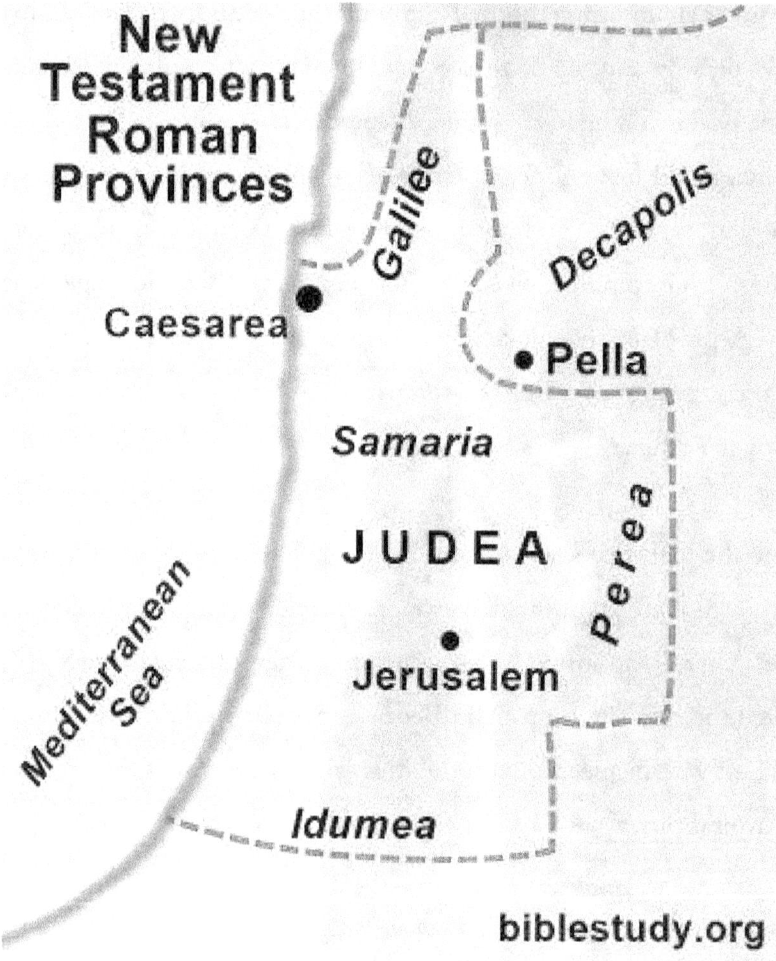

---

[52] "Idumea Meaning of Bible Names," Bible Study, accessed December 8, 2020, https://www.biblestudy.org/meaning-names/idumea.html.

2. Galilee – "**Galilee**, Hebrew **Ha-galil**, northernmost region of ancient Palestine, corresponding to modern northern <u>Israel</u>. Its biblical boundaries are indistinct; conflicting readings leave clear only that it was part of the territory of the northern tribe of Naphtali."[53]

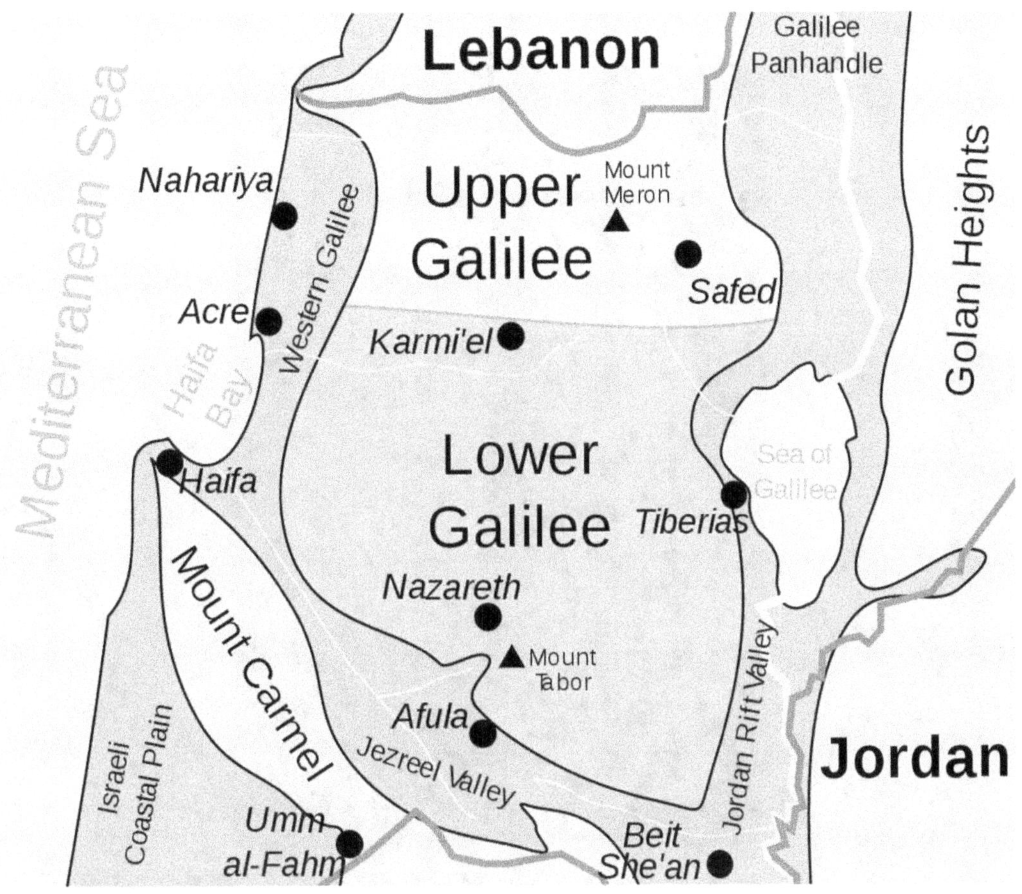

3. Judea – "Judea in Smiths Bible Dictionary (from Judah), a territorial division which succeeded to the overthrow of the ancient landmarks of the tribes of Israel and Judah in their respective captivities. The word first occurs Da 5:13 Authorized Version "Jewry," and the first mention of the "province of Judea" is in the book of Ezra, Ezr 5:8 It is alluded to in Ne 11:3 (Authorized Version "Judah"). In the apocryphal books the word "province" is dropped, and throughout them and the New Testament the expressions are "the land of Judea," "Judea." In a wide and more improper sense, the term Judea was sometimes extended to the whole country of the Canaanites, its ancient inhabitants; and even in the Gospels we read of the coasts of Judea "beyond Jordan." Mt 19:1; Mr 10:1 Judea was, in

---

[53] "Galilee," Encyclopædia Britannica (Encyclopædia Britannica, inc.), accessed December 8, 2020, https://www.britannica.com/place/Galilee-region-Israel.

strict language, the name of the third district, West of the Jordan and south of Samaria. It was made a portion of the Roman province of Syria upon the deposition of Archelaus, the ethnarch of Judea, in AD 6, and was governed by a procurator, who was subject to the governor of Syria."[54]

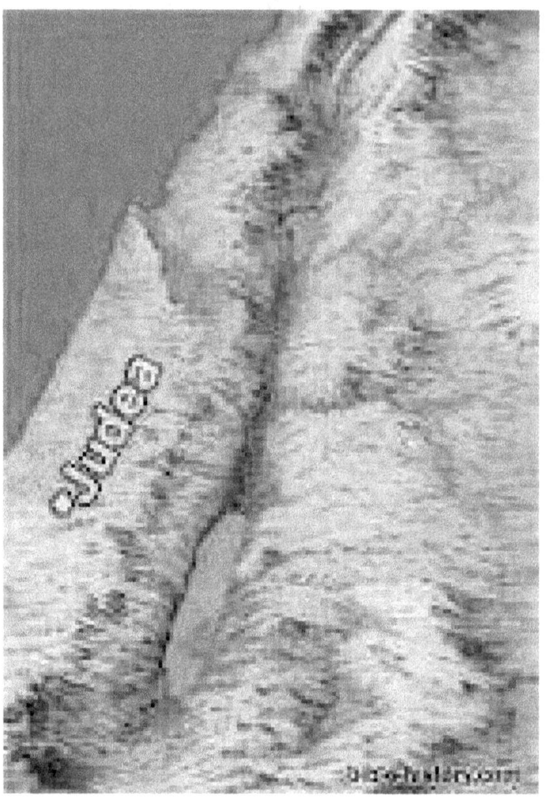

4. Tyre – "Tyre is an ancient Phoenician port city which, in myth, is known as the birthplace of Europa (who gave Europe its name) and Dido of Carthage (who gave aid to, and fell in love with, Aeneas of Troy). The name means 'rock' and the city consisted of two parts, the main trade centre on an island, and 'old Tyre', about a half mile opposite on the mainland. The old city, known as Ushu, was founded c. 2750 BCE and the trade centre grew up shortly after. In time, the island complex became more prosperous and populated than Ushu and was heavily fortified."[55]

---

[54] "Judea," Ark of the Covenant - Bible History Online, accessed December 8, 2020, https://www.bible-history.com/geography/ancient-israel/judea.html.

[55] Joshua J. Mark, "Tyre," Ancient History Encyclopedia (Ancient History Encyclopedia, December 8, 2020), https://www.ancient.eu/Tyre/.

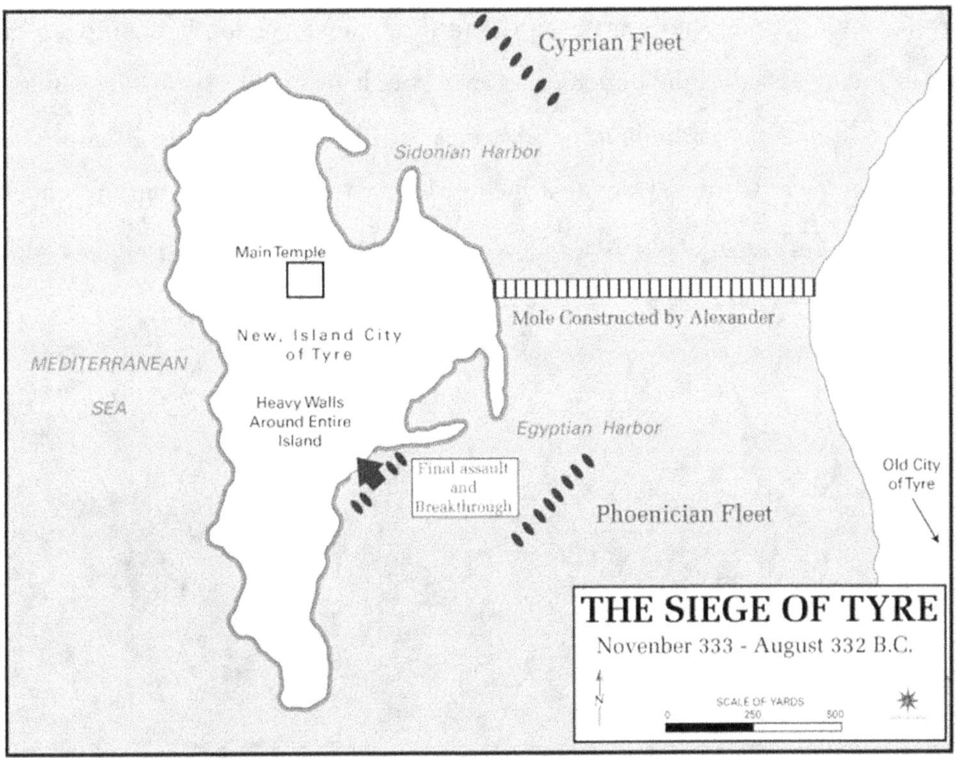

5. Sidon – "One of the oldest Phoenician cities, situated on a narrow plain between the range of Lebanon and the sea, in latitude 33 degrees 34 minutes nearly. The plain is well watered and fertile, about 10 miles long, extending from a little North of Sarepta to the Bostrenus (Nahr el-'Auly). The ancient city was situated near the northern end of the plain, surrounded with a strong wall. It possessed two harbors, the northern one about 500 yds. long by 200 wide, well protected by little islets and a breakwater, and a southern about 600 by 400 yards, surrounded on three sides by land, but open to the West, and thus exposed in bad weather. The date of the founding of the city is unknown, but we find it mentioned in the Tell el-Amarna Letters in the 14th century BC, and in <u>Genesis 10:19</u> it is the chief city of the Canaanites, and Joshua (<u>Joshua 11:8</u>) calls it Great Sidon. It led all the Phoenician cities in its early development of maritime affairs, its sailors being the first to launch out into the open sea out of sight of land and to sail by night, guiding themselves by the stars. They were the first to come into contact with the Greeks and we find the mention of them several times in Homer, while other Phoenician towns are not noticed. Sidon became early distinguished for its manufactures and the skill of its artisans, such as beautiful metal-work in silver and bronze and textile fabrics embroidered and dyed with the famous purple dye which became known as Tyrian, but which was earlier produced at Sidon. Notices of these choice articles

are found in Homer, both in the Iliad and the Odyssey. Sidon had a monarchical form of government, as did all the Phoenician towns, but it also held a sort of hegemony over those to the South as far as the limit of Phoenicia. It likewise made one attempt to establish an inland colony at Laish or Dan, near the headwaters of the Jordan, but this ended in disaster (Judges 18:7, 27, 28). The attempt was not renewed, but many colonies were established over-sea. Citium, in Cyprus, was one of the earliest."[56]

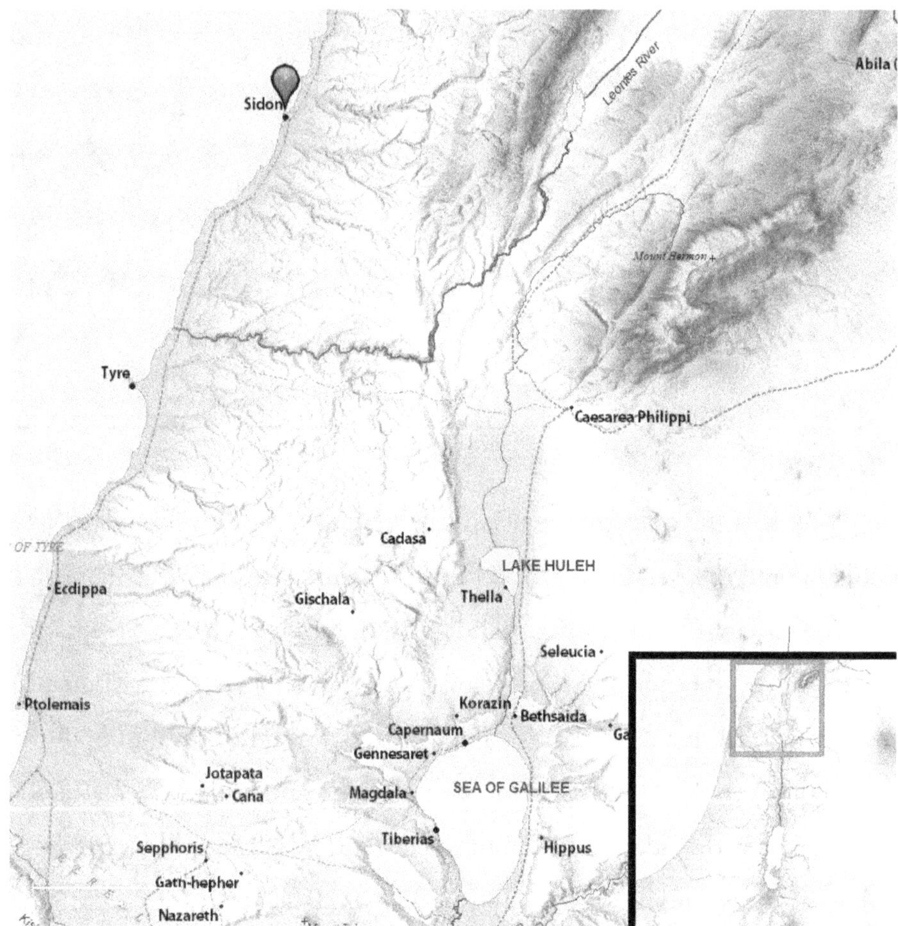

Culture Section

Questioning the passage

1. What does "unclean spirits" mean? (v. 11)

---

[56] Bible Map: Sidon, accessed December 8, 2020, https://bibleatlas.org/full/sidon.htm.

A person who had an unclean spirit meant that the person was mentally ill. It was believed that insane people had unclean spirits. Insane men knew when they were in the presence of a holy man. Most of the time, their garments told the insane person this information, i.e., the priestly garments. Yeshua did not have a priestly garment. Therefore, the insane person knew He was a holy man by how he projected Himself. The insane person wanted to be cured.[57]

2. What does the term "son of God" mean? (v. 12)

    This title was given to a person to show honor and respect. Holy men were given this title. It means that a person was godly or god-like.

3. Why did the people want to touch Yeshua (v. 10)

    In Yeshua's day, people believed that they could touch the holy man's *tallis*, especially the *tziztit*. The *tallis* was and still is a prayer shawl that is worn around the neck. At the four corners of the tallis are the *tziztit*. The *tzitzit* represent the Torah. Each has five knots in it to symbolize the first five books of the Torah.

Thoughts

A lesson for us from this passage is that the ruling class should silence no one. Yeshua did not agree with the ruling class. He told them so and quite directly. They worked to silence Him, and eventually, they did by having Yeshua executed. There was no tolerance for a different point of view. The religious elite worked hard to silence any other views. They did this to maintain their power. It does not matter that Yeshua was considered a liberal in his day because he was trying to reform a traditional system. He wanted to allow a free expression of worship and praise to the LORD. In His day, that was considered a liberal position. Today the idea of free expression of worship and praise has been classified as a conservative position. There are elements in the United States' society today who want to stop the free expression of devotion to the LORD. They want to remove all signs of the LORD from society. The followers of Yeshua MUST stop this from happening. It must also be

---

[57] Rocco A. Errico, George M. Lamsa, and George M. Lamsa, *Aramaic Light on the Gospels of Mark and Luke: a Commentary on the Teachings of Jesus from the Aramaic and Unchanged Near Eastern Customs* (Smyrna, GA: Noohra Foundation, 2001).

done by civil disobedience against this "new order." The lessons on how to combat the rise of the anti-God belief is to show them that Yeshua's love is also for them.

Reflections

Free speech was a movement in the 1960s on college campuses across the United States. It started at Berkley College in California and spread quickly. People with differing views to openly speak and debate with people of opposing views became a mainstay of society up to the year 2000. Then in the United States, that changed. The leaders of the free speech movement took over a large part of society and decided to implement a shutdown of free speech. They believe that only views that match their views are allowed to be heard. Many colleges do not include guest speakers and lecturers on their campuses who do not fully share their faculty and administration's opinions. The once free speech preaching colleges are now liberal views only colleges. Sadly, the free speech movement leaders have shut down free speech. The idea of free speech for all must be revived from the 1960s today. This restoration is necessary to heal a severely divided country.

MARK 3:13-19

Language

New American Standard 1995	Koine
[13] And He went up on the mountain and summoned those whom He Himself wanted, and they came to Him. [14] And He appointed twelve, so that they would be with Him and that He *could* send them out to preach, [15] and to have authority to cast out the demons. [16] And He appointed the twelve: Simon (to whom He gave the name Peter), [17] and James, the *son* of Zebedee, and John the brother of James (to them He gave the name Boanerges, which means, "Sons of Thunder"); [18] and Andrew, and Philip, and Bartholomew, and Matthew, and Thomas, and James the son of Alphaeus, and Thaddaeus, and Simon the Zealot; [19] and Judas Iscariot, who betrayed Him.	[13] Καὶ ἀναβαίνει εἰς τὸ ὄρος, καὶ προσκαλεῖται οὓς ἤθελεν αὐτός καὶ ἀπῆλθον πρὸς αὐτόν. [14] Καὶ ἐποίησεν δώδεκα, ἵνα ὦσιν μετ' αὐτοῦ, καὶ ἵνα ἀποστέλλῃ αὐτοὺς κηρύσσειν [15] καὶ ἔχειν ἐξουσίαν θεραπεύειν τὰς νόσους, καὶ ἐκβάλλειν τὰ δαιμόνια [16] καὶ ἐπέθηκεν τῷ Σίμωνι ὄνομα Πέτρον [17] καὶ Ἰάκωβον τὸν τοῦ Ζεβεδαίου, καὶ Ἰωάννην τὸν ἀδελφὸν τοῦ Ἰακώβου καὶ ἐπέθηκεν αὐτοῖς ὀνόματα Βοανεργές, ὅ ἐστιν, Υἱοὶ Βροντῆς [18] καὶ Ἀνδρέαν, καὶ Φίλιππον, καὶ Βαρθολομαῖον, καὶ Ματθαῖον, καὶ Θωμᾶν, καὶ Ἰάκωβον τὸν τοῦ Ἀλφαίου, καὶ Θαδδαῖον, καὶ Σίμωνα τὸν Κανανίτην, [19] καὶ Ἰούδαν Ἰσκαριώτην, ὃς καὶ παρέδωκεν αὐτόν.

Process of Discovery

Linguistics Section

Linguistic Structure

[13] And He went up on the mountain and summoned those whom He Himself wanted, and they came to Him. [14] And He appointed twelve, so that they would be with Him and that He *could* send them out to preach, [15] and to have authority to cast out the demons. [16] And He appointed the twelve: Simon (to whom He gave the name Peter), [17] and James, the *son* of Zebedee, and John the brother of James (to them He gave the name Boanerges, which means, "Sons of Thunder"); [18] and Andrew, and Philip, and Bartholomew, and Matthew, and Thomas, and James the son of Alphaeus, and Thaddaeus, and Simon the Zealot; [19] and Judas Iscariot, who betrayed Him.

Discussion

Yeshua created His inner circle of disciples.

Questioning the Passage

1. Why did Yeshua ascend a mountain? (v. 13)

   This is an echo of what Moses did at Mount Sinai. When Moses ascended Mount Sinai, he received the LORD's Law. This was a turning point for the new nation of Israel. They received a set of laws that was pleasing to the LORD and allowed them to create a community that thrived. The LORD's Law allowed Israel to grow as a nation. The author has Yeshua ascending a mountain and naming his inner group of disciples. Thus, Yeshua is creating the new "law" that His movement was to follow.[58]

2. Why is the list different than the list in the other Gospels? (v. 16 – 19)

   Levi, Philip, and Nathanael are not included in the list. This could indicate that Yeshua had an inner circle of twelve men but more disciples than twelve.

3. Why did Yeshua give the men the authority to cast out demons? (v. 15)

---

[58] Ched Myers, *Binding the Strong Man a Political Reading of Mark's Story of Jesus* (Maryknoll, NY: Orbis Books, 1988).

This was the commissioning by Yeshua of these twelve men. They were commissioned to take the Gospel message out into the world. These men received extra training about the message and how to present it. They were able to perform the miracle of casting out demons so that the people would believe in them and the Gospel message.

4. Why did Yeshua give Simon, James, and John nicknames? (v. 16 & 17)

There is no indication in the Gospel why Yeshua did this. Simon's nickname of Petra (the rock) stood the test of time. James and John, He called the sons of thunder. That nickname did not last. Later on in the Gospel, at the gates of Pan (the Greek god of the underworld), Yeshua said, "upon this rock, I will build my church." Yeshua was not referring to Simon (Peter), but rather He said that the Kingdom of Heaven would be built upon the Kingdom of Satan. Thus Satan would be powerless in the Kingdom of Heaven. The church interpreted this scene as Simon (Peter) becoming the church's first leader. Today's churches were not built on Simon (Peter) but on Paul's conversion of the Mithras House Churches. Since the New Testament contains many of Paul's letters. Since Paul has the most space in the New Testament, the church was built on Paul and his choices rather than Peter's. Today's church was built on Paul and not Peter.

Linguistic Echoes

Yeshua ascending a mountain to commission His disciples is echoed by Moses' ascent.

"*The first ascent.* After the exodus from Egypt, on the first day of the third month, the Israelites arrived at Mt. Sinai. Moses' first trip up Mt. Sinai is described in Exodus 19:2–7. He ascends the mountain in verse 3 and comes back down in verse 7. On the mountain God tells Moses that He is offering a covenant to the people of Israel: if they will keep the covenant, God will make them His own "treasured possession" and "a kingdom of priests and a holy nation" (verses 5–6). Moses reports this message to the people, and the people respond by saying, "We will do everything the Lord has said" (Exodus 19:8).

The second ascent. Moses returns to the top of Mt. Sinai in Exodus 19:8 in order to relay the people's response to the offer of a covenant. God then tells Moses that He will speak audibly to Moses in a thick cloud so that all the people will put their trust in Moses as God's chosen leader. Moses descends the mountain in verse 9 in order to relay this information to the children of Israel.

The third ascent. In Exodus 19:10, God is speaking to Moses again, which implies that Moses may have again climbed Mt. Sinai. (Some scholars believe God's words in verse 10 were part of the discourse in verse 9.) In any case, Moses is said to descend the mountain again in verse 14. Moses consecrates the people in preparation for the Lord's appearance on the mountain on the third day (verses 10–11).

On the third day, "there was thunder and lightning, with a thick cloud over the mountain, and a very loud trumpet blast" (Exodus 19:16). The people of Israel were understandably frightened. Then "Mount Sinai was covered with smoke, because the Lord descended on it in fire. The smoke billowed up from it like smoke from a furnace, and the whole mountain trembled violently. As the sound of the trumpet grew louder and louder" (verses 18–19).

The fourth ascent. Moses' fourth trip up Mt. Sinai is described in Exodus 19:20–25. God summons Moses to the top of the mountain in order to have him warn the people not to draw near the mountain while His presence is on Sinai. He also tells Moses to bring his brother, Aaron, up the mountain with him. Moses descends the mountain in verse 25. God then delivers the Ten Commandments audibly in Exodus 20:1–17. In fear, the people of Israel plead with Moses not to let God speak directly to them. Instead, they ask Moses to be their intercessor and they would listen to him (verses 18–19). Moses tells them to not be afraid but that God is testing them so that they would fear Him and not sin (verse 20).

The fifth ascent. Moses returns to Mt. Sinai in Exodus 20:21 as he "approached the thick darkness where God was." At this time, God gives Moses various laws, recorded in chapters 21–23, along with a promise to give the land of Canaan to the children of Israel (Exodus

23:20–33).

The sixth ascent. In Exodus 24:1 Moses is summoned again to climb Mt. Sinai. This time he is to bring Aaron, Aaron's sons Nadab and Abihu, and seventy of the elders of Israel with him. The next morning, Moses "built an altar at the foot of the mountain and set up twelve stone pillars representing the twelve tribes of Israel" (verse 4). He offered burnt offerings and fellowship offerings and read the Book of the Covenant and to the people, who responded, "We will do everything the Lord has said; we will obey" (verse 7). To ratify the covenant, Moses sprinkled the people with the blood of the sacrifice (verse 8)."[59]

---

[59] GotQuestions.org, "Home," GotQuestions.org, January 30, 2018, https://www.gotquestions.org/Moses-on-Mount-Sinai.html.

MARK 3:20-30

Language

New American Standard 1995	Koine Greek
[20] And He came home, and the crowd gathered again, to such an extent that they could not even eat a meal. [21] When His own people heard *of this*, they went out to take custody of Him; for they were saying, "He has lost His senses." [22] The scribes who came down from Jerusalem were saying, "He is possessed by Beelzebul," and "He casts out the demons by the ruler of the demons." [23] And He called them to Himself and began speaking to them in parables, "How can Satan cast out Satan? [24] "If a kingdom is divided against itself, that kingdom cannot stand. [25] "If a house is divided against itself, that house will not be able to stand. [26] "If Satan has risen up against himself and is divided, he cannot stand, but he is finished! [27] "But no one can enter the strong man's house and plunder his property unless he first binds the strong man, and then he will plunder his house. [28] "Truly I say to you, all sins shall be forgiven the sons of men, and whatever blasphemies they utter; [29] but whoever blasphemes against the Holy Spirit never has forgiveness, but is guilty of an eternal sin "-- [30] because they were saying, "He has an unclean spirit."	[20] καὶ συνέρχεται πάλιν ὄχλος, ὥστε μὴ δύνασθαι αὐτοὺς μήτε ἄρτον φαγεῖν. [21] Καὶ ἀκούσαντες οἱ παρ' αὐτοῦ ἐξῆλθον κρατῆσαι αὐτόν· ἔλεγον γὰρ ὅτι Ἐξέστη. [22] Καὶ οἱ γραμματεῖς οἱ ἀπὸ Ἱεροσολύμων καταβάντες ἔλεγον ὅτι Βεελζεβοὺλ ἔχει, καὶ ὅτι Ἐν τῷ ἄρχοντι τῶν δαιμονίων ἐκβάλλει τὰ δαιμόνια. [23] Καὶ προσκαλεσάμενος αὐτούς, ἐν παραβολαῖς ἔλεγεν αὐτοῖς, Πῶς δύναται Σατανᾶς Σατανᾶν ἐκβάλλειν; [24] Καὶ ἐὰν βασιλεία ἐφ' ἑαυτὴν μερισθῇ, οὐ δύναται σταθῆναι ἡ βασιλεία ἐκείνη. [25] Καὶ ἐὰν οἰκία ἐφ' ἑαυτὴν μερισθῇ, οὐ δύναται σταθῆναι ἡ οἰκία ἐκείνη. [26] Καὶ εἰ ὁ Σατανᾶς ἀνέστη ἐφ' ἑαυτὸν καὶ μεμέρισται, οὐ δύναται σταθῆναι, ἀλλὰ τέλος ἔχει. [27] Οὐδεὶς δύναται τὰ σκεύη τοῦ ἰσχυροῦ, εἰσελθὼν εἰς τὴν οἰκίαν αὐτοῦ, διαρπάσαι, ἐὰν μὴ πρῶτον τὸν ἰσχυρὸν δήσῃ, καὶ τότε τὴν οἰκίαν αὐτοῦ διαρπάσῃ. [28] Ἀμὴν λέγω ὑμῖν, ὅτι πάντα ἀφεθήσεται τὰ ἁμαρτήματα τοῖς υἱοῖς τῶν ἀνθρώπων, καὶ βλασφημίαι ὅσας ἂν βλασφημήσωσιν· [29] ὃς δ' ἂν βλασφημήσῃ εἰς τὸ πνεῦμα τὸ ἅγιον, οὐκ ἔχει ἄφεσιν εἰς τὸν αἰῶνα, ἀλλ' ἔνοχός ἐστιν αἰωνίου κρίσεως. [30] Ὅτι ἔλεγον, Πνεῦμα ἀκάθαρτον ἔχει.

Process of Discovery

Linguistics Section

Linguistic Structure

[Transition] [20] And He came home, and the crowd gathered again, to such an extent that they could not even eat a meal.

[Who confronted Yeshua] [21] When His own people heard *of this*, they went out to take custody of Him; for they were saying, "He has lost His senses." [22] The scribes who came down from Jerusalem were saying, "He is possessed by Beelzebul," and "He casts out the demons by the ruler of the demons." [23] And He called them to Himself and began speaking to them in parables, "How can Satan cast out Satan?

[Yeshua Answers them] [24] "If a kingdom is divided against itself, that kingdom cannot stand. [25] "If a house is divided against itself, that house will not be able to stand. [26] "If Satan has risen up against himself and is divided, he cannot stand, but he is finished! [27] "But no one can enter the strong man's house and plunder his property unless he first binds the strong man, and then he will plunder his house. [28] "Truly I say to you, all sins shall be forgiven the sons of men, and whatever blasphemies they utter; [29] but whoever blasphemes against the Holy Spirit never has forgiveness, but is guilty of an eternal sin "-- [30] because they were saying, "He has an unclean spirit."

Discussion

This narrative is the first part of a "sandwich" that Mark's author used. He commences with a story about Yeshua's family coming to see him. He then shifts the emphasis to the Jerusalem scribes. Then he concludes with Yeshua's family.

Questioning the Passage

1. Who were the scribes from Jerusalem? (v. 22)

    This group was another group of detractors that Mark's author identified. This group was commencing its insurgence against Yeshua's mission. It was not formally identified why these different groups were attacking the poor person from Nazareth. Perhaps a reason was that Yeshua was a poor peasant from Nazareth. In John's Gospel, Nathaniel said, "why good can come from Nazareth?" The people from Judea's general opinion is that Adonai (God) would not select a poor peasant from Nazareth to become the Messiah of Israel.

2. What is a war of myths?

The debate in this narrative is a demonstration of what was called a war of myths. Ancient people believed that there was a good God and a bad God. These two Gods were continually battling against each other. It was believed that the wars on Earth were caused by the Gods fighting amongst each other. They believed that a person was influenced by a good God or a bad God. A good God blessed Yeshua. The scribes of Jerusalem tried to brand Him as influenced by a bad God. Thus the war of myths commenced. Being good or bad is not because of the influence of a good or bad God. The two myths were battling each other.[60]

3. Why did the scribes of Jerusalem use two euphemisms for Satan? (v. 22)

This was done to emphasize their accusations against Yeshua.

4. What does the name Beelzebub mean? (v. 22)

The name Beelzebub, which is Aramaic, means "lord of the flies." Jews altered the name from *zebub* to the Hebrew *zebul,* which means "dung." The Hebrew version is Beelzebul, which means "lord of the dung." In the Greek New Testament, the word is for Beelzebub is **Βεελζεβούλ,** which is pronounced in the same manner as the Hebrew name. Interestingly, the author of Mark's would use Hebrew slang instead of the proper Aramaic name.[61] Beelzebub was a Canaanite deity. During Yeshua's time, Beelzebub was the "prince of the house of devils." Beelzebub becomes associated with Satan after the writing of 1 Enoch, which tells the story of how a fallen angel is condemned to the Pit (Hell) because of the angel's transgressions.

---

[60] Ched Myers, *Binding the Strong Man a Political Reading of Mark's Story of Jesus* (Maryknoll, NY: Orbis Books, 1988).

[61] Rocco A. Errico, George M. Lamsa, and George M. Lamsa, *Aramaic Light on the Gospels of Mark and Luke: a Commentary on the Teachings of Jesus from the Aramaic and Unchanged Near Eastern Customs* (Smyrna, GA: Noohra Foundation, 2001).

If a demon of Satan healed a man whom another demon of Satan had made ill, then Satan was working against himself. In Yeshua's time, people believed that illness and disease were caused by one's sin being punished by Satan. Therefore, Satan had dominion over sin and suffering. However, if a demon of Satan were to heal a person, then that demon of Satan would be a rebel against the kingdom of Satan. Therefore, saying that Yeshua was saying to the Pharisees who questioned His healing, He was not a demon of Satan because Yeshua would be rebelling. Therefore, a house divided against itself cannot stand. The kingdom of Satan falls if Satan's demons are healing people.

5. Who was a "strong man" in Yeshua's day? (v. 27)

    In Yeshua's day, men who had treasures and other valuables were armed continuously. When they slept, they kept their weapons on them just if anyone broke into their home to rob them. The strong man is symbolic of Yeshua because He was armed with the LORD's truth. Beelzebub could not have possessed Yeshua unless he could disarm him. The power of the LORD's truth is more powerful than any demon of Satan. The healing power of the LORD was with Yeshua. A demon of Satan would have to take possession of the LORD's spiritual power from Yeshua, which meant the demon would have to be victorious over the LORD.

6. What does verse twenty-five?

    The author of Mark's Gospel has Yeshua addressing the concept of unity. Yeshua came to gather people into the Kingdom of Heaven. In Yeshua's kingdom, there is unity among all souls. Love, peace, and mercy are the medium of the Kingdom of Heaven. The people who become disciples of Yeshua will work him to become gathers, fishers of men and women. The people who are against Yeshua do not want to gather. Therefore they are scattered of people attempting to keep them out of the Kingdom of Heaven. When Yeshua returns, He will gather the faithful disciples to Him and will protect them from the disaster that will occur on the Earth.[62]

7. What does blasphemy against the Holy Spirit mean? (v. 29)

In Aramaic, the word for Spirit is *rucha*. This word also refers to the LORD's healing power. The *rucha* passes from the healer to the sick person. The healer is an instrument for the healing power of the LORD. Yeshua's words and methods of healing were radical and not in harmony with the priests and elders. Therefore, they reasoned that Yeshua was invoking Satan's power when He was doing His healing. They did not understand how the power of the LORD worked.[63]

This verse can be understood as whenever an individual or group of individuals hold an attitude that evil attributes to the power of good when they are blaspheming against the LORD, and this is unforgivable. As long as the individual holds onto this assertion, then they will not be forgiven by the LORD. If they forgo that belief, then they will receive mercy and forgiveness from the LORD.

Culture Section

Discussion

Yeshua's people are his relatives. The Peshitta says that "his relative" came to see Him. The Aramaic word *hyanaw* is in the Peshitta, which means "his relatives." They were embarrassed at what Yeshua was preaching. They were afraid that the religious authorities would ban them from the synagogue and Temple, thus cutting them off from worshiping the LORD.

There were many genuine and fake healers in the Near East in Yeshua's day. The genuine healers derived their power from the LORD. The fake healers derived their power from Satan. People were superstitious and believed that healing power was either from goodness or badness. Which

---

[62] *The New Interpreter's Bible* – Matthew and Mark (Nashville: Abingdon Press, 2005).
[63] Rocco A. Errico, George M. Lamsa, and George M. Lamsa, *Aramaic Light on the Gospels of Mark and Luke: a Commentary on the Teachings of Jesus from the Aramaic and Unchanged Near Eastern Customs* (Smyrna, GA: Noohra Foundation, 2001).

power was Yeshua using? Ancient people believed in a good God and an evil god named Satan. This dualism even applied to angels and demons.

If a person was under the LORD's control, the person could prophesy, work miracles, and heal the sick. They practiced sorcery, curses, and black magic when a person was under Satan's power. At times it was difficult to determine which power controlled the healer.

The family's charge to Yeshua was that he had an unclean spirit in Him, which then implied that Satan had taken over control. They were trying to shut down Yeshua's mission as it was starting to gain momentum.

Thoughts

This narrative has a riddle to it. Can Satan clean up his own house? If Satan influenced Yeshua, then Satan was working against his own house. Yeshua was leading a revolt against the power of Satan. Evil inclination had infected so many of the people in Judea and Galilee, especially the ruling class. Satan was not going to rid the people of Evil inclination because Satan enjoyed a free reign on Earth when Evil inclination was winning. Therefore, Yeshua fought a battle against Satan and Evil inclination. He tried to bring a positive way to a life that was pleasing to the LORD.

Reflections

Sometimes it is difficult to determine if a person is influenced by the LORD or by Evil inclination (Satan). Yeshua's detractors publicly said that He was the problem. That is what Evil inclination does. It tried to confuse the person it has control of and everyone around the person. Confused people can be easily influenced. A part of Yeshua's mission was to break Satan's bonds with people. He wanted to open their eyes to reality. Once the people's eyes were open, they would be able to recognize Evil inclination and fight against it.

MARK 3:31-35

Language

New American Standard 1995	Koine Greek
[31] Then His mother and His brothers arrived, and standing outside they sent *word* to Him and called Him. [32] A crowd was sitting around Him, and they said to Him, "Behold, Your mother and Your brothers are outside looking for You." [33] Answering them, He said, "Who are My mother and My brothers?" [34] Looking about at those who were sitting around Him, He said, "Behold My mother and My brothers! [35] "For whoever does the will of God, he is My brother and sister and mother."	[31] Ἔρχονται οὖν οἱ ἀδελφοὶ καὶ ἡ μήτηρ αὐτοῦ, καὶ ἔξω ἑστῶτες ἀπέστειλαν πρὸς αὐτόν, φωνοῦντες αὐτόν. [32] Καὶ ἐκάθητο ὄχλος περὶ αὐτόν· εἶπον δὲ αὐτῷ, Ἰδού, ἡ μήτηρ σου καὶ οἱ ἀδελφοί σου καὶ αἱ ἀδελφαί σου ἔξω ζητοῦσίν σε. [33] Καὶ ἀπεκρίθη αὐτοῖς λέγων, Τίς ἐστιν ἡ μήτηρ μου ἢ οἱ ἀδελφοί μου; [34] Καὶ περιβλεψάμενος κύκλῳ τοὺς περὶ αὐτὸν καθημένους, λέγει, Ἴδε, ἡ μήτηρ μου καὶ οἱ ἀδελφοί μου. [35] Ὃς γὰρ ἂν ποιήσῃ τὸ θέλημα τοῦ θεοῦ, οὗτος ἀδελφός μου καὶ ἀδελφή μου καὶ μήτηρ ἐστίν.

Process of Discovery

Linguistics Section

Linguistic Structure

A [31] Then His mother and His brothers arrived, and standing outside they sent *word* to Him and called Him.

> **B** [32] A crowd was sitting around Him, and they said to Him, "Behold, Your mother and Your brothers are outside looking for You."

A' [33] Answering them, He said, "Who are My mother and My brothers?"

> **B'** [34] Looking about at those who were sitting around Him, He said, "Behold My mother and My brothers! [35] "For whoever does the will of God, he is My brother and sister and mother."

Discussion

This narrative forms an A-B-A'-B' chiasm. It centers around the social structure of the family as defined by Yeshua.

Questioning the Passage

1. Why did the family not enter the house to talk to Yeshua?

   By not entering the house, the family demonstrated that they were not interested in Yeshua's ministry or did not believe that He was the promised Messiah. Mark's Gospel does not have a birth narrative, so the angel Gabriel did not visit Mary and tell her about the virgin birth nor Yeshua's mission. Mark's Gospel does not mention that there was anything special about Yeshua's conception or birth. Therefore, according to Mark's author, Mary had no idea that Yeshua was the promised Messiah. In proving that Yeshua was the Messiah, Mark's author had to convince the family and the people. This view is a different view of Yeshua's family than what is portrayed in Matthew, Luke, and John.

2. How did Yeshua reject His family?

   When Yeshua was told that his family was outside waiting for Him, the response was that they were not His family. He broke away from the family. This was a radical move for Him to make. It was not natural for a family member to leave. The crisis began at verse twenty-one. The family insisted that Yeshua was insane. If He were declared insane, then the family honor would not have been stained by His actions. Yeshua tried to create a new family structure by saying to the disciples in the house that they were His new family. His family was trying to help Him within the bounds of the culture of the day. Kinship was critical. Yeshua said that it is not.

3. Could Yeshua have recognized his blood family?

The short answer is "yes." Eventually, in Mark's Gospel, the family will join Yeshua's mission. The social order of Yeshua's day was based on family structures. Yeshua desired to adopt a new definition. When the family accepted who Yeshua was and His mission, they became a part of the new family. Yeshua tore down the old fabric of society and tried to create a new fabric.

Culture Section

Discussion

The family was important in Yeshua's day. Each family was an independent unit. The family was not just a nuclear family but an extended family. In many villages and small towns, everyone who resided in them was family. The family had to stay together because of the farm's needs or trade that the family was involved in. A family member becoming independent was not the norm in small villages and towns.

Marrying family members was practiced and can be seen in the book of Genesis. When Abraham wanted to get a bride for Isaac, he sent his servant Eliezer to his extended family. Rebecca did the same thing for her son Jacob. This practice indicates the importance of the continuation of the family.

In Yeshua's day, there was the concern that a family member's actions could have consequences for the entire family. Yeshua's claim as the Messiah and His actions could affect the family. The family could have been excluded from worship at the local synagogue and the Temple in Jerusalem. This fear alone is a strong motivator for what the family did.

In this chapter of Mark's Gospel, the family's reaction indicates that the family did not want to be a part of the messianic movement. They did not believe that Yeshua was the long-awaited Messiah.

Thoughts

The old saying that "blood is thicker than water" was being upended in this narrative. In this case, one can say that water is thicker than blood. Water is referring to the initiation rite of baptism. At that ceremony, the person being baptized with water becomes a member of the Christian family. The idea is to leave the old self behind to become a new person and a member of a new family. Yeshua was able to leave His family behind Him. Eventually, the family joined Him. Yeshua was ready to give up the most valuable thing He possessed so that He could follow the LORD.

Reflections

Yeshua gave up his most treasured thing. It was not a material possession but rather His relationship with His family. He treasured his parents, siblings, and extended family members. His mission from the LORD forced Him to make a decision. Follow the LORD or remain a part of his family. He chose the LORD. Are you ready and willing to make a sacrifice of that magnitude for the LORD?

MARK 4:1-9

Language

New American Standard 1995	Koine Greek
[1] He began to teach again by the sea. And such a very large crowd gathered to Him that He got into a boat in the sea and sat down; and the whole crowd was by the sea on the land. [2] And He was teaching them many things in parables, and was saying to them in His teaching, [3] "Listen *to this!* Behold, the sower went out to sow; [4] as he was sowing, some *seed* fell beside the road, and the birds came and ate it up. [5] "Other *seed* fell on the rocky *ground* where it did not have much soil; and immediately it sprang up because it had no depth of soil. [6] "And after the sun had risen, it was scorched; and because it had no root, it withered away. [7] "Other *seed* fell among the thorns, and the thorns came up and choked it, and it yielded no crop. [8] "Other *seeds* fell into the good soil, and as they grew up and increased, they yielded a crop and produced thirty, sixty, and a hundredfold." [9] And He was saying, "He who has ears to hear, let him hear."	[1] Καὶ πάλιν ἤρξατο διδάσκειν παρὰ τὴν θάλασσαν· καὶ συνάγεται πρὸς αὐτὸν ὄχλος πλεῖστος, ὥστε αὐτὸν εἰς πλοῖον ἐμβάντα καθῆσθαι ἐν τῇ θαλάσσῃ, καὶ πᾶς ὁ ὄχλος πρὸς τὴν θάλασσαν ἐπὶ τῆς γῆς ἦσαν. [2] καὶ ἐδίδασκεν αὐτοὺς ἐν παραβολαῖς πολλὰ καὶ ἔλεγεν αὐτοῖς ἐν τῇ διδαχῇ αὐτοῦ· [3] Ἀκούετε. ἰδοὺ ἐξῆλθεν ὁ σπείρων σπεῖραι. [4] καὶ ἐγένετο ἐν τῷ σπείρειν ὃ μὲν ἔπεσεν παρὰ τὴν ὁδόν, καὶ ἦλθεν τὰ πετεινὰ καὶ κατέφαγεν αὐτό. [5] καὶ ἄλλο ἔπεσεν ἐπὶ τὸ πετρῶδες ὅπου οὐκ εἶχεν γῆν πολλήν, καὶ εὐθὺς ἐξανέτειλεν διὰ τὸ μὴ ἔχειν βάθος γῆς· [6] καὶ ὅτε ἀνέτειλεν ὁ ἥλιος ἐκαυματίσθη καὶ διὰ τὸ μὴ ἔχειν ῥίζαν ἐξηράνθη. [7] καὶ ἄλλο ἔπεσεν εἰς τὰς ἀκάνθας, καὶ ἀνέβησαν αἱ ἄκανθαι καὶ συνέπνιξαν αὐτό, καὶ καρπὸν οὐκ ἔδωκεν. [8] καὶ ἄλλα ἔπεσεν εἰς τὴν γῆν τὴν καλὴν καὶ ἐδίδου καρπὸν ἀναβαίνοντα καὶ αὐξανόμενα καὶ ἔφερεν ἐν τριάκοντα καὶ ἐν ἑξήκοντα καὶ ἐν ἑκατόν. [9] καὶ ἔλεγεν· Ὃς ἔχει ὦτα ἀκούειν ἀκουέτω.

Process of Discovery

Linguistics Section

Linguistic Structure

[Parable of the Sower] [1] He began to teach again by the sea. And such a very large crowd gathered to Him that He got into a boat in the sea and sat down; and the whole crowd was by the sea on the land. [2] And He was teaching them many things in parables, and was saying to them in His teaching, [3] "Listen *to this!* Behold, the sower went out to sow; [4] as he was sowing, some *seed* fell beside the road, and the birds came and ate it up. [5] "Other *seed* fell on the rocky *ground* where it did not have much soil; and immediately it sprang up because it had no depth of soil. [6] "And after the sun had risen, it was scorched; and because it had no root, it withered away. [7] "Other *seed* fell among the thorns, and the thorns came up and choked it, and it yielded no crop. [8] "Other *seeds* fell into the good soil, and as they grew up and increased, they yielded a crop and produced thirty, sixty, and a hundredfold." [9] And He was saying, "He who has ears to hear, let him hear."

Discussion

In Mark's Gospel, chapter four is the first time the reader is exposed to the parables. There are several parables in this chapter. "A parable is verbal imagery that portrays and illustrates an event or a teaching." Yeshua used parables to make an impression on His listeners. He did not create parables to be used to construct definitions or dogmas. Yeshua's parables' central theme in the Gospel of Matthew is to describe the kingdom of Heaven. The parables were to help His listeners focus on the kingdom of Heaven and know that the LORD's presence was with them. The parables are dramatic, poetic, humorous, and enlightening. Near Easterners would sing parables, proverbs, and riddles with musicians playing appropriate music.[64]

The Greek word for parable means "something cast beside." In Hebrew, the word is *masal,* which means parable, proverb, aphorism, riddle, or allegory. Matthew's understanding of the parables is from the Hebrew understanding. Yeshua's parables can be seen as presenting new truths to the people. The reason people needed help to understand the parables was that Yeshua's parable turned the culture upside down. A parable does not have a specific point that can be stated in the non-parabolic language. A parable is like a musical piece, a painting, or even a poem. As these

---

[64] Rocco A. Errico and George M. Lamsa, *Aramaic Light on the Gospel of Matthew: a Commentary on the Teachings of Jesus from the Aramaic and Unchanged Near Eastern Customs* (Santa Fe, NM: Noohra Foundation, 2000).

works of music and art, Yeshua's parables are words that give different feelings and ideas to each reader. The parables should not be limited to one single idea. To do so is to remove the original intent of the parable.[65]

Even though Yeshua was religious, His parables are secular. The content of the parables is drawn from everyday life. Yeshua's method of constructing the parables was unique to Him. It was a new form of communication required because Yeshua's ideas of the Kingdom of Heaven were new and unfamiliar.

Questioning the Passage

1. What does the metaphor "the sower" mean? (v. 3)

   "Sowing" is a metaphor for teaching or preaching. The sower was the person who was teaching something through the parable.

2. What does the reference to a hundred, sixty, or thirty times mean? (v. 8)

   This reference refers to the number of seeds that the farmer will gather from his crops. Selling excess seed would allow the farmer to earn some extra money. The farmer needed to gather the plants' seeds to replant them in the next year. The one-hundred times was a reference to Genesis 26:12 when Isaac was told that his harvest would be one-hundredfold.

Linguistic Echo

1. Deuteronomy 6:5 – the echo is listening. Yeshua tells us to listen in the same way Moses told the people to listen. Listening to Yeshua acknowledges that His words are from the LORD in the same way that Moses' words were from the LORD.

2. Daniel 12:4-10 – to hear and not understand is echoed in Daniel. The implication is that the Word of the LORD is not simple to understand. It is concealed so that evil people cannot

---

[65] Leander E. Keck, *The New Interpreter's Bible Commentary* (Nashville, TN: Abingdon Press, 2015).

gain the power of the Word of the LORD. Ancient people believed that the Word of the LORD had the power to control the world.

Culture Section

Discussion

In the first century CE in Judea, the religious attitude concerned apocalyptic expectations. Since the Hebrews were under the Romans' control, they believed that God was a far-off, mysterious, awesome deity who would come one day to judge the people and punish wicked people and nations. This belief originated from the books Daniel and Enoch. When the LORD's judgment came, the Hebrew people would be redeemed. In Daniel and Enoch, a redeemer was sent by the LORD to start the process. The Redeemer (Messiah) was to open the way to the world to come where the oppressed would not reside. There was to be divine punishment to the nations who hurt Israel. The evil that came to the world with the fall of Azazel (1 Enoch, the Book of the Watchers) and the Watchers from Genesis chapter six would finally be eradicated.

Yeshua's ideas differed from the general idea of the Redeemer. His parables turned the culture upside down, and a result was that when people heard His parables, they noticed and thought about what they believed was to come. Yeshua was unique in His understanding of what the Kingdom of Heaven on Earth was to become.

Sociology

The prophet Ezekiel used parables as political criticism. Yeshua could have used the same idea in creating this and other parables that are found in Mark's Gospel. The idea of hearing and not understanding is seen in the politics of Yeshua's day and our day. According to Yeshua, permanent change does not come from an armed revolt. It comes from working within the system and slowly introducing change. Eventually, the reform desired will occur. This view of the parable is because it follows Yeshua's attempt to change the definition of family, which makes it sociological.[66] What would the four persons be in sociological terms?

a. The seeds that fell on the ground and were eaten by the birds are the people that are used as cannon fodder. These are people whom the politicians consider the lowest class of society, in other words, the peasants. They do not care about the peasants because there were plenty of them. These types of persons would never rise against the government, no matter how much they were oppressed.

b. The seeds on the rocky ground are the people who showed some concern for what the government was doing to them. They would rise to voice an objection, but they would quickly back down when the government pushed back. Their conviction for change and reform was not something they would lay their lives down.

c. The seeds that grew and the thorns got to them are similar to the rocky ground except that they could cause an insurrection. They raised their objections but did not back down when the government pushed back. They raised arms against the government. The thorns were the soldiers that the government sent to meet the insurrectionists and to kill them.

d. The last group was seed on good soil. The metaphor here is that the people who objected to their treatment of the government found that they could bring reform by working inside the government. Over time they would be able to enact the changes that they were seeking. It took over three hundred years for Christianity's reforms to become a part of the Roman Empire. It took time, but the seeds did flourish and brought in a harvest.

---

[66] Ched Myers, *Binding the Strong Man a Political Reading of Mark's Story of Jesus* (Maryknoll, NY: Orbis Books, 1988).

Thoughts

The seeds that fell on good ground and grew tell us that Yeshua wanted us to understand that patience is the key to a revolution. It does not matter if the change is religious or cultural. For Judea's local government, culture and religion were linked together. Yeshua knew that He was not going to influence Rome directly. Do not forget that the influence of Yeshua's movement eventually did touch and change Rome. Consider the seeds as an influence. When would the influence of reform work? It takes time because the changes must be gradual so as not to upset the cultural or religious machine. People, in general, are not fans of change. Forcing change on people does not work. Rather subtle change works. That requires patience, which is something that most of us do not have.

Reflections

Any institution has a bureaucracy that does not like change. The institution's leaders like the way things are running because it makes life easier and because they like it. In the church today, people do not like change. People who enter the church and try to change it become like seeds on rocky soil. The congregational leaders will get that new person and their new ideas tossed out of the church before they can spread their insurrection to the old ways. This attitude toward change is what is causing so many mainline churches to close their doors. Change is something that is all around us. Today it is running at a faster pace than ever before. Maybe it is time to let the seeds of ideas hit the fertile ground. This action means the church needs to let new ideas and methods to flourish rather than swatting them away.

MARK 4:10-20

Language

New American Standard 1995	Koine Greek
[10] As soon as He was alone, His followers, along with the twelve, *began* asking Him *about* the parables. [11] And He was saying to them, "To you has been given the mystery of the kingdom of God, but those who are outside get everything in parables, [12] so that WHILE SEEING, THEY MAY SEE AND NOT PERCEIVE, AND WHILE HEARING, THEY MAY HEAR AND NOT UNDERSTAND, OTHERWISE THEY MIGHT RETURN AND BE FORGIVEN." [13] And He said to them, "Do you not understand this parable? How will you understand all the parables? [14] "The sower sows the word. [15] "These are the ones who are beside the road where the word is sown; and when they hear, immediately Satan comes and takes away the word which has been sown in them. [16] "In a similar way these are the ones on whom seed was sown on the rocky *places,* who, when they hear the word, immediately receive it with joy; [17] and they have no *firm* root in themselves, but are *only* temporary; then, when affliction or persecution arises because of the word, immediately they fall away. [18] "And others are the ones on whom seed was sown among the thorns; these are the ones who have heard the word, [19] but the worries of the world, and the deceitfulness of riches, and the desires for other things enter in and choke the word, and it becomes unfruitful. [20] "And those are the ones on whom seed was sown on the good soil; and they hear the word and accept it and bear fruit, thirty, sixty, and a hundredfold."	[10] Ὅτε δὲ ἐγένετο καταμόνας, ἠρώτησαν αὐτὸν οἱ περὶ αὐτὸν σὺν τοῖς δώδεκα τὴν παραβολήν. [11] Καὶ ἔλεγεν αὐτοῖς, Ὑμῖν δέδοται γνῶναι τὸ μυστήριον τῆς βασιλείας τοῦ θεοῦ ἐκείνοις δὲ τοῖς ἔξω, ἐν παραβολαῖς τὰ πάντα γίνεται [12] ἵνα βλέποντες βλέπωσιν, καὶ μὴ ἴδωσιν καὶ ἀκούοντες ἀκούωσιν, καὶ μὴ συνιῶσιν μήποτε ἐπιστρέψωσιν, καὶ ἀφεθῇ αὐτοῖς τὰ ἁμαρτήματα. [13] Καὶ λέγει αὐτοῖς, Οὐκ οἴδατε τὴν παραβολὴν ταύτην; Καὶ πῶς πάσας τὰς παραβολὰς γνώσεσθε; [14] Ὁ σπείρων τὸν λόγον σπείρει. [15] Οὗτοι δέ εἰσιν οἱ παρὰ τὴν ὁδόν, ὅπου σπείρεται ὁ λόγος, καὶ ὅταν ἀκούσωσιν, ευθέως ἔρχεται ὁ Σατανᾶς καὶ αἴρει τὸν λόγον τὸν ἐσπαρμένον ἐν ταῖς καρδίαις αὐτῶν. [16] Καὶ οὗτοί εἰσιν ὁμοίως οἱ ἐπὶ τὰ πετρώδη σπειρόμενοι, οἱ, ὅταν ἀκούσωσιν τὸν λόγον, ευθέως μετὰ χαρᾶς λαμβάνουσιν αὐτόν, [17] καὶ οὐκ ἔχουσιν ῥίζαν ἐν ἑαυτοῖς, ἀλλὰ πρόσκαιροί εἰσιν εἶτα γενομένης θλίψεως ἢ διωγμοῦ διὰ τὸν λόγον, ευθέως σκανδαλίζονται. [18] Καὶ οὗτοί εἰσιν οἱ εἰς τὰς ἀκάνθας σπειρόμενοι, οἱ τὸν λόγον ἀκούοντες, [19] καὶ αἱ μέριμναι τοῦ αἰῶνος τουτου, καὶ ἡ ἀπάτη τοῦ πλούτου, καὶ αἱ περὶ τὰ λοιπα ἐπιθυμίαι εἰσπορευόμεναι συμπνίγουσιν τὸν λόγον, καὶ ἄκαρπος γίνεται. [20] Καὶ οὗτοί εἰσιν οἱ ἐπὶ τὴν γῆν τὴν καλὴν σπαρέντες, οἵτινες ἀκούουσιν τὸν λόγον, καὶ παραδέχονται, καὶ καρποφοροῦσιν, ἐν τριάκοντα, καὶ ἐν ἐξήκοντα, καὶ ἐν ἑκατόν.

Process of Discovery

Linguistics Section

Linguistic Structure

[Why parables?] [10] As soon as He was alone, His followers, along with the twelve, *began* asking Him *about* the parables. [11] And He was saying to them, "To you has been given the mystery of the kingdom of God, but those who are outside get everything in parables, [12] so that WHILE SEEING, THEY MAY SEE AND NOT PERCEIVE, AND WHILE HEARING, THEY MAY HEAR AND NOT UNDERSTAND, OTHERWISE THEY MIGHT RETURN AND BE FORGIVEN."

[Explanation of Parable] [13] And He said to them, "Do you not understand this parable? How will you understand all the parables? [14] "The sower sows the word. [15] "These are the ones who are beside the road where the word is sown; and when they hear, immediately Satan comes and takes away the word which has been sown in them. [16] "In a similar way these are the ones on whom seed was sown on the rocky *places,* who, when they hear the word, immediately receive it with joy; [17] and they have no *firm* root in themselves, but are *only* temporary; then, when affliction or persecution arises because of the word, immediately they fall away. [18] "And others are the ones on whom seed was sown among the thorns; these are the ones who have heard the word, [19] but the worries of the world, and the deceitfulness of riches, and the desires for other things enter in and choke the word, and it becomes unfruitful. [20] "And those are the ones on whom seed was sown on the good soil; and they hear the word and accept it and bear fruit, thirty, sixty, and a hundredfold."

Discussion

The Yeshua Seminar met back in the late 1990s, and their task was to try to determine what Yeshua said and did. They believed that this parable was developed by Yeshua and spread orally throughout the Christian community.[67] When Christianity left its Jewish roots, it lost the ability to interpret parables. Mark's Gospel was edited to add explanations to the parables that Greek thinking Christians developed. Therefore, the explanation of the parable is not necessarily in line with Yeshua's original intent. This parable is examined as a social call for patient change, but it contradicts the Gospel's explanation. Since the editors claimed that Yeshua explained this, making it is difficult to impossible to challenge the church. The search

---

[67] Robert Walter Funk and Roy W. Hoover, *The Five Gospels: the Search for the Authentic Words of Yeshua: New Translation and Commentary* (San Francisco: Harper SanFrancisco, 2007).

for Yeshua's original meaning allows for the possibility that this explanation is church developed and not Yeshua developed.

Questioning the Passage

1. Why did Yeshua communicate privately with His disciples? (v. 10)

   The idea of Yeshua having an inner circle that would acquire private knowledge is introduced. With the backdrop of this section being written by the church, its purpose is to show that the church's leadership is an inner circle connected directly to Yeshua. Therefore, any interpretation of Scripture from church leadership is as valuable as if it came from Yeshua Himself.

2. Why does Yeshua use parables? (v. 11)

   Rabbis were using parables long before Yeshua's day. Isaiah chapter five has a parable from Isaiah. Hebrew people learned to utilize parables for centuries before and after Yeshua. The church needed to explain why the parables seem foreign and difficult to understand to the Gentiles. If the Jewish church in Jerusalem had survived, its leaders could have easily explained the parable. Semitic parables are written in a specific way to convey information by getting the listener to ask questions. The church has struggled with parables for over two millennia. In many places, it is questionable whether they have the original intention of Yeshua.

3. What is the church's interpretation of the parable?

   Since parables have multiple interpretations, the one offered by the church is valid. The sower is the proclaimer of the Kingdom of Heaven. The hostile soil represents the three obstacles to the success of the Kingdom. The blocks are what hinder or enhance discipleship to Yeshua.

   The first two seed scatterings represent people who immediately fall away from the faith. They hear the words of Yeshua, but the words never take root in their souls. Their discipleship is temporary.

What are the obstacles to discipleship? The first is Satan. When Satan comes upon them, these people hear the word, and they do not follow it. Social leaders of His day were in this category. They heard His words but stood in strong opposition. They refuse to listen to the word and ponder its meaning and implications. It is rejected without any thought.

The second obstacle is tribulation and persecution. New disciples who have faith in the word will be persecuted in many different ways. This action happens today. The disciple will find the suffering a stumbling block to maintaining their faith in the word when it comes. They leave the faith as soon as any hardship comes upon them. They do not understand that Yeshua's ministry fruits will come out of His disciples' suffering. That is what happened.

The third obstacle is the lie of riches, and desire for material objects is essential. The lure of wealth, which brings a more comfortable life, pulls the disciple away. An example is from Luke's Gospel about the rich man who turned down Yeshua because he could not imagine life without wealth.[68]

The emphasis of the church interpretation is on the barriers to discipleship. The explanation also says that it is not the obscurity of the word that makes discipleship hard. Rather, it is one's loyalty to the church's ideology that will drive discipleship. The argument against this statement is that one can be faithful to the word of Yeshua and reject the church's interpretation. The catholic church would not allow its members to have a Bible until 1964. The church fought hard against Luther, who translated the Bible into German so that Germans could read the word for themselves. Many people died to have the Bible translated into English. Christians today have Bibles in their vernacular language but do not know about the martyrs that made it possible.

---

[68] Ched Myers, *Binding the Strong Man a Political Reading of Mark's Story of Jesus* (Maryknoll, NY: Orbis Books, 1988).

Culture Section

Discussion

The leaders of the early proto-orthodox church wanted to control the definition of Christianity. They went out of their way to destroy and erase any brand of Christianity that developed. Unfortunately, the church eliminated the writings of these other brands. Most of what is known about these early Christianities is because the letters from Bishops to the churches were maintained. The proto-orthodox church which Paul established was based on the Mithras religion. A goal of Mithras through the centuries was to be the only true religion. It was known to fight against other religions. That belief came through to the early church since Paul converted many Mithras house churches into Yeshua house churches. The converted Mithras churches wanted nothing from Judaism, so it developed its answers to Yeshua's parable questions. Using their Greek philosophy, they tried to interpret the Semitic parables. Thus, the original message was either diluted or lost.

Thoughts

What are the obstacles to discipleship today? One block for me was the notion that the church only cared about getting my money. This idea is still widespread. An example from my past is attending a free Advent dinner at the church, after which the church was decorated for the season. After the dinner, the pastor announced that there would be a free-will offering for dinner. Wait, I thought this was a free dinner. President Ronald Regan said that there was no free lunch, and I should have realized that. When the basket came before me, I had to put something in it. Since there were five of us, I put a $20 bill in. I felt that all eyes were watching me. The next time a free dinner came up at the church, I knew that it was not free. False advertising from the church did not help me discover Yeshua's words' power. The reputation of the church is a big obstacle, and it is more far-reaching than just money.

Reflections

The explanation offered for the parable is to create a tight control of people by the church. One does not want to fall into Satan's hand. The church says that we need it to prevent that from happening. The church will happily show the ways to salvation through discipleship to Yeshua.

However, what is the road to discipleship? What does one have to do to get into Heaven? The Gospels are not clear; however, the church is. It says that one has to do good deeds. But who determines what the good deeds are? The Hebrew Scriptures, especially the Torah, tell us what good deeds, called mitzvot, will help one get into Heaven. The church must not become an obstacle to discipleship. The numerous denominations in the church tend to send the message that it is an obstacle. If a disciple does not agree with one denomination, one can always go to another denomination. Today Christianity has multiple independent churches. Certainly, a disciple of Yeshua can find a church that fits one's needs. The bottom line is discipleship to Yeshua, not a church.

MARK 4:21-25

Language

New American Standard 1995	Koine Greek
[21] And He was saying to them, "A lamp is not brought to be put under a basket, is it, or under a bed? Is it not *brought* to be put on the lampstand? [22] "*a*For nothing is hidden, except to be revealed; nor has *anything* been secret, but that it would come to light. [23] "If anyone has ears to hear, let him hear." [24] And He was saying to them, "Take care what you listen to. By your standard of measure it will be measured to you; and more will be given you besides. [25] "For whoever has, to him *more* shall be given; and whoever does not have, even what he has shall be taken away from him."	[21] Καὶ ἔλεγεν αὐτοῖς, Μήτι ὁ λύχνος ἔρχεται ἵνα ὑπὸ τὸν μόδιον τεθῇ ἢ ὑπὸ τὴν κλίνην; Οὐχ ἵνα ἐπὶ τὴν λυχνίαν ἐπιτεθῇ; [22] Οὐ γάρ ἐστίν τι κρυπτόν, ὃ ἐὰν μὴ φανερωθῇ οὐδὲ ἐγένετο ἀπόκρυφον, ἀλλ' ἵνα εἰς φανερὸν ἔλθῃ. [23] Εἴ τις ἔχει ὦτα ἀκούειν ἀκουέτω. [24] Καὶ ἔλεγεν αὐτοῖς, Βλέπετε τί ἀκούετε. Ἐν ᾧ μέτρῳ μετρεῖτε μετρηθήσεται ὑμῖν, καὶ προστεθήσεται ὑμῖν τοῖς ἀκούουσιν. [25] Ὃς γὰρ ἂν ἔχῃ, δοθήσεται αὐτῷ καὶ ὃς οὐκ ἔχει, καὶ ὃ ἔχει ἀρθήσεται ἀπ' αὐτοῦ.

Process of Discovery

Linguistics Section

Linguistic Structure

[Parable] [21] And He was saying to them, "A lamp is not brought to be put under a [1]basket, is it, or under a bed? Is it not *brought* to be put on the lampstand? [22] "For nothing is hidden, except to be revealed; nor has *anything* been secret, but that it would come to light. [23] "If anyone has ears to hear, let him hear."

[Parable] [24] And He was saying to them, "Take care what you listen to. By your standard of measure it will be measured to you; and more will be given you besides. [25] "For whoever has, to him *more* shall be given; and whoever does not have, even what he has shall be taken away from him."

Discussion

This pericope contains two parables. The lamp being hidden is talking about the power of the LORD being available to all people. It is not meant to be hidden from anyone. The second parable deals with the understanding that fairness does not exist in the world, but it will in Heaven.

Phrase Study

1. υπτός[69]

    1. pert. to being unknown because of being kept secret, *hidden, secret,* adj.

    2. a hidden entity, *something hidden*

    The word "mystery" was loaded with metaphysical implications. Mark's author used this term and followed it by explaining that it does mean that parables were not enshrined with arcane knowledge. The parables were a teaching mechanism to illuminate and reveal truth.[70]

---

[69] Frederick W. Danker, William Arndt, and Walter Bauer, *A Greek-English Lexicon of the New Testament and Other Early Christian Literature* (Chicago: University of Chicago Press, 2000).
[70] Ched Myers, *Binding the Strong Man a Political Reading of Mark's Story of Jesus* (Maryknoll, NY: Orbis Books, 1988).

Culture Section

Discussion

What was a standard measure? The measurement refers to an amount of wheat. In Yeshua's day in the Near East, most wheat farmers had one or two wheat measures that varied in size. A buyer would agree to a price for a particular measure. The seller would use a smaller measure, thus cheating the seller. The buyer and seller would agree whether the measure was to be shaken after the wheat was poured out. Shaking the measure would be advantageous to the buyer because he would get more. The seller was usually against shaking the measure. In Yeshua's time, cheating buyers was commonplace. Yeshua said that in the Kingdom of Heaven, one will always be given more than one expects.

Thoughts

A feature of early Christianity is that the movement was not meant to be for a particular people. The message Yeshua brought was meant for all people to hear. At first glance, the construction of the Bible and even Yeshua's parables appear to be restricted to the people who knew how to read it. The parable of the lamp seems to remove that restriction. History tells us that the church leaders held onto the faith's mysteries keeping the secrets to themselves; in some cases, that is still happening. If the church controls the secrets, it believes it controls people. Today people are seeing through this veil and are reacting to it. The search for the true meaning of Yeshua's words is a large movement and will never end. The church needs to return to Yeshua's ways and release all the secrets in the Vatican basements for the world to see.

Reflections

The lamp can be used as a metaphor for many different things. In the case of the people in Galilee and Judea, it was a metaphor for hope. The people had lost hope in freedom from the oppressive Roman rule. Yeshua said to them do not lose hope. It is also followed by the parable that says that life is not always fair, but in the Kingdom of Heaven, the world to come, life is fair. Do not lose hope in the ways of the LORD. We cannot understand His ways, but we must have hope in them.

MARK 4:26-29

Language

New American Standard 1995	Koine Greek
[26] And He was saying, "The kingdom of God is like a man who casts seed upon the soil; [27] and he goes to bed at night and gets up by day, and the seed sprouts and grows—how, he himself does not know. [28] "The soil produces crops by itself; first the blade, then the head, then the mature grain in the head. [29] "But when the crop permits, he immediately puts in the sickle, because the harvest has come."	[26] Καὶ ἔλεγεν, Οὕτως ἐστὶν ἡ βασιλεία τοῦ θεοῦ, ὡς ἐὰν ἄνθρωπος βάλῃ τὸν σπόρον ἐπὶ τῆς γῆς, [27] καὶ καθεύδῃ καὶ ἐγείρηται νύκτα καὶ ἡμέραν, καὶ ὁ σπόρος βλαστάνῃ καὶ μηκύνηται ὡς οὐκ οἶδεν αὐτός. [28] Αὐτομάτη γὰρ ἡ γῆ καρποφορεῖ, πρῶτον χόρτον, εἶτα στάχυν, εἶτα πλήρη σῖτον ἐν τῷ στάχυϊ. [29] Ὅταν δὲ παραδῷ ὁ καρπός, εὐθέως ἀποστέλλει τὸ δρέπανον, ὅτι παρέστηκεν ὁ θερισμός.

Process of Discovery

Linguistics Section

Linguistic Structure

[**Parable**] [26] And He was saying, "The kingdom of God is like a man who casts seed upon the soil; [27] and he goes to bed at night and gets up by day, and the seed sprouts and grows—how, he himself does not know. [28] "The soil produces crops by itself; first the blade, then the head, then the mature grain in the head. [29] "But when the crop permits, he immediately puts in the sickle, because the harvest has come."

Discussion

The main character in the parable is usually identified as the farmer. What would the parable say if the main character was the crop?

Questioning the Passage

1. What is the purpose of the farmer in the parable?

   The farmer is necessary for the parable because who else would cast the seed upon the soil. Once that is done, he goes to bed to sleep. The crop commands him to harvest it. The farmer does not make that decision. Instead, the crop decides when the harvest comes. This is the cultural twist of the parable.

2. How much time is indicated in verse 27?

   This period is an indeterminate amount of time. A farmer does not plant the seed on day one; he goes to bed, and on day two, he harvests the crop. Therefore, some time goes by before the harvest can be done.

3. What does it mean that the crop permits the harvest? (v. 29)

   Crops grow at different rates. Even wheat grows at different rates depending on what type of wheat it is.

4. How many types of wheat exist?

"Winter Wheat

Winter wheat is used for baking bread and rolls because of its good milling and making properties, and even a home gardener can produce enough to make a few batches of baked goods. It is planted in the fall, usually between October and December, and grows over the winter to be harvested in the spring or early summer. Typically it takes about seven to eight months to reach maturity and it creates pretty golden contrast in spring gardens.

Spring Wheat

Another popular wheat in the American diet and growing in American fields is spring wheat, the green shoots of which look lovely spaced in clumps among late spring and early summer flowers. Spring wheat is usually planted between March and May and should be harvested (or simply dug up) between July and September. That means a considerably shorter maturity time than winter wheat, around four months.

Durum Wheat

Used most commonly to make semolina flour for pasta, durum wheat's delicate flavor is balanced by its elegant, classic appearance: thick heads of braided wheat grain on long stalks. Its time to maturity is similar to spring wheat, with plantings in mid-spring and harvests in late summer. This again means a time to harvest of around four months, and pretty green shoots in spring gardens maturing to golden stalks in summer."[71]

5. Can the parable be a metaphor for spiritual growth?

Parables can take on many different interpretations. One way to examine this parable is that Yeshua was talking about spiritual growth. Yeshua met many people during

---

[71] Sarah Moore, "How Long Do Wheat Plants Take Before the Harvest?," Home Guides | SF Gate, November 17, 2020, https://homeguides.sfgate.com/long-wheat-plants-before-harvest-69823.html.

His ministry, and they immediately followed Him. Why? They determined that Yeshua was the Messiah that the LORD had promised to His people.

Nevertheless, did they remain as disciples? That is an impossible question to answer. Indeed, many of them did because their faith grew. Many probably did not. Yeshua was only with them for three years. How long does it take for spiritual growth to occur? It is a unique process for every individual. Similarities will exist between people. However, there is a uniqueness to spiritual development (growth).

Spiritual growth starts with a seed being planted. The seed is a metaphor for the idea that there is a need to come to know the LORD. That seed can be a basic understanding of the work of Yeshua. Today, many people would have to begin their spiritual growth with a seed that convinces them that the LORD exists. In Yeshua's day, that would not have been necessary. Today that situation exists for many people.

Spiritual growth can then occur by the study of the Bible, especially an understanding of the Gospels. It may be necessary for a mentor to help. The farmer does not intervene to help the crop grow in the parable. However, the seeds do receive help from the soil. It contains the nutrients and water necessary for growth. Therefore, it can be concluded that a mentor is necessary for spiritual growth. The soil is the spiritual mentor. Then the farmer is not necessarily a person. The farmer can be a metaphor for an event or feeling that sparks a person to learn about the LORD.

When is spiritual growth over? The answer is never. Unfortunately, many people today are not interested in continual spiritual growth. They get baptized and are satisfied. Many times a person comes to understand Yeshua, gets baptized, then never enters the church again. They believe that they have obtained salvation through baptism. However, that is not the truth. Baptism is only the beginning of the spiritual journey. Suppose the harvest is a metaphor for the completion of one's spiritual growth. In that case, the harvest is the disconnection from the LORD. When the sickle cuts the crop, all growth stops. Therefore, the crop should never tell the farmer that it is ready to be harvested. Why? Because the harvest of a crop is the crop's death. Spiritual growth must never be halted!

The Scripture is as deep as the LORD is infinite. Based on this, spiritual growth and learning never conclude. There is always more to learn. Using the parable metaphorically, the crop harvest never happens. If the soil is a metaphor for the LORD, then a harvest is a disconnection from the LORD. This situation is not a desirable event. The parable says that it is up to the crop to decide to harvest.

Several metaphors have been introduced in this examination. As one reads the parable, there are more ways to view it. This examination considers the parable to be about spiritual growth. The idea of learning everything about the LORD can take hold in a person. It will occur differently in each person. It will take a different amount of time for each person. Yeshua said that it would occur. The crop is the spiritual awareness of the individual. Once the growth starts, it should never be stopped because there is an infinite amount of learning about the LORD that has to be done. It is a lifelong adventure.

In this metaphorical analysis, spiritual growth never ends unless the person wants it to happen. It is unwise to stop spiritual growth. It should continue forever.

6. Can the parable be a metaphor for patience?

The obvious answer is "yes." This metaphor is a bit more challenging to grasp because farmers know how long it should take for their crops to grow. The exact amount of time between planting and harvest can vary from year to year. The farmer has to wait for the time of harvest patiently. Watching the plants grow will not cause them to grow faster. The same is right about spiritual development. The theological view is that the disciples of Yeshua plant seeds into the hearts of people who do not know Him. Then the planter has to be patient. Consultants say that the Gospel has to be introduced to a person up to nine times before they want to learn more. That takes much patience. The planter has to wait until the person is ready to learn more about Yeshua. Forcing the issue does not work. If the planter tries to push for spiritual growth, it can backfire and turn off the potential disciple.

Linguistic Echo

Joel 3:3 "Put in the sickle, for the harvest is ripe" is echoed in verse 29. This echo invoke the idea of a prophetic-apocalyptic holy-war. The Day of the LORD was expected to be a time when the LORD returned to Earth and separated the righteous and evil people. The righteous would receive their reward in Heaven while the sinners would be banish to Sheol.[72]

Culture Section

Discussion

What was farming like in Yeshua's day? "For one thing, farming is hard work. Farmers work 365 days a year, regardless of the weather. Animals have to be fed, crops have to be fertilized and watered, and it doesn't matter how the farmer feels on that particular day. The work still has to be done. In the same way, most of us don't understand how hard life is. We seemed to be surprised by the hard work required by life. Building a good life is harder work, and every day, just like the farmer, we have to show up and do the work. Every day, relationships have to be tended. Weeds have to be removed, watered, and fertilizer added. Neglect a relationship, and just like a field left unplowed, weeds will overrun everything, and whatever was planted will die.

Farming takes time. You can't speed up nature. Cows, like people, reproduce in about nine months. You can't speed that up. Corn takes anywhere from 90 to 100 days to be ready to be harvested. Nature takes its own time. A million factors can control the time it takes for the crop to ripen. The amount of rain, the warmth of the days, the cool of the nights, soil condition, insects – the lists goes on and on. On some days, the only thing the farmer can do is sit and wait.

---

[72] Ched Myers, *Binding the Strong Man a Political Reading of Mark's Story of Jesus* (Maryknoll, NY: Orbis Books, 1988).

Patience is a required virtue for a farmer. Patience is a needed virtue for life. Some things just take time. Some things dictate their own schedule. A baby will learn to walk when the baby is ready. Not before. Children, in fact, will do almost everything they do in their own time. Every parent has a horror story of trying to rush a child into something before they are ready. All of us had endured small disasters because we tried to do something before the moment was ready. We pushed to repair a relationship before there had been time for true healing. Farming takes time. Life takes time. The smart farmer knows when the moment is ready. So does the wisest of us is living."[73]

Another interpretation for this parable can be found when considering the social situation of the early Christian faith. The faith was under constant oppression. It was documented that some believers joined the local Christian community, suffered oppression, and left the community. There were social penalties to pay for becoming a member of the growing Christian faith. The harvest could be viewed as a cutting-off from the community. Thus, saying planted in the community was better than being harvested. While in the soil, the protection of Yeshua was offered. Once a person left the faith, they were cut off from Yeshua. The faith had to do something about the defection that was occurring. This is one way to do it.

Thoughts

Evangelism is a way to examine the parable. The farmer plants the idea of discipleship to Yeshua. The farmer knows that not every seed will germinate and grow when he plants the seed. He also knows that each plant will grow at a slightly different rate. Evangelists have to have patience! A large amount of the time, discussing religion with a nonbeliever will not change their mind. Many factors come into play when evangelizing. Some of this art was lost when Constantine made Christianity the religion of the Roman Empire. The need to evangelize was unnecessary. After 1960 C.E., the need for evangelism has returned, especially in the United States. Currently, the U.S. is the largest mission field in the world. In the late 1800s, U.S. churches sent missionaries out into the world.

---

[73] Mike Glenn et al., "Why Jesus Talked So Much about Agriculture," Jesus Creed | A Blog by Scot McKnight, accessed February 3, 2021, https://www.christianitytoday.com/scot-mcknight/2020/january/why-jesus-talked-so-much-about-agriculture.html.

Now the rest of the world is sending evangelists into the U.S. It is well past time for U.S. churches to start planting seeds.

Reflections

Evangelism is one of the most challenging things to do. In general, people do not like rejection. It is taken as a personal thing. Also, are the churches training disciples to become evangelists? If you are a member of a church, is there training? A more straightforward question, is there an outreach effort at the church? Outreach ministries are supposed to be designed to bring the grace and love of Yeshua to the general public. If outreach ministry is not happening where your church is, then where does the church expect to get its next generation of members? Church membership and attendance have been sliding in the U.S. since 1960. It may be too late to return to Yeshua's way and spread some spiritual seeds.

MARK 4:30-32

Language

New American Standard 1995	Koine Greek
[30] And He said, "How shall we picture the kingdom of God, or by what parable shall we present it? [31] "*It is* like a mustard seed, which, when sown upon the soil, though it is smaller than all the seeds that are upon the soil, [32] yet when it is sown, it grows up and becomes larger than all the garden plants and forms large branches; so that THE BIRDS OF THE AIR can NEST UNDER ITS SHADE."	[30] Καὶ ἔλεγεν, Τίνι ⸀ ὁμοιώσωμεν ⸀ τὴν βασιλείαν τοῦ θεοῦ; Ἢ ἐν ποίᾳ παραβολῇ παραβάλωμεν αὐτήν; [31] Ὡς κόκκον σινάπεως, ὅς, ὅταν σπαρῇ ἐπὶ τῆς γῆς, μικρότερος πάντων τῶν σπερμάτων ἐστὶν τῶν ἐπὶ τῆς γῆς· [32] καὶ ὅταν σπαρῇ, ἀναβαίνει, καὶ γίνεται πάντων τῶν λαχάνων μείζων, καὶ ποιεῖ κλάδους μεγάλους, ὥστε δύνασθαι ὑπὸ τὴν σκιὰν αὐτοῦ τὰ πετεινὰ τοῦ οὐρανοῦ κατασκηνοῦν.

Process of Discovery

Linguistics Section

Linguistic Structure

[Parable] [30] And He said, "How shall we picture the kingdom of God, or by what parable shall we present it? [31] "*It is* like a mustard seed, which, when sown upon the soil, though it is smaller than all the seeds that are upon the soil, [32] yet when it is sown, it grows up and becomes larger than all the garden plants and forms large branches; so that THE BIRDS OF THE AIR can NEST UNDER ITS SHADE."

Discussion

Yeshua continues His parables about the Kingdom of Heaven. This parable contains references from Ezekiel, which makes it an apocalyptic parable.

Verse Comparison of citations or proof text

1. [23] "On the high mountain of Israel I will plant it, that it may bring forth boughs and bear fruit and become a stately cedar. And birds of every kind will nest under it; they will nest in the shade of its branches. (Ezek. 17:23 NAU)

    The apocalyptic description Ezekiel uses is about plants that give shade to birds. The mustard plant gave shade to birds on warm days. Yeshua was saying that the birds will nest in the trees, which invokes the apocalyptic imagery of Ezekiel. The apocalypse will occur when the items described in Ezekiel occur. Yeshua said that the Kingdom of God would be ushered in at that time.

Phrase Study

1. κόκκῳ σινάπεως (v. 32) – is translated in the NAU as "mustard seed." According to the Bauer-Danker lexicon, the precise plant species this phrase refers to cannot be determined. The mustard seed was considered the smallest seed at that time. Since the species is unclear from

the Greek, many interpreters have determined that Yeshua was referring to a large mustard tree while others refer to it as a large bush.[74]

Scripture cross-references

This parable can be found in Luke and Mark.

Culture Section

Discussion

In Judea and Galilee, the mustard seed was the smallest of the seeds known to the people. Mustard bushes grew wild like weeds. It is believed that farmers never planted mustard seeds. The people believed that eating mustard would cause insanity. However, they did use the plant for medicinal purposes. When the mustard plant grows, it looks like a large bush. The mustard plant does not grow into a tree. The Scripture should not have said that it grows into a tree in the Middle East. The plant grows to around three feet in height. Small birds, especially wild sparrows, nest in the mustard plant. During the heat of the day, birds rest under the mustard plant because of the shadow that it creates.

The mustard seed was considered hot and authoritative. It was the smallest of seeds but produced a massive bush-like plant. Yeshua used the mustard seed as an example in this parable because everyone thought of the Kingdom of God as enormous, but, instead, people missed the LORD's sovereign presence because it was so small. The LORD's presence was small because so many people of the time ignored the ways of the LORD. Therefore, in order to generate the LORD's presence, one must live by the words of the LORD. If one is not living by the words of the LORD, then one cannot feel His presence.

---

[74] Danker, Frederick W., and Walter Bauer. *A Greek-English Lexicon of the New Testament and Other Early Christian Literature*. Chicago: The University of Chicago Press, 2014.

Yeshua used the mustard seed for the sovereign presence of the LORD as humor. He made the omnipresent, omniscient, omnipotent LORD as tiny as a mustard seed.

The mustard seed is round and cannot be divided into two pieces like other seeds. The Gospel of the Kingdom is based on the truth of the LORD alone and cannot be divided! When the mustard seed grows, it kills any seeds that are near it. The Kingdom of God will supplant all and any religious notions and ideologies that separate, alienate, and divide one person against another. The Kingdom of God cannot grow next to idol worship and other erroneous, materialistic teaching and philosophies.

Yeshua is also referring to His words and beliefs about the Kingdom of Heaven. When the mustard seed germinates, it proliferates. When the Kingdom of Heaven grows, it is fast growing. For example, the Gospel of Yeshua is growing like mustard plants in Africa and Asia and is supplanting the pagan religions of those parts of the world. Yeshua expected His word and the Kingdom of Heaven to spread around the world.[75]

Thoughts

Yeshua tells us that the Kingdom of Heaven will flourish and grow once it is started. However, the parable does not say who is going to plant the seed? One view is that Yeshua came to Earth to plant the seeds. Yeshua is the one who commences the Kingdom of Heaven. However, history has proven that the Kingdom of Heaven is not here on Earth, at least not yet. The "man" in the parable could represent every follower of Yeshua. If all Christians planted their mustard seed, then the Kingdom of Heaven would flourish. The mustard seed is an individual's belief in the power of the Messiahship of Yeshua. The mustard seed has to be planted in one's heart before it can be planted elsewhere. Once it is planted, it should grow fast.

Reflections

---

[75] Rocco A. Errico and George M. Lamsa, *Aramaic Light on the Gospel of Matthew: a Commentary on the Teachings of Jesus from the Aramaic and Unchanged Near Eastern Customs* (Santa Fe, NM: Noohra Foundation, 2000).

An aspect of the mustard seed is that it cannot be divided. Applying this fact to the parable leaves the idea that the faith of Yeshua cannot be divided. However, a vehicle to demonstrate faith in Yeshua, the church, is very divided. Yeshua said the mustard seed is the Kingdom of Heaven, and the Kingdom cannot be divided. Since the church is divided, it cannot be a part of the Kingdom of Heaven. Those who are waiting in church for the "Jesus bus" to pick them up will never be picked up. Even inside individual churches, there is division. The Kingdom of heaven cannot grow in a divided church. So, the first thing that has to happen is that Christ's love, agape, must flow inside the church, and FULL unity must be restored. The division of the church occurred in 48 CE with the first church council. This trend of division must stop and must be reversed. The idea of unity among all Christian sects would be fantastic but will never happen. Most church people are looking out for themselves and not for the Kingdom of God. As long as the church's leadership is self-centered, the divisions will continue to occur, which will inhibit the growth of the Kingdom of Heaven. Suppose the politics are removed and the people who are attending church for their glory are removed. In that case, all church denominations could come back together. Until the churches become one church under Yeshua, the Kingdom of Heaven will not spread.

MARK 4:33-41

Language

New American Standard 1995	Koine Greek
[33] With many such parables He was speaking the word to them, so far as they were able to hear it; [34] and He did not speak to them without a parable; but He was explaining everything privately to His own disciples. [35] On that day, when evening came, He said to them, "Let us go over to the other side." [36] Leaving the crowd, they took Him along with them in the boat, just as He was; and other boats were with Him. [37] And there arose a fierce gale of wind, and the waves were breaking over the boat so much that the boat was already filling up. [38] Jesus Himself was in the stern, asleep on the cushion; and they woke Him and said to Him, "Teacher, do You not care that we are perishing?" [39] And He got up and rebuked the wind and said to the sea, "Hush, be still." And the wind died down and it became perfectly calm. [40] And He said to them, "Why are you afraid? Do you still have no faith?" [41] They became very much afraid and said to one another, "Who then is this, that even the wind and the sea obey Him?"	[33] Καὶ τοιαύταις παραβολαῖς πολλαῖς ἐλάλει αὐτοῖς τὸν λόγον καθὼς ἠδύναντο ἀκούειν· [34] χωρὶς δὲ παραβολῆς οὐκ ἐλάλει αὐτοῖς, κατ᾽ ἰδίαν δὲ τοῖς ἰδίοις μαθηταῖς ἐπέλυεν πάντα. [35] Καὶ λέγει αὐτοῖς ἐν ἐκείνῃ τῇ ἡμέρᾳ ὀψίας γενομένης· διέλθωμεν εἰς τὸ πέραν. [36] καὶ ἀφέντες τὸν ὄχλον παραλαμβάνουσιν αὐτὸν ὡς ἦν ἐν τῷ πλοίῳ, καὶ ἄλλα πλοῖα ἦν μετ᾽ αὐτοῦ. [37] καὶ γίνεται λαῖλαψ μεγάλη ἀνέμου καὶ τὰ κύματα ἐπέβαλλεν εἰς τὸ πλοῖον, ὥστε ἤδη γεμίζεσθαι τὸ πλοῖον. [38] καὶ αὐτὸς ἦν ἐν τῇ πρύμνῃ ἐπὶ τὸ προσκεφάλαιον καθεύδων. καὶ ἐγείρουσιν αὐτὸν καὶ λέγουσιν αὐτῷ· διδάσκαλε, οὐ μέλει σοι ὅτι ἀπολλύμεθα; [39] καὶ διεγερθεὶς ἐπετίμησεν τῷ ἀνέμῳ καὶ εἶπεν τῇ θαλάσσῃ· σιώπα, πεφίμωσο. καὶ ἐκόπασεν ὁ ἄνεμος καὶ ἐγένετο γαλήνη μεγάλη. [40] καὶ εἶπεν αὐτοῖς· τί δειλοί ἐστε; οὔπω ἔχετε πίστιν; [41] καὶ ἐφοβήθησαν φόβον μέγαν καὶ ἔλεγον πρὸς ἀλλήλους· τίς ἄρα οὗτός ἐστιν ὅτι καὶ ὁ ἄνεμος καὶ ἡ θάλασσα ὑπακούει αὐτῷ;

Process of Discovery

Linguistics Section

Linguistic Structure

[A reason for parables] [33] With many such parables He was speaking the word to them, so far as they were able to hear it; [34] and He did not speak to them without a parable; but He was explaining everything privately to His own disciples.

[Transition] [35] On that day, when evening came, He said to them, "Let us go over to the other side." [36] Leaving the crowd, they took Him along with them in the boat, just as He was; and other boats were with Him.

A [37] And there arose a fierce gale of wind, and the waves were breaking over the boat so much that the boat was already filling up.

    B [38] Jesus Himself was in the stern, asleep on the cushion; and they woke Him and said to Him, "Teacher, do You not care that we are perishing?"

        C [39] And He got up and rebuked the wind and said to the sea, "Hush, be still." And the wind died down and it became perfectly calm.

    B' [40] And He said to them, "Why are you afraid? Do you still have no faith?"

A' [41] They became very much afraid and said to one another, "Who then is this, that even the wind and the sea obey Him?"

Discussion

The narrative of Yeshua conquering the wind brings to mind the narratives about the prophets of old who were able to control nature. The disciples were convinced that they would die from the storm. Their faith should have been in Yeshua, who would not let that happen.

Questioning the passage

1. How does the narrative of the great storm discuss discipleship? (v. 35-41)
   Mountains surround the Sea of Galilee, and sudden gusts of wind from all directions can occur at any time and without warning. It may not have been a storm that the disciples felt

but rather the wind gust. If the boat were near the shoreline, it would not be as big a problem if the wind blew over the boat. If the boat was near the center of the sea, the concern of the disciples could be understood. People in Yeshua's day believed that the great abyss was in the center of the Sea of Galilee. The abyss was the entrance to Hell. Certainly, they did not want to end up there.

Yeshua calms the gusts of wind. This demonstrates that Yeshua was a prophet sent by the LORD. Prophets of the past had these kinds of powers. This impressed the disciples, who realized that they were following a prophet of the LORD.

Discipleship is a hard life. It will not be easy. The storm is a metaphor for the hard life ahead for the disciples. If they trusted in Yeshua, the road could be difficult, but Yeshua would always be there.

2. Why did Jesus' followers ask what kind of man is this? (v. 41)

The discussion was about Yeshua being a prophet of the LORD. The days of the prophets were over after the Persian period. The people did not recognize prophets during the time of the Greek and Roman occupation of Judea and the Galilee. Then Yeshua was born, and the disciples were trying to determine who He was. Was this Yeshua a prophet of the LORD? Rejoicing would be in order since a prophet of the LORD had not been sent in many centuries. Controlling nature was something that Elijah and other prophets of old could do. Therefore, the answer to the question of what kind of man Yeshua was is that He was a prophet of the LORD.

Linguistic Echoes

The narrative about Yeshua and the disciples on a boat is an echo of the Jonah story. The same images are used in the Mark story as in the Jonah story. The LORD sent a violent wind on the sea with terrible waves and water coming over the boat. Jonah was asleep in the boat in the same manner that Yeshua was asleep in the boat. Jonah was a prophet of the LORD since the same thing happened to Yeshua. The disciples concluded that Yeshua was a prophet of the LORD.

Culture Section

Discussion

This is a parable that places Yeshua against the powers of nature. This struggle can be categorized as to who is stronger, Yeshua or nature? For a moment, consider the wind storm as a metaphor for evil. Can the power of evil prevail over the power of good? Yeshua is the power of good, and He wins the battle. Since Yeshua won the battle, He has the authority to forgive sins. Why? Yeshua proved that he could beat the forces of evil. Sin is caused by the evil powers of the world overtaking a person. Therefore, Yeshua can forgive sins because He is always victorious over evil.

Several parables and statements of Yeshua in the Gospel offer the promise of radical sociopolitical change on behalf of the disenfranchised. Yeshua looks to subvert the current cultural ideals and not to legitimate them. Hellenistic miracle stories originated from the aristocracy. These stories were written to maintain the status quo. The aristocracy had the best life under their culture and did not want any change to occur.[76]

There is a bit of mystery to the parable. The disciples were not only fascinated at what Yeshua did but more interested in how He did it. The only explanation the Gospel offers is that He has divine powers. One thing to look for in a Yeshua parable is to find the mystery in it. Sometimes the mystery can be found in an anticultural statement. Either way, there is something special that Yeshua did.

Mark built His Gospel around a dialect of public discourse that Yeshua offers, followed by a withdrawal from the people. He either goes off by Himself to recharge through prayer or

---

[76] Ched Myers, *Binding the Strong Man a Political Reading of Mark's Story of Jesus* (Maryknoll, NY: Orbis Books, 1988).

explains the parable to His disciples. Many of Mark's stories revolve around action, then reflection. The action, in this case, is Yeshua stopping the storm. The reflection is His question to His disciples about faith.

Thoughts

Let us view this parable differently. It can be interpreted as a metaphor for good versus evil. It is not a view that you will find in the standard lesson books or even most academic commentaries. Yeshua's work was to show that good always triumphs over evil. Some people say that Yeshua and the forces of good had lost the battle at the cross. However, Yeshua and the forces of good won because of the resurrection. Evil thought it won the battle, but frankly, it did not. The forces of evil are all around us. Whether we are on land or sea, evil will find us. What will you do if evil finds you? Yeshua stood up to evil, the storm, and fought against it. The Gospel passage does not tell us more than he rebuked the wind. What was this rebuke? A fair question with no answer. How do you rebuke evil?

Reflections

Yeshua rebuked the evil that came to attack His disciples. Satan wanted to scare the disciples to the point that they would abandon Yeshua. The disciples were shocked that Yeshua was asleep. Was He asleep or waiting to see what His disciples were going to do? It did not take long to realize that they panicked. They were confident that they would die. Yeshua rebuked the storm, and all became calm. A lesson is that faith in Yeshua will take you through any storm.

MARK 5:1-20

Language

New American Standard 1995	Koine Greek
[1] They came to the other side of the sea, into the country of the Gerasenes. [2] When He got out of the boat, immediately a man from the tombs with an unclean spirit met Him, [3] and he had his dwelling among the tombs. And no one was able to bind him anymore, even with a chain; [4] because he had often been bound with shackles and chains, and the chains had been torn apart by him and the shackles broken in pieces, and no one was strong enough to subdue him. [5] Constantly, night and day, he was screaming among the tombs and in the mountains, and gashing himself with stones. [6] Seeing Jesus from a distance, he ran up and bowed down before Him; [7] and shouting with a loud voice, he said, "What business do we have with each other, Jesus, Son of the Most High God? I implore You by God, do not torment me!" [8] For He had been saying to him, "Come out of the man, you unclean spirit!" [9] And He was asking him, "What is your name?" And he said to Him, "My name is Legion; for we are many." [10] And he *began* to implore Him earnestly not to send them out of the country. [11] Now there was a large herd of swine feeding nearby on the mountain. [12] *The demons* implored Him, saying, "Send us into the swine so that we may enter them." [13] Jesus gave them permission. And coming out, the unclean spirits entered the swine; and the herd rushed down the steep bank into the sea, about two thousand *of them*; and they were drowned in the sea. [14] Their herdsmen ran away and reported it in the city and in the country. And *the people* came to see what it was that had happened.	[1] Καὶ ἦλθον εἰς τὸ πέραν τῆς θαλάσσης εἰς τὴν χώραν τῶν Γερασηνῶν. [2] καὶ ἐξελθόντος αὐτοῦ ἐκ τοῦ πλοίου εὐθὺς ὑπήντησεν αὐτῷ ἐκ τῶν μνημείων ἄνθρωπος ἐν πνεύματι ἀκαθάρτῳ, [3] ὃς τὴν κατοίκησιν εἶχεν ἐν τοῖς μνήμασιν, καὶ οὐδὲ ἁλύσει οὐκέτι οὐδεὶς ἐδύνατο αὐτὸν δῆσαι [4] διὰ τὸ αὐτὸν πολλάκις πέδαις καὶ ἁλύσεσιν δεδέσθαι καὶ διεσπάσθαι ὑπ' αὐτοῦ τὰς ἁλύσεις καὶ τὰς πέδας συντετρῖφθαι, καὶ οὐδεὶς ἴσχυεν αὐτὸν δαμάσαι· [5] καὶ διὰ παντὸς νυκτὸς καὶ ἡμέρας ἐν τοῖς μνήμασιν καὶ ἐν τοῖς ὄρεσιν ἦν κράζων καὶ κατακόπτων ἑαυτὸν λίθοις. [6] Καὶ ἰδὼν τὸν Ἰησοῦν ἀπὸ μακρόθεν ἔδραμεν καὶ προσεκύνησεν αὐτῷ [7] καὶ κράξας φωνῇ μεγάλῃ λέγει· τί ἐμοὶ καὶ σοί, Ἰησοῦ υἱὲ τοῦ θεοῦ τοῦ ὑψίστου; ὁρκίζω σε τὸν θεόν, μή με βασανίσῃς. [8] ἔλεγεν γὰρ αὐτῷ· ἔξελθε τὸ πνεῦμα τὸ ἀκάθαρτον ἐκ τοῦ ἀνθρώπου. [9] καὶ ἐπηρώτα αὐτόν· τί ὄνομά σοι; καὶ λέγει αὐτῷ· λεγιὼν ὄνομά μοι, ὅτι πολλοί ἐσμεν. [10] καὶ παρεκάλει αὐτὸν πολλὰ ἵνα μὴ αὐτὰ ἀποστείλῃ ἔξω τῆς χώρας. [11] Ἦν δὲ ἐκεῖ πρὸς τῷ ὄρει ἀγέλη χοίρων μεγάλη βοσκομένη· [12] καὶ παρεκάλεσαν αὐτὸν λέγοντες· πέμψον ἡμᾶς εἰς τοὺς χοίρους, ἵνα εἰς αὐτοὺς εἰσέλθωμεν. [13] καὶ ἐπέτρεψεν αὐτοῖς. καὶ ἐξελθόντα τὰ πνεύματα τὰ ἀκάθαρτα εἰσῆλθον εἰς τοὺς χοίρους, καὶ ὥρμησεν ἡ ἀγέλη κατὰ τοῦ κρημνοῦ εἰς τὴν θάλασσαν, ὡς δισχίλιοι, καὶ ἐπνίγοντο ἐν τῇ θαλάσσῃ. [14] Καὶ οἱ βόσκοντες αὐτοὺς ἔφυγον καὶ ἀπήγγειλαν εἰς τὴν πόλιν καὶ εἰς τοὺς ἀγρούς· καὶ ἦλθον ἰδεῖν τί ἐστιν τὸ γεγονὸς

<table>
<tr>
<td>

[15] They came to Jesus and observed the man who had been demon-possessed sitting down, clothed and in his right mind, the very man who had had the "legion"; and they became frightened.

[16] Those who had seen it described to them how it had happened to the demon-possessed man, and *all* about the swine.

[17] And they began to implore Him to leave their region.

[18] As He was getting into the boat, the man who had been demon-possessed was imploring Him that he might accompany Him.

[19] And He did not let him, but He said to him, "Go home to your people and report to them what great things the Lord has done for you, and *how* He had mercy on you."

[20] And he went away and began to proclaim in Decapolis what great things Jesus had done for him; and everyone was amazed.

</td>
<td>

[15] καὶ ἔρχονται πρὸς τὸν Ἰησοῦν καὶ θεωροῦσιν τὸν δαιμονιζόμενον καθήμενον ἱματισμένον καὶ σωφρονοῦντα, τὸν ἐσχηκότα τὸν λεγιῶνα, καὶ ἐφοβήθησαν.

[16] καὶ διηγήσαντο αὐτοῖς οἱ ἰδόντες πῶς ἐγένετο τῷ δαιμονιζομένῳ καὶ περὶ τῶν χοίρων.

[17] καὶ ἤρξαντο παρακαλεῖν αὐτὸν ἀπελθεῖν ἀπὸ τῶν ὁρίων αὐτῶν.

[18] Καὶ ἐμβαίνοντος αὐτοῦ εἰς τὸ πλοῖον παρεκάλει αὐτὸν ὁ δαιμονισθεὶς ἵνα μετ᾽ αὐτοῦ ᾖ.

[19] καὶ οὐκ ἀφῆκεν αὐτόν, ἀλλὰ λέγει αὐτῷ· ὕπαγε εἰς τὸν οἶκόν σου πρὸς τοὺς σοὺς καὶ ἀπάγγειλον αὐτοῖς ὅσα ὁ κύριός σοι πεποίηκεν καὶ ἠλέησέν σε.

[20] καὶ ἀπῆλθεν καὶ ἤρξατο κηρύσσειν ἐν τῇ Δεκαπόλει ὅσα ἐποίησεν αὐτῷ ὁ Ἰησοῦς, καὶ πάντες ἐθαύμαζον.

</td>
</tr>
</table>

Process of Discovery

Linguistics Section

Linguistic Structure

[Transition] [1] They came to the other side of the sea, into the country of the Gerasenes.

[Meeting Legion] [2] When He got out of the boat, immediately a man from the tombs with an unclean spirit met Him, [3] and he had his dwelling among the tombs. And no one was able to bind him anymore, even with a chain; [4] because he had often been bound with shackles and chains, and the chains had been torn apart by him and the shackles broken in pieces, and no one was strong enough to subdue him. [5] Constantly, night and day, he was screaming among the tombs and in the mountains, and gashing himself with stones. [6] Seeing Jesus from a distance, he ran up and bowed down before Him; [7] and shouting with a loud voice, he said, "What business do we have with each other, Jesus, Son of the Most High God? I implore You by God, do not torment me!" [8] For He had been saying to him, "Come out of the man, you unclean spirit!" [9] And He was asking him, "What is your name?" And he said to Him, "My name is Legion; for we are many."

[Exorcism] [10] And he *began* to implore Him earnestly not to send them out of the country. [11] Now there was a large herd of swine feeding nearby on the mountain. [12] *The demons* implored Him, saying,

"Send us into the swine so that we may enter them." [13] Jesus gave them permission. And coming out, the unclean spirits entered the swine; and the herd rushed down the steep bank into the sea, about two thousand *of them*; and they were drowned in the sea.

[Result of the Exorcism] [14] Their herdsmen ran away and reported it in the city and in the country. And *the people* came to see what it was that had happened. [15] They came to Jesus and observed the man who had been demon-possessed sitting down, clothed and in his right mind, the very man who had had the "legion"; and they became frightened. [16] Those who had seen it described to them how it had happened to the demon-possessed man, and *all* about the swine.

[Continued Result] [17] And they began to implore Him to leave their region. [18] As He was getting into the boat, the man who had been demon-possessed was imploring Him that he might accompany Him. [19] And He did not let him, but He said to him, "Go home to your people and report to them what great things the Lord has done for you, and *how* He had mercy on you."

[20] And he went away and began to proclaim in Decapolis what great things Jesus had done for him; and everyone was amazed.

Discussion

The description of this narrative is longer than it is in Matthew's Gospel but is essentially the same.

Questioning the Passage[77]

1. What is the "other side?" (v. 1)

    This means that Yeshua's boat had sailed from the west side, where He was previously, to the east side of the sea.

2. Whom did the people of Yeshua's day believe were demons?

    This is a reference to the belief that the fallen spirits of the Watchers possessed the demon-possessed people.

    The demons were believed to be the spirits of the 199 angels, called the Watchers. In Genesis chapter six, there is a short overview of what happened. The story is expanded in the Book of

---

[77] (The questions and answers offered are for discussion purposes. You may have different questions and answers. Remember all questions are valid and all answers must be defendable from Scripture. This applies to this section and to the Culture Section.)

the Watchers, which is the first thirty-six chapters of 1 Enoch. The Ethiopian Orthodox church has the books of Enoch as a part of their Canonical (Bible) books.[78]

There a several possible reasons why the proto-orthodox church (which became the catholic, orthodox and protestant churches) rejected the books of Enoch. There are theological thoughts in Enoch that did not fit the beliefs the church had about God, angels, and humans. Paul did not seem to be a fan of Enoch and infers that Enoch and other such writings are false teachings. Paul was a student who studied Scripture and would have been familiar with Enoch along with several other extra-Biblical writings. It appears that if a writer did not comply with Paul's view of Christ, he labeled it false teaching. If Paul's theory using the Mithras cult as a basis for his view of Yeshua is correct, then Enoch would not fit the narrative.

The Gospel of Matthew contains several encounters between Yeshua and demons. Examining Genesis chapter six and the Book of the Watchers, it can be seen how the demons came into being. There is a midrash about Azazel and Shemihazah (they were angels) coming before God's throne and asking if they could have permission to visit the humans on the Earth. The LORD warned them against doing this because the humans' evil would influence the two angels. Azazel and Shemihazah decided to visit the Earth anyway. While in human form, the two angels experienced the evil of the world. The Midrash stops there. It is possible to continue the Midrash using the events that occurred in Genesis chapter six and the Book of Watchers. When the two angels return to Heaven, the LORD made them part of a group of angels called the Watchers. Their job can be described as being guardian angels. Since Azazel and Shemihazah lived on the Earth, they would know what humans did and how they thought. It is stated in Genesis six that the Watchers saw how beautiful the daughters of men were. Why would the angels be concerned about this? Speculation is that when Azazel and Shemihazah were on the Earth, they could have experienced the joys of knowing the women on the Earth. They could have desired to have that union with women again and convinced 198 other Watchers to join them. It is unclear in the Book of the Watchers why the 198 Watchers joined them.

---

[78]http://www.ethiopianorthodox.org/english/canonical/books.html. Accessed on January 24, 2018

The 200 Watchers came to Earth and took human male form. Genesis six says that the Watchers took wives for themselves. This tells us that they had sex with the women who got pregnant and gave birth to children who were the Giants. The Scripture calls them the Nephilim. According to the Book of the Watchers, Genesis chapter six is a very sketchy overview of what happened. That book says that the offspring of the union of the Watchers and the women were called the Giants. The Giants had offspring called the Nephilim, and their offspring were called the Elioud. It was the actions of the Elioud that caused all the problems.

The Elioud and the humans of that day entered into a war against each other. The Elioud were physically large in comparison to the humans, and they were killing humans. The Elioud committed the one sin that inflamed the LORD more than any other sin. They drank human blood.

[26] 'You are not to eat any blood, either of bird or animal, in any of your dwellings. [27] 'Any person who eats any blood, even that person shall be cut off from his people.'" (Lev. 7:26-27 NAU)

Azazel and Shemihazah knew that they had brought sin upon their fellow Watchers and upon the Earth. They attempted to repair the problem. The angels were divided into groups of ten with a lead angel. Each leader of the group of ten offered a secret of Heaven to the humans. Azazel offered humans the knowledge of metallurgy. This enabled the humans to create weapons that would help them to destroy the Elioud. This secret and several others were given to the humans against the wishes of the LORD. If the LORD wanted the humans to know these secrets, He would have dispatched angels to transmit the information. Instead, the Watchers decided to offer the information.

The LORD was angered by what the Watchers did and the evil growing on upon the Earth. Unfortunately, by giving a free choice to the humans, the LORD enabled them to create their sin. Humans do not need help from anyone to sin. However, with Heaven's secrets that the Watchers gave the humans, sin and evil spread rapidly. The Flood that the LORD brought upon the Earth was to cleanse the Earth of this sin. Perhaps the flood was also necessary to kill the Elioud and their descendants. The Flood could have served this dual purpose.

The LORD court was held, and the indictment about the Watchers was read before the LORD. The Watchers were found guilty of sin, and the LORD pronounced punishment. Azazel was thrown into the Pit (which becomes Hell). He was the fallen angel that became Satan. The other 199 Watchers were punished by being condemned to live in the foundations of the Earth. Ancient people believed that pillars of rock held up the land of the Earth. They also believed that a river of water flowed under the Earth. They believed this because when they dug into the ground, they hit the rock, and in other cases, they hit the water in some cases. The 199 Watchers were believed to have been placed inside the rock, the foundation of the Earth.

Therefore, when the LORD brought the Flood upon the Earth the Watchers were not destroyed. Since they were forced to live in the Earth's foundation, they were not affected by the Flood. The Flood killed the evil and sinful people, Giants, Nephilim and Elioud of the Earth. Noah and his family were righteous people, so God spared them. There are various midrashim about the Flood because the following verse can be found in the book of Numbers.

[33] "There also we saw the Nephilim (the sons of Anak are part of the Nephilim); and we became like grasshoppers in our own sight, and so we were in their sight." (Num. 13:33 NAU)

There is a legend that the King of the Nephilim begged Noah to save him. The King was told that he could ride on Ark. several beams stuck out of the Ark, and the King sat on one. Noah cut a special window into the Ark, which allowed him to give the King food and water. According to Numbers, the Nephilim seemed to survive the Flood. The King's mate must have also survived. The Midrash does not tell us about her. Perhaps she was on a beam on the opposite side of the Ark. If only the King was on a beam, the Ark certainly would have tipped over because of the King's weight. Therefore, logically speaking, there had to be a counterweight on the opposite side. The easiest counterweight would have been the queen of the Nephilim. It is believed that Goliath was a descendant of the Nephilim, thus giving rise to this type of legend.

So, the 199 Watchers survived the Flood. Chronologically there is nothing written about their activities until Yeshua's time. The purpose of the Flood was to eliminate evil and sin from the Earth. Then how come evil and sin continued after the Flood? A reason is that the earthly bound Watchers took revenge against the humans because of their punishment from the LORD. The Watchers' influence could account for history's horrific events of people killing each other before Yeshua's arrival.

How could the LORD remove the Watchers' evil influence on the Earth? In Yeshua's day, the Watchers were known as demons. Yeshua, the Son of God, exorcised the demons out of humans and condemned them to the Pit to join Azazel. The Book of the Watchers was well-read in Yeshua's day. The Hebrew people believed that the demons were those spirits of the condemned Watchers. From the narratives in the Gospels, the demons knew who Yeshua was.

In the book of the Watchers, the Watchers are called unclean spirits. The Watchers became unclean spirits, which prohibited them from returning to Heaven. Only the perfect, the pure, and the clean spirits are permitted into Heaven. Instead of destroying the Watchers' spirits, the LORD had them condemned into the Foundations of the Earth.

3. Why did the citizens of the city ask Yeshua to leave? (v. 17)
    The citizen of the city wanted Yeshua to leave and not enter their town because raising swine and selling them to the Romans was the basis of their economy. If more residents were converted to Judaism, they would want to destroy their swine. Therefore, they were thinking about their economic life and not their spiritual life.

Biblical Locations

1. Where was the country of Gadarenes located? (v. 20)

[79]

Culture Section

Discussion

When Yeshua reached the other side of Galilee's Sea, he was approached by a demon-possessed man. In Yeshua's day, lunatics, people with profound mental illness, were said to be possessed by demons. They lived in the cemeteries near the town where they were born. Verse 28 says that they "came out of the tombs," which is saying that they were in the cemetery. Even with their mental illness, they recognized Yeshua as a Jewish prophet. Word must have reached the eastern side of the Sea of Galilee about Yeshua. Besides, a man traveling with twelve other men was either a religious teacher or a high official. This would attract everybody's attention[80].

Questioning the passage

1. Why did the demons want to be sent to the pigs? (v. 12)

    "Cast out" is an Aramaic phrase meaning "to restore sanity, to remove the cause that produces insanity." The demons asked to attack the pigs. To send them to the pigs is the same as saying

---

[79] "Gergesa." Wikipedia. May 30, 2018. Accessed November 14, 2018. https://en.wikipedia.org/wiki/Gergesa.
[80] Errico, Rocco A., and George M. Lamsa. Aramaic Light on the Gospel of Matthew: A Commentary on the Teachings of Jesus from the Aramaic and Unchanged Near Eastern Customs. Santa Fe, NM: Noohra Foundation, 2000.

let them enter the pigs. In Aramaic, to enter someone is to wrestle or fight them. Semites would say that two oxen enter each other when they attack each other or fight with each other. The two men were mentally ill and were Syrians. Syrians kept large swine herds.

Pigs were an abomination to the Hebrews. The two men converted to the Jewish faith because of Yeshua's healing. Therefore, as proof of their conversion and appreciation, they wanted to destroy the pigs because they were now an abomination to them. They might have gone to the prophets of their false gods and could not be healed. Yeshua was able to heal them. When a person converted to a new faith in the Near East, they discontinued their previous religious practices. Today, if a Christian wants to become a Muslim, he must sell or kill his swine and repudiate Christianity's customs and practices.[81]

Thoughts

In this narrative, we have evidence that a Gentile was converted to Judaism because they met Yeshua. The narrative says that the demons went into the pigs, the pigs jumped into the sea, and when this is understood through the culture, the result is a conversion of religion because the two men gave up something that they had while Gentiles. Hebrews did not eat pork, while Gentiles did. The pigs are a metaphor for giving up something to become a disciple of Yeshua. Not only did they become disciples of Yeshua, but they also converted to Judaism. This feature of the story is never understood this way by the church because the church, which survived from the first century CE, was based on Paul, who believed that being Jewish was not crucial to becoming a disciple of Christ. Paul's proto-orthodox church would never say that one had to become Jewish before coming to know Christ. Interestingly, Matthew's Gospel has this narrative. If the church's theologians understood the passage's original meaning, they might have had it removed.

Reflections

What have you given up for Christ? When adults come to believe in Christ, they generally give up something. That something may not be a physical object. It could be anything. For example, the author used to go to flea markets on Sunday morning. After coming to know Yeshua, he gave up

---

[81] IBID.

flea marketing to go to church and start tithing. The money spent at the flea markets was now being given to help a local church. People who grew up in the church give up not sinning, which is not partaking in sinful actions. There is plenty of sin in the world that one can participate in without much effort. Not participating in those events or anti-biblical habits is a way of giving something up for one's discipleship to Christ. People who say they are a disciple of Christ but partake in sinful actions are not disciples and will be saddened on judgment day. A New Testament professor at a seminar said, "there are sins I like that I will not give up." So, is this New Testament professor a true disciple of Yeshua? The answer is no. This is a continuation of the theme from the previous narrative that discipleship is hard.

MARK 5:21-43

Language

New American Standard 1995	Koine Greek
21 When Jesus had crossed over again in the boat to the other side, a large crowd gathered around Him; and so He stayed by the seashore. 22 One of the synagogue officials named Jairus came up, and on seeing Him, fell at His feet 23 and implored Him earnestly, saying, "My little daughter is at the point of death; *please* come and lay Your hands on her, so that she will get well and live." 24 And He went off with him; and a large crowd was following Him and pressing in on Him.	21 Καὶ διαπεράσαντος τοῦ Ἰησοῦ ἐν τῷ πλοίῳ πάλιν εἰς τὸ πέραν, συνήχθη ὄχλος πολὺς ἐπ' αὐτόν, καὶ ἦν παρὰ τὴν θάλασσαν. 22 Καὶ ἰδού, ἔρχεται εἷς τῶν ἀρχισυναγώγων, ὀνόματι Ἰάειρος, καὶ ἰδὼν αὐτόν, πίπτει πρὸς τοὺς πόδας αὐτοῦ, 23 καὶ παρεκάλει αὐτὸν πολλά, λέγων ὅτι Τὸ θυγάτριόν μου ἐσχάτως ἔχει ἵνα ἐλθὼν ἐπιθῇς αὐτῇ τὰς χεῖρας, ὅπως σωθῇ καὶ ζήσεται. 24 Καὶ ἀπῆλθεν μετ' αὐτοῦ καὶ ἠκολούθει αὐτῷ ὄχλος πολύς, καὶ συνέθλιβον αὐτόν.
25 A woman who had had a hemorrhage for twelve years, 26 and had endured much at the hands of many physicians, and had spent all that she had and was not helped at all, but rather had grown worse — 27 after hearing about Jesus, she came up in the crowd behind *Him* and touched His cloak. 28 For she thought, "If I just touch His garments, I will get well." 29 Immediately the flow of her blood was dried up; and she felt in her body that she was healed of her affliction. 30 Immediately Jesus, perceiving in Himself that the power *proceeding* from Him had gone forth, turned around in the crowd and said, "Who touched My garments?" 31 And His disciples said to Him, "You see the crowd pressing in on You, and You say, 'Who touched Me?'" 32 And He looked around to see the woman who had done this. 33 But the woman fearing and trembling, aware of what had happened to her, came and fell down before Him and told Him the whole truth. 34 And He said to her, "Daughter, your faith has [1]made you well; go in peace and be healed of your affliction."	25 Καὶ γυνή τις οὖσα ἐν ῥύσει αἵματος ἔτη δώδεκα, 26 καὶ πολλὰ παθοῦσα ὑπὸ πολλῶν ἰατρῶν, καὶ δαπανήσασα τὰ παρ' αὐτῆς πάντα, καὶ μηδὲν ὠφεληθεῖσα, ἀλλὰ μᾶλλον εἰς τὸ χεῖρον ἐλθοῦσα, 27 ἀκούσασα περὶ τοῦ Ἰησοῦ, ἐλθοῦσα ἐν τῷ ὄχλῳ ὄπισθεν, ἥψατο τοῦ ἱματίου αὐτοῦ 28 ἔλεγεν γὰρ ὅτι Κἂν τῶν ἱματίων αὐτοῦ ἅψωμαι, σωθήσομαι. 29 Καὶ εὐθέως ἐξηράνθη ἡ πηγὴ τοῦ αἵματος αὐτῆς, καὶ ἔγνω τῷ σώματι ὅτι ἴαται ἀπὸ τῆς μάστιγος. 30 Καὶ εὐθέως ὁ Ἰησοῦς ἐπιγνοὺς ἐν ἑαυτῷ τὴν ἐξ αὐτοῦ δύναμιν ἐξελθοῦσαν, ἐπιστραφεὶς ἐν τῷ ὄχλῳ, ἔλεγεν, Τίς μου ἥψατο τῶν ἱματίων; 31 Καὶ ἔλεγον αὐτῷ οἱ μαθηταὶ αὐτοῦ, Βλέπεις τὸν ὄχλον συνθλίβοντά σε, καὶ λέγεις, Τίς μου ἥψατο; 32 Καὶ περιεβλέπετο ἰδεῖν τὴν τοῦτο ποιήσασαν. 33 Ἡ δὲ γυνὴ φοβηθεῖσα καὶ τρέμουσα, εἰδυῖα ὃ γέγονεν ἐπ' αὐτῇ, ἦλθεν καὶ προσέπεσεν αὐτῷ, καὶ εἶπεν αὐτῷ πᾶσαν τὴν ἀλήθειαν. 34 Ὁ δὲ εἶπεν αὐτῇ, Θύγατερ, ἡ πίστις σου σέσωκέν σε ὕπαγε εἰς εἰρήνην, καὶ ἴσθι ὑγιὴς ἀπὸ τῆς μάστιγός σου.
35 While He was still speaking, they came from the *house of* the synagogue official, saying, "Your daughter has died; why trouble the Teacher anymore?" 36 But Jesus, overhearing what was being spoken, said to the synagogue official, "Do	35 Ἔτι αὐτοῦ λαλοῦντος, ἔρχονται ἀπὸ τοῦ ἀρχισυναγώγου, λέγοντες ὅτι Ἡ θυγάτηρ σου ἀπέθανεν τί ἔτι σκύλλεις τὸν διδάσκαλον; 36 Ὁ δὲ Ἰησοῦς εὐθέως ἀκούσας τὸν λόγον λαλούμενον λέγει τῷ ἀρχισυναγώγῳ, Μὴ φοβοῦ, μόνον πίστευε. 37 Καὶ οὐκ ἀφῆκεν οὐδένα αὐτῷ συνακολουθῆσαι, εἰ μὴ Πέτρον καὶ Ἰάκωβον καὶ

not be afraid *any longer,* only believe." [37] And He allowed no one to accompany Him, except Peter and James and John the brother of James. [38] They came to the house of the synagogue official; and He saw a commotion, and *people* loudly weeping and wailing. [39] And entering in, He said to them, "Why make a commotion and weep? The child has not died, but is asleep." [40] They *began* laughing at Him. But putting them all out, He took along the child's father and mother and His own companions, and entered *the room* where the child was. [41] Taking the child by the hand, He said to her, "Talitha kum!" (which translated means, "Little girl, I say to you, get up!"). [42] Immediately the girl got up and *began* to walk, for she was twelve years old. And immediately they were completely astounded. [43] And He gave them strict orders that no one should know about this, and He said that *something* should be given her to eat.

Ἰωάννην τὸν ἀδελφὸν Ἰακώβου. [38] Καὶ ἔρχεται εἰς τὸν οἶκον τοῦ ἀρχισυναγώγου, καὶ θεωρεῖ θόρυβον, κλαίοντας καὶ ἀλαλάζοντας πολλά. [39] Καὶ εἰσελθὼν λέγει αὐτοῖς, Τί θορυβεῖσθε καὶ κλαίετε; Τὸ παιδίον οὐκ ἀπέθανεν, ἀλλὰ καθεύδει. [40] Καὶ κατεγέλων αὐτοῦ. Ὁ δέ, ἐκβαλὼν πάντας, παραλαμβάνει τὸν πατέρα τοῦ παιδίου καὶ τὴν μητέρα καὶ τοὺς μετ' αὐτοῦ, καὶ εἰσπορεύεται ὅπου ἦν τὸ παιδίον ἀνακείμενον. [41] Καὶ κρατήσας τῆς χειρὸς τοῦ παιδίου, λέγει αὐτῇ, Ταλιθά, κούμι ὅ ἐστιν μεθερμηνευόμενον, Τὸ κοράσιον, σοὶ λέγω, ἔγειραι. [42] Καὶ εὐθέως ἀνέστη τὸ κοράσιον καὶ περιεπάτει, ἦν γὰρ ἐτῶν δώδεκα καὶ ἐξέστησαν ἐκστάσει μεγάλῃ. [43] Καὶ διεστείλατο αὐτοῖς πολλὰ ἵνα μηδεὶς γνῶ τοῦτο καὶ εἶπεν δοθῆναι αὐτῇ φαγεῖν.

Process of Discovery

Linguistics Section

Linguistic Structure

[Healing Story #1] [21] When Jesus had crossed over again in the boat to the other side, a large crowd gathered around Him; and so He stayed by the seashore. [22] One of the synagogue officials named Jairus came up, and on seeing Him, fell at His feet [23] and implored Him earnestly, saying, "My little daughter is at the point of death; *please* come and lay Your hands on her, so that she will get well and live." [24] And He went off with him; and a large crowd was following Him and pressing in on Him.

[Healing Story #2] [25] A woman who had had a hemorrhage for twelve years, [26] and had endured much at the hands of many physicians, and had spent all that she had and was not helped at all, but rather had grown worse — [27] after hearing about Jesus, she came up in the crowd behind *Him* and touched His cloak. [28] For she thought, "If I just touch His garments, I will get well." [29] Immediately the flow of her blood was dried up; and she felt in her body that she was healed of her affliction. [30] Immediately Jesus, perceiving in Himself that the power *proceeding* from Him had gone forth, turned around in the crowd and said, "Who touched My garments?" [31] And His disciples said to Him, "You see the crowd pressing in on You, and You say, 'Who touched Me?'" [32] And He looked around to see the woman who had done this. [33] But the woman fearing and trembling, aware of what had happened to her, came and fell down before Him and told Him the whole truth. [34] And He said to her, "Daughter, your faith has [1]made you well; go in peace and be healed of your affliction."

[Healing Story #3] [35] While He was still speaking, they came from the *house of* the synagogue official, saying, "Your daughter has died; why trouble the Teacher anymore?" [36] But Jesus, overhearing what was being spoken, said to the synagogue official, "Do not be afraid *any longer*, only believe." [37] And He allowed no one to accompany Him, except Peter and James and John the brother of James. [38] They came to the house of the synagogue official; and He saw a commotion, and *people* loudly weeping and wailing. [39] And entering in, He said to them, "Why make a commotion and weep? The child has not died, but is asleep." [40] They *began* laughing at Him. But putting them all out, He took along the child's father and mother and His own companions, and entered *the room* where the child was. [41] Taking the child by the hand, He said to her, "Talitha kum!" (which translated means, "Little girl, I say to you, get up!"). [42] Immediately the girl got up and *began* to walk, for she was twelve years old. And immediately they were completely astounded. [43] And He gave them strict orders that no one should know about this, and He said that *something* should be given her to eat.

Discussion

This section consists of three miracle healings. Each miracle needs to be understood culturally separate, but then the overall message about Yeshua and discipleship needs to be examined as one whole. The three healing stories revolve around the need for faith. Each person(s) had to have a strong faith in Yeshua that He could heal them. Perhaps the faith was not in Yeshua as much as it was in the LORD who could promise anything He wished.

Questioning the Passage

1. Why did the author of Mark's Gospel break up the narrative about the dead girl with another healing story?

    The break in the story might have been done for drama. Today this can be seen in storytelling, especially in TV shows. The idea is to captivate the reader (or viewer) to stay with the story so that he/she can hear or see the result of the story that is being told.

2. Is there a significance that the woman approached Yeshua from behind Him? (v. 27)

    The woman probably feared a direct approach. What would have happened if Yeshua saw her coming and did not want to her touch because He would have become ritualistically unclean? Therefore, the woman took no chances. She came up behind Yeshua and touched Him. Yeshua would have been aware of what she wanted to do and could have avoided her. The woman was not taking a chance, so she came from behind.

3. Why did the bleeding woman want to touch Yeshua's garment? (v. 28)

    A bleeding woman's touch would have made Yeshua unclean. It is possible that the crowd did not know that she was experiencing a continual menstrual cycle. If they did, then they would have instantly pulled away from Yeshua and her because they feared to become ritualistically unclean. She wanted to touch the fringes of His clothing. The "fringes" are the *tzitzi* that are found on the four corners of the *tallis*. They represent the Word of the LORD. The LORD commanded that the Word be worn on the four corners of a Hebrew's garment. To make that happen the fringes were added to the prayer shawl. The woman believed that the power of the LORD was in Yeshua and that it could be transmitted by touching the Word of the LORD, which was hanging off Yeshua's garment. Yeshua was not concerned about being declared unclean by a priest. Yeshua was counter-cultural and was not concerned about the purity law in this case. He demonstrated his desire to help people.

4. Why did the people laugh at Yeshua? (v. 40)

   This statement does not coincide with the culture of the day. Either Mark's author is showing his lack of cultural education or created this situation to say that the Hebrew people rejected the LORD's Messiah. Since a theme in all four Gospels is that the Hebrew people rejected Yeshua as the Messiah, it is fitting that this story also says that Yeshua was rejected.

5. What house did Yeshua enter in verse thirty-five?

   It is not known what house Yeshua entered. It is not crucial to understand the passage which the house is identified.

Culture Section

Discussion

How did Semites mourn for their dead in Yeshua's day? Their mourning was overwhelming grief. The only suitable conduct at a funeral was to manifest your respect for the dead by showing grief emotionally. To be silent at a funeral meant that you had no feelings for the departed. The attendees of the funeral weep over their dead. They would slap their faces with their hands, tear their clothes, and even inflict wounds on themselves. "Women cut their hair and beat their breasts; men stop shaving as a sign of mourning." The weeping and wailing reached its high point when professional singers chanted songs of lamentation and men and women eulogized. Relatives would join the professional singers. Sometimes the wailing was so loud and lamenting that a deep hysteria and disorder could result.

Yeshua understood how people viewed death. He entered the home and ordered the people to leave the room and told the professional singers to stop making noise. He did not want the girl to be frightened by the crying and laments. "The girl is not dead, but she is sleeping" is a Semitic expression that was used to quiet distressed parents. Yeshua believed that death was nothing more but sleep. To Yeshua the deceased were really alive because their souls were still alive.

Middle Eastern people in Yeshua's day thought that a person suffering from a coma was dead. Perhaps the girl was in a coma and Yeshua was able to revive her.[82]

Thoughts

This might sound a bit radical, however it is a proper interpretation of the triad. Could Yeshua's power be limited by the faith of the individual. The knee jerk reaction is that if Yeshua is divine that His power cannot be limited. Stop for a moment and think about it. Those who deny Yeshua may never experience the feeling of comfort and joy that disciples do. People who deny Yeshua have to answer the question about what happens to the soul after physical death. Disciples of Yeshua have the promise of salvation and eternal life. They lead a life led by the Gospels, therefore they are following the ways of Yeshua. Loving God and neighbor with all of one's heart brings one close to Yeshua. These individuals would be able to feel the presence of Yeshua through the Holy Spirit. There is comfort in knowing that one's actions and words are pleasing to the LORD. People who reject Yeshua will have a difficult time in accepting the LORD's gift of salvation.

Reflections

Before I became a disciple of Yeshua the world seemed black and white. Wake up, go to work, come home, have some personal time then repeat the cycle the next day. There had to be more to life than just that cycle. When I became a disciple of Yeshua I learned that life is more than the repetitive cycle. Yeshua opened pathways for an exploration of the spiritual realm. Coming to understand the ways of the LORD through Yeshua is a building block of faith. Faith is strengthened as one submits to the ways of Yeshua and follows Him. This passage offers three examples of how faith is strengthened when one becomes a disciple of Yeshua. For a disciple of Yeshua a spiritual growth plan must be established. A person with a deeper understanding of the ways of will become a stronger disciple and will be able to touch the divine.

---

[82] Errico, Rocco A., and George M. Lamsa. Aramaic Light on the Gospel of Matthew: A Commentary on the Teachings of Jesus from the Aramaic and Unchanged Near Eastern Customs. Santa Fe, NM: Noohra Foundation, 2000.

MARK 6:1-6

Language

New American Standard 1995	Koine Greek
[1] Jesus went out from there and came into His hometown; and His disciples followed Him. [2] When the Sabbath came, He began to teach in the synagogue; and the many listeners were astonished, saying, "Where did this man *get* these things, and what is *this* wisdom given to Him, and such miracles as these performed by His hands? [3] "Is not this the carpenter, the son of Mary, and brother of James and Joses and Judas and Simon? Are not His sisters here with us?" And they took offense at Him. [4] Jesus said to them, "A prophet is not without honor except in his hometown and among his *own* relatives and in his *own* household." [5] And He could do no miracle there except that He laid His hands on a few sick people and healed them. [6] And He wondered at their unbelief. And He was going around the villages teaching.	[1] Καὶ ἐξῆλθεν ἐκεῖθεν, καὶ ἦλθεν εἰς τὴν πατρίδα αὐτοῦ· καὶ ἀκολουθοῦσιν αὐτῷ οἱ μαθηταὶ αὐτοῦ. [2] Καὶ γενομένου σαββάτου, ἤρξατο ἐν τῇ συναγωγῇ διδάσκειν· καὶ πολλοὶ ἀκούοντες ἐξεπλήσσοντο, λέγοντες, Πόθεν τούτῳ ταῦτα; Καὶ τίς ἡ σοφία ἡ δοθεῖσα αὐτῷ, καὶ δυνάμεις τοιαῦται διὰ τῶν χειρῶν αὐτοῦ γίνονται; [3] Οὐχ οὗτός ἐστιν ὁ τέκτων, ὁ υἱὸς Μαρίας, ἀδελφὸς δὲ Ἰακώβου καὶ Ἰωσῆ καὶ Ἰούδα καὶ Σίμωνος; Καὶ οὐκ εἰσὶν αἱ ἀδελφαὶ αὐτοῦ ὧδε πρὸς ἡμᾶς; Καὶ ἐσκανδαλίζοντο ἐν αὐτῷ. [4] Ἔλεγεν δὲ αὐτοῖς ὁ Ἰησοῦς ὅτι Οὐκ ἔστιν προφήτης ἄτιμος, εἰ μὴ ἐν τῇ πατρίδι αὐτοῦ, καὶ ἐν τοῖς συγγενέσιν καὶ ἐν τῇ οἰκίᾳ αὐτοῦ. [5] Καὶ οὐκ ἠδύνατο ἐκεῖ οὐδεμίαν δύναμιν ποιῆσαι, εἰ μὴ ὀλίγοις ἀρρώστοις ἐπιθεὶς τὰς χεῖρας, ἐθεράπευσεν. [6] Καὶ ἐθαύμαζεν διὰ τὴν ἀπιστίαν αὐτῶν. Καὶ περιῆγεν τὰς κώμας κύκλῳ διδάσκων.

Process of Discovery

Linguistics Section

Linguistic Structure

[Transition] [1] Jesus went out from there and came into His hometown; and His disciples followed Him.

[Action] [2] When the Sabbath came, He began to teach in the synagogue; and the many listeners were astonished, saying, "Where did this man *get* these things, and what is *this* wisdom given to Him, and such miracles as these performed by His hands?

[Reaction] [3] "Is not this the carpenter, the son of Mary, and brother of James and Joses and Judas and Simon? Are not His sisters here with us?" And they took offense at Him.

[Response] [4] Jesus said to them, "A prophet is not without honor except in his hometown and among his *own* relatives and in his *own* household."

[Result] [5] And He could do no miracle there except that He laid His hands on a few sick people and healed them. [6] And He wondered at their unbelief. And He was going around the villages teaching.

Discussion

Mark's author notes again that Yeshua was a poor peasant. How can a poor peasant become the LORD's Messiah? He is also disclosing the culture of the day with Yeshua's rejection.

Questioning the Passage

1. What does the expression "son of Mary" mean? (v. 3.)

   This expression means that Joseph had more than one wife.[83] Tradition says that Joseph was an older man. Therefore, he would have been married at least once before. It was

---

[83] Rocco A. Errico, George M. Lamsa, and George M. Lamsa, *Aramaic Light on the Gospels of Mark and Luke: a Commentary on the Teachings of Jesus from the Aramaic and Unchanged Near Eastern Customs* (Smyrna, GA: Noohra Foundation, 2001).

very common for women to die in childbirth. A church tradition is that Mary only had one child, Yeshua. If that is true then the brothers and sisters mentioned in the Gospel had to be the children of a different wife of Joseph.

Phrase Study

1. τέκτων, ονος, ὁ; one who constructs, *builder, carpenter* (Hom.+; SEG XXVIII, 1186' worker in wood, carpenter, joiner'. Acc. to Maximus Tyr. 15, 3c, a τ. makes ἄροτρα; Just. , D. 88, 8, states that Joseph made ἄροτρα καὶ ζυγά' plows and yokes'; acc. to Epict. 1, 15, 2 a τ. works w. wood, in contrast to a worker in bronze; for the latter, less freq., Eur., Alc. 5; in Ael. Aristid. 46 p. 211 D. τέκτων signifies worker in stone. GJs 9:3 al. Joseph's work is οἰκοδομῆσαι τὰς οἰκοδομάς; the word. τ. is not used.—CMcCown, ὁ τέκτων: Studies in Early Christ., ed. SCase 1928, 173–89). In Mt 13:55 Jesus is called ὁ τοῦ τέκτονος υἱός, in Mk 6:3 ὁ τέκτων (cp. Just., D. 88, 8=ASyn. 18, 55f; the difference may perh. be explained on the basis of a similar one having to do with Sophillus, the father of Sophocles: Aristoxenus, fgm. 115 calls him τέκτων, but the Vita Sophoclis 1 [=OxfT. of Soph., ed. Pearson p. xviii; not printed in NWilson's ed. '90] rejects this and will admit only that he may possibly have possessed τέκτονες as slaves. Considerations of social status may have something to do with the variation in the gospel tradition).—HHöpfl, Nonne hic est fabri filius?: Biblica 4, 1923, 41–55; ELombard, Charpentier ou maçon: RTP '48, 4; EStauffer, Jeschua ben Mirjam (Mk 6:3): MBlack Festschr., '69, 119–28; RBatey, NTS 30, '84, 249–58.—B. 589. BHHW III 2341. DELG. M-M. EDNT.[84]

The entire DBAG entry is included because several commentators have interchanged the translation of "carpenter" or "stoneworker" over the years. Was Yeshua a stoneworker or a carpenter? The Peshitta uses the Aramaic word *nagara*. This word means "carpenter." Thus Yeshua is described by Mark's Gospel as a wood carpenter.

---

[84] Frederick W. Danker, William Arndt, and Walter Bauer, *A Greek-English Lexicon of the New Testament and Other Early Christian Literature* (Chicago: University of Chicago Press, 2000).

Culture Section

Questioning the passage

1. What did people think about being a carpenter? (v. 3)

    Carpentry was a low-tech and insignificant occupation in Yeshua's day. In Yeshua's day, a carpenter would fix broken doors and plows. They made wooden spoons. There was little demand for carpenters because nearly every family made their wooden objects. A carpenter would be called to assist in building a house or to manufacture wooden keys from time to time. Such work was not paid for. The carpenter was offered a good meal or perhaps a few eggs and some cheese. Yokes and plows were cut from trees and manufactured in the field by the farmer.[85]

    The people in Galilee were not wealthy. They would have repaired their wooden items until a point came that repairs could not be accomplished. The demand for new wooden objects was low. Yeshua might not have been a carpenter. Mark's author could have used this occupation to remind the reader that Yeshua was a lowly peasant. The Gospel's premise is to prove that the lowly peasant from Galilee is the Messiah of the LORD.

2. What is the culture about not honoring prophets? (v. 4)

    Church tradition says that Yeshua was not accepted in His hometown. Nevertheless, the reason for the rejection is not what the church espouses. The culture of Yeshua's day is essential to know when considering this question. The people of Galilee had a robust cultural presence from the Assyrian people. When the Assyrians conquered the Northern Kingdom of Israel, they moved a large portion of the population to other parts of their empire. They brought people from different parts of their empire to populate the land that became Galilee. The Assyrians did this in an attempt to eliminate the culture of the people they conquered. Near Eastern culture does not change much over time. Many aspects of Galilean culture were initially from the Assyrian Empire.

---

[85] Rocco A. Errico, George M. Lamsa, and George M. Lamsa, *Aramaic Light on the Gospels of Mark and Luke: a Commentary on the Teachings of Jesus from the Aramaic and Unchanged Near Eastern Customs* (Smyrna, GA: Noohra Foundation, 2001).

Not honoring a prophet of their nationality was one of these cultural traits. People were jealous and envious of each other. This attitude was a cultural trait of the Assyrian peoples. Assyrians did not like to see their countrymen attain prominence. When an Assyrian gained wealth or became well known, some of his people would attempt to ruin him. Interestingly is that a poor man was pitied him.

Yeshua grew up in Galilee with Galilean and Assyrian customs. The emotions of resentment and jealousy were dominant. The people in Nazareth would not object to a religious leader from another town. However, they did reject a religious leader of their town. Even Yeshua's brothers were jealous of Him and denounced him.

3. Why was Yeshua's family identify? (v. 3)
Family lineage generally determined a person's social position and trade.[86]

Yeshua was defining a new sociological definition for the family. In this narrative, it is essential to note that Yeshua said that family lineage does not determine who an individual is. The family structure was solid in Yeshua's day. If the father was a farmer, then the sons became farmers. One's trade or occupation became what his father was. That trend was being challenged. Yeshua's father was not a religious man, certainly not a rabbi. Yeshua presented Himself as a rabbi. His teachings were new, and the question of authority came. In this narrative, the question of authority is because of His family line. Yeshua's family were farming peasants. They were not rabbis. Therefore, how can Yeshua be a rabbi? That was the question that Mark was addressing. In the new family order, anyone can do what the LORD leads them to do.

Thoughts

Guilty by association comes to mind. Yeshua was rejected as a teacher of the Word of the LORD because the culture of His day said so. The first point is that the people of the town He grew up in

---

[86] E. Randolph Richards and Brandon J. O'Brien, *Misreading Scripture with Western Eyes: Removing Cultural Blinders to Better Understand the Bible* (Downers Grove, IL: InterVarsity Press, 2012).

rejected him as a religious man because centuries of culture told them. Mark's author adds the question of family. Yeshua's family was not a leading religious family. Therefore, Yeshua could not have had the LORD's spirit with Him. He was not rejected because the people did not like the message. That is a church tradition in which the church wants to condemn Jews. The peoples' cultural beliefs prevented them from seeing the truth of Yeshua's words.

Reflections

Have you ever been guilty because of association? When looking at the family point, Yeshua was guilty of not being from the LORD because of His family. Today it may not be because of your family but rather by your friends. While I was in college, I became friends with Douglas. Several persons in the Hillel group (an organization for Jewish people) rejected me because I was friends with Douglas. Guilt by association. It was not fair that others judged me because of my friends. Guilt by association occurred to me in the church. My first appointment was as the Associate Pastor at a United Methodist church. After the first year, I was told by one member that the mistreatment I received was because of guilt by association. The people believed that I was appointed because of the Senior Pastor (who was not well-liked). It took the people a year to realize that I was not like him—guilt by association.

MARK 6:7-13

Language

New American Standard 1995	Koine Greek
[7] And He summoned the twelve and began to send them out in pairs, and gave them authority over the unclean spirits; [8] and He instructed them that they should take nothing for *their* journey, except a mere staff-- no bread, no bag, no money in their belt-- [9] but *to* wear sandals; and *He added,* "Do not put on two tunics." [10] And He said to them, "Wherever you enter a house, stay there until you leave town. [11] "Any place that does not receive you or listen to you, as you go out from there, shake the dust off the soles of your feet for a testimony against them." [12] They went out and preached that *men* should repent. [13] And they were casting out many demons and were anointing with oil many sick people and healing them.	[6] Καὶ ἐθαύμαζεν διὰ τὴν ἀπιστίαν αὐτῶν. Καὶ περιῆγεν τὰς κώμας κύκλῳ διδάσκων. [7] Καὶ προσκαλεῖται τοὺς δώδεκα, καὶ ἤρξατο αὐτοὺς ἀποστέλλειν δύο δύο, καὶ ἐδίδου αὐτοῖς ἐξουσίαν τῶν πνευμάτων τῶν ἀκαθάρτων. [8] Καὶ παρήγγειλεν αὐτοῖς ἵνα μηδὲν αἴρωσιν εἰς ὁδόν, εἰ μὴ ῥάβδον μόνον· μὴ πήραν, μὴ ἄρτον, μὴ εἰς τὴν ζώνην χαλκόν· [9] ἀλλ’ ὑποδεδεμένους σανδάλια· καὶ μὴ ἐνδύσησθε δύο χιτῶνας. [10] Καὶ ἔλεγεν αὐτοῖς, Ὅπου ἐὰν εἰσέλθητε εἰς οἰκίαν, ἐκεῖ μένετε ἕως ἂν ἐξέλθητε ἐκεῖθεν. [11] Καὶ ὅσοι ἂν μὴ δέξωνται ὑμᾶς, μηδὲ ἀκούσωσιν ὑμῶν, ἐκπορευόμενοι ἐκεῖθεν, ἐκτινάξατε τὸν χοῦν τὸν ὑποκάτω τῶν ποδῶν ὑμῶν εἰς μαρτύριον αὐτοῖς. Ἀμὴν λέγω ὑμῖν, ἀνεκτότερον ἔσται Σοδόμοις ἢ Γομόρροις ἐν ἡμέρᾳ κρίσεως, ἢ τῇ πόλει ἐκείνῃ. [12] Καὶ ἐξελθόντες ἐκήρυσσον ἵνα μετανοήσωσιν· [13] καὶ δαιμόνια πολλὰ ἐξέβαλλον, καὶ ἤλειφον ἐλαίῳ πολλοὺς ἀρρώστους καὶ ἐθεράπευον.

Process of Discovery

Linguistics Section

Linguistic Structure

[Jesus' instructions] [7] And He summoned the twelve and began to send them out in pairs, and gave them authority over the unclean spirits; [8] and He instructed them that they should take nothing for *their* journey, except a mere staff-- no bread, no bag, no money in their belt-- [9] but *to* wear sandals; and *He added*, "Do not put on two tunics." [10] And He said to them, "Wherever you enter a house, stay there until you leave town. [11] "Any place that does not receive you or listen to you, as you go out from there, shake the dust off the soles of your feet for a testimony against them."

[Disciples react] [12] They went out and preached that *men* should repent. [13] And they were casting out many demons and were anointing with oil many sick people and healing them.

Discussion

This narrative is a cause-and-effect passage. The cause is Yeshua's orders. The effect is the disciples carrying out the orders.

Questioning the Passage

1. Why did Yeshua have to summon the disciples? (v. 7)

    The verb "to summon" could indicate that the twelve men were not together and not with Yeshua. Perhaps the men did not yet know each other to the extent that they would work together when they were not with Yeshua. Therefore, Yeshua summoned them to join Him. As the Gospel continues, He will not have to gather them because the disciples will be with Him and each other.

2. Why did Yeshua send the disciples out in pairs? (v. 7)

    "The sending in pairs corresponds to the early Christian mission practice as frequently illustrated in Acts (e.g., Acts 13:1–3). A similar pairing appears in the sending of the Seventy (Luke 10:1) and in the listing of the Twelve in Matt 10:2–4 (cf. Acts 1:13). Jeremias lists numerous illustrations of similar use of pairs in Judaism, though missing from the OT, as well as in the NT (Abba, 133–34). The background may lie in Jewish legal practice where two witnesses established the evidence (Deut 17:6; 19:15; cf. Matt 18:16; John 8:17; 2 Cor 13:1; 1 Tim 5:19). But it also may reflect the travel conditions and the need for personal and moral support (Jeremias, Abba, 135)."[87]

3. Why did Yeshua tell the disciples not to take money nor food? (v. 8)

The lesson was for them to learn how to live detached from materialism. The disciples were instructed on how to survive in the materialistic world without the benefits of materials. It was their spirituality that was being tested and bolstered. They needed to rely on the LORD for their basic needs. They could preach the Kingdom of Heaven and prove that the Kingdom was all that one needed.

4. What is the significance of sandals? (v. 9)

"Hence forth footwear and bare feet took on major symbolic significance in the Jewish religion. These are seen in the Torah , (Laws of Moses) and the Shulchan Aruch, (Code of Jewish law) which was written in the 16th century. Every day event were to be seen as something to worship the glory of God include Hence forth footwear and bare feet took on major symbolic significance in the Jewish religion. These are seen in the Torah , (Laws of Moses) and the Shulchan Aruch, (Code of Jewish law) which was written in the 16th century. Every day event were to be seen as something to worship the glory of God including putting on sandals. The Jewish laws prescribed the order in which you put them on. The right went on first followed by the left. (Shulchan Aruch/Orach Chaim 2:4). The left shoe was to be tied firs and the whole process reversed when taking the shoes off (Shulchan Aruch/Orach Chaim 2:5). It is thought this custom was based on the belief the right side was more important than the left and subsequently the right foot should not remain uncovered while the left was covered. Shoes were tied from the left because knotted teffilin was worn on the left arm. This refers to the children of Israel being out of Egypt as an act of God. When walking outdoors, Jews were required to cover the entire body including their feet (Shulchan Aruch/Orach Chaim 2:6). By the end of the first century CE shoes were considered an item of sensuousness, comfort, luxury and pleasure. Rabbi Akiva (ca.50–ca.135 CE) instructed his son Joshua not to go

---

[87] Guelich, R. A. (1989). *Mark 1–8:26* (Vol. 34A, p. 321). Dallas: TX, Word, Incorporated.

barefooting putting on sandals. The Jewish laws prescribed the order in which you put them on. The right went on first followed by the left. (Shulchan Aruch/Orach Chaim 2:4). The left shoe was to be tied firs and the whole process reversed when taking the shoes off (Shulchan Aruch/Orach Chaim 2:5). It is thought this custom was based on the belief the right side was more important than the left and subsequently the right foot should not remain uncovered while the left was covered. Shoes were tied from the left because knotted teffilin was worn on the left arm. This refers to the children of Israel being out of Egypt as an act of God. When walking outdoors, Jews were required to cover the entire body including their feet (Shulchan Aruch/Orach Chaim 2:6). By the end of the first century CE shoes were considered an item of sensuousness, comfort, luxury and pleasure. Rabbi Akiva (ca.50–ca.135 CE) instructed his son Joshua not to go barefoot."[88]

Wearing sandals was a way for Yeshua to tell His disciples that they were to follow all of the day's Hebraic customs and Laws. They were not permitted to deviate from anything. This would indicate that they were only allowed to enter Hebraic homes. They were not allowed to go to any Gentiles at this time.

5. Why did Yeshua tell the disciples to stay at the first house that welcomed them? (v. 10) Yeshua did not want His disciples to search through a town looking for the best place to stay. Whoever showed hospitality first was the house they were to reside. This would emphasize to the disciples that materialism was not a part of Yeshua's mission.

6. What did Yeshua mean when he said, "shake the dust off your feet? (v. 11) "Shaking the dust off the feet is a symbolic indication that one has done all that can be done in a situation and therefore carries no further responsibility for it. In the scriptural examples, He told His disciples that they were to preach the Gospel to everyone. Where

---

[88] Footalk, "Sandals in Biblical Times," Sandals in Biblical Times, accessed February, 23, 2021, https://historyofsandals.blogspot.com/2010/11/biblical-sandals.html.

they were received with joy, they should stay and teach. But where their message was rejected, they had no further responsibility."[89]

There was a cultural practice that when a Hebrew left a Gentile house, they would shake the dust off their feet. Yeshua probably told His disciples that the Hebrew people who did not listen to them were acting like pagans and thus should be treated that way.

Phrase Study

1. προσκαλέω (v. 7)

    1. "to call to or notify in order to secure someone's presence

        a. of a call issued for presence with the speaker summon, call on, call to oneself, invite

        b. in transf. sense of God's invitation to share in the benefits of salvation call (to) God or Christ, to faith, etc.

    2. to call in a legal or official sense

        a. as a legal) call in, summon for inquiry

        b. call to a special task or office—issued by the Holy Spirit."[90]

Culture Section

Questioning the passage

1. Why did Yeshua tell His disciples to take a staff but nothing else? (v. 8)
   A person could travel in the ancient Near East without money or food because hospitality was a significant part of the culture. When strangers came to a house, he would be welcomed with open arms. Hospitality was that important to Semitic people. A staff was always carried when traveling. It was used for protection against bandits, dogs, wild animals, and snakes. The staff was also used to help them climb hills and cross streams.

---

[89] GotQuestions.org, "Home," GotQuestions.org, April 7, 2015, https://www.gotquestions.org/shake-dust-off-feet.html.

[90] Frederick W. Danker, William Arndt, and Walter Bauer, *A Greek-English Lexicon of the New Testament and Other Early Christian Literature* (Chicago: University of Chicago Press, 2000).

A Semitic parable is "a staff is a friend on the road." Even if the traveler had weapons, the staff was still brought.[91]

2. Why did Yeshua tell the disciples to anoint the ill with oil? (v. 13)

The use of anointing the sick was not a Hebraic practice. Anointing with oil was done for Kings and prophets. The early proto-orthodox church started this practice. It may have been a part of the Mithras religion. Since Paul converted Mithras house churches into Yeshua house churches, anointing the sick with oil would have continued. Mark's author says that Yeshua instructed His disciples to anoint the sick with oil to legitimize the practice.

Thoughts

Several themes are in this narrative. Materialism is one of them. Yeshua had to get his disciples to divest themselves of material needs before they could be useful at building the Kingdom of Heaven. However, the disciples were not yet trained in how to accomplish this. How could they be expected to release all of their beliefs about materialism so quickly? Therefore, Yeshua could have been testing them to learn how much work He needed to put into their re-education.

Reflections

Take a moment and reflect on your giving to the work of your church. How much of your total income do you give? This is a taboo subject in most churches. When tithing sermons are presented, they generally are accompanied by rejection. The Bible says that a tithe is ten percent. Where did this come from? When Abraham met Melchizedek, the priest of Salem (old name for Jerusalem) he immediately gave him ten percent of everything he had in thanksgiving to the LORD. Imagine if tithing was considered offering thanksgiving to the LORD. Would members of the church give more then? United Methodist reports indicate that people give 1.8% of their income to the church. A far cry from 10%. So, what do you give to thank the LORD for your blessings?

---

[91] Rocco A. Errico, George M. Lamsa, *Aramaic Light on the Gospels of Mark and Luke: a Commentary on the Teachings of Jesus from the Aramaic and Unchanged Near Eastern Customs* (Smyrna, GA: Noohra Foundation, 2001).

MARK 6:14-32

Language

New American Standard 1995	Koine Greek
[14] And King Herod heard *of it*, for His name had become well known; and *people* were saying, "John the Baptist has risen from the dead, and that is why these miraculous powers are at work in Him." [15] But others were saying, "He is Elijah." And others were saying, "*He is* a prophet, like one of the prophets *of old*." [16] But when Herod heard *of it*, he kept saying, "John, whom I beheaded, has risen!" [17] For Herod himself had sent and had John arrested and bound in prison on account of Herodias, the wife of his brother Philip, because he had married her. [18] For John had been saying to Herod, "It is not lawful for you to have your brother's wife." [19] Herodias had a grudge against him and wanted to put him to death and could not *do so*; [20] for Herod was afraid of John, knowing that he was a righteous and holy man, and he kept him safe. And when he heard him, he was very perplexed; but he used to enjoy listening to him. [21] A strategic day came when Herod on his birthday gave a banquet for his lords and military commanders and the leading men of Galilee; [22] and when the daughter of Herodias herself came in and danced, she pleased Herod and his dinner guests; and the king said to the girl, "Ask me for whatever you want and I will give it to you." [23] And he swore to her, "Whatever you ask of me, I will give it to you; up to half of my kingdom." [24] And she went out and said to her mother, "What shall I ask for?" And she said, "The head of John the Baptist." [25] Immediately she came in a hurry to the king and asked, saying, "I want you to give me at once the head of John the Baptist on a platter."	[14] Καὶ ἤκουσεν ὁ βασιλεὺς Ἡρῴδης, φανερὸν γὰρ ἐγένετο τὸ ὄνομα αὐτοῦ, καὶ ἔλεγεν ὅτι Ἰωάννης ὁ βαπτίζων ἐκ νεκρῶν ἠγέρθη, καὶ διὰ τοῦτο ἐνεργοῦσιν αἱ δυνάμεις ἐν αὐτῷ. [15] Ἄλλοι ἔλεγον ὅτι Ἡλίας ἐστίν· ἄλλοι δὲ ἔλεγον ὅτι Προφήτης ἐστίν, ὡς εἷς τῶν προφητῶν. [16] Ἀκούσας δὲ Ἡρῴδης εἶπεν ὅτι Ὃν ἐγὼ ἀπεκεφάλισα Ἰωάννην, οὗτός ἐστιν· αὐτὸς ἠγέρθη ἐκ νεκρῶν. [17] Αὐτὸς γὰρ ὁ Ἡρῴδης ἀποστείλας ἐκράτησεν τὸν Ἰωάννην, καὶ ἔδησεν αὐτὸν ἐν φυλακῇ, διὰ Ἡρῳδιάδα τὴν γυναῖκα Φιλίππου τοῦ ἀδελφοῦ αὐτοῦ, ὅτι αὐτὴν ἐγάμησεν. [18] Ἔλεγεν γὰρ ὁ Ἰωάννης τῷ Ἡρῴδῃ ὅτι Οὐκ ἔξεστίν σοι ἔχειν τὴν γυναῖκα τοῦ ἀδελφοῦ σου. [19] Ἡ δὲ Ἡρῳδιὰς ἐνεῖχεν αὐτῷ, καὶ ἤθελεν αὐτὸν ἀποκτεῖναι· καὶ οὐκ ἠδύνατο· [20] ὁ γὰρ Ἡρῴδης ἐφοβεῖτο τὸν Ἰωάννην, εἰδὼς αὐτὸν ἄνδρα δίκαιον καὶ ἅγιον, καὶ συνετήρει αὐτόν· καὶ ἀκούσας αὐτοῦ, πολλὰ ἐποίει, καὶ ἡδέως αὐτοῦ ἤκουεν. [21] Καὶ γενομένης ἡμέρας εὐκαίρου, ὅτε Ἡρῴδης τοῖς γενεσίοις αὐτοῦ δεῖπνον ἐποίει τοῖς μεγιστᾶσιν αὐτοῦ καὶ τοῖς χιλιάρχοις καὶ τοῖς πρώτοις τῆς Γαλιλαίας, [22] καὶ εἰσελθούσης τῆς θυγατρὸς αὐτῆς τῆς Ἡρῳδιάδος καὶ ὀρχησαμένης, καὶ ἀρεσάσης τῷ Ἡρῴδῃ καὶ τοῖς συνανακειμένοις, εἶπεν ὁ βασιλεὺς τῷ κορασίῳ, Αἴτησόν με ὃ ἐὰν θέλῃς, καὶ δώσω σοί· [23] καὶ ὤμοσεν αὐτῇ ὅτι Ὃ ἐάν με αἰτήσῃς, δώσω σοί, ἕως ἡμίσους τῆς βασιλείας μου. [24] Ἡ δὲ ἐξελθοῦσα εἶπεν τῇ μητρὶ αὐτῆς, Τί αἰτήσομαι; Ἡ δὲ εἶπεν, Τὴν κεφαλὴν Ἰωάννου τοῦ βαπτιστοῦ. [25] Καὶ εἰσελθοῦσα εὐθέως μετὰ σπουδῆς πρὸς τὸν βασιλέα, ἠτήσατο, λέγουσα, Θέλω ἵνα μοι

²⁶ And although the king was very sorry, *yet* because of his oaths and because of his dinner guests, he was unwilling to refuse her.

²⁷ Immediately the king sent an executioner and commanded *him* to bring *back* his head. And he went and had him beheaded in the prison,

²⁸ and brought his head on a platter, and gave it to the girl; and the girl gave it to her mother.

²⁹ When his disciples heard *about this*, they came and took away his body and laid it in a tomb.

³⁰ The apostles gathered together with Jesus; and they reported to Him all that they had done and taught.

³¹ And He said to them, "Come away by yourselves to a secluded place and rest a while." (For there were many *people* coming and going, and they did not even have time to eat.)

³² They went away in the boat to a secluded place by themselves.

δῶς ἐξαυτῆς ἐπὶ πίνακι τὴν κεφαλὴν Ἰωάννου τοῦ βαπτιστοῦ.

²⁶ Καὶ περίλυπος γενόμενος ὁ βασιλεύς, διὰ τοὺς ὅρκους καὶ τοὺς συνανακειμένους οὐκ ἠθέλησεν αὐτὴν ἀθετῆσαι.

²⁷ Καὶ εὐθέως ἀποστείλας ὁ βασιλεὺς σπεκουλάτορα ἐπέταξεν ἐνεχθῆναι τὴν κεφαλὴν αὐτοῦ.

²⁸ Ὁ δὲ ἀπελθὼν ἀπεκεφάλισεν αὐτὸν ἐν τῇ φυλακῇ, καὶ ἤνεγκεν τὴν κεφαλὴν αὐτοῦ ἐπὶ πίνακι, καὶ ἔδωκεν αὐτὴν τῷ κορασίῳ· καὶ τὸ κοράσιον ἔδωκεν αὐτὴν τῇ μητρὶ αὐτῆς.

²⁹ Καὶ ἀκούσαντες οἱ μαθηταὶ αὐτοῦ ἦλθον, καὶ ἦραν τὸ πτῶμα αὐτοῦ, καὶ ἔθηκαν αὐτὸ ἐν μνημείῳ.

³⁰ Καὶ συνάγονται οἱ ἀπόστολοι πρὸς τὸν Ἰησοῦν, καὶ ἀπήγγειλαν αὐτῷ πάντα, καὶ ὅσα ἐποίησαν καὶ ὅσα ἐδίδαξαν.

³¹ Καὶ εἶπεν αὐτοῖς, Δεῦτε ὑμεῖς αὐτοὶ κατ᾽ ἰδίαν εἰς ἔρημον τόπον, καὶ ἀναπαύεσθε ὀλίγον. Ἦσαν γὰρ οἱ ἐρχόμενοι καὶ οἱ ὑπάγοντες πολλοί, καὶ οὐδὲ φαγεῖν εὐκαίρουν.

³² Καὶ ἀπῆλθον εἰς ἔρημον τόπον τῷ πλοίῳ κατ᾽ ἰδίαν.

Process of Discovery

Linguistics Section

Linguistic Structure

A [14] And King Herod heard *of it*,

> **B** for His name had become well known; and *people* were saying, "John the Baptist has risen from the dead, and that is why these miraculous powers are at work in Him." [15] But others were saying, "He is Elijah." And others were saying, "*He is* a prophet, like one of the prophets *of old*." [16] But when Herod heard *of it*, he kept saying, "John, whom I beheaded, has risen!"

> > **C** [17] For Herod himself had sent and had John arrested and bound in prison on account of Herodias, the wife of his brother Philip, because he had married her. [18] For John had been saying to Herod, "It is not lawful for you to have your brother's wife." [19] Herodias had a grudge against him and wanted to put him to death and could not *do so*; [20] for Herod was afraid of John, knowing that he was a righteous and holy man, and he kept him safe. And when he heard him, he was very perplexed; but he used to enjoy listening to him.

> > > **D** [21] A strategic day came when Herod on his birthday gave a banquet for his lords and military commanders and the leading men of Galilee; [22] and when the daughter of Herodias herself came in and danced, she pleased Herod and his dinner guests; and the king said to the girl, "Ask me for whatever you want and I will give it to you." [23] And he swore to her, "Whatever you ask of me, I will give it to you; up to half of my kingdom."

> > **C'** [24] And she went out and said to her mother, "What shall I ask for?" And she said, "The head of John the Baptist." [25] Immediately she came in a hurry to the king and asked, saying, "I want you to give me at once the head of John the Baptist on a platter." [26] And although the king was very sorry, *yet* because of his oaths and because of his dinner guests, he was unwilling to refuse her.

> **B'** [27] Immediately the king sent an executioner and commanded *him* to bring *back* his head. And he went and had him beheaded in the prison, [28] and brought his head on a platter, and gave it to the girl; and the girl gave it to her mother.

A' [29] When his disciples heard *about this*, they came and took away his body and laid it in a tomb.

[Disciples return from their mission] [30] The apostles gathered together with Jesus; and they reported to Him all that they had done and taught. [31] And He said to them, "Come away by yourselves to a secluded place and rest a while." (For there were many *people* coming and going, and they did not even have time to eat.) [32] They went away in the boat to a secluded place by themselves.

A: Hearing. B: Beheaded. C: Hostility of Herodias. D: The permission of Herod.[92]

Discussion

Mark's author created another sandwich of events. The first part of the chapter was Yeshua's calling of His disciples and sending them out into the world. The insertion divides that narrative about John the Baptist. Verses 30 to 32 are the conclusion of the story about the disciples being sent out into the world.

Questioning the Passage

1. Why was the story of John the Baptist's murder told in the past tense?

   Mark's author had not reported on the situation with John the Baptist. The question arose as to who Yeshua was. Many people, along with Herod Antipas, believed that Yeshua was Elijah, the prophet. Since it was important for Mark's author to record this situation, he had to tell the reader what had happened to John. The other synoptic Gospels tell the story of John as it occurred. Mark's author did not. Therefore, the author has to tell the story in the past tense.

2. Why did some people call Yeshua Elijah the prophet? (v. 15)

   Jewish tradition said that the prophet Elijah would return to introduce the Messiah to the world. The people did not think that Yeshua was the Messiah at this point in the Gospel. They believed that Yeshua was either the risen from the dead John the Baptist or Elijah.

3. Why was Herod Antipas afraid of John the Baptist? (v. 20)

   If Herod Antipas considered Yeshua was the LORD's Messiah, he would have to step down from the throne. The Messiah was to become the ultimate king of Israel and would usher at the end of time. Herod Antipas, like any king, did not want to give up his power

---

92 "Literary Structure (Chiasm, Chiasmus) of Gospel of Mark," Literary structure (chiasm, chiasmus) of each pericopes of Gospel of Mark, accessed March 2, 2021, http://www.bible.literarystructure.info/bible/41_Mark_pericope_e.html.

and wealth. He was afraid of John the Baptist because John told him what prophets had told kings for years. That message was that Herod Antipas was corrupt and broke the Laws of Moses. A sinful king was not suitable to be on the throne of Israel.

4. Why is Herod Antipas' birthday called a strategic day? (v. 21)

   A better translation would be "a favorable time for an event" had occurred. Herod Antipas' birthday would have been a time to hold a banquet.

5. What does it mean that Herod Antipas said "up to half of my kingdom?" (v. 23)

   This phrase means that Herod Antipas told Herodias' daughter that she could have any extravagant gift that she wanted. He was not offering the girl half of the kingdom. This phrase can be found in the book of Esther. The extravagant gift that the girl chose was for her mother. Herodias wanted John the Baptist dead. She found an opportunity to get her way at the party.

Biblical Personalities

1. Herod Antipas was the tetrarch of the territory of Galilee and Paraea. He was the son of Herod the Great. When Herod died, his will called for his kingdom's to be divided into four parts and given to his sons.

2. Philip was the tetrarch of the territory of Iturea and Trachonitis. He was the son of Herod the Great.

3. Herodias was the wife of Philip. She divorced Philip and married Herod Antipas.

Phrase Study

1. εὔκαιρος, ον (v. 41) - a time that is considered a favorable occasion for some event or circumstance, well-timed, suitable.[93]

---

[93] Frederick W. Danker, William Arndt, and Walter Bauer, *A Greek-English Lexicon of the New Testament and Other Early Christian Literature* (Chicago: University of Chicago Press, 2000).

Culture Section

Discussion

A brother was allowed to marry his sister-in-law only if the brother died and had no children. Philip and Herodias had children. Therefore, this marriage was forbidden by the Laws of Moses. Herod Antipas was an Idumean by race. He followed the Jewish laws and declared himself to be a Jew. Consequently, he was subject to the Laws of Moses. He broke that law by marrying his brother's wife. Herod Antipas murdered John the Baptist because he told Herod that he sinned before the LORD.

Thoughts

The Law of Moses was given by the LORD to the people of Israel so that the people could live with high morals and ethics. During the prophet's times, the LORD would send messages to Israel and Judea's leadership through prophets. The prophets' common thread is that the government officials, especially the kings, did not appreciate the message from the LORD. So, they killed the messenger. The time of the prophets was considered over several hundred years before the birth of John the Baptist. It is the LORD who determines the time for people and events and not humans. The LORD decided to send a prophet and the Messiah at the same time. Herod Antipas should have listened to John as opposed to murdering him

Reflections

Herod Antipas hid his repentance behind his royal position. He owned the power on Earth to do what he wanted to in Galilee. He must have forgotten that the LORD sees the sin of Israel's leaders and takes action. Herod Antipas was known for his extravagant parties and loose morality. Each person must determine if one is going to follow the Laws of Moses. Living by the Laws of Moses leads to a life of high character and outstanding ethics. This is a blessing to the LORD and is treated as treasures in Heaven.

MARK 6:33-44

Language

New American Standard 1995	Koine Greek
[33] *The people* saw them going, and many recognized *them* and ran there together on foot from all the cities, and got there ahead of them. [34] When Jesus went ashore, He saw a large crowd, and He felt compassion for them because they were like sheep without a shepherd; and He began to teach them many things. [35] When it was already quite late, His disciples came to Him and said, "This place is desolate and it is already quite late; [36] send them away so that they may go into the surrounding countryside and villages and buy themselves something to eat." [37] But He answered them, "You give them *something* to eat!" And they said to Him, "Shall we go and spend two hundred denarii on bread and give them *something* to eat?" [38] And He said to them, "How many loaves do you have? Go look!" And when they found out, they said, "Five, and two fish." [39] And He commanded them all to sit down by groups on the green grass. [40] They sat down in groups of hundreds and of fifties. [41] And He took the five loaves and the two fish, and looking up toward heaven, He blessed *the food* and broke the loaves and He kept giving *them* to the disciples to set before them; and He divided up the two fish among them all. [42] They all ate and were satisfied, [43] and they picked up twelve full baskets of the broken pieces, and also of the fish. [44] There were five thousand men who ate the loaves.	[33] Καὶ εἶδον αὐτοὺς ὑπάγοντας καὶ ἐπέγνωσαν αὐτὸν πολλοί, καὶ πεζῇ ἀπὸ πασῶν τῶν πόλεων συνέδραμον ἐκεῖ, καὶ προῆλθον αὐτούς, καὶ συνῆλθον πρὸς αὐτόν. [34] Καὶ ἐξελθὼν εἶδεν ὁ Ἰησοῦς πολὺν ὄχλον, καὶ ἐσπλαγχνίσθη ἐπ᾽ αὐτοῖς, ὅτι ἦσαν ὡς πρόβατα μὴ ἔχοντα ποιμένα· καὶ ἤρξατο διδάσκειν αὐτοὺς πολλά. [35] Καὶ ἤδη ὥρας πολλῆς γενομένης, προσελθόντες αὐτῷ οἱ μαθηταὶ αὐτοῦ λέγουσιν ὅτι Ἔρημός ἐστιν ὁ τόπος, καὶ ἤδη ὥρα πολλή· [36] ἀπόλυσον αὐτούς, ἵνα ἀπελθόντες εἰς τοὺς κύκλῳ ἀγροὺς καὶ κώμας ἀγοράσωσιν ἑαυτοῖς ἄρτους. Τί γὰρ φάγωσιν οὐκ ἔχουσιν. [37] Ὁ δὲ ἀποκριθεὶς εἶπεν αὐτοῖς, Δότε αὐτοῖς ὑμεῖς φαγεῖν. Καὶ λέγουσιν αὐτῷ, Ἀπελθόντες ἀγοράσωμεν δηναρίων διακοσίων ἄρτους, καὶ δῶμεν αὐτοῖς φαγεῖν; [38] Ὁ δὲ λέγει αὐτοῖς, Πόσους ἄρτους ἔχετε; Ὑπάγετε καὶ ἴδετε. Καὶ γνόντες λέγουσιν, Πέντε, καὶ δύο ἰχθύας. [39] Καὶ ἐπέταξεν αὐτοῖς ἀνακλῖναι πάντας συμπόσια συμπόσια ἐπὶ τῷ χλωρῷ χόρτῳ. [40] Καὶ ἀνέπεσον πρασιαὶ πρασιαί, ἀνὰ ἑκατὸν καὶ ἀνὰ πεντήκοντα. [41] Καὶ λαβὼν τοὺς πέντε ἄρτους καὶ τοὺς δύο ἰχθύας, ἀναβλέψας εἰς τὸν οὐρανόν, εὐλόγησεν, καὶ κατέκλασεν τοὺς ἄρτους, καὶ ἐδίδου τοῖς μαθηταῖς αὐτοῦ ἵνα παραθῶσιν αὐτοῖς· καὶ τοὺς δύο ἰχθύας ἐμέρισεν πᾶσιν. [42] Καὶ ἔφαγον πάντες, καὶ ἐχορτάσθησαν· [43] καὶ ἦραν κλασμάτων δώδεκα κοφίνους πλήρεις, καὶ ἀπὸ τῶν ἰχθύων. [44] Καὶ ἦσαν οἱ φαγόντες τοὺς ἄρτους πεντακισχίλιοι ἄνδρες.

Process of Discovery

Linguistics Section

Linguistic Structure

[Transition] [33] *The people* saw them going, and many recognized *them* and ran there together on foot from all the cities, and got there ahead of them.

[Actions] [34] When Jesus went ashore, He saw a large crowd, and He felt compassion for them because they were like sheep without a shepherd; and He began to teach them many things.

[Disciples] [35] When it was already quite late, His disciples came to Him and said, "This place is desolate and it is already quite late; [36] send them away so that they may go into the surrounding countryside and villages and buy themselves something to eat."

[Yeshua] [37] But He answered them, "You give them *something* to eat!"

[Disciples] And they said to Him, "Shall we go and spend two hundred denarii on bread and give them *something* to eat?"

[Yeshua] [38] And He said to them, "How many loaves do you have? Go look!"

[Disciples] And when they found out, they said, "Five, and two fish."

[Yeshua] [39] And He commanded them all to sit down by groups on the green grass. [40] They sat down in groups of hundreds and of fifties. [41] And He took the five loaves and the two fish, and looking up toward heaven, He blessed *the food* and broke the loaves and He kept giving *them* to the disciples to set before them; and He divided up the two fish among them all.

[Conclusion of the feeding] [42] They all ate and were satisfied, [43] and they picked up twelve full baskets of the broken pieces, and also of the fish. [44] There were five thousand men who ate the loaves.

Discussion

This narrative is a description of an event where Yeshua feed 5,000 people.

Questioning the Passage

1. Why did it matter that the place they were at was desolate? (v. 35)

    The verse indicates that the hour was late, which means that it must have been late in the day, and the village markets would have been closed for the day. Therefore, the people who came to see Yeshua would have gone hungry that night. Yeshua became concerned about the situation and told his disciples that they needed to offer dinner to all those who came to see him.

2. Is there significance to five loaves of bread and two fish? (v. 38)

    "The number 5 symbolizes God's grace, goodness and favor toward humans and is mentioned 318 times in Scripture. Five is the number of grace, and multiplied by itself, which is 25, is 'grace upon grace' (John 1:16)."[94] The Ten Commandments contain two sets of 5 commandments. The first five commandments are related to our treatment and relationship with God, and the last five concern our relationship with other humans.

    Appearances of the number five

    There are five primary types of offerings God commanded Israel to bring to him. They are the Burnt Offering (Leviticus 1; 8:18 - 21; 16:24), Sin (Leviticus 4; 16:3 - 22), Trespass (Leviticus 5:14 - 19; 6:1 - 7; 7:1 - 6), Grain (Leviticus 2) and Peace Offering (Leviticus 3; 7:11-34)."

    The Book of Psalms is divided into 5 major sections. Section 1 (Psalm 1 to 41) refers to the Passover, Israel's beginning, and the start of God's plan of salvation that centers around Christ.

---

94 "Meaning of Numbers in the BibleThe Number 5," Bible Study, accessed October 9, 2019, https://www.biblestudy.org/bibleref/meaning-of-numbers-in-bible/5.html.

Section 2 (42 to 72) sings about a unified Israel in the land and pictures the creation of the New Testament Church." [95]

The number two signifies a union of two into one. This number can be viewed as Yeshua in collaboration with people.

3. Is there a significance to 12 baskets of leftovers? (v. 43)

    The church interpretation is that the 12 baskets represent the 12 tribes of Israel. Another view is that the 12 baskets of leftovers emphasize the Semitic story that a miracle had occurred. Not only were all the people fed, but there were leftovers. The leftovers indicate that the LORD is so good that he will give us more than we need.

Linguistic Echoes

Corresponding echoes.

Yeshua in the wilderness	Israel in the wilderness
Yeshua supplies food	God provided manna in the wilderness
Yeshua calls people to him	God calls people to him (i.e., Psalm 23)

Culture Section

Discussion

Yeshua used his divine power to meet the people's needs, thus supplying the food for all those who came to seek him out as the bread of life. Prophets of the past demonstrated God's power by blessing and increasing the substance of men and women who revered God and were persecuted for the truth.[96]

---

[95] IBID.

[96] Rocco A. Errico and George M. Lamsa, *Aramaic Light on the Gospel of Matthew: a Commentary on the Teachings of Jesus from the Aramaic and Unchanged Near Eastern Customs* (Santa Fe, NM: Noohra Foundation, 2000).

People in the Middle East generally traveled with food and water. There are few restaurants along the path, especially along with the more secluded places.

This narrative may be about the sharing of resources. By Yeshua sharing the five fish in the two loaves of bread with the people, He gave them the desire to be like the rabbi and share whatever they might have.

1. What does "sheep without a shepherd" means? (v. 34)

    This phrase means "a congregation without a shepherd," or "an army without a general," or "a nation without a leader."

Culture

In Yeshua's day, the people hearing this narrative would have understood this concept. The question that needs to be asked is there a significance to the numbers in the story? The obvious answer is yes. The author could have said six fish and three loaves of bread were used to feed 10,000 people, and it would have been a miracle. Almost any number above 1000 would indicate a miracle.

The number 5000 is symbolic of an abundance. In Yeshua's day, people did not count past 1000. If a person had 1000 sheep, that person was considered wealthy. It did not matter how many sheep a person owned passed 1000. Therefore, any number over 1000 would tell us that there was an abundance available to all the people.

The number five is symbolic of divine grace. The number two is symbolic of the union of two different things. Yeshua said that if a person comes into partnership with the LORD, they will receive divine grace in abundance.

From the book of Exodus, we learn about the abundance of God's grace.

> [6] Then the LORD passed by in front of him and proclaimed, "The LORD, the LORD God, ªcompassionate and gracious, slow to anger, and abounding in lovingkindness and [1]truth; [7] who ªkeeps lovingkindness for thousands, who forgives iniquity, transgression and sin; yet He [b]will by no means leave *the guilty* unpunished, ªvisiting the iniquity of fathers on the children and on the grandchildren to the third and fourth generations."

Divine grace can be defined as the blessings of life from the goodwill of the LORD, the privileges they enjoyed, and their continued existence despite sinfulness through the goodwill of the LORD.[97]

Thoughts

This story is a beautiful Semitic story that teaches about the grace of the LORD. The story's main event is when Yeshua takes five loaves of bread and two fish and makes it possible to feed over 5000 men and an unknown number of women and children. The number five is symbolic of the LORD's grace. The number two is symbolic of a union, and in this case, the union between the LORD and His people. If one is to live under the grace of Yeshua in union with the LORD, then one has to learn to release concerns about needs and allow God to supply all needs. In our very self-centered society, we are taught that success means one has to be self-sufficient. It is difficult to get today's followers of Yeshua to trust in him fully.

Reflections

This narrative could be seen as symbolic of the need to receive spiritual direction, thus feeding on life's spiritual bread. The narrative talks about bread and fish, and the emphasis are that a vast amount of people came to hear the words of Yeshua. Yeshua sharing the bread and fish reminds us that we need to stay close to Yeshua, called the bread of life. The bread of life will supply a person's physical needs and spiritual needs. The narrative also says that we need to trust the LORD, who will take care of all requirements. Thus, it is imperative in all circumstances to maintain faith and belief in the LORD's Messiah, Yeshua of Nazareth.

---

[97] *The New Interpreter's Dictionary of the Bible* (Nashville, TN: Abingdon Press, 2006).

MARK 6:45-52

Language

New American Standard 1995	Koine Greek
[45] Immediately Jesus made His disciples get into the boat and go ahead of *Him* to the other side to Bethsaida, while He Himself was sending the crowd away. [46] After bidding them farewell, He left for the mountain to pray. [47] When it was evening, the boat was in the middle of the Sea, and He was alone on the land. [48] Seeing them straining at the oars, for the wind was against them, at about the fourth watch of the night He came to them, walking on the Sea; and He intended to pass by them. [49] But when they saw Him walking on the Sea, they supposed that it was a ghost, and cried out; [50] for they all saw Him and were terrified. But immediately He spoke with them and said to them, "Take courage; it is I, do not be afraid." [51] Then He got into the boat with them, and the wind stopped; and they were utterly astonished, [52] for they had not gained any insight from the *incident of* the loaves, but their heart was hardened.	[45] Καὶ εὐθέως ἠνάγκασε τοὺς μαθητὰς αὐτοῦ ἐμβῆναι εἰς τὸ πλοῖον καὶ προάγειν εἰς τὸ πέραν πρὸς Βηθσαϊδάν, ἕως αὐτὸς ἀπολύσει τὸν ὄχλον [46] καὶ ἀποταξάμενος αὐτοῖς ἀπῆλθεν εἰς τὸ ὄρος προσεύξασθαι. [47] καὶ ὀψίας γενομένης ἦν τὸ πλοῖον ἐν μέσῳ τῆς θαλάσσης, καὶ αὐτὸς μόνος ἐπὶ τῆς γῆς. [48] καὶ εἶδεν αὐτοὺς βασανιζομένους ἐν τῷ ἐλαύνειν ἦν γὰρ ὁ ἄνεμος ἐναντίος αὐτοῖς καὶ περὶ τετάρτην φυλακὴν τῆς νυκτὸς ἔρχεται πρὸς αὐτοὺς περιπατῶν ἐπὶ τῆς θαλάσσης, καὶ ἤθελε παρελθεῖν αὐτούς. [49] οἱ δὲ ἰδόντες αὐτὸν περιπατοῦντα ἐπὶ τῆς θαλάσσης ἔδοξαν φάντασμα εἶναι, καὶ ἀνέκραξαν [50] πάντες γὰρ αὐτὸν εἶδον καὶ ἐταράχθησαν. καὶ εὐθέως ἐλάλησε μετ' αὐτῶν καὶ λέγει αὐτοῖς θαρσεῖτε, ἐγώ εἰμι, μὴ φοβεῖσθε. [51] καὶ ἀνέβη πρὸς αὐτοὺς εἰς τὸ πλοῖον, καὶ ἐκόπασεν ὁ ἄνεμος καὶ λίαν ἐκ περισσοῦ ἐν ἑαυτοῖς ἐξίσταντο καὶ ἐθαύμαζον. [52] οὐ γὰρ συνῆκαν ἐπὶ τοῖς ἄρτοις, ἦν γὰρ αὐτῶν ἡ καρδία πεπωρωμένη.

Process of Discovery

Linguistics Section

Linguistic Structure

[Transition] [45] Immediately Jesus made His disciples get into the boat and go ahead of *Him* to the other side to Bethsaida, while He Himself was sending the crowd away. [46] After bidding them farewell, He left for the mountain to pray.

A [47] When it was evening, the boat was in the middle of the Sea, and He was alone on the land. [48] Seeing them straining at the oars, for the wind was against them, at about the fourth watch of the night He came to them, walking on the Sea; and He intended to pass by them.

> **B** [49] But when they saw Him walking on the Sea, they supposed that it was a ghost, and cried out; [50] for they all saw Him and were terrified. But immediately He spoke with them and said to them, "Take courage; it is I, do not be afraid."

A' [51] Then He got into the boat with them, and the wind stopped; and they were utterly astonished, [52] for they had not gained any insight from the *incident of* the loaves, but their heart was hardened.

Discussion

Yeshua had fed 5,000 people with a meager amount of bread and fish. He sent His disciples to Bethsaida ahead of Him. A simple chiasm is formed, which emphasizes that His disciples needed to learn courage. Only the courageous was going to be able to bring the Gospel into the world.

Questioning the Passage

1. Why did Yeshua send His disciples off in a boat? (v. 45)

   This narrative follows the feeding of the 5,000. It is possible that Yeshua was willing to chat with any of the people. The disciples were always protective of Yeshua and kept people at a distance whenever possible. Yeshua could now do what He wanted to do by sending the disciples away.

2. What is the significance of it being a night? (v. 47)

Nighttime was a time for Evil inclination to be its most potent. This was believed because darkness was associated with evil while the light was related to the LORD. Yeshua sent His disciples out at night on the Sea of Galilee. It was pretty unusual for anyone to attempt to navigate the Sea during the night. At the center of the Sea, it was believed that an abyss could swallow the boat and its passengers. Therefore, this could be a test of how the disciples dealt with evil.

3. When was the four[th] watch of the night? (v. 48)

"The Jews, since their conquest by Pompeii's, had adopted the Roman division of the night into four watches, and this was accordingly between 3 A.M. and 6 A.M., in the dimness of the early dawn."[98]

4. What is the significance of Yeshua walking on water? (v. 48)

The first point to contemplate is how far the boat was from the land. Since the sea waves were battering the ship, and because it was 9+ hours after Yeshua's command, it is safe to assume that the boat was several miles from shore. The miracle is Yeshua walking on water and Yeshua being able to cover the distance between the coast and the boat. The exact length is unknown. The author of Matthew is showing the reader that not only is Yeshua the replacement for Moses, but also Yeshua had divine qualities. Only the divine could rebuke nature by first walking on water and then stopping the storm.

5. What does it mean that Yeshua intended to pass by them? (v. 48)

"Thus to "pass by them" (παρελθεῖν αὐτούς) most probably has its significance in the similar language used in an epiphany of God to Moses (Exod 33:19–23; 34:6) and Elijah (1 Kgs 19:11) as the One who "passed by them" in a moment of self-revelation (Lohmeyer, 133–34; Kremer, BibLeb 10 [1969] 226–28; Pesch, 1:361). Therefore,

---

[98] Matthew 14:25 Commentaries: And in the Fourth Watch of the Night He Came to Them, Walking on the Sea. Accessed August 09, 2017. http://biblehub.com/commentaries/matthew/14-25.htm.

instead of a story about Jesus' rescue of his disciples who are distressed but not in danger (cf. 4:35–41), this is an epiphany story about Jesus' self-revelation to his own followers."[99].

Culture Section

Discussion

The fear of demons and evil spirits played a vital part in the lives of Semitic people. They even created specific religious laws about ghosts. In Assyria, when a man entered a house at night and was unknown to the family, he would be tested by sticking him with a large needle. If he was a spirit, he would change into a donkey. Yeshua's disciples believed in ghosts. That is why they were scared. Yeshua quickly assured them that he was not a ghost.[100]

Questioning the passage

1. What does verse fifty-five mean?

    Mark's author makes a note of the miracle of feeding the 5,000. The cultural significance is that the disciples discounted that event. Many Hebrew prophets through the centuries were able to multiply loaves of bread. When people went to visit a religious man, they always took food with them as a gift. The people wanted to see something spectacular. Something that no prophet had ever done. Tradition said that the Messiah would be able to do miracles and signs that would overly impress the people. Thus far in Mark's Gospel, Yeshua had not done anything impressive.[101]

Thoughts

Yeshua's disciples were sent out to the next city that He wanted to visit. They ran into trouble. A weather event took place, and that made it difficult to continue their voyage. They were scared about

---

[99] Word Commentary from Logos Bible Software
[100] Errico, Rocco A., and George M. Lamsa. "Matthew 14." *Aramaic Light on the Gospel of Matthew: a Commentary on the Teachings of Jesus from the Aramaic and Unchanged Near Eastern Customs*, Noohra Foundation, 2000.
[101] Errico, Rocco A., and George M. Lamsa. "Matthew 14." *Aramaic Light on the Gospel of Mark and Luke: a Commentary on the Teachings of Jesus from the Aramaic and Unchanged Near Eastern Customs*, Noohra Foundation, 2001.

what was about to happen to them. In the narrative, they did not call out to the LORD or to Yeshua to help them. They struggled against the Sea to take control of the situation. But they could not do it. Yeshua knew that they did not have complete faith in Him. So, He walked out toward the boat. The Scripture says that He was going to walk past them. Could this mean that if they did not ask for His help, He intended to let them die on the Sea? It was a test. They realized that the ghost was really their Messiah and asked Him to join them on the boat. The storm was then over. The spiritual lesson is to have faith in the power of Yeshua and call upon Him.

Reflections

There are always complications in life. No one can say that their life has been free of pain, sorrow, or distress. Who do you turn to in times of trouble? The disciples were given that choice and did not turn to Yeshua. A little more dialogue would help in this narrative. Since Yeshua got into the boat and calmed the storm, they spoke with Him. They had to have asked Him to save them. The lesson of surrender to the LORD and Yeshua is the critical point. Have you surrendered your life to Yeshua?

MARK 6:53-56

Language

New American Standard 1995	Koine Greek
[53] When they had crossed over they came to land at Gennesaret, and moored to the shore. [54] When they got out of the boat, immediately *the people* recognized Him, [55] and ran about that whole country and began to carry here and there on their pallets those who were sick, to the place they heard He was. [56] Wherever He entered villages, or cities, or countryside, they were laying the sick in the market places, and imploring Him that they might just touch the fringe of His cloak; and as many as touched it were being cured.	[53] Καὶ διαπεράσαντες ἦλθον ἐπὶ τὴν γῆν Γενησαρὲτ καὶ προσωρμίσθησαν. [54] καὶ ἐξελθόντων αὐτῶν ἐκ τοῦ πλοίου εὐθέως ἐπιγνόντες αὐτὸν [55] περιδραμόντες ὅλην τὴν περίχωρον ἐκείνην ἤρξαντο ἐπὶ τοῖς κραββάτοις τοὺς κακῶς ἔχοντας περιφέρειν ὅπου ἤκουον ὅτι ἐκεῖ ἐστι [56] καὶ ὅπου ἂν εἰσεπορεύετο εἰς κώμας ἢ πόλεις ἢ ἀγρούς, ἐν ταῖς ἀγοραῖς ἐτίθουν τοὺς ἀσθενοῦντας καὶ παρεκάλουν αὐτὸν ἵνα κἂν τοῦ κρασπέδου τοῦ ἱματίου αὐτοῦ ἅψωνται καὶ ὅσοι ἂν ἥπτοντο αὐτοῦ, ἐσῴζοντο.

Process of Discovery

Linguistics Section

Linguistic Structure

[Transition] [53] When they had crossed over they came to land at Gennesaret, and moored to the shore.

[At Gennesaret] [54] When they got out of the boat, immediately *the people* recognized Him, [55] and ran about that whole country and began to carry here and there on their pallets those who were sick, to the place they heard He was. [56] Wherever He entered villages, or cities, or countryside, they were laying the sick in the market places, and imploring Him that they might just touch the fringe of His cloak; and as many as touched it were being cured.

Discussion

Yeshua and His disciples journey from Bethsaida to Gennesaret. When they arrived, they discover that the knowledge of what Yeshua was doing and their arrival was known. At this point in the Gospel, Yeshua did many healings.

Questioning the Passage

1. Why did Mark's author say that people were brought to Yeshua on pallets? (v. 55) Using the word "pallets," the reader would recognize that the people being brought to Yeshua were the poor and peasants. These were people that did not have much to live for. They lived under terrible conditions of oppression and famine. Yeshua's healing was a boost to their lives.

Biblical Locations

1. Gennesaret

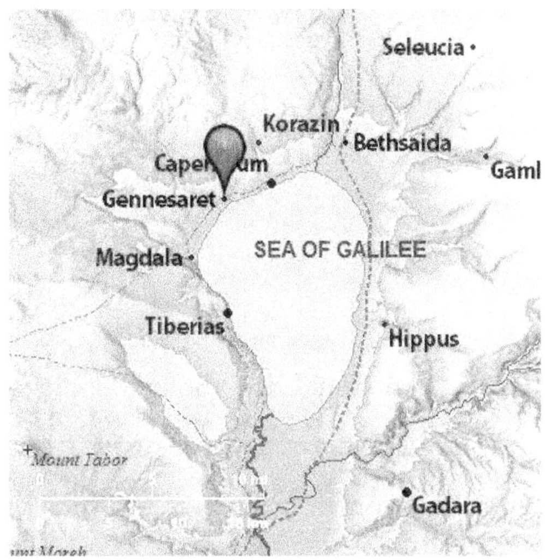

Phrase Study

1. κράσπεδον, ου, τό (v. 56)[102]

    1. edge, border, hem of a garment

    2. *tassel* (צִיצָה), which an Israelite was obligated to wear on the four corners of his outer garment, acc. to Num 15:38; Dt 22:12

2. κράβαττος, ου, ὁ *mattress, pallet,* the poor man's *bed* (v. 55) [103]

Culture Section

Discussion

It was in Yeshua's day and today for Hebrew males to wear a *tallis.* Today reformed Jews will allow women to wear the *tallis.* This cloth is worn to fulfill the LORD's commandment to wear the Word of God on the corners of the garment. The *tallis* is a rectangular cloth. It is worn over the shoulders. The wearer determines the length of it. At each corner of the *tallis* is the *tzitzit.*

---

[102] Frederick W. Danker, William Arndt, and Walter Bauer, *A Greek-English Lexicon of the New Testament and Other Early Christian Literature* (Chicago: University of Chicago Press, 2000).
[103] IBID.

Each of the four corners have a *tzitzit*. The *tzitzit* consists of several strands of string. There are five knots on a *tzitzit*. These knots represent the first five books of the Scripture, the Torah. The Torah is the book of the Law Moses received from the Lord. It was believed that the *tzitzit* had a "magical" power that could be invoked by touching them. Healing was available by touching *tzitzit* of a holy man.

Thoughts

Why would people think that a tzitzit could heal them? People in Yeshua's day were superstitious. Amulets and special clothes were considered to have divine powers. Yeshua was like the prophets of centuries earlier. These men and women could perform such things. Messianic tradition says that the Messiah would be able to perform the same healings as the prophets of the past.

Reflections

Yeshua wanted to have a following of people who were ready to rid themselves of the corruption of their own government and Temple leadership. Healing was considered a sign from the LORD. Every time that Yeshua cured a person, they would bolster His claim to be the Messiah.

MARK 7:1-13

Language

New American Standard 1995	Koine Greek
[1] The Pharisees and some of the scribes gathered around Him when they had come from Jerusalem, [2] and had seen that some of His disciples were eating their bread with *a*mpure hands, that is, unwashed. [3] (For the Pharisees and all the Jews do not eat unless they carefully wash their hands, *thus* observing the traditions of the elders; [4] and *when they come* from the market place, they do not eat unless they cleanse themselves; and there are many other things which they have received in order to observe, such as the washing of cups and pitchers and copper pots.) [5] The Pharisees and the scribes asked Him, "Why do Your disciples not walk according to the tradition of the elders, but eat their bread with impure hands?" [6] And He said to them, "Rightly did Isaiah prophesy of you hypocrites, as it is written: 'THIS PEOPLE HONORS ME WITH THEIR LIPS, BUT THEIR HEART IS FAR AWAY FROM ME. [7] 'BUT IN VAIN DO THEY WORSHIP ME, TEACHING AS DOCTRINES THE PRECEPTS OF MEN.' [8] "Neglecting the commandment of God, you hold to the tradition of men." [9] He was also saying to them, "You are experts at setting aside the commandment of God in order to keep your tradition. [10] "For Moses said, "HONOR YOUR FATHER AND YOUR MOTHER'; and, 'HE WHO SPEAKS EVIL OF FATHER OR MOTHER, IS TO BE PUT TO DEATH'; [11] but you say, 'If a man says to *his* father or *his* mother, whatever I have that would help you is Corban (that is to say, given *to God*),' [12] you no longer permit him to do anything for *his* father or *his* mother; [13] *thus* invalidating the word of God by your tradition which you have	[1] Καὶ συνάγονται πρὸς αὐτὸν οἱ Φαρισαῖοι, καί τινες τῶν γραμματέων, ἐλθόντες ἀπὸ Ἱεροσολύμων· [2] καὶ ἰδόντες τινὰς τῶν μαθητῶν αὐτοῦ κοιναῖς χερσίν, τοῦτ' ἔστιν ἀνίπτοις, ἐσθίοντας ἄρτους ἐμέμψαντο [3] Οἱ γὰρ Φαρισαῖοι καὶ πάντες οἱ Ἰουδαῖοι, ἐὰν μὴ πυγμῇ νίψωνται τὰς χεῖρας, οὐκ ἐσθίουσιν, κρατοῦντες τὴν παράδοσιν τῶν πρεσβυτέρων· [4] καὶ ἀπὸ ἀγορᾶς, ἐὰν μὴ βαπτίσωνται, οὐκ ἐσθίουσιν· καὶ ἄλλα πολλά ἐστιν ἃ παρέλαβον κρατεῖν, βαπτισμοὺς ποτηρίων καὶ ξεστῶν καὶ χαλκίων καὶ κλινῶν. [5] Ἔπειτα ἐπερωτῶσιν αὐτὸν οἱ Φαρισαῖοι καὶ οἱ γραμματεῖς, Διὰ τί οἱ μαθηταί σου οὐ περιπατοῦσιν κατὰ τὴν παράδοσιν τῶν πρεσβυτέρων, ἀλλὰ ἀνίπτοις χερσὶν ἐσθίουσιν τὸν ἄρτον; [6] Ὁ δὲ ἀποκριθεὶς εἶπεν αὐτοῖς ὅτι Καλῶς προεφήτευσεν Ἡσαΐας περὶ ὑμῶν τῶν ὑποκριτῶν, ὡς γέγραπται, Οὗτος ὁ λαὸς τοῖς χείλεσίν με τιμᾷ, ἡ δὲ καρδία αὐτῶν πόρρω ἀπέχει ἀπ' ἐμοῦ. [7] Μάτην δὲ σέβονταί με διδάσκοντες διδασκαλίας ἐντάλματα ἀνθρώπων. [8] Ἀφέντες γὰρ τὴν ἐντολὴν τοῦ θεοῦ, κρατεῖτε τὴν παράδοσιν τῶν ἀνθρώπων, βαπτισμοὺς ξεστῶν καὶ ποτηρίων· καὶ ἄλλα παρόμοια τοιαῦτα πολλὰ ποιεῖτε. [9] Καὶ ἔλεγεν αὐτοῖς, Καλῶς ἀθετεῖτε τὴν ἐντολὴν τοῦ θεοῦ, ἵνα τὴν παράδοσιν ὑμῶν τηρήσητε. [10] Μωσῆς γὰρ εἶπεν, Τίμα τὸν πατέρα σου καὶ τὴν μητέρα σου· καί, Ὁ κακολογῶν πατέρα ἢ μητέρα θανάτῳ τελευτάτω· [11] ὑμεῖς δὲ λέγετε, Ἐὰν εἴπῃ ἄνθρωπος τῷ πατρὶ ἢ τῇ μητρί, Κορβᾶν, ὅ ἐστιν, δῶρον, ὃ ἐὰν ἐξ ἐμοῦ ὠφεληθῇς· [12] καὶ οὐκέτι ἀφίετε αὐτὸν οὐδὲν ποιῆσαι τῷ πατρὶ αὐτοῦ ἢ τῇ μητρὶ αὐτοῦ, [13] ἀκυροῦντες τὸν λόγον τοῦ θεοῦ τῇ παραδόσει ὑμῶν ᾗ παρεδώκατε· καὶ παρόμοια τοιαῦτα πολλὰ ποιεῖτε.

handed down; and you do many things such as that."

196

Process of Discovery

Linguistics Section

Linguistic Structure

[Transition and narrative description] [1] The Pharisees and some of the scribes gathered around Him when they had come from Jerusalem, [2] and had seen that some of His disciples were eating their bread with 'mpure hands, that is, unwashed. [3] (For the Pharisees and all the Jews do not eat unless they carefully wash their hands, *thus* observing the traditions of the elders; [4] and *when they come* from the market place, they do not eat unless they cleanse themselves; and there are many other things which they have received in order to observe, such as the washing of cups and pitchers and copper pots.)

[The Question] [5] The Pharisees and the scribes asked Him, "Why do Your disciples not walk according to the tradition of the elders, but eat their bread with impure hands?"

[Yeshua's answer] [6] And He said to them, "Rightly did Isaiah prophesy of you hypocrites, as it is written:

'THIS PEOPLE HONORS ME WITH THEIR LIPS,

BUT THEIR HEART IS FAR AWAY FROM ME.

[7] BUT IN VAIN DO THEY WORSHIP ME,

TEACHING AS DOCTRINES THE PRECEPTS OF MEN.'

[8] "Neglecting the commandment of God, you hold to the tradition of men."

[Yeshua's second answer] [9] He was also saying to them, "You are experts at setting aside the commandment of God in order to keep your tradition. [10] "For Moses said, "HONOR YOUR FATHER AND YOUR MOTHER'; and, 'HE WHO SPEAKS EVIL OF FATHER OR MOTHER, IS TO BE PUT TO DEATH'; [11] but you say, 'If a man says to *his* father or *his* mother, whatever I have that would help you is Corban (that is to say, given *to God*),' [12] you no longer permit him to do anything for *his* father or *his* mother; [13] *thus* invalidating the word of God by your tradition which you have handed down; and you do many things such as that."

Discussion

The Pharisees enter into a discussion with Yeshua about tradition and Scripture. They were trying to discover what tradition Yeshua followed. Was Yeshua a Pharisee or a Sadducee? The church has interpreted the questioning about traditions to be an attack against Yeshua. It was not an attack at this point in Mark's Gospel. The Hebraic leaders wanted to know what group Yeshua belonged to.

Verse Comparison of citations or proof text

1. 'THIS PEOPLE HONORS ME WITH THEIR LIPS, BUT THEIR HEART IS FAR AWAY FROM ME. 'BUT IN VAIN DO THEY WORSHIP ME, TEACHING AS DOCTRINES THE PRECEPTS OF MEN.'

> Isaiah 29:13 (NAS95S)   Then the Lord said, "Because *this people draw near with their words   And honor Me with their lip service,   But they remove their hearts far from Me, And their reverence for Me consists of tradition learned *by rote*, [14]   Therefore behold, I will once again deal *marvelously with this people, wondrously marvelous;   And the wisdom of their wise men will perish,   And the discernment of their discerning men will be concealed."

Yeshua was repeating a prophecy from the prophet Isaiah that the people in His day were giving the LORD lip service because they were saying that they honored and loved the LORD, but their actions showed that their hearts truly did not belong to the Lord. The tradition that they were learning from the Pharisees and Sadducees was taking them away from true worship of the LORD. The Isaiah passage also says that the truth of the LORD's way would eventually return to the people.

Phrase Study

1. κορβᾶν (-άν; קָרְבָּן) Hebrew word, explained by the notation ὅ ἐστι δῶρον (transl. corresponding to the LXX Lev 2:1, 4, 12, 13) something consecrated as a gift for God and closed to ordinary human use, a gift to God. It is offered in English as Corban.[104]

---

[104] Frederick W. Danker, William Arndt, and Walter Bauer, *A Greek-English Lexicon of the New Testament and Other Early Christian Literature* (Chicago: University of Chicago Press, 2000).

Culture Section

Questioning the passage

1. What does the reference to honoring mother and father mean in verse ten?

    Near Eastern culture says that children were supposed to support their parents when they reached retirement. The fourth commandment of the Ten Commandments reinforces that custom. The Pharisees were able to change that custom to benefit themselves. They claimed that any money put aside for the parents' retirement could be donated as an offering in the Temple in Jerusalem. This would exempt children from taking care of their parents in retirement. The Pharisees saw a gift to the LORD as a sacrifice was far more critical than honoring and caring for one's parents. This human-made tradition and incorrect interpretation of the LORD's law allowed the Pharisees and Sadducees to become wealthy at the expense of the elderly. Essentially they obscured the teachings of the prophets, which were based on the Torah.[105]

2. What was the cultural significance of washing hands before eating bread?

    The washing of hands before eating bread was an ordinance created by the community elders. These ordinances were not a part of the Torah nor the teaching of the prophets. Therefore, it was not a part of God's law but rather a human-made law. The ordinances tended to take the people's attention away from the Torah's spiritual and moral truths by supplanting the weightier meaning of the Word of the LORD with their teaching and traditions. Essentially it allowed the elders to control the people. Unfortunately, some human-made traditions and incorrect amplification of the Torah nullified the LORD's law and obscured the prophets' teachings.[106]

    These ordinances became popular because it was easier to follow them established by the elders than it was to follow the Torah and the laws established by the Lord. Following the Laws of the Lord is not an easy thing.

---

[105] Rocco A. Errico and George M. Lamsa, *Aramaic Light on the Gospel of Matthew: a Commentary on the Teachings of Jesus from the Aramaic and Unchanged Near Eastern Customs* (Santa Fe, NM: Noohra Foundation, 2000).
[106] IBID.

Thoughts

For 2000 years, the church has been creating ordinances for the people of God to follow. Many of these ordinances are not based on biblical Scripture but on the theological beliefs developed over the centuries. For example, in the Catholic Church, a priest cannot be married. This ordinance came from feudalism when the inheritance was based on the firstborn male of the family. When priests had children, the church building and its property could be passed down to the firstborn child; thus, the church would lose income. An ordinance was created to stop this income loss that prevented priests from marrying. Illegitimate children could not inherit property during feudalism. There is no commandment in the Scripture that says that the people of God cannot be married. This is just one example of many places where the church has created ordinances to control people and sometimes obscure the Scripture's true meaning.

Reflections

Martin Luther, in 1517 CE, started what is called the Reformation. He was not the first reformer but rather the first reformer whom the church did not kill. Luther's first beef with the church was over the paying of indulgences for the forgiveness of sin. When Luther started to translate the New Testament into German, he discovered many ordinances that the church had created that were not biblical. Besides, the Catholic Church stated that tradition trumped the Bible. The Protestant churches that arose from Luther's Reformation changed based on Luther's belief that the Bible must be first. Today, several Protestant churches will say that the Bible comes first but put their ordinance books and regulations ahead of the Scripture. When a Protestant denomination places its ordinance book before the Bible, then that denomination is no longer Protestant.

Afterthoughts

This is an exciting encounter between Jesus and the Pharisees. The Sadducees are mentioned, not by name, but by being called "teachers of the Law." The Sadducees are silent in the exchange as if they are merely observers of the situation. The discussion between Jesus and the Pharisees concerned the Pharisee Halakah (Midrash interpretation of the Torah Laws). The Halakah is presented as the need to purify oneself before touching food. The need for handwashing was prominent in Pharisee Halakah Midrash. Today, we know that washing hands before handling food is good hygiene and prevents diseases. Perhaps the Pharisees understood this (not the mechanics of spreading illness but also distributed by what is left on our hands during the day). Whatever the reason, they decided hand washing is necessary.

Jesus uses an Isaiah proof text to show the Pharisees the more significant issue than just hand washing. We defile ourselves by what we say does not match what we are doing or when our words and/or actions are not biblically sanctioned. Christians over the years have used this passage, especially the allegory (v. 14-15), to believe Jesus allowed un-kosher food to be consumed. Since Jesus came to fulfill the Torah and the prophets, it would seem very unlikely Jesus was declaring non-kosher food as acceptable. Of course, most of the church around 90 CE was gentile, and Paul had previously introduced non-kosher food to this church.

What Jesus is really doing here is: "Jesus was condemning the general practice of the Pharisees of bypassing God's laws and substituting them with their own traditions through Corban.

So, the Pharisees created a Halakah Midrash that overrode the Torah (the Law). Jesus is clearly saying this is unacceptable. No one can override or rewrite God's Word than God. Therefore, to follow Jesus is to follow the Word of God!

MARK 7:24-23

Language

New American Standard 1995	Koine Greek
[14] After He called the crowd to Him again, He *began* saying to them, "Listen to Me, all of you, and understand: [15] there is nothing outside the man which can defile him if it goes into him; but the things which proceed out of the man are what defile the man. [16] ["If anyone has ears to hear, let him hear."] [17] When he had left the crowd *and* entered the house, His disciples questioned Him about the Parable. [18] And He said to them, "Are you so lacking in understanding also? Do you not understand that whatever goes into the man from outside cannot defile him, [19] because it does not go into his heart, but into his stomach, and is eliminated?" (*Thus He* declared all foods clean.) [20] And He was saying, "That which proceeds out of the man, that is what defiles the man. [21] "For from within, out of the heart of men, proceed the evil thoughts, fornications, thefts, murders, adulteries, [22] deeds of coveting *and* wickedness, *as well as* deceit, sensuality, envy, slander, pride *and* foolishness. [23] "All these evil things proceed from within and defile the man."	[14] Καὶ προσκαλεσάμενος πάντα τὸν ὄχλον, ἔλεγεν αὐτοῖς, Ἀκούετέ μου πάντες, καὶ συνίετε. [15] Οὐδέν ἐστιν ἔξωθεν τοῦ ἀνθρώπου εἰσπορευόμενον εἰς αὐτόν, ὃ δύναται αὐτὸν κοινῶσαι· ἀλλὰ τὰ ἐκπορευόμενα ἀπ᾽ αὐτοῦ, ἐκεῖνα ἐστιν τὰ κοινοῦντα τὸν ἄνθρωπον. [16] Εἴ τις ἔχει ὦτα ἀκούειν ἀκουέτω. [17] Καὶ ὅτε εἰσῆλθεν εἰς οἶκον ἀπὸ τοῦ ὄχλου, ἐπηρώτων αὐτὸν οἱ μαθηταὶ αὐτοῦ περὶ τῆς παραβολῆς. [18] Καὶ λέγει αὐτοῖς, Οὕτως καὶ ὑμεῖς ἀσύνετοί ἐστε; Οὐ νοεῖτε ὅτι πᾶν τὸ ἔξωθεν εἰσπορευόμενον εἰς τὸν ἄνθρωπον οὐ δύναται αὐτὸν κοινῶσαι, [19] ὅτι οὐκ εἰσπορεύεται αὐτοῦ εἰς τὴν καρδίαν, ἀλλ᾽ εἰς τὴν κοιλίαν· καὶ εἰς τὸν ἀφεδρῶνα ἐκπορεύεται, καθαρίζον πάντα τὰ βρώματα. [20] Ἔλεγεν δὲ ὅτι Τὸ ἐκ τοῦ ἀνθρώπου ἐκπορευόμενον, ἐκεῖνο κοινοῖ τὸν ἄνθρωπον. [21] Ἔσωθεν γάρ, ἐκ τῆς καρδίας τῶν ἀνθρώπων οἱ διαλογισμοὶ οἱ κακοὶ ἐκπορεύονται, μοιχεῖαι, πορνεῖαι, φόνοι, [22] κλοπαί, πλεονεξίαι, πονηρίαι, δόλος, ἀσέλγεια, ὀφθαλμὸς πονηρός, βλασφημία, ὑπερηφανία, ἀφροσύνη· [23] πάντα ταῦτα τὰ πονηρὰ ἔσωθεν ἐκπορεύεται, καὶ κοινοῖ τὸν ἄνθρωπον.

Process of Discovery

Linguistics Section

Linguistic Structure

[Parable] [14] After He called the crowd to Him again, He *began* saying to them, "Listen to Me, all of you, and understand: [15] there is nothing outside the man which can defile him if it goes into him; but the things which proceed out of the man are what defile the man. [16] ["If anyone has ears to hear, let him hear."]

[Parable discussed] [17] When he had left the crowd *and* entered the house, His disciples questioned Him about the Parable. [18] And He said to them, "Are you so lacking in understanding also? Do you not understand that whatever goes into the man from outside cannot defile him, [19] because it does not go into his heart, but into his stomach, and is eliminated?" (*Thus He* declared all foods clean.) [20] And He was saying, "That which proceeds out of the man, that is what defiles the man. [21] "For from within, out of the heart of men, proceed the evil thoughts, fornications, thefts, murders, adulteries, [22] deeds of coveting *and* wickedness, *as well as* deceit, sensuality, envy, slander, pride *and* foolishness. [23] "All these evil things proceed from within and defile the man."

Discussion

Yeshua offered a parable which He then explained to His disciples.

Questioning the Passage

1. What is the Parable indicating?

The Parable is Yeshua's way of saying that it is the intent that a person has that matters. When a person allows outside influences to determine their actions, there is a potential problem. If an outside influence moves a person to sin, they already had that notion in their hearts.

Eating or not eating Kosher is not the issue. The food purity law is being used as a metaphor. The Laws of the LORD are a guide for living a godly life. It influences one's behavior but is not what is entirely driving a person's actions.

A person can defile themselves without the Laws of the LORD. There is an ethical and moral standard that each person adopts as their own. Personal ethics and morals are derived from culture and society. Ethics are canonized, which means a person selects which ones to follow. This is similar to the usage of the Bible. Church denominations have selected certain books that they preach heavily and other books they ignore. For example, the Amish and Mennonite churches favor the book of James. According to the liturgical calendar, many protestant denominations will use James twice every three years. So denominations select the books they emphasize to their members. That is canonizing the Bible.

The same canonizing is done for ethics and morals. For example, decades ago, divorce was considered taboo. It was not an integral part of the ethics code of society. Married couples still got divorced. They were frowned upon by society. For the divorced couple, they saw nothing wrong with divorce. They canonized the cultural ethics not to include the shame but rather the acceptance of divorce. There are plenty of examples of this type of canonizing.

Yeshua got to the heart of what should be canonized and what should not. In this passage, the Kosher laws were not being challenged, but the interpretation and implementation of the laws were challenged.

Culture Section

Discussion

Mark's author provides this Parable and its definition to show that Yeshua conflicted with the religious leaders. The conflict, in this case, starts with chapter seven, verse one. The author sets up the scene. The practices of the Pharisees are challenged. The first one is ritual hand washing. Yeshua did not challenge the purity code but rather the Pharisaic oral tradition that surrounded the purity code. In this pericope, the dispute is about kosher regulations. It is believed that a small group only kept the extreme rules of the Pharisees with the Pharisees and perhaps the priests. It was challenging to follow the Leviticus purity code in the manner the Pharisees demanded, even for them.[107]

---

[107] Ched Myers, *Binding the Strong Man a Political Reading of Mark's Story of Jesus* (Maryknoll, NY: Orbis Books, 1988).

The Pharisees created their codes to control the people. They went far beyond the meaning and intent of the Torah. People can be controlled when they are told what they wear and what they can or cannot eat. The power base was attacked by Yeshua, asking what authority the Pharisees had to impose their will on the people. Yeshua believed that the people needed to be free. He concentrated on Pharisaic control of the people. He did not challenge Roman control. He said, "give Ceaser what is due to Ceaser." In this narrative and others in the Gospels, Yeshua is found challenging the religious establishment.

Thoughts

The LORD gave us His Word as a guide for us to have a spotless life. There are so many rules and regulations that it is virtually impossible to live on Earth and not break a code here and there. The LORD established forgiveness into His system because He was aware that this would indeed happen. What did humans do? They determined which of the Laws they wanted to follow. For example, Paul's Kosher laws were a big problem when he converted to Mithras churches. The pork was cheap and readily available meat. How can you tell people to follow the LORD's Word and eat pork? According to the purity code in Leviticus, pork is off the menu. Each person has to decide which of the biblical laws one will follow.

Reflections

A problem arises when society decides to enact some of its own laws instead of biblical ones. If the new society's law or custom is not in violation of anything written in the Bible, then all is good. What happens when the society cannon is against the Bible. For example, today, homosexual laws are heavily challenged. Society and culture have determined laws against them to be obsolete, and new regulations in favor of this act are in place. Please take note of the acceptance of the changes not is in question in this writing. Instead, one has to examine these changes and determine whether they violate the tenents of the Bible and if so, does it matter to you? Each person has to decide the answer to that question.

MARK 7:24–30

Language

New American Standard 1995	Koine Greek
[24] Jesus got up and went away from there to the region of Tyre. And when He had entered a house, He wanted no one to know *of it;* yet He could not escape notice. [25] But after hearing of Him, a woman whose little daughter had an unclean spirit immediately came and fell at His feet. [26] Now the woman was a Gentile, of the Syrophoenician race. And she kept asking Him to cast the demon out of her daughter. [27] And He was saying to her, "Let the children be satisfied first, for it is not good to take the children's bread and throw it to the dogs." [28] But she answered and said to Him, "Yes, Lord, *but* even the dogs under the table feed on the children's crumbs." [29] And He said to her, "Because of this answer go; the demon has gone out of your daughter." [30] And going back to her home, she found the child lying on the bed, the demon having left.	[27] Καὶ ἐκεῖθεν ἀναστὰς ἀπῆλθεν εἰς τὰ μεθόρια Τύρου καὶ Σιδῶνος. Καὶ εἰσελθὼν εἰς οἰκίαν, οὐδένα ἤθελεν γνῶναι, καὶ οὐκ ἠδυνήθη λαθεῖν. [25] Ἀκούσασα γὰρ γυνὴ περὶ αὐτοῦ, ἧς εἶχεν τὸ θυγάτριον αὐτῆς πνεῦμα ἀκάθαρτον, ἐλθοῦσα προσέπεσεν πρὸς τοὺς πόδας αὐτοῦ· [26] ἦν δὲ ἡ γυνὴ Ἑλληνίς, Συραφοινίκισσα τῷ γένει· καὶ ἠρώτα αὐτὸν ἵνα τὸ δαιμόνιον ἐκβάλῃ ἐκ τῆς θυγατρὸς αὐτῆς. [27] Ὁ δὲ Ἰησοῦς εἶπεν αὐτῇ, Ἄφες πρῶτον χορτασθῆναι τὰ τέκνα· οὐ γὰρ καλόν ἐστιν λαβεῖν τὸν ἄρτον τῶν τέκνων καὶ βαλεῖν τοῖς κυναρίοις. [28] Ἡ δὲ ἀπεκρίθη καὶ λέγει αὐτῷ, Ναί, κύριε· καὶ γὰρ τὰ κυνάρια ὑποκάτω τῆς τραπέζης ἐσθίει ἀπὸ τῶν ψιχίων τῶν παιδίων. [29] Καὶ εἶπεν αὐτῇ, Διὰ τοῦτον τὸν λόγον ὕπαγε· ἐξελήλυθεν τὸ δαιμόνιον ἐκ τῆς θυγατρός σου. [30] Καὶ ἀπελθοῦσα εἰς τὸν οἶκον αὐτῆς, εὗρεν τὸ δαιμόνιον ἐξεληλυθός, καὶ τὴν θυγατέρα βεβλημένην ἐπὶ τῆς κλίνης.

Process of Discovery

Linguistics Section

Linguistic Structure

A [24] Jesus got up and went away from there to the region of Tyre. And when He had entered a house, He wanted no one to know *of it;* yet He could not escape notice.

> **B** [25] But after hearing of Him, a woman whose little daughter had an unclean spirit immediately came and fell at His feet. [26] Now the woman was a Gentile, of the Syrophoenician race. And she kept asking Him to cast the demon out of her daughter.

> > **C** [27] And He was saying to her, "Let the children be satisfied first, for it is not good to take the children's bread and throw it to the dogs."

> **B'** [28] But she answered and said to Him, "Yes, Lord, *but* even the dogs under the table feed on the children's crumbs."

A' [29] And He said to her, "Because of this answer go; the demon has gone out of your daughter." [30] And going back to her home, she found the child lying on the bed, the demon having left.

Discussion

This narrative forms an A-B-C chiasm. One question of this narrative is, are Gentiles included in Yeshua's plan for salvation?

Questioning the Passage

1. Is there a significance that Yeshua was in the district of Tyre? (v. 24)

   The district of Tyre was a Gentile area. Therefore, the listener is prepared to experience a Yeshua-Gentile encounter.

2. What does it mean to be demon-possessed? (v. 25)

   An unclean spirit was also called a demon in Yeshua's day. Demons were considered angels or messengers of destruction. Like angels, they could cause people to live in darkness. Also, demons could punish the wicked. The understanding of demons was from the Book of the Watchers, from 1 Enoch. The demons were the spirits of the Watchers. They were punished because they gave several secrets of the Universe to humans. When demons possessed a person, they blocked them from the love and light of the LORD.[108]

Culture Section

Discussion

In Yeshua's day, dogs were regarded as unclean animals. Dogs were not treated well and were seldom fed. Many Semites believed that they would become unclean if they touched a dog. Dogs roamed the streets in search of food. They ate meat that humans would not because of religious laws. Dogs also ate the carcass of any animal.

Semites did not use tables when eating. Instead, their food was served on a tray and placed on a cloth spread on the floor. When the tray was lifted, small pieces of bread often fell onto the floor. Dogs would patiently wait and watch people who were eating. The dogs knew that eventually, the tray would be lifted, and crumbs would be available. Near Easterners would usually give the crumbs to beggars. It was considered a sin to throw bread at dogs because the bread was sacred and scarce. No parent would want to see their child hungry while dogs were being fed.

People of different religious faiths called people of other faiths dogs because they would eat meat unlawful. The Gentiles who lived around Judea and the Galilee ate swine meat. Because of this practice, Hebrews thought of them as dogs.

Questioning the passage

1. What did Yeshua mean in verse twenty-seven?

   The culture in Yeshua's day was first to ensure that the requestor had genuine faith. At first, Yeshua refused to help the woman. One reason was that Yeshua's loyalty was with His people. Yeshua wanted to minister to His people first. Semitic teachers and healers

---

[108] "Demons - in Volume Two." In *The New Interpreter's Dictionary of the Bible*. Nashville, TN: Abingdon, 2008.

often tested the sincerity of the people making requests of them. The woman's response to Yeshua was about dogs receiving crumbs. This response showed Yeshua that this Gentile woman had faith in His capabilities. Therefore, He granted her request.[109]

Thoughts

The story of Yeshua's encounter with a Gentile woman and curing her daughter of a demon has the literal meaning that Yeshua's love and grace is available to all people, Gentile and Jew. Unfortunately, throughout the history of the church, the church has learned how to reverse that lesson. In many churches, Jews are not received with gladness but rather with anti-Semitism. Not only are Jews steered away but also people of different races. The motto of such a church is that Yeshua is available to everyone, just not here.

An allegorical approach is to realize that people in the world are searching for Yeshua. It is the responsibility of the church and its members to greet these people and help them in their journey to seek out God. Yeshua's grace and love are meant for all people. It is the responsibility of the disciples of Yeshua to help others to find Him. The woman knew that she wanted to find the LORD. Her benefit was that she knew of the Messiah.

The mini-parable of the dog tells us that there are people we know who are searching for God's love and grace. Instead of ignoring them, like one does when the dog sits at the dinner table, one must embrace that person and introduce them to the love of God through Yeshua.

Reflections

Jesus' attitude and language used in the narrative are shocking to the reader. How can our Lord and Savior treat anyone in the way He is portrayed in this narrative? The pagan woman is simply looking for a way that her daughter can be cured of having been possessed by a demon. Instead of immediately helping her, He calls her a dog, thus insulting her. Was Jesus forced to confront His prejudice?

---

[109] Rocco A. Errico, George M. Lamsa, and George M. Lamsa, *Aramaic Light on the Gospels of Mark and Luke: a Commentary on the Teachings of Jesus from the Aramaic and Unchanged Near Eastern Customs* (Smyrna, GA: Noohra Foundation, 2001).

However, how can the Savior of the world, whom God sent for all, have any prejudice. Is this a Markian example of showing us that Jesus was human? The woman taught Jesus a lesson that He must drop any earthly prejudices that He may have picked up and offer mercy, which He does.

MARK 7:31-37

Language

New American Standard 1995	Koine Greek
[31] Again He went out from the region of Tyre, and came through Sidon to the Sea of Galilee, within the region of Decapolis. [32] They brought to Him one who was deaf and spoke with difficulty, and they implored Him to lay His hand on him. [33] Jesus took him aside from the crowd, by himself, and put His fingers into his ears, and after spitting, He touched his tongue *with the saliva;* [34] and looking up to heaven with a deep sigh, He said to him, "Ephphatha!" that is, "Be opened!" [35] And his ears were opened, and the impediment of his tongue was removed, and he *began* speaking plainly. [36] And He gave them orders not to tell anyone; but the more He ordered them, the more widely they continued to proclaim it. [37] They were utterly astonished, saying, "He has done all things well; He makes even the deaf to hear and the mute to speak."	Καὶ πάλιν ἐξελθὼν ἐκ τῶν ὁρίων Τύρου καὶ Σιδῶνος, ἦλθεν πρὸς τὴν θάλασσαν τῆς Γαλιλαίας, ἀνὰ μέσον τῶν ὁρίων Δεκαπόλεως. [32] Καὶ φέρουσιν αὐτῷ κωφὸν ˹ μογγιλάλον, ˺ καὶ παρακαλοῦσιν αὐτὸν ἵνα ἐπιθῇ αὐτῷ τὴν χεῖρα. [33] Καὶ ἀπολαβόμενος αὐτὸν ἀπὸ τοῦ ὄχλου κατ' ἰδίαν, ἔβαλεν τοὺς δακτύλους αὐτοῦ εἰς τὰ ὦτα αὐτοῦ, καὶ πτύσας ἥψατο τῆς γλώσσης αὐτοῦ, [34] καὶ ἀναβλέψας εἰς τὸν οὐρανόν, ἐστέναξεν, καὶ λέγει αὐτῷ, Ἐφφαθά, ὅ ἐστιν, Διανοίχθητι. [35] Καὶ εὐθέως διηνοίχθησαν αὐτοῦ αἱ ἀκοαί· καὶ ἐλύθη ὁ δεσμὸς τῆς γλώσσης αὐτοῦ, καὶ ἐλάλει ὀρθῶς. [36] Καὶ διεστείλατο αὐτοῖς ἵνα μηδενὶ εἴπωσιν· ὅσον δὲ αὐτὸς αὐτοῖς διεστέλλετο, μᾶλλον περισσότερον ἐκήρυσσον. [37] Καὶ ὑπερπερισσῶς ἐξεπλήσσοντο, λέγοντες, Καλῶς πάντα πεποίηκεν· καὶ τοὺς κωφοὺς ποιεῖ ἀκούειν, καὶ τοὺς ἀλάλους λαλεῖν.

Process of Discovery

Linguistics Section

Linguistic Structure

[Transition] [31] Again He went out from the region of Tyre, and came through Sidon to the Sea of Galilee, within the region of Decapolis.

A [32] They brought to Him one who was deaf and spoke with difficulty, and they implored Him to lay His hand on him.

> **B** [33] Jesus took him aside from the crowd, by himself, and put His fingers into his ears, and after spitting, He touched his tongue *with the saliva;* [34] and looking up to heaven with a deep sigh, He said to him, "Ephphatha!" that is, "Be opened!"

> > **C** [35] And his ears were opened, and the impediment of his tongue was removed, and he *began* speaking plainly.

> **B'** [36] And He gave them orders not to tell anyone; but the more He ordered them, the more widely they continued to proclaim it.

A' [37] They were utterly astonished, saying, "He has done all things well; He makes even the deaf to hear and the mute to speak."

Discussion

This narrative is another example of Yeshua's power to heal.

Questioning the Passage

1. Is there an allegorical meaning to the various healings? (v. 30 & 31)

    There are several healing stories in Matthew's Gospel. This narrative has a longer list than most of the other ones. It is also a part of the triad, which contains the feeding of 4000 people. Why the repetition? This narrative indicates that Yeshua's healing is a prime reason for believing Yeshua is the LORD's Messiah.

    Lame – this is a condition where a body limb cannot be used for the function that the LORD designed it to do. Usually, it is used for someone who cannot walk healthily. The followers of Yeshua must learn to walk in the ways of righteousness, which is healthy living. Yeshua's cure for the lame demonstrates how to walk in the ways of the LORD.

No matter what a person's economic condition or societal position is, one can walk upright when the words of Yeshua are incorporated into the soul. Yeshua cures the spiritually lame who may be walking in the ways of Satan to see the Light of the LORD and walk with Him toward sanctification.

Crippled – society's religious rules and regulations have damaged disabled people. The priests of the Temple at Jerusalem had special rules and regulations about disabled people entering the courts. The court for the Hebrews was limited, not only by one having to be a member of the tribe but also not being crippled. Being crippled was considered a result of the individual's sin or the parents' sin. Yeshua cured the crippled, instructing the people that a disabled person is not the result of sin. Some people become disabled through a random accident and are not injured because of sin. This reference can also be applied to one's hands. If the hands are crippled, then a person cannot hold the Torah or any other sacred object. To hold onto Yeshua as the Messiah, a disabled person would have to have their hands repaired to a healthy state. Yeshua cured disabled persons by repairing their disability to be a part of worship to the LORD. Therefore, Yeshua says that all broken people, the disabled, have a place in the Kingdom of Heaven. The love of the LORD is for them as much as if the person was completely whole.

Blind – meaning of the Greek word indicates comprehension. Therefore, one who is blind can be viewed as a person who is blind to the Word of the LORD. That is that the person does not understand the Word and ways of the LORD. Yeshua explained and clarified the original meaning of the Torah and Prophets. The religious leaders of the day had corrupted by creating their ordinances for the Law. Curing the blind is Yeshua teaching them about the "code" that is used in the Scripture. In order to understand the original meaning of Scripture, the blindness caused by the interpretations of the church must be removed. In Yeshua's day, the interpretations of the Pharisees blinded the people from seeing the true meaning of the Scripture. When the filters of the church are removed, the blind to the original and true meaning of the Scripture will be able to see what the Scripture means. Yeshua's way of interpreting the Torah and Prophets enlightens all who come to Him as the Messiah.

Mute – the Greek word used can also mean deaf. First, the examination of the mute says that Yeshua teaches people that it is essential to preach the Word of the LORD for all people to hear. How can the Gospel of Yeshua be spread in the world if the church and its people are mute? Evangelism should not be a scary thing to do but rather something that Yeshua energizes in you. Speaking about Yeshua is power. There will be people who will not listen, and that has to be accepted. With the cure from Yeshua, any disciple should be able to speak about faith in Yeshua. For the deaf, Yeshua cures deafness by offering other learning methods about Him. Disciples of Yeshua must demonstrate what Yeshua's words say. The deaf can see Yeshua's words in action, and that will bring the deaf into the faith. Also, the writings of the Scripture are another vehicle to learn about Yeshua. Some people are not physically deaf but are deaf to the Word of the LORD. Yeshua offers ways to remove deafness. He uses his disciples to show the deaf, those who either have not or do not want to hear the Word of the LORD, what it means to come into faith in Yeshua as the LORD's Messiah.

Biblical Locations

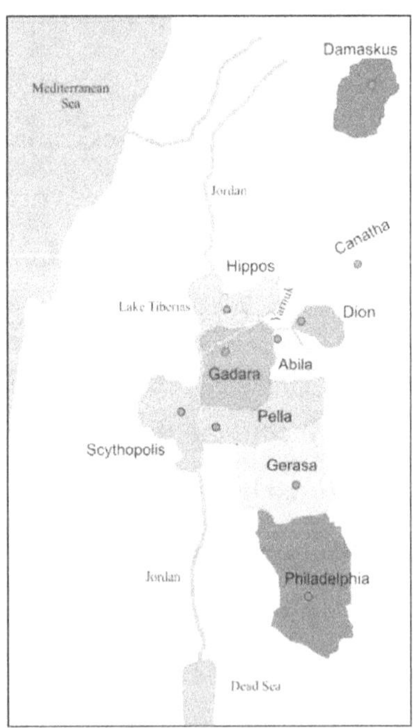

Culture Section

Discussion

Healers in the Near East believe that spit cured blindness. Yeshua respected His culture, and whenever it was possible, He was in sync with it. Therefore, He kept the tradition.

Thoughts

Near Eastern people in Yeshua's (and later on) wrote allegories, metaphors, and parables. Is this healing story real? In the minds of Near Eastern people, it does not matter. The lesson of the story is the key. The lesson is that everyone must open their eyes to reading the Torah and live by the Torah. The LORD gave us the Torah to help us in our lives. Too many people view the Bible as a blockade and not as a gift from God. Open your eyes to the LORD's way.

Reflections

What would the world look like if everyone followed the Laws of the LORD? One of Yeshua's tasks was to enlighten the people on the Torah. The people were following what the religious leaders were telling them. Quite a bit of the religious leaders' demands was not biblical. Yeshua fought against proclamations that were not biblical. The religious leaders also interpreted the Torah and Prophets to best suit them.

MARK 8:1–10

Language

New American Standard 1995	Koine Greek
[1] In those days, when there was again a large crowd and they had nothing to eat, Jesus called His disciples and said to them, [2] "I feel compassion for the [1]people because they have remained with Me now three days and have nothing to eat. [3] "If I send them away hungry to their homes, they will faint on the way; and some of them have come from a great distance." [4] And His disciples answered Him, "Where will anyone be able *to find enough* bread here in *this* desolate place to satisfy these people?" [5] And He was asking them, "How many loaves do you have?" And they said, "Seven." [6] And He directed the people to sit down on the ground; and taking the seven loaves, He gave thanks and broke them, and started giving them to His disciples to serve to them, and they served them to the people. [7] They also had a few small fish; and after He had blessed them, He ordered these to be served as well. [8] And they ate and were satisfied; and they picked up seven large baskets full of what was left over of the broken pieces. [9] About four thousand were *there;* and He sent them away. [10] And immediately He entered the boat with His disciples and came to the district of Dalmanutha.	[1] Ἐν ἐκείναις ταῖς ἡμέραις, παμπόλλου ὄχλου ὄντος, καὶ μὴ ἐχόντων τί φάγωσιν, προσκαλεσάμενος ὁ Ἰησοῦς τοὺς μαθητὰς αὐτοῦ λέγει αὐτοῖς, [2] Σπλαγχνίζομαι ἐπὶ τὸν ὄχλον· ὅτι ἤδη ⸀ ἡμέραι ⸀ τρεῖς προσμένουσίν μοι, καὶ οὐκ ἔχουσιν τί φάγωσιν· [3] καὶ ἐὰν ἀπολύσω αὐτοὺς νήστεις εἰς οἶκον αὐτῶν, ἐκλυθήσονται ἐν τῇ ὁδῷ· τινὲς γὰρ αὐτῶν μακρόθεν ἥκουσιν. [4] Καὶ ἀπεκρίθησαν αὐτῷ οἱ μαθηταὶ αὐτοῦ, Πόθεν τούτους δυνήσεταί τις ὧδε χορτάσαι ἄρτων ἐπ' ἐρημίας; [5] Καὶ ἐπηρώτα αὐτούς, Πόσους ἔχετε ἄρτους; Οἱ δὲ εἶπον, Ἑπτά. [6] Καὶ παρήγγειλεν τῷ ὄχλῳ ἀναπεσεῖν ἐπὶ τῆς γῆς· καὶ λαβὼν τοὺς ἑπτὰ ἄρτους, εὐχαριστήσας ἔκλασεν καὶ ἐδίδου τοῖς μαθηταῖς αὐτοῦ, ἵνα παραθῶσιν· καὶ παρέθηκαν τῷ ὄχλῳ. [7] Καὶ εἶχον ἰχθύδια ὀλίγα· καὶ εὐλογήσας εἶπεν ⸀ παραθεῖναι ⸀ καὶ αὐτά. [8] Ἔφαγον δέ, καὶ ἐχορτάσθησαν· καὶ ἦραν περισσεύματα κλασμάτων ἑπτὰ σπυρίδας. [9] Ἦσαν δὲ οἱ φαγόντες ὡς τετρακισχίλιοι· καὶ ἀπέλυσεν αὐτούς. [10] Καὶ εὐθέως ἐμβὰς εἰς τὸ πλοῖον μετὰ τῶν μαθητῶν αὐτοῦ, ἦλθεν εἰς τὰ μέρη Δαλμανουθά.

Process of Discovery

Linguistics Section

Linguistic Structure

[Transition] [1] In those days, when there was again a large crowd and they had nothing to eat,

[Jesus' words] Jesus called His disciples and said to them, [2] "I feel compassion for the people because they have remained with Me now three days and have nothing to eat. [3] "If I send them away hungry to their homes, they will faint on the way; and some of them have come from a great distance."

[Response] [4] And His disciples answered Him, "Where will anyone be able *to find enough* bread here in *this* desolate place to satisfy these people?"

[Jesus' words][5] And He was asking them, "How many loaves do you have?"

[Response] And they said, "Seven."

[Feeding] [6] And He directed the people to sit down on the ground; and taking the seven loaves, He gave thanks and broke them, and started giving them to His disciples to serve to them, and they served them to the people. [7] They also had a few small fish; and after He had blessed them, He ordered these to be served as well. [8] And they ate and were satisfied; and they picked up seven large baskets full of what was left over of the broken pieces. [9] About four thousand were *there;* and He sent them away.

[Transition] [10] And immediately He entered the boat with His disciples and came to the district of Dalmanutha.

Discussion

The feeding story in Mark's Gospel indicates that there were 4,000 people present.

Questioning the Passage
1. What is the significance of the number three? (v. 2)
    The number three is used in the Scripture to designate the divine. In this case, the three days tell the reader that something of a divine nature was about to occur. The divine event was Yeshua taking seven loaves of bread and feeding a large crowd of people. Unfortunately, the

number of people at this event is unknown. Mark's Gospel indicates 4,000 persons. Matthew's Gospel does not indicate how many people were present.

This event was three days long. How did the people get fed for the three days? Since they were located near the shoreline of the Sea of Galilee, some men could have gone to the water and tried to capture some fish. Since there were no ovens mentioned, it would not be possible to cook bread. A mystery is how people feed themselves for three days. If the three days are viewed symbolically, then it tells the reader that something divine and, therefore, amazing was about to occur.

2. What is the significance of the number seven? (v. 6 & 8)
    The number is symbolic in the Scripture as indicating completion. The LORD created the Heavens and Earth in seven days. On the seventh day, the LORD rested. The Sabbath day, the seventh day is considered a part of the creation story. Thus, on the Sabbath day, creation was complete.

3. What is the significance of seven being repeated? (v. 6 & 8)
    The narrative states that there were seven loaves and a few small fish available. After Yeshua fed the people, there were seven baskets of leftovers remaining. The author is repeating the number seven for emphasis. The narrative is about completeness.

An Allegorical Interpretation of the Narrative

The three days allegorically tell the listener that something divine is about to happen. The LORD had created His chosen people. The chosen people had accepted the Torah from the LORD. A part of their responsibility was to bring the Torah to the world. Since that had not happened, the LORD sent His Messiah, Yeshua. The author of Matthew's Gospel needed to create Gentile stories to show that Yeshua's saving grace was for all.

This Gentile story talks about the completeness of the Kingdom of Heaven, which leads to inclusion. The LORD wanted the Gentiles to be included in the Kingdom of Heaven. Until the

Messiah arrived, only the Chosen People of the LORD were to be freely admitted into the Kingdom of Heaven. Seven being repeated says that through divine intervention, the Gentiles would become a part of the Kingdom of Heaven, which then brings completion to the Kingdom of Heaven. Of course, the Kingdom of Heaven is not complete, but the inclusion of all people is complete – well, at least started.

The Kingdom of Heaven was to include all the peoples of the Earth. That is the basic lesson of the narrative.

Biblical Locations

1. "Dalmanutha a place on the west of the Sea of Galilee, mentioned only in Mark 8:10 . In the parallel passage it is said that Christ came "into the borders of Magdala" (Matthew 15:39). It is plain, then, that Dalmanutha was near Magdala, which was probably the Greek name of one of the many Migdols (i.e., watch-towers) on the western side of the lake of Gennesaret. It has been identified in the ruins of a village about a mile from Magdala, in the little open valley of 'Ain-el-Barideh, "the cold fountain," called el-Mejdel, possibly the "Migdal-el" of Joshua 19:38 ."[110]

Speculation about this narrative and the Gentiles

[Matthew 15:24] But He answered and said, "I was sent only to the lost sheep of the house of Israel."

I will commence this speculation by saying that I am not convinced that this speculation is true in the same way that John Crossan, in his book "Jesus a Revolutionary Biography," said in the chapter "Dogs under the Cross." Taking into account Matthew 15:24 and that there are two almost identical feeding stories, the speculation is that Yeshua did not visit and perform miracles for the Gentiles during His ministry. The stories are duplicated to include the Gentiles by the author. At the 48 CE council in Jerusalem, Peter demanded that new "Christians" had to convert to Judaism first. Paul heavily objected to the proposal.

---

[110] Michael Jakes et al., "Dalmanutha Definition and Meaning - Bible Dictionary," biblestudytools.com, accessed May 11, 2021, https://www.biblestudytools.com/dictionary/dalmanutha/.

Paul converted Mithras Churches into Christian Churches. He left behind the rituals of the Mithras religion and most of the morals and ethics of that religion. He did attempt to change some of the pagan beliefs and actions to be in line with Yeshua's view of the world. The epistles Paul wrote to the churches to make that clear. Christianity has kept most of the Mithras rituals and beliefs, just changing them to fit Yeshua as the son of God instead of Mithras as the son of God.

The converted Mithras churches took over Christianity, and Jewish Christianity disappeared. Their people wrote the Gospels. They had stories about Yeshua and what He did when in the presence of the Hebrew people. They needed Yeshua to do similar things for the Gentiles, if not the same. A prime example is the feeding stories. Essentially they are identical stories with minor changes.

Yeshua says in verse 24 that He came only for the lost sheep of Israel is the lynchpin of this analysis. The church has demanded that Yeshua come for the Gentiles. It was the incident described in verse twenty-four for Yeshua to realize the second half of His Mission. So, why would Yeshua say that He only came for the Jews if He also came for the Gentiles? Indeed, Yeshua would have known what His Mission was.

One of the purposes of the Messiah was to bring people to the LORD. Indeed, the lost sheep of Israel needed to come back to the LORD. Also, the Gentiles who were Pagan needed to come to the LORD. The Messiah Yeshua came to bring all people to the LORD. Did Yeshua's work occur with only the Hebrew people, then Paul was commissioned to perform the second part of the mission? If so, then it was Paul's task to bring Yeshua's message to the Gentiles. That would fit the conversion of the Mithras churches by Paul. He brought Yeshua the Messiah to the Gentiles.

So, this analysis concludes that Yeshua, the Messiah's mission was to bring the message of salvation, grace, and hope of the LORD to the Hebrew people, the first part of the mission. Yeshua selected Paul to bring the message of salvation, grace, and hope of the LORD through the

Messiah to the Gentiles. The new Christianized Mithras churches eventually needed some writings of their own. That would be the reason for writing the Gospels and other books. These books would have to demonstrate that Yeshua came for the Gentiles in addition to the Hebrews. The duplication of the feeding story, and others like it, confirm this possibility.

Allegorical speculation of this event

Yeshua held a three-day seminar for the people in the Decapolis. Even Yeshua needed some sleep during this period. Probably people came out during the day to hear from the young teacher and then returned home that evening. They would get some food to eat and prepare for the next day at home. On the second day, people would have returned to hear more. The crowd could have consisted of people who were there on the first day and new attendees. The same thing would have happened at the end of the second day.

On the third day, when Yeshua was done teaching, He decided to have a meal with the people. This meal would signify the end of his visit and teaching to the Decapolis people. It could be viewed as a "Last Supper" with the Gentiles. The Last Supper was with His inner circle, of which all the members were Hebrew. This supper could be a foreshadowing of what was going to happen later in the narrative.

Thoughts

The number seven is the key to the meaning of this feeding. The Kingdom of Heaven is not complete until the Gentiles were included. Seven is the symbol of completion. Yeshua's work in saving humankind is not complete until all the people of the world are included. The divine intervention of the LORD is indicated to us by having a three-day event. Three is symbolic of divinity and divine intervention. The seven loaves and seven baskets of left-overs symbolize the inclusion of all people, Hebrew, and Gentiles.

Reflections

The number seven in the Scripture indicates completeness. The LORD was completing the Kingdom with the inclusion of the Gentiles.

MARK 8:14-21

Language

New American Standard 1995	Koine Greek
[14] And they had forgotten to take bread, and did not have more than one loaf in the boat with them. [15] And He was giving orders to them, saying, "Watch out! Beware of the leaven of the Pharisees and the leaven of Herod." [16] They *began* to discuss with one another *the fact* that they had no bread. [17] And Jesus, aware of this, said to them, "Why do you discuss *the fact* that you have no bread? Do you not yet see or understand? Do you have a hardened heart? [18] "HAVING EYES, DO YOU NOT SEE? AND HAVING EARS, DO YOU NOT HEAR? And do you not remember, [19] when I broke the five loaves for the five thousand, how many baskets full of broken pieces you picked up?" They said to Him, "Twelve." [20] "When *I broke* the seven for the four thousand, how many large baskets full of broken pieces did you pick up?" And they said to Him, "Seven." [21] And He was saying to them, "Do you not yet understand?"	[14] Καὶ ἐπελάθοντο λαβεῖν ἄρτους, καὶ εἰ μὴ ἕνα ἄρτον οὐκ εἶχον μεθ' ἑαυτῶν ἐν τῷ πλοίῳ. [15] Καὶ διεστέλλετο αὐτοῖς, λέγων, Ὁρᾶτε, βλέπετε ἀπὸ τῆς ζύμης τῶν Φαρισαίων καὶ τῆς ζύμης Ἡρώδου. [16] Καὶ διελογίζοντο πρὸς ἀλλήλους, λέγοντες ὅτι Ἄρτους οὐκ ἔχομεν. [17] Καὶ γνοὺς ὁ Ἰησοῦς λέγει αὐτοῖς, Τί διαλογίζεσθε ὅτι ἄρτους οὐκ ἔχετε; Οὔπω νοεῖτε, οὐδὲ συνίετε; Ἔτι πεπωρωμένην ἔχετε τὴν καρδίαν ὑμῶν; [18] Ὀφθαλμοὺς ἔχοντες οὐ βλέπετε; Καὶ ὦτα ἔχοντες οὐκ ἀκούετε; Καὶ οὐ μνημονεύετε; [19] Ὅτε τοὺς πέντε ἄρτους ἔκλασα εἰς τοὺς πεντακισχιλίους, πόσους κοφίνους πλήρεις κλασμάτων ἤρατε; Λέγουσιν αὐτῷ, Δώδεκα. [20] Ὅτε δὲ τοὺς ἑπτὰ εἰς τοὺς τετρακισχιλίους, πόσων σπυρίδων πληρώματα κλασμάτων ἤρατε; Οἱ δὲ εἶπον, Ἑπτά. [21] Καὶ ἔλεγεν αὐτοῖς, Πῶς οὐ συνίετε;

Process of Discovery

Linguistics Section

Linguistic Structure

[Transition] [14] And they had forgotten to take bread, and did not have more than one loaf in the boat with them.

[Yeshua's words][15] And He was giving orders to them, saying, "Watch out! Beware of the leaven of the Pharisees and the leaven of Herod."

[Disciples react] [16] They *began* to discuss with one another *the fact* that they had no bread.

[Yeshua's words] [17] And Jesus, aware of this, said to them, "Why do you discuss *the fact* that you have no bread? Do you not yet see or understand? Do you have a hardened heart? [18] "HAVING EYES, DO YOU NOT SEE? AND HAVING EARS, DO YOU NOT HEAR? And do you not remember, [19] when I broke the five loaves for the five thousand, how many baskets full of broken pieces you picked up?"

[Disciples react] They said to Him, "Twelve."

[Yeshua's words] [20] "When *I broke* the seven for the four thousand, how many large baskets full of broken pieces did you pick up?"

[Disciples react] And they said to Him, "Seven."

[Yeshua's final words] [21] And He was saying to them, "*Do you not yet understand?"

Discussion

This narrative is composed of Yeshua giving directions and instructions. For each item, the disciples respond to Yeshua.

Questioning the Passage

1. Who were the Pharisees?

   The Pharisees were a socio-religious movement within the Jewish state. They were not politically oriented but were preferably religiously oriented. History records that the Pharisees appeared in the year 168 BCE when the Maccabean revolt against Greek oppression. The Greek controllers of Galilee and Judea tried to Hellenize the Hebrew people. The Pharisees sect was a response to Hebrews that did not want to be Hellenized because it was considered paganism.

   The Pharisees were a part of the revolt against the Seleucid government, which controlled Galilee and Judea. The high priests had lost favor with the masses of the religious people because of their scandalous acts with the Seleucid government. The spark that started the revolution was when the offering of swine's blood was used, and the offering was made to Zeus on the altar in the temple in Jerusalem.

   The Pharisee's name means separatists. They wanted to set themselves apart, that is, separate from the Hellenize Jews that had taken over the political arm of Judea. Pharisees believed in the resurrection of the body and the life hereafter. They also believed in helping their enemies if they were in distress while traveling from place to place. Finally, they believed that enmity and anger blinded one's eyes to the reality of the day. However, love opens eyes and makes one aware of how they can improve their situation.

   The Pharisee's principal idea was to follow the Torah while adhering to their forefathers' interpretations of the writings from the time of Ezra and Nehemiah when the Hebrews had returned from Babylon. They also followed the oral law, which was the tradition of the fathers. In the Gospels, this is called the tradition of the elders. They believed in God's omnipotence, human responsibility, free will, and the soul's resurrection.[111]

2. Who was Herod?

    Herod the Great became the ruling King of Judah and the Galilee a few years before Yeshua's birth. When Herod the Great died, he divided his kingdom into four parts. The Galilee was under the control of Herod Antipas, a son of Herod the Great. Herod Antipas was known for his lavish lifestyle and disregard for Hebraic customs and traditions. Herod Antipas allowed the materialism of the world to oversee his policies. Yeshua warned His disciples not to allow the world's materialism to overshadow their spirituality and relationship to the LORD.

3. What is the significance of the number seven? (v. 20)

    The number seven symbolizes completeness. This is derived from the number of days that the LORD used to create the Heavens and the Earth.

4. What is the significance of the number twelve? (v. 19)

    This number symbolizes the nation of Israel. There were twelve tribes to Israel. Jacob had twelve sons. Each became a tribe. Since ten of the tribes were destroyed by the Assyrian invasion, the number twelve symbolizes all of humankind.

Verse Comparison of citations or proof text

1. [18] "HAVING EYES, DO YOU NOT SEE? AND HAVING EARS, DO YOU NOT HEAR?

    'Now hear this, O foolish and senseless people, who have *eyes but do not see; Who have ears but do not hear. Jeremiah 5:21

    [2] "Son of man, you live in the *midst of the *rebellious house, who *have eyes to see but do not see, ears to hear but do not hear; for they are a rebellious house. Ezekiel 12:2

---

[111] Rocco A. Errico and George M. Lamsa, *Aramaic Light on the Gospel of Matthew: a Commentary on the Teachings of Jesus from the Aramaic and Unchanged Near Eastern Customs* (Santa Fe, NM: Noohra Foundation, 2000).

This verse can be interpreted as how can one see and hear what is happening yet be blind to it? There are always people who see the corruption of the government and turn a blind eye. One reason is that they are benefitting from corruption. The religion and government of Yeshua's day were corrupt. The common people knew this, but they could not do anything about it. John the Baptist spoke out about the corruption of Herod Antipas and was executed for speaking out.

Culture Section

Discussion

The disciples of Yeshua would have known that when he spoke about the leaven of bread, it was a symbol of the teachings of the Pharisees and Sadducees. Therefore, Mark's author probably included this sentence to help the Gentile Christians understand what Yeshua was talking about.

Yeshua's referring to the feeding of the four thousand symbolizes that He is the bread of life and from the bread of life comes eternal life. If one believes in the bread of life, Yeshua, they will have everything they need to live in this world and promise to join Yeshua in the world to come. Yeshua is giving an explanation of the feeding stories to his disciples. Yeshua said that if one believes in him as God's Messiah sent to save all people, they will indeed be saved. No matter how bad things look in society, if one continues to believe in the power of Yeshua, then one will be saved. The bread of life is Yeshua. He was born in Bethlehem, the house of bread. Humans tried to take his life away from him. The result was God raised him from the dead to show all people that everything that Yeshua said was the truth about God and the Messiah.

Questioning the passage

1. What was leaven in Yeshua's day?

   After women had needed their bread, they would set aside a handful of dough as leaven to be mixed with the next day's supply of bread. This handful of bread would be placed in a large wooden basin, and hot water would be poured over it. The handful of bread dough then dissolved into the water and was mixed, creating a solution. Yeast is the leavening agent that was used. This solution would start to rise as the yeast caused fermentation to occur. Eastern people believe the increase in the leaven solution was caused by a sacred and hidden blessing, which was found in the leaven. Therefore the leavening solution was considered sacred.

When men were on good terms with each other, they would bless each other's leaven and be careful not to make the slightest remark against it. When men were fighting or disputing with one another, they would curse each other's leaven. Common phrases are statements like "he has grown up eating bread made of bad leaven" and "is leaven his blood" were common phrases. If a man committed murder or was a known sinner or a known blasphemer, his family leaven would be considered defiled. No one in the town would borrow the leaven or even touch it if you belong to such a man.

The term leaven in this narrative is allegorical and means teaching. When people talked about the leaven of others, they could also be talking about the government's policies or even about specific people. Teaching is like leaven because it permeates human behavior and attitudes so that the leaven spreads throughout the bread dough.

Yeshua said that the leaven of the Pharisees was evil leaven and corrupt. The Pharisees had substituted some of their own beliefs in place of God's word. This meant that social teachings were taking precedence over divine teachings. It was believed that many of these Pharisee doctrines fermented in the Jewish mind to such an extent that many of the people had lost their spiritual vision and understanding of the Lord.

Many Pharisees prayed to act a certain way, but their hands were smeared with the blood of the innocent. In other words, they did not walk in their walk or talk their talk. Yeshua did not want any of his disciples to be misguided by the corrupt teachings of the Pharisees. Yeshua ignored the doctrine of the elders, and he questioned all religious notions about God. Yeshua did not teach any theology. Instead, he talked about the messianic political and religious hopes that would come when the Messiah would be with the people when the messianic age would occur.[112]

---

[112] IBID.

Thoughts

It is notable that when a given number of people are brought together to form an organization, a core set of beliefs and behaviors develop. When 50 people, or 150 people, or 350 people, or over 500 people, come together to create an organization, the core beliefs and behaviors are the same from individual units to individual units. For example, a church whose number is 50 members or less has the same core beliefs and behaviors as other churches of the same number. The same occurs at the 150, 350, and 500 levels. The same thing happens in the church. A United Methodist Church of 50 or fewer Sunday attendees develops the same beliefs and behaviors as any other UMC church of 50 persons or less anywhere else in the same country. The development of a core set of beliefs and behavior happens naturally. There is no magic formula to prevent this development of the organization; it just happens. As a person moves from church to church of the same Sunday attendance size, one will be able to note the sameness between churches.

Reflections

The Pharisees started as a sect with a noble and perhaps a divine purpose. They were organized to resist the Hellenization of the Holy Land. The Seleucids wanted to change Galilee and Judah into a paradise of Greek Hellenism. The Pharisee sect was formed in 168 B.C.E. to combat this infringement on the people of the LORD. They were very successful in helping many Hebrews from losing their love of the LORD and turning to the Greek pagan Gods. Unfortunately, as the sect grew, corruption entered its core. Corruption can enter the organization when an organization learns that it can use its clout to oppress its people. It does not matter how large the organization is or might become. Corruption accompanies the organization once people learn that they can control other people by their wills. The goodwill of the Pharisees disappeared when they learned that they held a strong influence over the people they initially tried to save. Corruption took the place of goodwill.

Unfortunately, this can be seen in all of human history. The church is no exception. It started with the noble purpose of spreading the Gospel of Jesus Christ. Unfortunately, over the centuries, it developed its own set of rules and regulations that are mainly outside the scope of the true meaning of the Gospel. The Reformation, which started in 1517, is a prime example of the people striking out against the Catholic Church's corruption. Today in 2021, there are numerous church denominations, all with their charters and books outside of the Bible, which define its members' beliefs and accepted behavior and allow for its members' exploitation.

Jesus warns us not to fall into the same trap that the Pharisees and the Sadducees did. These were, at one time, reputable organizations that fell from grace. The LORD created each disciple of Jesus Christ to serve the LORD through His Messiah. Each disciple must ask themselves the question, "Are you doing that which is pleasing to the LORD?"

MARK 8:22-26

Language

New American Standard 1995	Koine Greek
[22] And they came to Bethsaida. And they brought a blind man to Jesus and implored Him to touch him. [23] Taking the blind man by the hand, He brought him out of the village; and after spitting on his eyes and laying His hands on him, He asked him, "Do you see anything?" [24] And he looked up and said, "I see men, for I see *them* like trees, walking around." [25] Then again He laid His hands on his eyes; and he looked intently and was restored, and *began* to see everything clearly. [26] And He sent him to his home, saying, "Do not even enter the village."	[22] Καὶ ἔρχεται εἰς Βηθσαιδάν. Καὶ φέρουσιν αὐτῷ τυφλόν, καὶ παρακαλοῦσιν αὐτὸν ἵνα αὐτοῦ ἅψηται. [23] Καὶ ἐπιλαβόμενος τῆς χειρὸς τοῦ τυφλοῦ, ἐξήγαγεν αὐτὸν ἔξω τῆς κώμης· καὶ πτύσας εἰς τὰ ὄμματα αὐτοῦ, ἐπιθεὶς τὰς χεῖρας αὐτῷ, ἐπηρώτα αὐτὸν εἴ τι βλέπει. [24] Καὶ ἀναβλέψας ἔλεγεν, Βλέπω τοὺς ἀνθρώπους ὅτι ὡς δένδρα ὁρῶ περιπατοῦντας. [25] Εἶτα πάλιν ἐπέθηκεν τὰς χεῖρας ἐπὶ τοὺς ὀφθαλμοὺς αὐτοῦ, καὶ ἐποίησεν αὐτὸν ἀναβλέψαι. Καὶ ἀποκατεστάθη, καὶ ἐνέβλεψεν τηλαυγῶς ἅπαντας. [26] Καὶ ἀπέστειλεν αὐτὸν εἰς τὸν οἶκον αὐτοῦ, λέγων, Μηδὲ εἰς τὴν κώμην εἰσέλθῃς, μηδὲ εἴπῃς τινι ἐν τῇ κώμῃ.

Process of Discovery

Linguistics Section

Linguistic Structure

A [22] And they came to Bethsaida. And they brought a blind man to Jesus and implored Him to touch him.

> **B** [23] Taking the blind man by the hand, He brought him out of the village; and after spitting on his eyes and laying His hands on him, He asked him, "Do you see anything?"

> **B'** [24] And he looked up and said, "I see men, for I see *them* like trees, walking around." [25] Then again He laid His hands on his eyes; and he looked intently and was restored, and *began* to see everything clearly.

A' [26] And He sent him to his home, saying, "Do not even enter the village."

Discussion

Mark's narratives are short and to the point. In this case, healing was done for a blind man. Yeshua had to perform the healing twice. In the other Gospels, Yeshua never has to do it twice.

Questioning the Passage

1. Why did Yeshua have to leave Bethsaida to heal the blind man? (v. 23)

   Yeshua took the man outside the village to avoid a crowd surrounding Him. Eastern people generally came together to watch a healer. Many were just curious, while others could be enemies. Yeshua wanted to avoid a crowd. It is possible that Yeshua would not have felt comfortable spitting on the man. Spitting on a person was considered a great insult. However, only holy men could use spit as a healing tool.[113]

2. Why did it take two applications to heal the man? (v. 24)

   The author may have been using this narrative to foreshadow Peter's confession, which follows this narrative. Even though Peter exclaimed that Yeshua was the Messiah, he was

---

[113] Rocco A. Errico, George M. Lamsa, *Aramaic Light on the Gospels of Mark and Luke: a Commentary on the Teachings of Jesus from the Aramaic and Unchanged Near Eastern Customs* (Smyrna, GA: Noohra Foundation, 2001).

not wholly convinced. It was going to take the resurrection of Yeshua for Peter to be fully convinced. This logical argument could be applied to Yeshua's disciples. Their blindness to the Messiah had been half removed when Yeshua was with them and completely removed after Yeshua's resurrection.[114]

3. Why did Yeshua tell the man not to enter the village? (v. 26)

Yeshua did not want the healed man to go back into Bethsaida and tell people about his healing. The verse implies that the blind man lived outside of the village. Yeshua did this for most of His healing in that he did not want His work to be shared. Even though this was His desire, His fame for healing spread quickly throughout Galilee and Judea.

Biblical Locations

1. Bethsaida was formally a fishing village at the mouth of the Jordan River. Herod the Great rebuilt the village and upgraded it to become a Hellenistic city and renamed the village Bethsaida Julius.[115]

Linguistic Echoes

Yeshua adopted the theme of healing the deaf and the blind from the prophet Isaiah.

> On that day the deaf will hear words of a book, and out of *their* gloom and darkness the eyes of the blind will see. Isaiah 29:18

> Then the eyes of the blind will be opened And the ears of the deaf will be unstopped. Isaiah 35:5

> Bring out the people who are blind, even though they have eyes, and the deaf, even though they have ears. Isaiah 43:8

The healing stories would have reminded the people about the prophet Isaiah. The prophet Isaiah was a sign of a new order in the LORD's world. Thus, Yeshua is using healing to tell the people that new order was coming. This new order was a spiritual revolution by the establishment of the kingdom of Heaven.

---

[114] *The New Interpreter's Bible: General Articles & Introduction, Commentary, & Reflections for Each Book of the Bible, Including the Apocryphal/Deuterocanonical Books* (Nashville: Abingdon Press, 1994).

[115] Ched Myers, *Binding the Strong Man a Political Reading of Mark's Story of Jesus* (Maryknoll, NY: Orbis Books, 1988).

Culture Section

Questioning the passage

1. Why did Yeshua use spit? (v. 23)

    In Yeshua's day, spitting was often a way of repudiating disease and people's belief in sickness. The clay with spit did not heal the man. Yeshua did the healing. The clay and spit were to symbolize the repudiation of blindness. People needed to see signs in order to believe that the healing had occurred.

Thoughts

Many readers of this narrative will see it as an insult to Yeshua. Why? Because Yeshua had to repeat the healing process twice. Instead of viewing this as an insult, the question to be asked is why twice? The narrative is a foreshadowing of what was to happen with Peter and the disciples. Yeshua had removed some of their spiritual blindness. They may have viewed Yeshua as the Messiah, but they're always seemed to be some doubt. Even after the resurrection, Thomas doubted that it was Yeshua. Mark's author could be saying that it takes two experiences to accept Yeshua truly.

Reflections

In the vain of a double experience to accept Yeshua as the Messiah, it reflects on the "born again" groups of the past and the present. The Puritans believed that a follower of Yeshua had to be born again. Thus they had two experiences. The problem with this idea was that most of the second-generation Puritans did not have the "born again" experience, which led to the dissolving of the Puritans.

Perhaps the double experience is what is missing in today's churches. How many people say they believe in Yeshua? However, their experience is because their parents had them baptized and perhaps confirmed in the church. Perhaps they attended worship now and then, usually Easter and Christmas. So many people who call themselves Christians really need that second experience. The church should call upon Yeshua to send a second experience to Christians around the world. This would certainly change the direction of the dying church into a living growing church.

MARK 8:27-30

Language

New American Standard 1995	Koine Greek
[27] Jesus went out, along with His disciples, to the villages of Caesarea Philippi; and on the way He questioned His disciples, saying to them, "Who do people say that I am?" [28] They told Him, saying, "John the Baptist; and others *say* Elijah; but others, one of the prophets." [29] And He *continued* by questioning them, "But who do you say that I am?" Peter answered and said to Him, "You are the Christ." [30] And He warned them to tell no one about Him.	[27] Καὶ ἐξῆλθεν ὁ Ἰησοῦς καὶ οἱ μαθηταὶ αὐτοῦ εἰς τὰς κώμας Καισαρείας τῆς Φιλίππου· καὶ ἐν τῇ ὁδῷ ἐπηρώτα τοὺς μαθητὰς αὐτοῦ, λέγων αὐτοῖς, Τίνα με λέγουσιν οἱ ἄνθρωποι εἶναι; [28] Οἱ δὲ ἀπεκρίθησαν, Ἰωάννην τὸν βαπτιστήν· καὶ ἄλλοι Ἠλίαν, ἄλλοι δὲ ἕνα τῶν προφητῶν. [29] Καὶ αὐτὸς λέγει αὐτοῖς, Ὑμεῖς δὲ τίνα με λέγετε εἶναι; Ἀποκριθεὶς δὲ ὁ Πέτρος λέγει αὐτῷ, Σὺ εἶ ὁ χριστός. [30] Καὶ ἐπετίμησεν αὐτοῖς, ἵνα μηδενὶ

Process of Discovery

Linguistics Section

Linguistic Structure

A [27] Jesus went out, along with His disciples, to the villages of Caesarea Philippi; and on the way He questioned His disciples, saying to them, "Who do people say that I am?"

> **B** [28] They told Him, saying, "John the Baptist; and others *say* Elijah; but others, one of the prophets."

A' [29] And He *continued* by questioning them, "But who do you say that I am?"

> **B'** Peter answered and said to Him, "You are the Christ." [30] And He warned them to tell no one about Him.

Discussion

The two questions and answers form an A-B-A'-B' chiasm.

Questioning the Passage[116]

1. What was Peter's role in this narrative? (v. 27-30)

   Shimon was Peter's name. It is derived from the root word "shm" which means to hear. Shimon means "one who is keen, sharp, and perceptive." It was a common name during Yeshua's day. Shimon's friends had given him the nickname "Kepa" because instead of being quick-witted and alert, his name implies, he was slow in his comprehension of matters and situations. "Kepa" metaphorically means "protection, shelter, and support." When Yeshua asked who He was, Kepa answered that He was the Messiah. Because of his confession, Yeshua calls him Peter because he was a supporter of Yeshua as the Messiah, and he offered the truth.[117]

---

[116] (The questions and answers offered are for discussion purposes. You may have different questions and answers. Remember all questions are valid and all answers must be defendable from Scripture. This applies to this section and to the Culture Section.)

[117] Rocco A. Errico and George M. Lamsa, *Aramaic Light on the Gospel of Matthew: a Commentary on the Teachings of Jesus from the Aramaic and Unchanged Near Eastern Customs* (Santa Fe, NM: Noohra Foundation, 2000).

Biblical Locations

1. Caesarea Philippi – "Καισάρεια ἡ Φιλίππου *C. Philippi*, a city at the foot of Mt. Hermon, once known as Paneas, rebuilt by Philip the Tetrarch and made an important city; he named it Caesarea in honor of Tiberius Caesar"[118]

[119]

Culture Section

Questioning the passage

1. What was Yeshua looking for when He asked His disciples who He was? (v. 27)

    In Yeshua's day, when a man began a religious career or became prominent, he became the subject of public discussion. People strived to learn all they could say about him. They wanted to know his ancestry, qualifications, and mission. Yeshua had heard the rumors about Him and that people were debating what His role in the community was. Yeshua wanted to know what His disciples thought about Him. The Aramaic text reads, "Whom do

---

[118] BDAG from Accordance Bible Software V. 13.

[119] "Caesarea Philippi (Banias)-From The God Pan To The God-Man," 2. Caesarea Philippi (Banias)-From The God Pan To The God-Man | Bible.org, accessed November 20, 2019, https://bible.org/seriespage/2-caesarea-philippi-banias-god-pan-god-man.

men say that I am, the Son of man?" To be a "Son of Man" in Aramaic meant to be an ordinary person. To be ordinary meant that the person held no credentials.[120]

2. Why would people believe that Elijah would come before the Messiah? (v. 28)

The Pharisees and Sadducees taught that Elijah, Jeremiah, or some other old prophet would come to prepare the way for the Messiah. In Yeshua's day, kings, princes, and high government officials sent their emissaries ahead of them to clean the streets, thus preparing the way for the official.

The Pharisees believed that the Messiah could not come and walk on the streets of Jerusalem until the pagan Romans were removed because they ruled the streets. They believed the great prophet would come to prepare the way, which meant to overthrow the Gentile rule so that the Messiah could arrive.[121]

Culture and Linguistics Section

Yeshua took His disciples to Caesarea Philippi, which was a holy place for the pagan religion of the Gentiles. The Grotto of Pan, the Lord of the Underworld, was located in this city. The people of Yeshua's day believed that once one died and was placed in Sheol (the grave), they no longer had any communication with the LORD. They believed that the LORD did not influence the dead. Yeshua needed to make them understand that the LORD is God over everything and everyone. The LORD created all things and had control even over Sheol. The Grotto of Pan represented Sheol to the disciples.

Here, Yeshua has a discussion with His disciples about who He was. Rumors had run ramped around the Galilee and Judea as to who this new religious man was. In chapter eleven, John's disciples came before Yeshua and said they had heard about the works of the Messiah. Yeshua

---

[120] Rocco A. Errico and George M. Lamsa, *Aramaic Light on the Gospel of Matthew: a Commentary on the Teachings of Jesus from the Aramaic and Unchanged Near Eastern Customs* (Santa Fe, NM: Noohra Foundation, 2000).
[121] IBID.

told them to return to John and tell him what they saw. However, Yeshua did not admit to being the Messiah.

Peter's revelation that Yeshua was the Messiah did not come from man but rather was an inspiration from the LORD. Peter's name was Shimon, which meant that he was to be keen and sharp in thought. However, Peter was not, and that is why he received the nickname Kepa. The revelation of the LORD that Yeshua was the Messiah changed Peter. He became sharp and insightful and worthy of the name Shimon. Verse eighteen says that Yeshua calls Shimon Peter and implies that Shimon has received this new name. Shimon is referred to as Peter in several places in Matthew's Gospel before chapter sixteen.

The god Pan was believed to be the master of the underworld. The concept of Satan in Hebraic thought was in its infancy, but there was a connection between the two. The Grotto of Pan was viewed as a place of evil. The primary tool of evil was the lies that Pan, or Satan, told people. To get people to worship Pan or Satan, they had to be brainwashed into believing a lie.

Thoughts

If a non-believer approached you and asked about Yeshua (Jesus) Christ, could you give an adequate answer? Peter's answer was short and sweet, "You are the Messiah." For the Disciples, this answer contained quite a lot of information. The people of Yeshua's day knew exactly what it meant to be called the Messiah. Likewise, the Hebrew people studied their Torah and Prophets. They knew precisely what they were looking for in the LORD's Messiah. Their understanding of the Messiah is different then what the church espouses today. So, can you adequately explain Yeshua? It will strengthen your faith to be able to answer that question.

Reflections

Who is Yeshua? Most Christians offer an easy answer. He is God. What exactly does that mean? Can we define God? For if we do, we are actually placing God in a box. By defining God, we are determining what God can and cannot do. It is incorrect to try to define God. In the Kabbalah, God is known as Ein Sof. God is considered everything, and God is considered nothing. Without the power of Ein Sof, the Universe and we would not exist. Therefore Ein Sof is the God of nothing. However, Ein Sof sent His power to create the Universe. This makes God everything. In the Kabbalah Yeshua, the Messiah is considered a spiritual entity that resides in the Tree of Life. There will always be discussions about which Sefirot of the Tree of Life Yeshua is from. Regardless of which of the ten Sefirot contains Yeshua Spirit this passage clearly states that the Disciples had determined that He was the Messiah, the special Spirit that the LORD would send to usher in a new World.

MARK 8:31-33

Language

New American Standard 1995	Koine Greek
[31] And He began to teach them that the Son of Man must suffer many things and be rejected by the elders and the chief priests and the scribes, and be killed, and after three days rise again. [32] And He was stating the matter plainly. And Peter took Him aside and began to rebuke Him. [33] But turning around and seeing His disciples, He rebuked Peter and said, "Get behind Me, Satan; for you are not setting your mind on God's interests, but man's."	[31] Καὶ ἤρξατο διδάσκειν αυτούς, ὅτι δεῖ τὸν υἱὸν τοῦ ἀνθρώπου πολλὰ παθεῖν, καὶ ἀποδοκιμασθῆναι ἀπὸ τῶν πρεσβυτέρων καὶ τῶν ἀρχιερέων καὶ τῶν γραμματέων, καὶ ἀποκτανθῆναι, καὶ μετὰ τρεῖς ἡμέρας ἀναστῆναι [32] καὶ παρρησίᾳ τὸν λόγον ἐλάλει. Καὶ προσλαβόμενος αὐτὸν ὁ Πέτρος ἤρξατο ἐπιτιμᾶν αὐτῷ. [33] Ὁ δὲ ἐπιστραφείς, καὶ ἰδὼν τοὺς μαθητὰς αὐτοῦ, ἐπετίμησεν τῷ Πέτρῳ, λέγων, Ὕπαγε ὀπίσω μου, Σατανᾶ ὅτι οὐ φρονεῖς τὰ τοῦ θεοῦ, ἀλλὰ τὰ τῶν ἀνθρώπων.

Process of Discovery

Linguistics Section

Linguistic Structure

A [31] And He began to teach them that the Son of Man must suffer many things and be rejected by the elders and the chief priests and the scribes, and be killed, and after three days rise again.

> **B** [32] And He was stating the matter plainly. And Peter took Him aside and began to rebuke Him.

A' [33] But turning around and seeing His disciples, He rebuked Peter and said, "Get behind Me, Satan; for you are not setting your mind on God's interests, but man's."

Discussion

This short narrative creates a chiasm based on who spoke.

Questioning the Passage

1. Why did Yeshua talk about His death? (general question)

    There is a scholarly belief that the early Christian communities needed to create precise stories that Yeshua told His disciples about His life and death. It was well known from history that prophets died in Jerusalem. Kings and princes did not like being told that they were violating the Laws of the LORD. The LORD commissioned the prophets of old to bring the words of repentance to Kings and princes. The usual response from the authority figures was to put the prophetic messenger to death. The King and princes might acknowledge that their actions were against the Word of the LORD, but few wanted to be told what they had to do.

    Yeshua was no different. During His life, He learned what happened to John the Baptist. John told Herod Antipas that marrying his brother's wife was against the Laws of the LORD. Instead of repenting, Herod had John killed for speaking out against the King. The idea of killing off the LORD's prophet was still in play in Yeshua's day.

Yeshua went to Jerusalem to tell the religious leaders that the LORD was not pleased with them. History says that Yeshua would suffer and die because of the message that He needed to bring because He would have been viewed as a prophet.

2. What did Yeshua mean about Peter's interest and not that of the LORD's? (v. 33)

Yeshua believed that Peter's words were instigated by Peter's desired not to lose his best friend, mentor, and religious leader. Peter received the divine revelation that Yeshua was the Messiah. In the following verse, he is told that his Messiah had to die to fulfill the LORD's plan. Acknowledging the LORD's plan was very difficult for Peter to handle. Peter's reaction was a natural human reaction, and that was to save his friend. Yeshua had to tell Peter that the LORD's plan had to be implemented. The human plan that came into Peter's mind was not the answer.

Culture Section

Discussion

Yeshua's disciples believed that all the Gentile and pagan kingdoms would bow down to the Davidic Kingdom when the Messiah arrived. The new Hebraic Kingdom would conquer all the Gentile kingdoms and end the annihilation threat since Abraham walked the Earth. Besides, the Isaiah prophecy about the suffering Messiah was unknown to them. So when Yeshua spoke of His suffering and death at the hands of the religious leadership in Jerusalem, the disciples became concerned and alarmed. Peter did not understand that Yeshua had to suffer a humiliating death so that the gates of Heaven would be opened to the LORD's people.[122]

Yeshua taught His disciples about the Kingdom of Heaven, not the Davidic Kingdom. Yeshua was probably surprised at Peter's response, and that drew some anger. In His anger, Yeshua said to Peter to get behind Him and called him Satan. However, as we call the personification of evil today, Satan had a different name in Yeshua's day, which is found in Matthew's Gospel. That name

---

[122] Rocco A. Errico and George M. Lamsa, *Aramaic Light on the Gospel of Matthew: a Commentary on the Teachings of Jesus from the Aramaic and Unchanged Near Eastern Customs* (Santa Fe, NM: Noohra Foundation, 2000).

is Beelzebul. The question is, if Yeshua were calling Peter Satan, even in anger, He would have used the Word Beelzebul.

The name Satan which is derived from the Hebrew word שָׂטָן has become almost universal in languages around the world to mean the personification of evil, the Devil, Satan. However, in its original Hebraic שָׂטָן and Aramaic, it has a different meaning. Since Yeshua would have been speaking Aramaic when talking to His disciples, the examination of satan in its Aramaic form is necessary. The Word *satan* is derived from the root word *sata*. *Sata* means "to mislead, miss the mark, slip, slide, or to deviate from one's course."[123]

From Yeshua's point of view, Peter was trying to mislead and deviate Yeshua from the divine course that He had to follow. Yeshua was making it clear that Peter and the other disciples did not understand the real purpose of the Messiah and that the traditional view of the Messiah was not the path of the Messiah. They were not aware of the Suffering Servant prophecy of the Messiah. Indeed they did not want the Messiah to be killed because of their understanding of the Messiah. The disciples expected Yeshua to rid them of the Roman oppressors. Yeshua must have thought that He communicated the actual path of the Messiah as the Suffering Servant and was surprised that Peter did not understand it. Yeshua said to Peter to get out of His way and not deviate Yeshua from the divine path.

YESHUA DID NOT CALL PETER SATAN!

The disciples did not know the Suffering Servant path of the Messiah. The incorrect understanding of the Hebrew word שָׂטָן, which is the same Word in Aramaic, is where the current church interpretation of what Yeshua said to Peter originated. As was said earlier, if Yeshua wanted to call Peter Satan, He would have said: "Get behind me, Beelzebub!"

---

[123] IBID.

The problem with the mistranslation of שָׂטָן starts with the Koine Greek. The translation used in the Greek is Σατανᾶ. From the Koine Greek, the name Satan spread out to the translations of Matthew's Gospel. The English translation in the King James version is Satan. From that point on, English translations of Matthew's Gospel say, "Get behind me, Satan." Church tradition is dominant with Bible publishers. Publishers are in business to make money and not necessarily to offer the proper translations. Since church tradition out trumps the actual biblical text in so many Christianity areas, it is not surprising that it is done here.

Until the church is ready to return to the original meaning of Matthew's Gospel, this mistranslation and others like it will continue to be made.

Thoughts

Peter thought that he knew what the LORD's plan was for the restoration of Israel. When Yeshua said that he would die at the hands of the Hebraic leadership, Peter was compelled to say, "not going to happen." How many people today believe that they know the LORD's plan? Many Christians say that they know that they are going to Heaven. How do they know that? In the case of Peter, he believed that he knew the LORD's plan for the Messiah. It turned out that he did not. So, how does one discover the LORD's actual plan for their life? That is a part of the discernment that is necessary to discover the plan. In ancient days prayer was the way to discover the plan. Prayer was a time to be quiet and listen to the voice of the LORD telling His people what He wanted to be done. Today people offer their words of prayer and rarely sit back and listen to the LORD. Listening to the LORD takes time and patience. The needed patience to wait for the LORD's answer is not an integral part of society today.

Reflections

The idea of the stumbling block is in several places in the Christian Scriptures. Sometimes a stumbling block is created when a person believes that they have the only meaning of the Scripture. Each denomination of the church preaches that it has the only and correct interpretation of the

Scripture. What is seen in this short narrative is that the church can have an incorrect interpretation? The mistranslation of the Hebrew and Aramaic word *satan* as the personification of evil, Satan, made Yeshua's followers believe that he called Peter Satan when He did not. What this shows is that the church has locked the interpretation of Scripture, and for centuries anyone who challenged the church interpretation was called heretics and put to death in many different ways. The idea of questioning the Scripture for a deeper understanding is not allowed. Those days are coming to an end. How could Yeshua call His number one disciple, Satan? Well, the church said so. The prevailing belief for 2000 years is that the church must be right. In this case, the church is incorrect. However, many Christians may read the case presented that Yeshua did not call Peter Satan and will reject it before even reading it. Why? The church has learned over its 2000 years how to enforce its beliefs on Christians. Today, Christians should arise and question everything the church says to be the truth, no matter the denomination. Searching and discovering the original meaning of Scripture is paramount today so that the questions of the younger generation can be answered.

MARK 8:34-38

Language

New American Standard 1995	Koine Greek
[34] And He summoned the crowd with His disciples, and said to them, "If anyone wishes to come after Me, he must deny himself, and take up his cross and follow Me. [35] "For whoever wishes to save his life will lose it, but whoever loses his life for My sake and the gospel's will save it. [36] "For what does it profit a man to gain the whole world, and forfeit his soul? [37] "For what will a man give in exchange for his soul? [38] "For whoever is ashamed of Me and My words in this adulterous and sinful generation, the Son of Man will also be ashamed of him when He comes in the glory of His Father with the holy angels."	[34] Καὶ προσκαλεσάμενος τὸν ὄχλον σὺν τοῖς μαθηταῖς αὐτοῦ, εἶπεν αὐτοῖς, Ὅστις θέλει ὀπίσω μου ἀκολουθεῖν, ἀπαρνησάσθω ἑαυτόν, καὶ ἀράτω τὸν σταυρὸν αὐτοῦ, καὶ ἀκολουθείτω μοι. [35] Ὃς γὰρ ἂν θέλῃ τὴν ψυχὴν αὐτοῦ σῶσαι, ἀπολέσει αὐτήν· ὃς δ' ἂν ἀπολέσῃ τὴν ἑαυτοῦ ψυχὴν ἕνεκεν ἐμοῦ καὶ τοῦ εὐαγγελίου, οὗτος σώσει αὐτήν. [36] Τί γὰρ ὠφελήσει ἄνθρωπον, ἐὰν κερδήσῃ τὸν κόσμον ὅλον, καὶ ζημιωθῇ τὴν ψυχὴν αὐτοῦ; [37] Ἢ τί δώσει ἄνθρωπος ἀντάλλαγμα τῆς ψυχῆς αὐτοῦ; [38] Ὃς γὰρ ἐὰν ἐπαισχυνθῇ με καὶ τοὺς ἐμοὺς λόγους ἐν τῇ γενεᾷ ταύτῃ τῇ μοιχαλίδι καὶ ἁμαρτωλῷ, καὶ ὁ υἱὸς τοῦ ἀνθρώπου ἐπαισχυνθήσεται αὐτόν, ὅταν ἔλθῃ ἐν τῇ δόξῃ τοῦ πατρὸς αὐτοῦ μετὰ τῶν ἀγγέλων τῶν ἁγίων.

Process of Discovery

Linguistics Section

Linguistic Structure

[Yeshua's sayings] [34] And He summoned the crowd with His disciples, and said to them, "If anyone wishes to come after Me, he must deny himself, and take up his cross and follow Me. [35] "For whoever wishes to save his life will lose it, but whoever loses his life for My sake and the gospel's will save it. [36] "For what does it profit a man to gain the whole world, and forfeit his soul? [37] "For what will a man give in exchange for his soul? [38] "For whoever is ashamed of Me and My words in this adulterous and sinful generation, the Son of Man will also be ashamed of him when He comes in the glory of His Father with the holy angels."

Discussion

This passage consists of five statements that Yeshua made to his disciples.

Questioning the Passage

1. Why would Yeshua say that one had to take up the cross to be a disciple? (v. 34)

   Crucifixion was the "Suffocation, loss of body fluids, and multiple organ failure. It was not pleasant, but for those with a strong constitution, take a deep breath and read on. "The weight of the body pulling down on the arms makes breathing extremely difficult," says Jeremy Ward, a physiologist at King's College London. Besides, the heart and lungs would stop working as the blood drained through wounds. Crucifixion was invented by the Persians in 300-400BC and developed, during Roman times, into a punishment for the most serious of criminals. The upright wooden cross was the most common technique, and the time victims took to die would depend on how they were crucified."[124]

   Crucifixion was the execution of criminals of the state. The Roman government used it for most executions in Judea and the Galilee during Yeshua's time. Crucifixion was not new to the Near East. Yeshua knew that if he was to be executed for his preaching about the kingdom of heaven, his execution would be on a cross. He also knew that if his disciples

---

[124] Alok Jha, "How Did Crucifixion Kill?," The Guardian (Guardian News and Media, April 8, 2004), https://www.theguardian.com/science/2004/apr/08/thisweekssciencequestions.

were true disciples and followed him, they too would be executed. That execution would be on a cross.

There has been some debate as to whether Yeshua could have said, "pick up your cross." The question was, how would Yeshua know that he was going to die on the cross? That debate should be closed when one realizes that crucifixion was a form of execution for almost 400 years in the Middle East before Yeshua also knew that he was usually executed when a prophet went to Jerusalem to confront the king or religious leaders. He also knew that his disciples would be viewed as prophets and executed in the same manner that he was.

2. What does it mean that the Son of Man will come in glory with his father and the angels? (v. 38)
Angels are spirits whose primary purpose is to bring messages from the Lord to humankind and to bring God's counsel everywhere. Angels' wings symbolize God's omnipresence and the presence of the Holy Spirit.

Yeshua's teaching was rejected by the religious leaders of His time, and was crucified with criminals. From a practical point of view, Yeshua was a defeated man. However, this statement by Yeshua says that his death would be the beginning of his mission. His death symbolizes the end of his mission on earth, but that was not the end of the overall mission. Yeshua's mission was to begin to establish the kingdom of heaven on earth. His disciples would carry this mission up to and including today.

In the Near East, when a man suffers defeat or loss of his political or economic power, it is said that he is dead. When a man succeeds, they say, he has come back again. Yeshua's followers knew that he would return in glory in the hearts of the believers. The believers in Yeshua's day and the believers that were to be born in the future no this party of the story. When a person accepts Yeshua in their heart as Lord and Savior, then the glory of Yeshua has returned. Yeshua's "second coming."

As the kingdom of heaven is established on Earth, it can be said that Yeshua has returned. It is possible that this misunderstanding of the Semitic words "he has come back again."

The idea of the second coming of Yeshua will not be a physical one as described in the book of the Revelation but rather a spiritual return. When the kingdom of heaven has spread throughout the Earth, Yeshua has returned. He has not returned physically, but he has returned spiritually.

When the kingdom of heaven is established on Earth, Yeshua will have been successful in his mission to bring God's love and grace to all people. Yeshua will then live in the hearts of believers, and we can say that his glory has returned. Yeshua also told us that he will always be with us. That means that through the Holy Spirit, we can feel his presence with us and if we are following His ways and words, then His memory is always with us. As long as we are following the ways of Yeshua as laid out in the Gospel, then Yeshua is always with us.

The establishment of the kingdom of heaven has brushed up against the secular world throughout the centuries. One could look at the battles that are described in the book of Revelation as a battle between secularists and the religious. Today in the United States, the battle is between the secularists who want to push God out of the public sector and the religious peoples in the country who demand that God must remain. The United States was formed under a Christian Judeo moral and ethics base. The laws of the country, including the Constitution, were built on the laws of God.

Today that original structure is being attacked by secularists who desire to take God out of the picture. When God and Yeshua are removed from the culture, the morality and ethics established by God's laws are removed. The culture would then revert to the ways culture word during the Roman Empire. The ethics of civility and sexuality are being replaced by secularists who do not wish to live by the Bible's restrictions on one's life. They want the return of sexual promiscuity and other forms of behavior that are not in line with the Bible. That is the battle that we are facing right now that corresponds to the battle we find in Revelation.

The book of Revelation says that Yeshua would return with an army one day. That is based on the two Messiah theology from Zechariah chapter nine verse nine. The first appearance of the Messiah was to be the Messiah, son of Joseph. This Messiah's task was to establish the beginning of the Kingdom of Heaven and the restoration of pure spirituality to the LORD. The Messiah would then return as Messiah, son of David, who would rid the world of the remaining secularists who do not believe in the LORD and use arms and force. The reason for the second return of the Messiah is because it is easy for secularists to hide under the blankets of being religious when, Indeed, they are not religious. These people can be seen today, especially politicians who say they believe in the Bible and the ways of Jesus Christ, but then the laws and actions that they act upon while in their political office are the opposite of that.

The second coming of Yeshua will not be this physical return but is instead the full establishment of the Kingdom of Heaven on Earth. When every heart has the glory of the LORD in it, Yeshua will have fully returned. There may need to be some intervention by Yeshua to make this finally occur. The world has been waiting for Yeshua's return for 2000 years. A question that arises is, why has he not returned? He is not returned because it is up to his disciples to spread the Kingdom of Heaven on Earth, thus bringing the glory of God in Yeshua into every heart. Viewing it this way, the return of Yeshua is within each of his disciples. This is the view of the second coming using the original language and culture of Yeshua's day.

The church's view of the second coming of Yeshua is that he will physically return and cause some revolution that would cause all wickedness and evil to be removed from the Earth. However, it is up to the the disciples of Yeshua to make this happen. It is too easy to relinquish the responsibility of spreading the word of the gospel and in the idea of loving each other. It is evident in this verse of Matthew's Gospel that it is our responsibility to bring the Kingdom of Heaven sufficiently to Earth, and thus Yeshua will return because his mission will have succeeded. "He has come back," is the expression used in Yeshua day that His mission was successful. Yeshua's church will make His mission successful, and thus he will have come back.

Thoughts

Yeshua spoke about the need to do what is right by the LORD's law so that the soul would be saved. According to Yeshua, the soul is more important to save then the body. To be a disciple of Yeshua can mean to give up the material world and possibly one's life. In Yeshua's day, new disciples did give up materially and physically. Anyone who worked for the Roman government lost their job when it was discovered that they came into discipleship to Yeshua. Many of the first Christians were killed for joining the faith. Today the cost in many countries is not very high. In those countries, the number of disciples of Yeshua is shrinking. In countries where the risk is high, many disciples are growing. What are you willing to give up for Yeshua?

Reflections

The Second Coming is the idea that Yeshua would come again in the flesh. The book of Revelation makes its argument that this is a truth. However, when the phrase "for the Son of Man is going to come in the glory" is an Aramaic phrase, "my mission will become a success in the future." This original meaning says that the mission that Yeshua started and many believed that He had failed, would become a successful movement. The Yeshua movement became a sweeping world movement. Thus the mission of Yeshua became a success. Yeshua did return! The mission of the creation of the Kingdom of Heaven on Earth did take off. Yeshua did, does, and will always come into the hearts of those who would allow Him. The "second coming" is not a specific date on the calendar. Instead, it is a process that will terminate when every person on the Earth knows and loves the LORD and Yeshua.

MARK 9:1-13

Language

New American Standard 1995	Koine Greek
[1] And Jesus was saying to them, "Truly I say to you, there are some of those who are standing here who will not taste death until they see the kingdom of God after it has come with power." [2] Six days later, Jesus took with Him Peter and James and John, and brought them up on a high mountain by themselves. And He was transfigured before them; [3] and His garments became radiant and exceedingly white, as no launderer on earth can whiten them. [4] Elijah appeared to them along with Moses; and they were talking with Jesus. [5] Peter said to Jesus, "Rabbi, it is good for us to be here; let us make three tabernacles, one for You, and one for Moses, and one for Elijah." [6] For he did not know what to answer; for they became terrified. [7] Then a cloud formed, overshadowing them, and a voice came out of the cloud, "This is My beloved Son, listen to Him!" [8] All at once they looked around and saw no one with them anymore, except Jesus alone. [9] As they were coming down from the mountain, He gave them orders not to relate to anyone what they had seen, until the Son of Man rose from the dead. [10] They seized upon that statement, discussing with one another what rising from the dead meant. [11] They asked Him, saying, *Why is it* that the scribes say that Elijah must come first?" [12] And He said to them, "Elijah does first come and restore all things. And *yet* how is it written of the Son of Man that He will suffer many things and be treated with contempt? [13] "But I say to you that Elijah has indeed come, and they did to him whatever they wished, just as it is written of him."	[1] Καὶ ἔλεγεν αὐτοῖς, Ἀμὴν λέγω ὑμῖν, ὅτι εἰσίν τινες τῶν ὧδε ἑστηκότων, οἵτινες οὐ μὴ γεύσωνται θανάτου, ἕως ἂν ἴδωσιν τὴν βασιλείαν τοῦ θεοῦ ἐληλυθυῖαν ἐν δυνάμει. [2] Καὶ μεθ' ἡμέρας ἓξ παραλαμβάνει ὁ Ἰησοῦς τὸν Πέτρον καὶ τὸν Ἰάκωβον καὶ ῀ Ἰωάννην, ῀ καὶ ἀναφέρει αὐτοὺς εἰς ὄρος ὑψηλὸν κατ' ἰδίαν μόνους καὶ μετεμορφώθη ἔμπροσθεν αὐτῶν [3] καὶ τὰ ἱμάτια αὐτοῦ ῀ ἐγένοντο ῀ στίλβοντα, λευκὰ λίαν ὡς χιών, οἷα γναφεὺς ἐπὶ τῆς γῆς οὐ δύναται λευκᾶναι. [4] Καὶ ὤφθη αὐτοῖς Ἠλίας σὺν ῀ Μωσῇ, ῀ καὶ ἦσαν συλλαλοῦντες τῷ Ἰησοῦ. [5] Καὶ ἀποκριθεὶς ὁ Πέτρος λέγει τῷ Ἰησοῦ, Ῥαββί, καλόν ἐστιν ἡμᾶς ὧδε εἶναι καὶ ποιήσωμεν σκηνὰς τρεῖς, σοὶ μίαν, καὶ ῀ Μωσῇ ῀ μίαν, καὶ Ἠλίᾳ μίαν. [6] Οὐ γὰρ ᾔδει τί λαλήσει ἦσαν γὰρ ἔκφοβοι. [7] Καὶ ἐγένετο νεφέλη ἐπισκιάζουσα αὐτοῖς καὶ ἦλθεν φωνὴ ἐκ τῆς νεφέλης, Οὗτός ἐστιν ὁ υἱός μου ὁ ἀγαπητός αὐτοῦ ἀκούετε. [8] Καὶ ἐξάπινα περιβλεψάμενοι, οὐκέτι οὐδένα εἶδον, ἀλλὰ τὸν Ἰησοῦν μόνον μεθ' ἑαυτῶν. [9] Καταβαινόντων δὲ αὐτῶν ἀπὸ τοῦ ὄρους, διεστείλατο αὐτοῖς ἵνα μηδενὶ διηγήσωνται ἃ εἶδον, εἰ μὴ ὅταν ὁ υἱὸς τοῦ ἀνθρώπου ἐκ νεκρῶν ἀναστῇ. [10] Καὶ τὸν λόγον ἐκράτησαν πρὸς ἑαυτούς, συζητοῦντες τί ἐστιν τὸ ἐκ νεκρῶν ἀναστῆναι. [11] Καὶ ἐπηρώτων αὐτόν, λέγοντες ὅτι Λέγουσιν οἱ γραμματεῖς ὅτι Ἠλίαν δεῖ ἐλθεῖν πρῶτον; [12] Ὁ δὲ ἀποκριθείς, εἶπεν αὐτοῖς, Ἠλίας μὲν ἐλθὼν πρῶτον, ἀποκαθιστᾷ πάντα καὶ πῶς γέγραπται ἐπὶ τὸν υἱὸν τοῦ ἀνθρώπου, ἵνα πολλὰ πάθῃ καὶ ἐξουδενωθῇ. [13] Ἀλλὰ λέγω ὑμῖν ὅτι καὶ Ἠλίας ἐλήλυθεν, καὶ ἐποίησαν αὐτῷ ὅσα ἠθέλησαν, καθὼς γέγραπται ἐπ' αὐτόν.

Process of Discovery

Linguistics Section

Linguistic Structure

[Transition] [1] And Jesus was saying to them, "Truly I say to you, there are some of those who are standing here who will not taste death until they see the kingdom of God after it has come with power."

A [2] Six days later, Jesus took with Him Peter and James and John, and brought them up on a high mountain by themselves. And He was transfigured before them; [3] and His garments became radiant and exceedingly white, as no launderer on earth can whiten them. [4] Elijah appeared to them along with Moses; and they were talking with Jesus.

> **B** [5] Peter said to Jesus, "Rabbi, it is good for us to be here; let us make three tabernacles, one for You, and one for Moses, and one for Elijah."

> > **C** [6] For he did not know what to answer; for they became terrified.

> > > **D** [7] Then a cloud formed, overshadowing them, and a voice came out of the cloud, "This is My beloved Son, listen to Him!"

> > > > **E** [8] All at once they looked around and saw no one with them anymore, except Jesus alone.

> > > **D'** [9] As they were coming down from the mountain, He gave them orders not to relate to anyone what they had seen, until the Son of Man rose from the dead.

> > **C'** [10] They seized upon that statement, discussing with one another what rising from the dead meant.

> **B** [11] They asked Him, saying, "*Why is it* that the scribes say that Elijah must come first?"

A' [12] And He said to them, "Elijah does first come and restore all things. And *yet* how is it written of the Son of Man that He will suffer many things and be treated with contempt? [13] "But I say to you that Elijah has indeed come, and they did to him whatever they wished, just as it is written of him."

A: Elijah is coming. B: Words of disciples. C: Lack of understandings of the disciples. D: The Son of God and the Son of Man. E: Jesus alone with them.[125]

Discussion

This narrative is a deep chiasm. The central point of the chiasm is Yeshua.

Questioning the Passage

1. What does verse one mean?

   This verse is better placed at the end of chapter eight. It refers to the apocalyptic nature of the future. The taste of death refers to the release of the souls in Sheol. These souls will travel to Heaven to be with the LORD.

2. What mountain did the Transfiguration occur? (v. 2)

   Mount Tabor is the traditional location for the Transfiguration. However, Mount Hermon is a higher mountain in the Galilee region. The Scripture calls it a highly esteemed mountain. Since the belief was the closer one was to the firmament (the sky), the closer one was to God. Mount Hermon seems like a better fit.

   At Mount Tabor:

   - Deborah the Judge called her troops together to rid the area of the Canaanites.
   - The mount was a strategic location bordering on Zebulun, Issachar, and Naphtali.
   - During the Second Temple, period beacons were placed on Mount Tabor to tell Hebrews in the north when the month and holy days began.
   - In 55 BCE, a Hasmonean army was defeated by the Greeks. Ten thousand soldiers died.

---

125 "Literary Structure (Chiasm, Chiasmus) of Gospel of Mark." Literary structure (chiasm, chiasmus) of each pericopes of Gospel of Mark. Accessed March 2, 2021. http://www.bible.literarystructure.info/bible/41_Mark_pericope_e.html.

At Mount Hermon:

- The highest mountain in Israel.
- In the book of Enoch, the Watchers came to Mount Hermon before coming to Earth.

3. What does it mean that his clothes were white as light? (v. 3)

Yeshua's clothing glowing is a repetition of the light beaming from His face. The light shining from His face is an echo of Moses. Adding that the light is also shining through His clothes separates Yeshua from Moses. Matthew's author spends a lot of time showing Yeshua as the substitute of Moses; the author has to show Yeshua on a higher spiritual plane.

4. What is the significance of Moses and Elijah appearing with Yeshua? (v. 4)

Moses was the Law Giver and the most prominent prophet of the LORD. The light of God shined through Moses' face when we came down from Mount Sinai after his time with the LORD. The power of God was with Moses.

Elijah had the power of God with him, as shown when he called down fire when he battled the prophets of Baal on Mount Carmel. Elijah also left the Earth on a chariot which was described as being on fire. Fire displays light. In biblical days fire was a demonstration of the power of God.

Therefore, both Moses and Elijah were conduits for the power of God.

Also, the LORD told the people that Elijah would be sent before the coming of the Messiah. Malachi 4:5-6 refers to this event:

> [5] "Behold, I am going to send you Elijah the prophet before the coming of the great and **terrible** day of the LORD. [6] "He will restore the hearts of the fathers to *their* children and the hearts of the children to their fathers, so that I will not come and smite the land with a curse." (Mal. 4:5-6 NAU)

The word in red could also be translated as "awesome" (the Hebrew word is *yare*). Using this translation, it would be an awesome day of the LORD when the Messiah came to Earth. Since Elijah was supposed to come first, the Transfiguration event takes care of Elijah's arrival before Yeshua. Now Yeshua turned toward His Messianic work (more fully turned).

5. What is the significance of the "tabernacles" in verse five?

    The tabernacles could be a reference to the festival of Sukkot. The following comes from: http://www.hebrew4christians.com/Holidays/Fall_Holidays/Sukkot/sukkot.html

    > "The seventh (and final) feast given to Israel is called Sukkot (ni•o) or the "Feast of Tabernacles." Sukkot is observed in the fall, from the 15th to the 22nd of Tishri. During this time many Jewish families construct a sukkah (n•o), a small hastily built hut in which meals are eaten throughout the festival. The sukkah is used to remember the huts [plural: sukkot] Israel lived in during their 40 year sojourn in the desert after the exodus from Egypt.

    > Since it immediately follows the Days of Awe and Repentance, Sukkot represents the time of restored fellowship with the LORD. In fact, the Mish kan (and later, the Temple) represents God's Presence dwelling among His redeemed people (Exod. 29:44-45).

    > The modern observance of Sukkot allows just a few days -- from the time Yom Kippur ends on Tishri 11 to Tishri 15 -- to begin assembling and decorating the sukkah for the festivities. If the High Holidays focus on the LORD as our Creator, our Judge, and the One who atones for our sins, the festival of Sukkot is the time when we celebrate all that the LORD has done for us. Prophetically understood, the seven days picture olam haba, the world to come, and the 1,000 Millennial Kingdom age. If Yeshua was born during Sukkot (i.e., conceived during Chanukah), then another (and prophetic) meaning of the "word became flesh and 'tabernacled with us" (John 1 :14) foretells the coming Millennial kingdom, when King Messiah will again "tabernacle with us" during his reign from Zion.

The holiday of Sukkot therefore represents a time of renewed fellowship with God, remembering His sheltering provision and care for us as we travel in the desert, surrounded the Clouds of Glory... In practical terms, the festival is celebrated for eight days (i.e., from Tishri 15-22) during which we are commanded to "dwell" in a sukkah - a structure of temporary construction - with a roof covering (schach) of branches, bamboo, etc. The sukkah itself symbolizes our dependence upon God's care and sustenance. We eat meals in the sukkah and recite a special blessing (leshev Ba-Sukkah) at this time.

In light of the work of Yeshua as our Kohen Gadol (high priest) of the New Covenant, we now have access to the Heavenly Temple of God (Heb. 4:16). We are now members of the greater Temple of His body; we are now part of His great Sukkah!"[126]

Elul & the Season of Teshuvah

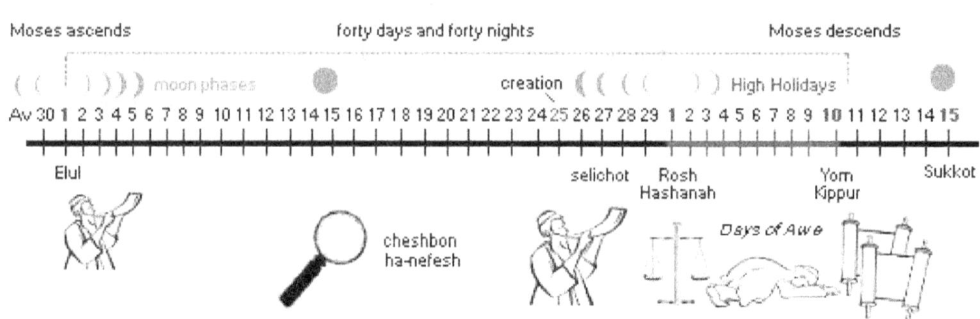

If the Transfiguration story mimicks Sukkot, it is a celebration of the beginning of the Millennial Kingdom. Peter is saying that he believes that Yeshua is the Messiah. The desire to build the Sukkot is the first indicator. The second is the cloud which represents the Cloud of Glory which followed Israel throughout the desert. A purpose for the Messiah was to reestablish the relationship between God and all people. It would be a time of celebration because the forgiveness of sin would have occurred.

---

[126] "Sukkot - the Feast of Tabernacles." Sukkot - the Feast of Tabernacles. Accessed February 22, 2017.

Then the Messiah can accept us into the Kingdom of Heaven. Sukkot reminds us that we are accepted by God and forgiven by God for our sins.

6. What is the significance of the cloud and its description? (v. 6)

    The cloud at the transfiguration is a reminder of the Cloud of Glory, which followed Israel throughout the desert.

7. Whose voice was heard? (v. 7)

    The voice was that of God the Father.

8. Why were the men terrified when they heard the voice? (v. 6)

    It is hard to imagine the voice of God. God's voice would have power and glory. Hearing God's voice would also tell you that God was near. That alone would terrify Peter, James, and John. There is an echo of God's voice here and God's voice at Yeshua's immersion. It is almost a perfect repetition.

9. Why would Yeshua tell them not to talk about this event? (v. 9)

    Perhaps it was because the event revealed the messianic purpose of Yeshua. Yeshua wanted to have His purpose announced in His way and at His time. The interesting point would be why Yeshua took the three men with Him if He knew that this event would take place? There would become a time where the men could talk about this event.

Biblical Personalities

1. Ἰησοῦς *Iesous* Meaning: *Jesus* or *Joshua,* the name of the Messiah, also three other Israelites

2. Πέτρος *Petros* Meaning: 'a stone' or 'a boulder,' *Peter,* one of the twelve apostles

3. Ἰάκωβος *Iakobos* Meaning: James, the name of several Israelites

4. Ἰωάννης *Ioannes* Meaning: *John,* the name of several Israelites

5. Μωϋσῆς *Mouses* Meaning: *Moses,* a leader of Israelites

6. Ἠλίας *Elias* Meaning: *Elijah,* an Israelite prophet

Linguistic Echoes

Yeshua's face of light and Moses' face of light.

[29] It came about when Moses was coming down from Mount Sinai (and the two tablets of the testimony *were* in Moses' hand as he was coming down from the mountain), that Moses did not know that the skin of his face shone because of his speaking with Him. [30] So when Aaron and all the sons of Israel saw Moses, behold, the skin of his face shone, and they were afraid to come near him. (Exod. 34:29-30 NAU)

When Moses came in contact with the divine, the power of God shined from his face with radiating beams of light. Yeshua being God would also have that same shine on His face. Since Yeshua had to return to the world after the Transfiguration, He could not have his face show the power of God, so He lost that outward shine but had an inward shine. The light of God came through Yeshua differently through his love and kindness for all people.

Thoughts

The Transfiguration is an event that brings together the theological perspectives of Sukkot and Yeshua being the Messiah. Peter's calling to build a Sukkot and the Cloud of glory which surrounded Yeshua, Moses, and Elijah brings up the imagery of that holiday. The Sukkot was a celebration of God's forgiveness for the previous year's sins. Yeshua was sent to tell the people of the forgiveness of sin and to die for their sins. Therefore, the event is connected to Sukkot in that way because during the Sukkot celebration, a prayer is offered for the beginning of the Messianic period. The Messiah was to bring people back to God and to tell us of God's forgiveness for sin. This is a critical component of the Sukkot celebration.

The forgiveness of sin by God is accompanied by a time for a person to confess their sins before the LORD. An admittance of sin would not be sufficient. Following the celebrations of the Holy

Days and Sukkot, one would confess to the LORD of their sins during the days of repentance. On Yom Kippur, prayers are offered for forgiveness. Sukkot follows, which celebrates God's forgiveness of sin. In a way, Sukkot is Yeshua's celebration. How much power would the Transfiguration have been if it occurred on Sukkot?

Also, Yeshua is declared the Messiah by the appearance of Elijah. God said in Malachi that Elijah would come to announce the Messiah. Elijah's appearance at the Transfiguration completes the prophecy. The idea of Yeshua as the Messiah becomes revealed further in Matthew's Gospel after this event.

Reflections

The Greek influence from the Stoics of antiquity is so present in our society. If we want not to be hurt in this society, we can cut ourselves off from emotion. We would keep everyone at a distance so that no risk could hurt us. Because of this influence, too many Christians are unwilling to accept our Savior Jesus's horrific death. The path to the cross starts at the Transfiguration in Mark's Gospel. The acceptance of Jesus' death in the manner of the cross is not acceptable to many modern-day Christians. The attendance of the Good Friday worship bears this out very clearly. A terrible day for attendance to the point where you wonder if the church should hold the worship. We like the good things of Christianity but not the pain of Christianity. The Transfiguration reminds us that we are moving in Lent and towards Holy Week. Easter worship brings out the people to hear the Good News of the Resurrection while they deny the events leading up to it. It is a good thing Jesus is forgiving. However, what will He say about those Christians who do not accept His pain in order for them to receive their salvation?

MARK 9:14–29

Language

New American Standard 1995	Koine Greek
[14] When they came *back* to the disciples, they saw a large crowd around them, and *some* scribes arguing with them. [15] Immediately, when the entire crowd saw Him, they were amazed and *began* running up to greet Him. [16] And He asked them, "What are you discussing with them?" [17] And one of the crowd answered Him, "Teacher, I brought You my son, possessed with a spirit which makes him mute; [18] and whenever it seizes him, it slams him *to the ground* and he foams *at the mouth,* and grinds his teeth and stiffens out. I told Your disciples to cast it out, and they could not *do it.*" [19] And He answered them and said, "O unbelieving generation, how long shall I be with you? How long shall I put up with you? Bring him to Me!" [20] They brought the boy to Him. When he saw Him, immediately the spirit threw him into a convulsion, and falling to the ground, he *began* rolling around and foaming *at the mouth.* [21] And He asked his father, "How long has this been happening to him?" And he said, "From childhood. [22] "It has often thrown him both into the fire and into the water to destroy him. But if You can do anything, take pity on us and help us!" [23] And Jesus said to him, "'If You can?' *"*All things are possible to him who believes." [24] Immediately the boy's father cried out and said, "I do believe; help my unbelief." [25] When Jesus saw that a crowd was rapidly gathering, He rebuked the unclean spirit, saying to it, "You deaf and mute spirit, I [2]command you, come out of him and do not enter him again." [26] After crying out and throwing him into terrible convulsions, it came out; and *the boy* became so much like a corpse that most *of them* said, "He is dead!" [27] But Jesus took him by the hand and raised him; and he got up. [28] When He came *"*into *the* house, His disciples *began* questioning Him privately, "Why could we not drive it out?" [29]	[14] Καὶ ἐλθόντες πρὸς τοὺς μαθητὰς εἶδον ὄχλον πολὺν περὶ αὐτοὺς καὶ γραμματεῖς συζητοῦντας πρὸς αὐτούς. [15] καὶ εὐθὺς πᾶς ὁ ὄχλος ἰδόντες αὐτὸν ἐξεθαμβήθησαν καὶ προστρέχοντες ἠσπάζοντο αὐτόν. [16] καὶ ἐπηρώτησεν αὐτούς· τί συζητεῖτε πρὸς αὐτούς; [17] Καὶ ἀπεκρίθη αὐτῷ εἷς ἐκ τοῦ ὄχλου· διδάσκαλε, ἤνεγκα τὸν υἱόν μου πρὸς σέ, ἔχοντα πνεῦμα ἄλαλον· [18] καὶ ὅπου ἐὰν αὐτὸν καταλάβῃ ῥήσσει αὐτόν, καὶ ἀφρίζει καὶ τρίζει τοὺς ὀδόντας καὶ ξηραίνεται· καὶ εἶπα τοῖς μαθηταῖς σου ἵνα αὐτὸ ἐκβάλωσιν, καὶ οὐκ ἴσχυσαν. [19] ὁ δὲ ἀποκριθεὶς αὐτοῖς λέγει· ὦ γενεὰ ἄπιστος, ἕως πότε πρὸς ὑμᾶς ἔσομαι; ἕως πότε ἀνέξομαι ὑμῶν; φέρετε αὐτὸν πρός με. [20] καὶ ἤνεγκαν αὐτὸν πρὸς αὐτόν. καὶ ἰδὼν αὐτὸν τὸ πνεῦμα εὐθὺς συνεσπάραξεν αὐτόν, καὶ πεσὼν ἐπὶ τῆς γῆς ἐκυλίετο ἀφρίζων. [21] καὶ ἐπηρώτησεν τὸν πατέρα αὐτοῦ· πόσος χρόνος ἐστὶν ὡς τοῦτο γέγονεν αὐτῷ; ὁ δὲ εἶπεν· ἐκ παιδιόθεν· [22] καὶ πολλάκις καὶ εἰς πῦρ αὐτὸν ἔβαλεν καὶ εἰς ὕδατα ἵνα ἀπολέσῃ αὐτόν· ἀλλ' εἴ τι δύνῃ, βοήθησον ἡμῖν σπλαγχνισθεὶς ἐφ' ἡμᾶς. [23] ὁ δὲ Ἰησοῦς εἶπεν αὐτῷ· τὸ εἰ δύνῃ, πάντα δυνατὰ τῷ πιστεύοντι. [24] εὐθὺς κράξας ὁ πατὴρ τοῦ παιδίου ἔλεγεν· πιστεύω· βοήθει μου τῇ ἀπιστίᾳ. [25] ἰδὼν δὲ ὁ Ἰησοῦς ὅτι ἐπισυντρέχει ὄχλος, ἐπετίμησεν τῷ πνεύματι τῷ ἀκαθάρτῳ λέγων αὐτῷ· τὸ ἄλαλον καὶ κωφὸν πνεῦμα, ἐγὼ ἐπιτάσσω σοι, ἔξελθε ἐξ αὐτοῦ καὶ μηκέτι εἰσέλθῃς εἰς αὐτόν. [26] καὶ κράξας καὶ πολλὰ σπαράξας ἐξῆλθεν· καὶ ἐγένετο ὡσεὶ νεκρός, ὥστε τοὺς πολλοὺς λέγειν ὅτι ἀπέθανεν. [27] ὁ δὲ Ἰησοῦς κρατήσας τῆς χειρὸς αὐτοῦ ἤγειρεν αὐτόν, καὶ ἀνέστη. [28] Καὶ εἰσελθόντος αὐτοῦ εἰς οἶκον οἱ μαθηταὶ αὐτοῦ κατ' ἰδίαν ἐπηρώτων αὐτόν· ὅτι ἡμεῖς οὐκ ἠδυνήθημεν ἐκβαλεῖν αὐτό; [29] καὶ εἶπεν αὐτοῖς·

And He said to them, "This kind cannot come out by anything but prayer."	τοῦτο τὸ γένος ἐν οὐδενὶ δύναται ἐξελθεῖν εἰ μὴ ἐν προσευχῇ.

Process of Discovery

Linguistics Section

Linguistic Structure

A [14] When they came *back* to the disciples, they saw a large crowd around them, and *some* scribes arguing with them. [15] Immediately, when the entire crowd saw Him, they were amazed and *began* running up to greet Him. [16] And He asked them, "What are you discussing with them?" [17] And one of the crowd answered Him, "Teacher, I brought You my son, possessed with a spirit which makes him mute; [18] and whenever it seizes him, it slams him *to the ground* and he foams *at the mouth,* and grinds his teeth and stiffens out. I told Your disciples to cast it out, and they could not *do it.*" [19] And He answered them and said, "O unbelieving generation, how long shall I be with you? How long shall I put up with you? Bring him to Me!"

> **B** [20] They brought the boy to Him. When he saw Him, immediately the spirit threw him into a convulsion, and falling to the ground, he *began* rolling around and foaming *at the mouth.*

> > **C** [21] And He asked his father, "How long has this been happening to him?"

> > > **D** And he said, "From childhood. [22] "It has often thrown him both into the fire and into the water to destroy him. But if You can do anything, take pity on us and help us!"

> > > > **E** [23] And Jesus said to him, "'If You can?' *a*All things are possible to him who believes."

> > > **D'** [24] Immediately the boy's father cried out and said, "I do believe; help my unbelief."

> > **C'** [25] When Jesus saw that a crowd was rapidly gathering, He rebuked the unclean spirit, saying to it, "You deaf and mute spirit, I *2*command you, come out of him and do not enter him again."

> **B'** [26] After crying out and throwing him into terrible convulsions, it came out; and *the boy* became so much like a corpse that most *of them* said, "He is dead!" [27] But Jesus took him by the hand and raised him; and he got up.

A' [28] When He came *a*into *the* house, His disciples *began* questioning Him privately, "Why could we not drive it out?" [29] And He said to them, "This kind cannot come out by anything but prayer."

Discussion

This narrative is a layered chiasm, with the center being about faith. This is a healing story.

Healing is considered a spiritual matter, not a physical matter.

Questioning the Passage

1. Whom was Yeshua addressing in verse seventeen?

   The conventional Christian interpretation is that Yeshua was referring to the people who came to see Him. Why would a man beg for Yeshua to cure his son if he did not believe in His power? Therefore, this statement must be directed elsewhere. The man said that he brought the boy to Yeshua's disciples, but they could not heal him. Therefore, the unbelieving generation was directed at Yeshua's disciples. Perhaps Yeshua did teach them the power of healing. The disciples did not have confidence in themselves to perform the recovery? The disciples may have doubted that the cures that Yeshua taught them would work. Sometimes, for the treatment of a disease to work, the caregiver and person must believe that the treatment will work.

2. What does it mean that the boy falls into the fire? (v. 15)

   During Yeshua's time, the typical home in the Near East was constructed with several dung ovens dug into the floor for the cooking of food and the baking of bread. The ovens were left uncovered often. Family members and visitors in the home could fall into the oven and suffer severe burns. A boy with epilepsy could easily fall into an oven if he suffered a seizure.[127]

3. What does it mean that the boy often fell into the water? (v. 15)

   Many of the towns in the Near East in Yeshua's day were built near streams. Many times the streams ran through the towns. Besides streams, towns might have wadis in them. During the rainy season, the streams would overflow their banks, and the wadis would fill with water, making both unsafe to cross, especially for children. Small towns did not have bridges. In the rainy season, people would have to wade through the stream. Stones were placed at different points in the creek or wadi bed to tell people where it was safe to walk across the water.

---

[127] Rocco A. Errico and George M. Lamsa, *Aramaic Light on the Gospel of Matthew: a Commentary on the Teachings of Jesus from the Aramaic and Unchanged Near Eastern Customs* (Santa Fe, NM: Noohra Foundation, 2000).

If the epileptic boy had a seizure while near an overflowing stream or wadi, he could fall into the water; if this occurred, the boy would not be able to pull himself out of the water and would drown.[128]

Culture Section

Questioning the passage

1. What was known about epilepsy?

   "The history of epilepsy and its treatment in the western world dates back at least 4 millennia to the ancient civilization of the middle east. Past and present treatments have been empirical, usually reflecting the prevailing views of epilepsy, be they medical, theological or superstitious. Ancient physicians relied on clinical observation to distinguish between epileptic syndromes and infer their cause. Early pathophysiological theories of epilepsy correctly identified the brain as the site of the problem, but emphasized incorrect causes such as an excess of phlegm in the brain. Treatments consisted of prescribed diets or living conditions, occasional surgery such as bloodletting or skull trephination and medicinal herbs. These treatments, often ineffective, had the intellectual advantage of being based on pathophysiological principles, unlike current, more empirical, therapies. The unfortunate but widely held view of epilepsy as being due to occult or evil influences gained adherents even in the medical world during ancient times, and the later acceptance of Christianity allowed theological interpretations of seizures as well. Magical or religious treatments were more frequently prescribed as a result, practices which persist to this day. In the Renaissance an attempt was made to view epilepsy as a manifestation of physical illness rather than a moral or occult affliction, but it was during the Enlightenment that epilepsy was viewed along more modern lines, helped by advances in anatomy and pathology and the development of chemistry, pharmacy and physiology. The idea that focal irritation may cause seizures came about from clinical and experimental work, and was supported by the successful control of seizures by the (sedative) bromides and barbiturates in the late 19th century. The introduction of phenytoin showed that non-sedative drugs could be effective in controlling seizures as well, and the development of in vivo seizure models widened the scope of

---

[128] IBID.

pharmaceutical agents tested for their efficacy against epilepsy. Increasing knowledge of the cellular mechanisms of epilepsy will, hopefully, allow the development and introduction of drugs with increasing specificity against seizure activity and the development of epilepsy."[129]

Thoughts

This narrative is a beautiful example of why biblical readers need to look deeper into the Scripture and learn about the culture of Yeshua's day. The narrative unfolds into a healing story about epilepsy. Yeshua knew how to use herbs and plant roots to create a compound that cured the body. Today that knowledge is called modern medicine. The discoveries of medical science are from the LORD. As physicians continue to learn about how the human body functions, they also learned about ways to cure the body when it breaks down.

An example is vaccines. There is a movement in the United States to stop giving children vaccines. Sometimes a vaccine will have horrible side effects, but overall, they work well. Vaccines are discoveries the LORD has set up for us to find. The LORD wants the vaccines discovered. The outbreak of measles in 2019 is a prime example of the vaccination problem. Many parents do not vaccinate their children. By not vaccinating, they are allowing a cured disease to reemerge. All the discoveries in all areas of life are gifts from the LORD. They need to be used in that manner.

---

[129] R A Gross, "A Brief History of Epilepsy and Its Therapy in the Western Hemisphere," Epilepsy research (U.S. National Library of Medicine, July 1992), https://www.ncbi.nlm.nih.gov/pubmed/1396542. Accessed 7/21/2021.

Reflections

Faith is usually expressed in spiritual terms. Perhaps faith should be examined as trusting the LORD both spiritually and physically. When praying for healing for oneself or another person, remember to include prayers for the caregivers and doctors. The wisdom of the LORD is given to people to help us live long and fruitful lives. Faith becomes faith in the LORD and faith in the wisdom the LORD gives to people who help others.

MARK 9:30-37

Language

New American Standard 1995	Koine Greek
[30] From there they went out and *began* to go through Galilee, and He did not want anyone to know *about it.* [31] For He was teaching His disciples and telling them, "The Son of Man is to be delivered into the hands of men, and they will kill Him; and when He has been killed, He will rise three days later." [32] But they did not understand *this* statement, and they were afraid to ask Him. [33] They came to Capernaum; and when He was in the house, He *began* to question them, "What were you discussing on the way?" [34] But they kept silent, for on the way they had discussed with one another which *of them was* the greatest. [35] Sitting down, He called the twelve and said to them, "If anyone wants to be first, he shall be last of all and servant of all." [36] Taking a child, He set him before them, and taking him in His arms, He said to them, [37] "Whoever receives one child like this in My name receives Me; and whoever receives Me does not receive Me, but Him who sent Me."	[30] Καὶ ἐκεῖθεν ἐξελθόντες παρεπορεύοντο διὰ τῆς Γαλιλαίας Καὶ οὐκ ἤθελεν ἵνα τις γνῷ. [31] Ἐδίδασκεν γὰρ τοὺς μαθητὰς αὐτοῦ, καὶ ἔλεγεν αὐτοῖς ὅτι Ὁ υἱὸς τοῦ ἀνθρώπου παραδίδοται εἰς χεῖρας ἀνθρώπων, καὶ ἀποκτενοῦσιν αὐτὸν καὶ ἀποκτανθείς, τῇ τρίτῃ ἡμέρᾳ ἀναστήσεται [32] Οἱ δὲ ἠγνόουν τὸ ῥῆμα, καὶ ἐφοβοῦντο αὐτὸν ἐπερωτῆσαι. [33] Καὶ ἦλθεν εἰς Καπερναοὺμ καὶ ἐν τῇ οἰκίᾳ γενόμενος ἐπηρώτα αὐτούς, Τί ἐν τῇ ὁδῷ πρὸς ἑαυτοὺς διελογίζεσθε; [34] Οἱ δὲ ἐσιώπων πρὸς ἀλλήλους γὰρ διελέχθησαν ἐν τῇ ὁδῷ, τίς μείζων. [35] Καὶ καθίσας ἐφώνησεν τοὺς δώδεκα, καὶ λέγει αὐτοῖς, Εἴ τις θέλει πρῶτος εἶναι, ἔσται πάντων ἔσχατος, καὶ πάντων διάκονος. [36] Καὶ λαβὼν παιδίον, ἔστησεν αὐτὸ ἐν μέσῳ αὐτῶν καὶ ἐναγκαλισάμενος αὐτό, εἶπεν αὐτοῖς [37] Ὃς ἐὰν ἐν τῶν τοιούτων παιδίων δέξηται ἐπὶ τῷ ὀνόματί μου, ἐμὲ δέχεται καὶ ὃς ἐὰν ἐμὲ δέξηται, οὐκ ἐμὲ δέχεται, ἀλλὰ τὸν ἀποστείλαντά με.

Process of Discovery

Linguistics Section

Linguistic Structure

[Transition] [30] From there they went out and *began* to go through Galilee, and He did not want anyone to know *about it*. [31] For He was teaching His disciples and telling them, "The Son of Man is to be delivered into the hands of men, and they will kill Him; and when He has been killed, He will rise three days later." [32] But they did not understand *this* statement, and they were afraid to ask Him.

A [33] They came to Capernaum; and when He was in the house, He *began* to question them, "What were you discussing on the way?"

> **B** [34] But they kept silent, for on the way they had discussed with one another which *of them was* the greatest.

> > **C** [35] Sitting down, He called the twelve and said to them, "If anyone wants to be first, he shall be last of all and servant of all."

> **B'** [36] Taking a child, He set him before them, and taking him in His arms, He said to them,

A' [37] "Whoever receives one child like this in My name receives Me; and whoever receives Me does not receive Me, but Him who sent Me."

Discussion

Mark 9:30-32 is a transition paragraph. It is believed that Yeshua took His disciples to the Grotto of Pan in the northern section of Galilee. Pan was the Greek god of the underworld (Hell). Yeshua could have been saying that the evil of the world was going to condemn Him to death. It was believed that the world's evil was caused by the presence of Satan (Pan). Therefore, Yeshua's statement about his death was a foreshadowing of what was to occur. It was known that prophets went to Jerusalem to die. The LORD sends a message through a prophet, the leaders do not like the message, and generally, the leaders kill the prophet.

Questioning the Passage

1   Why did Yeshua's disciples ask about a hierarchy in Heaven? (v. 1)

Mark does not have the words "in the Kingdom of Heaven," which appear in Matthew's Gospel. Christian tradition says that the disciples were talking about their position in Heaven. It is possible that they were talking about the leadership structure of their group. Since Yeshua said He would be killed, the group would have wondered who would lead after Yeshua's death. To hold this discussion while Yeshua was alive seems to be insensitive. Therefore, Matthew's Gospel added the words about the Kingdom of Heaven.

In Mark's Gospel, the discussion is based on who would lead the group after Yeshua's death.

2   What is the symbolism of being like a child and being the greatest? (v. 37)

A child is trusting his/her parents that they will provide for them. In Yeshua's day, even needy parents ensured that their children had what they needed to survive. Children were considered a blessing from the LORD and were to be treated that way. A child is ready to learn whatever they are taught. They trust their teachers and parents that they will be taught properly; for an adult to become like a child means surrendering everything learned in exchange for the truth. This infers that the disciples of Yeshua had been taught incorrectly and needed to forget those ideas for new ones. Yeshua taught a new way to examine the Scripture and to relate to the LORD using the Torah. To accomplish most of what Yeshua taught, a disciple would have to let go of everything they believed and absorb a new way of thinking.

Culture Section

Discussion

"Receiving a child in my name" is an ancient Near Eastern saying which means "receive a child the way I would receive him." When a holy person, government official, or other dignitaries would enter a town or city, children would gather around said person. The officials with the important person would chase the children away. They would rebuke the children, tell them to stay away, and sometimes curse them. It was considered an embarrassment to a host to have children playing in the house when he was entertaining guests. When guests reclined to eat a meal, the children would be sent out of the house.

Yeshua's disciples would have rebuked any children who came to see Him. After all, that was their cultural norm. Yeshua was against this practice and rebuked His disciples for rebuking the children. To emphasize His teaching, He took one child in his arms and told them that they must become like the child if they wanted to enter the Kingdom of Heaven. Yeshua was also telling His disciples that children were of value and should be treated that way.

Children are a blessing from the LORD. The culture of rebuking them when they came to see a holy person was wrong. This is another aspect of Yeshua's anti-cultural attitude.[130]

Thoughts

To fully interpret and understand Jesus' words, one must understand the culture in which he lived. Children were treated differently than they are today. That does not mean that parents did not love their children as much as parents do today. Parents loved their children because they were blessings from the LORD. Creating a family was essential to every married couple. It must be noted that there were aspects of the culture where children were expected to become invisible. Perhaps it was because politics or some other subject was being discussed. Children tend to repeat what they hear even if they are told that it is a secret. If several adults met at home to discuss some aspect of Herod's rule and if discovered that they disagreed, they could be put to death or imprisoned. Therefore, it had to be kept quiet.

Reflections

I remember saying to one of my children when they were very young that they needed to keep a purchase I made a secret. The child assured me that they would be quiet. Unfortunately, I was a new parent and soon discovered that I was rated out by the child. So, I asked the child why she rated me out to mommy? After a couple of minutes of thinking the response from the child was, "I don't know." I learned quickly that kids do not keep secrets. In Judea or the Galilee in Yeshua's day a child saying something about their parents felt about the local or Roman government could easily lead to death. The culture around children may have developed from the fear of the government. Yeshua tells us to include children and is saying that adults should not say anything around children that they do not want repeated.

---

[130] Rocco A. Errico, George M. Lamsa, and George M. Lamsa, *Aramaic Light on the Gospels of Mark and Luke: a Commentary on the Teachings of Jesus from the Aramaic and Unchanged Near Eastern Customs* (Smyrna, GA: Noohra Foundation, 2001).

MARK 9:38-41

Language

New American Standard 1995	Koine Greek
[38] John said to Him, "Teacher, we saw someone casting out demons in Your name, and we tried to prevent him because he was not following us." [39] But Jesus said, "Do not hinder him, for there is no one who will perform a miracle in My name, and be able soon afterward to speak evil of Me. [40] "For he who is not against us is for us. [41] "For whoever gives you a cup of water to drink because of your name as *followers* of Christ, truly I say to you, he will not lose his reward.	[38] Ἀπεκρίθη δὲ αὐτῷ ʼ Ἰωάννης, ʼ λέγων, Διδάσκαλε, εἴδομεν τινα τῷ ὀνόματί σου ἐκβάλλοντα δαιμόνια, ὃς οὐκ ἀκολουθεῖ ἡμῖν καὶ ἐκωλύσαμεν αὐτόν, ὅτι οὐκ ἀκολουθεῖ ἡμῖν. [39] Ὁ δὲ Ἰησοῦς εἶπεν, Μὴ κωλύετε αὐτόν οὐδεὶς γάρ ἐστιν ὃς ποιήσει δύναμιν ἐπὶ τῷ ὀνόματί μου, καὶ δυνήσεται ταχὺ κακολογῆσαί με. [40] Ὃς γὰρ οὐκ ἐστιν καθ' ὑμῶν, ὑπὲρ ὑμῶν ἐστιν. [41] Ὃς γὰρ ἂν ποτίσῃ ὑμᾶς ποτήριον ὕδατος ἐν ὀνόματι μου, ὅτι χριστοῦ ἐστε, ἀμὴν λέγω ὑμῖν, οὐ μὴ ἀπολέσῃ τὸν μισθὸν αὐτοῦ.

Process of Discovery

Linguistics Section

Linguistic Structure

[John's statement] [38] John said to Him, "Teacher, we saw someone casting out demons in Your name, and we tried to prevent him because he was not following us."

[Yeshua's reply] [39] But Jesus said, "Do not hinder him, for there is no one who will perform a miracle in My name, and be able soon afterward to speak evil of Me. [40] "For he who is not against us is for us. [41] "For whoever gives you a cup of water to drink because of your name as *followers* of Christ, truly I say to you, he will not lose his reward.

Discussion

This narrative is a simple statement by John followed by Yeshua's reply. The question of casting out demons is discussed. Who had the power to do it? The disciples saw another person doing this, and they felt that they were the only persons allowed.

Questioning the Passage

1. Why did the disciples try to stop the person who cast out a demon? (v. 38)
   The disciples wanted to be the only persons who learned the trade of casting out demons. This skill would have given them an edge over others. It is a verse that the church has used for centuries to hold power over the members of the faith. Only the church clergy were allowed to have specific knowledge of the Scriptures. Knowledge is power.

2. Why did Yeshua tell the disciples not to hinder people from casting out demons in His name? (v. 39, 40)
   Yeshua knew that a person doing anything "in His name" would not become an enemy; rather, that person would be a supporter and friend.

3. What does verse forty-one mean?

Water was scarce in the Near East. For someone to offer another person a cup of water was a "big deal." When a person wants to help in your ministry, Yeshua encourages you to allow that person to help. Do not stop anyone who believes in Christ from doing Christ's work. Desiring to do anything for Christ, especially in Christ's manner, is a blessing to Christ and the person.

Linguistic Echoes

1. [27] So a young man ran and told Moses and said, "Eldad and Medad are prophesying in the camp." [28] Then ⸀Joshua the son of Nun, the attendant of Moses from his youth, said, "⸆Moses, my lord, restrain them." [29] But Moses said to him, "Are you jealous for my sake? ⸀Would that all the LORD'S people were prophets, that the LORD would put His Spirit upon them!" [30] Then Moses ⸀returned to the camp, *both* he and the elders of Israel. (Numbers 11:27-29)

Mark is alluding to this story. Joshua wanted Moses to restrain the persons prophesying in the camp. The disciples wanted Yeshua to stop the men who were casting out demons.[131]

Culture Section

Discussion

Near Eastern traders and professionals receive their training and "secrets" from father to son. They are cautious not to give away the secrets of the trade openly. However, when an artist discovers a trade's secrets, others in the trade will praise him. Trade secrets were valuable.

Questioning the passage

---

[131] Ched Myers, *Binding the Strong Man a Political Reading of Mark's Story of Jesus* (Maryknoll, NY: Orbis Books, 1988).

1. What does it mean to perform miracles in Yeshua's name? (v. 38)

   The phrase is a Semitic phrase that means "by Yeshua's method." Whenever the Scripture says "in Yeshua's name," it means to be doing something in the manner Yeshua did and taught us to do. The phrase had lost its original meaning through the church when it broke away from its Hebraic and Semitic roots. The words "in Yeshua's name" have been appended to prayers. People in the church believe that their words are equivalent to Yeshua's words. The phrase "in Yeshua's name" is not always appropriate to the prayer being offered when one considers its original meaning. To end any statement with "in Yeshua's name" indicates that the speaker wants to perform a task the way Yeshua would have.[132]

2. What does it mean to cast out demons? (v. 38)

   Demons in Yeshua's day were the 199 Watchers who were condemned to live in the foundation of the Earth because they brought evil upon the world. The story of the Watchers can be found in Genesis chapter six and expanded in 1 Enoch, the Book of the Watchers. Yeshua was able to rid people of the influence of the Watchers and banned them from Sheol and Satan.

Thoughts

I think that it is sad that when I read this narrative, it made me think about the control the church has held over people for almost 2000 years. The church used only one verse, thus out of context, to control people. Catholics could not own a Bible until 1964 CE. The idea that a person has to confess to a priest, who then prays to Mary, then to Jesus, then to God for forgiveness, presents a hierarchy. Jesus said many times that every person could come before His throne and ask for forgiveness. The reality is not a need for an intermediary. Read the book of Hebrews if you disagree. However, the church insists that one is necessary, and that person is Jesus Christ. In the movie "The Empire

---

[132] Rocco A. Errico, George M. Lamsa, and George M. Lamsa, *Aramaic Light on the Gospels of Mark and Luke: a Commentary on the Teachings of Jesus from the Aramaic and Unchanged Near Eastern Customs* (Smyrna, GA: Noohra Foundation, 2001).

Strikes Back, "Yoda told Luke Skywalker, "control, you must have control "that is true for the Force, but not for an individual who comes before God.

Reflections

Another controlling mechanism of the church is the phrase "in Jesus' name." The church's interpretation is not accurate. This phrase means that the speaker wants to do something like Jesus would (or did). The church grabbed power by saying that this phrase means doing it the church's way because the church represents Jesus. Therefore, the church determined what it meant. Its original meaning is that you have a desire to do something in the same way Jesus did. Also, using this phrase allows the person to show allegiance to Jesus. Following the ways of your rabbi (teacher) was influential in Jesus' day. Even today, some groups of Christians and Jews follow the ways of their teacher. The Disciples learned to do things the way Jesus wanted them done. In other words, He taught them. When this is done to show honor and respect to the teacher, it is good. When it is used to control people, well, that is bad.

MARK 10:1-12

Language

New American Standard 1995	Koine Greek
[1] Getting up, He went from there to the region of Judea and beyond the Jordan; crowds gathered around Him again, and, according to His custom, He once more *began* to teach them. [2] *Some* Pharisees came up to Jesus, testing Him, and *began* to question Him whether it was lawful for a man to divorce a wife. [3] And He answered and said to them, "What did Moses command you?" [4] They said, "Moses permitted *a man* TO WRITE A CERTIFICATE OF DIVORCE AND SEND *her* AWAY." [5] But Jesus said to them, " Because of your hardness of heart he wrote you this commandment. [6] "But from the beginning of creation, *God* MADE THEM MALE AND FEMALE. [7] "FOR THIS REASON A MAN SHALL LEAVE HIS FATHER AND MOTHER[1], [8] AND THE TWO SHALL BECOME ONE FLESH; so they are no longer two, but one flesh. [9] "What therefore God has joined together, let no man separate." [10] In the house the disciples *began* questioning Him about this again. [11] And He said to them, "Whoever divorces his wife and marries another woman commits adultery against her; [12] and if she herself divorces her husband and marries another man, she is committing adultery."	[1] Κἀκεῖθεν ἀναστὰς ἔρχεται εἰς τὰ ὅρια τῆς Ἰουδαίας διὰ τοῦ πέραν τοῦ Ἰορδάνου Καὶ συμπορεύονται πάλιν ὄχλοι πρὸς αὐτόν καί, ὡς εἰώθει, πάλιν ἐδίδασκεν αὐτούς. [2] Καὶ προσελθόντες ˹ Φαρισαῖοι ˺ ἐπηρώτησαν αὐτόν, Εἰ ἔξεστιν ἀνδρὶ γυναῖκα ἀπολῦσαι, πειράζοντες αὐτόν. [3] Ὁ δὲ ἀποκριθεὶς εἶπεν αὐτοῖς, Τί ὑμῖν ἐνετείλατο Μωσῆς; [4] Οἱ δὲ εἶπον, Μωσῆς ἐπέτρεψεν βιβλίον ἀποστασίου γράψαι, καὶ ἀπολῦσαι. [5] Καὶ ἀποκριθεὶς ὁ Ἰησοῦς εἶπεν αὐτοῖς, Πρὸς τὴν σκληροκαρδίαν ὑμῶν ἔγραψεν ὑμῖν τὴν ἐντολὴν ταύτην [6] ἀπὸ δὲ ἀρχῆς κτίσεως, ἄρσεν καὶ θῆλυ ἐποίησεν αὐτοὺς ὁ θεός. [7] Ἕνεκεν τούτου καταλείψει ἄνθρωπος τὸν πατέρα αὐτοῦ καὶ τὴν μητέρα καὶ προσκολληθήσεται πρὸς τὴν γυναῖκα αὐτοῦ, [8] καὶ ἔσονται οἱ δύο εἰς σάρκα μίαν. Ὥστε οὐκέτι εἰσὶν δύο, ἀλλὰ μία σάρξ. [9] Ὃ οὖν ὁ θεὸς συνέζευξεν, ἄνθρωπος μὴ χωριζέτω. [10] Καὶ ἐν τῇ οἰκίᾳ πάλιν οἱ μαθηταὶ αὐτοῦ περὶ τοῦ αὐτοῦ ἐπηρώτησαν αὐτόν. [11] Καὶ λέγει αὐτοῖς, Ὃς ἐὰν ἀπολύσῃ τὴν γυναῖκα αὐτοῦ καὶ γαμήσῃ ἄλλην, μοιχᾶται ἐπ᾽ αὐτήν [12] καὶ ἐὰν γυνὴ ἀπολύσῃ τὸν ἄνδρα αὐτῆς καὶ γαμηθῇ ἄλλῳ, μοιχᾶται

Process of Discovery

Linguistics Section

Linguistic Structure

A [1] Getting up, He went from there to the region of Judea and beyond the Jordan; crowds gathered around Him again, and, according to His custom, He once more *began* to teach them. [2] *Some* Pharisees came up to Jesus, testing Him, and *began* to question Him whether it was lawful for a man to divorce a wife. [3] And He answered and said to them, "What did Moses command you?" [4] They said, "Moses permitted *a man* TO WRITE A CERTIFICATE OF DIVORCE AND SEND *her* AWAY."

> **B** [5] But Jesus said to them, "'Because of your hardness of heart he wrote you this commandment. [6] "But from the beginning of creation, *God* MADE THEM MALE AND FEMALE.
>
>> **C** [7] "FOR THIS REASON A MAN SHALL LEAVE HIS FATHER AND MOTHER, [8] AND THE TWO SHALL BECOME ONE FLESH; so they are no longer two, but one flesh.
>
> **B'** [9] "What therefore God has joined together, let no man separate."

A' [10] In the house the disciples *began* questioning Him about this again. [11] And He *said to them, "Whoever divorces his wife and marries another woman commits adultery against her; [12] and if she herself divorces her husband and marries another man, she is committing adultery."

Discussion

This section of the text discusses the Torah law of divorce and how it was being applied in Yeshua's day.

Questioning the Passage

1. Where did Yeshua go? (v. 1)

    The land beyond the Jordan near Judea was Perea.[133]

---

[133] Matthew 19:1 Commentaries: When Jesus had finished these words, He departed from Galilee and came into the region of Judea beyond the Jordan; accessed February 19, 2020, https://biblehub.com/commentaries/matthew/19-1.htm.

134

2. What does it mean that some Pharisees came up to test Yeshua? (v. 22)

    The use of the word "test" is unfortunate. The Pharisees were not testing Yeshua but rather questioning him in a debate format. They wanted to know if Yeshua was a part of there movement. In Yeshua's day people debated issues to determine which political group they belonged.

Culture Section

Discussion

Near Eastern people do not recognize nor practice civil marriages. The bond between a man and woman in marriage came from the priest and the payment of a dowry. Marriage was considered a sacred institution and was never mixed with politics or courts. Women viewed marriage as a lottery because the marriages were prearranged, and they had no say in whom they married. The sole authority in a marriage was the husband, who could exercise unlimited power over his wife.

Men could divorce their wives for not bearing children, not working hard enough (according to his standard), and were considered and treated as property. Divorce became so easy in Yeshua's day that religious laws had to be instituted.

---

[134] Google Search

Yeshua condemned the laxity of the divorce laws of His day and wanted to strengthen them. Yeshua was against the practice of men divorcing their wives for arbitrary reasons. He also saw how husbands would mistreat their wives. Yeshua believed in the equality of men and women. Therefore, He believed that a woman was not be divorced except on the grounds of adultery.

The House of Hillel believed that divorce should be easy to obtain, while the House of Shammai held onto the Torah code about divorce. The question of divorce between these two different houses of study came to a head about seventy years before Yeshua's birth. During the time between Hillel and Yeshua, the society had expanded divorce. It would have been equivalent to today's no-fault divorce.

The question that most people have when reading this passage is what divorce means today while trying to understand the passage about divorce in Matthew's Gospel. When reading about divorce in the Gospels, the cultural background has to be what the Old Testament said about divorce. The two rabbis of the day spoke about divorce. The sage Hillel and the sage Shammai had very different opinions about divorce.

Verse three says that some Pharisees came to Jesus to test him. Most readers believe that the Pharisees were testing him to find some heresy that they could convict and kill him for, and that is not what they were doing. The Pharisees wanted to see whether Jesus agreed with Hillel or Shammai. Therefore, it is essential to look at what Hillel said about divorce and Shammai's statement about divorce.

In the Hebrew Scriptures, there is no definitive answer about divorce. One thing is sure is that it was the husband's prerogative to divorce his wife. The key passage that is used to tell us about divorce is from Deuteronomy chapter 24, verses one through four.

Deuteronomy 24:1 (NAS95S)   "When a man takes a wife and marries her, and it happens that she finds no favor in his eyes because he has found some indecency in her, and he writes her a certificate of divorce and puts *it* in her hand and sends her out from his house, [2] and she leaves his house and goes and becomes another man's *wife,* [3] and if the latter husband turns against her and writes her a certificate of divorce and puts *it* in her hand and sends her out of his house, or if the latter husband dies who took her to be his wife, [4] *then* her former husband who sent her away is not allowed to take her again to be his wife, since she has been defiled; for that is an abomination before the LORD, and you shall not bring sin on the land which the LORD your God gives you as an inheritance.

This passage mainly says that it is prohibited for a man to divorce his wife and then re-marry her. Leviticus chapter 21 verse seven gives some additional rules about priests getting married. Priests were not allowed to marry divorced women or harlots.

[7] 'They shall not take a woman who is profaned by harlotry, nor shall they take a woman divorced from her husband; for he is holy to his God. (Leviticus 21:7)

In the Gospel of Matthew and Luke, it reads that Joseph betrothed Mary. A betrothal was a contractual agreement between the two families for marriage to occur. Since there was a period between the betrothal and the actual marriage date, a divorce could dissolve the on consummated marriage.

The followers of Shammai believed in the strict interpretation of the Torah. Today we would say that they were followers of the letters of the law. The followers of Hillel would be considered more liberal and allowed a man to divorce his wife far beyond the Deuteronomy chapter 4, verses one through four. The Pharisees came to talk to Jesus to see which side he was going to agree with. The answer Jesus gives in verse eight places him in the strict interpretation of the Torah and agreement with Shammai. On the other hand, Hillel believed in what we call today no-fault divorce. Hillel believed it should be easy for his followers to dissolve a marriage.

In the Jewish world, the political leadership of that day was the Herod family. Herod the great had multiple wives. History says he divorced his first wife, Doris, to marry Mariame, the high priest's daughter. Herod's sister Salome sent the document to her husband, Costobarus dissolving their marriage. Herod Antipas divorced his wife, the daughter of Nabatean king of Aretas to marry Herodias. Herodias was able to get a divorce from her uncle Herod Philip in order to marry Herod Antipas.

Herod Agrippa I had three daughters who had multiple marriages. Drusilla divorced Azizus, king of Emeasa in Syria, to marry the Roman governor Felix. Bernice married her uncle Herod of Chalcis. After his death, she married Polemo, king of Cilicia, whom she divorced to have sexual relations with her brother Herod Agrippa II. Mariamme divorced her husband Julius Archelaus so that she could marry Demetrius, the alabarch of Alexandria. The Herod family agreed with Hillel about a no-fault divorce.

The debate between Hillel and Shammai centered over the Deuteronomy passage, chapter 24, verses one through four. The actual argument is found in the first verse.

עֶרְוַת דָּבָר

What Shammai did was to invert this phrase to read:

דָּבָר עֶרְוַת

English translation of these two words is "a matter of decency." By flipping these two words, Shammai said that divorce was only possible in the case of adultery. While Hillel said that the words in their original order meant that any defect that could cause a husband to be dissatisfied was legal grounds for divorce. Under Hillel's view, any matter brought up by a husband could result in a divorce. Hillel's view became the dominant factor in the culture during Yeshua's lifetime. It is clear that this view was accepted by the Herod family, as shown by the number of divorces each one of them had.

The Mishnah and the Talmud list many reasons why a husband could divorce his wife. For example, if a wife went out into public with her hair unbound, spins in the street, or speaks - if she curses her husband's parents in his presence, the husband could divorce her and give her a writ of divorce. The Tosefta says that divorce was possible if a wife went out in public with messy clothes or bathed in the public bath with a man present. It even said that a husband could divorce his wife if she exposed her arms in public. These three writings also said that divorce was obligatory if the wife had committed adultery.

When a marriage was arranged, a written agreement was drawn up called the *ketubah*. The *ketubah* was an agreement between the groom and the father or another male guardian of the bride. Usually, the bride was in her early teens when the agreement was made. It also contained a pledge payment to the wife in case there was a divorce. The standard divorce payment was set at 200 sacred shekels, which would pay for the wife's sustenance for seven or eight months. The wife usually came with the dowry, and if a divorce occurred, the dowry needed to be returned. The husband was liable for the payment of any divorce money and the return of the dowry. To validate a divorce, the papers would be given to the wife, and it would be registered in the Jewish court.[135]

Thoughts

Verses one through nine was a debate between Jesus and the Pharisees about divorce. The people who followed Hillel (a sage who lived about 70 years before Jesus) believed that divorce should exist for just about any reason. This situation favored men and was a detriment to women. Jesus consistently demonstrated his concern for the disenfranchised. Women were the largest segment of the disenfranchised. When her husband divorced, her world was shattered. Hillel made it easy to divorce. Jesus disagreed with that view. Jesus was on the side of Shammai (a rival sage who lived during the time of Hillel), who believed that a divorce required strict adherence to the Torah.

---

[135] Edwin M. Yamauchi and Marvin R. Wilson, *Dictionary of Daily Life: in Biblical and Post-Biblical Antiquity,* Peabody Massachusetts: Hendrickson Publishers, 2015.

Reflections

In the United States and other countries, divorce has become no-fault. There are fancy legal words used for no-fault, but the bottom line is that we know have a no-fault divorce option. How do we deal with a culture that wants an easy divorce when Jesus was against it. I am not taking any stand for or against the way divorce occurs in the US today. I do pray that the couples that I united in marriage will stay married.

On the other hand, life is too short to be miserable. If a marriage is not working and cannot be reconciled, then why continue it? Divorce releases the two people from the difficulties of living together, and each can decide what their next step in life will be. A marriage covenant should be respected, and everything possible should be done to save it. Unfortunately, some marriages will not continue even after all of the attempts to bandage it. A divorce may become the only way to cure the marriage. Divorce should be used as a last resort.

MARK 10:13-16

Language

New American Standard 1995	Koine Greek
[13] And they were bringing children to Him so that He might touch them; but the disciples rebuked them. [14] But when Jesus saw this, He was indignant and said to them, "Permit the children to come to Me; do not hinder them; for the kingdom of God belongs to such as these. [15] "Truly I say to you, whoever does not receive the kingdom of God like a child will not enter it *at all.*" [16] And He took them in His arms and *began* blessing them, laying His hands on them.	[13] Καὶ προσέφερον αὐτῷ παιδία ἵνα ἅψηται αὐτῶν οἱ δὲ μαθηταὶ ἐπετίμων τοῖς προσφέρουσιν. [14] Ἰδὼν δὲ ὁ Ἰησοῦς ἠγανάκτησεν, καὶ εἶπεν αὐτοῖς, Ἄφετε τὰ παιδία ἔρχεσθαι πρός με, μὴ κωλύετε αὐτα τῶν γὰρ τοιουτων ἐστιν ἡ βασιλεία τοῦ θεοῦ. [15] Ἀμὴν λέγω ὑμῖν, ὃς ἐὰν μὴ δέξηται τὴν βασιλείαν τοῦ θεοῦ ὡς παιδίον, οὐ μὴ εἰσέλθῃ εἰς αὐτήν. [16] Καὶ ἐναγκαλισάμενος αὐτά, τιθεὶς τὰς χεῖρας ἐπ᾽ αὐτά, εὐλογεῖ αὐτά.

Process of Discovery

Linguistics Section

Linguistic Structure

A [13] And they were bringing children to Him so that He might touch them; but the disciples rebuked them.

> **B** [14] But when Jesus saw this, He was indignant and said to them, "Permit the children to come to Me; do not hinder them; for the kingdom of God belongs to such as these. [15] "Truly I say to you, *a*whoever does not receive the kingdom of God like a child will not enter it *at all*."

A' [16] And He *a*took them in His arms and *began* blessing them, laying His hands on them.

Discussion

The chiasm is developed around the action of Yeshua with the children.

Culture Section

Discussion

This event has much meat to it. Surprisingly, Christian academic commentaries have very little information about the passage. These commentaries say that children were brought to Yeshua, and the disciples tried to stop the parents from doing it. Yeshua tells the disciples to bring the children forward. The authors of these commentaries do not take into account the culture of Yeshua's day. Projecting twenty-first century culture to events in the Scripture offers the least accurate interpretation. This event is an excellent example of this problem. When the culture is examined, it will become clear what is happening in this passage.

Questioning the passage

1. What was the view of children in Yeshua's day in the Middle East?
   Middle Eastern parents in Yeshua's day treated their children differently than Western parents did. Middle Eastern parents loved their children just as much as Western parents did. One difference between their parenting was that Middle Easter parents, at times,

disciplined their children too severely. Middle Eastern children did not receive training concerning good manners and cleanliness. Their behavior was often neglected, which allowed them to develop bad habits.

When parents entertained honorable guests, they swept the house clean before the guests arrived. They would send their children out of the house with the instructions not to return until the guests left. The host and the guests' servants kept a steady vigilance to prevent unwanted noise, people entering the home with soiled clothing and children with dirty faces. Children tended to do acts that embarrassed the host. They would also ask foolish questions and make uncalled-for remarks.[136]

The custom was different when a holy man visited the home. Every man would present his boys to the holy man to bless them and protect them from diseases.

2. Why did the disciples rebuke the children?
The disciples did not view Yeshua as a holy man at that time. They saw him as a king rather than as a prophet. The disciples expected Yeshua to restore the Davidic kingdom with Yeshua as the king. Since the custom was to bring the boys to a holy man and not an honored guest, the disciples rebuked the boys.

The parents who brought their children to Yeshua saw him as a holy man and followed their custom. They did not see Yeshua as a political ruler but rather as the Messiah who was going to bring the LORD's kingdom to the Earth.

3. Why did Yeshua allow the children to come to him?
Children are open-minded, free from dogmatic traditions, and did not harbor hatred for anyone. To the children, all men were equal, and none were more important than their parents. Yeshua was demonstrating that there is no rank in the Kingdom of Heaven. All

---

[136] Rocco A. Errico and George M. Lamsa, *Aramaic Light on the Gospel of Matthew: a Commentary on the Teachings of Jesus from the Aramaic and Unchanged Near Eastern Customs* (Santa Fe, NM: Noohra Foundation, 2000).

humans are equal in the LORD's eyes. Yeshua showed that the children were the future recruits of His kingdom and needed to learn about Him while young.[137]

Additional analysis

This passage says that the disciples thought of Yeshua as a new King at the moment of the event. The disciples did not imagine Yeshua as the Messiah nor as a holy man. If the disciples understood Yeshua to be a holy man, they would have never stopped the fathers from bringing their sons to see the holy man. The disciples viewed Yeshua as the military king who would rid the country of the Romans. It is easy for the twenty-first-century reader to condemn the disciples for not understanding the true nature of Yeshua. That is an unfair analysis. Even after the resurrection, the disciples will grapple with the question of who Yeshua was. The author of Matthew's Gospel wanted to make a clear statement that Yeshua was not the king the disciples were looking for but instead was the Messiah, the Holy Man, that Yeshua indeed was. The author of the Gospel probably had people in the Christian community who questioned what Messiah Yeshua was. The idea of two Messiahs was prevalent and came from Zechariah 9:9. So which Messiah was Yeshua? Having the boys come to Him to be blessed, Yeshua demonstrated that He is the holy man, the LORD's Messiah. Therefore, the boys coming to Yeshua for blessings were in the context of the culture.

Thoughts

The boys (custom says that girls were not taken to the holy men) were clay that could be molded to any shape for their entrance into the Kingdom of Heaven. Young children do not have the paradigms that tradition will force them into as they learn and grow up. It may be challenging to discover Heaven's kingdom because the paradigms that the church teaches may not be the valid paradigms of Heaven. Where did the church's views on theology develop from? Today's churches started with the conversion of Mithras churches. The paradigms of Mithras became paradigms of the church. As the church evangelized and expanded, it picked up paradigms from the religions it was converting. Christianity absorbed pagan beliefs and rituals, applying them to Yeshua's words found in the Gospels. Is the Kingdom of Heaven that the church espouses today the Kingdom of Heaven that Yeshua spoke? Probably not. The core paradigms of Judaism that survived the centuries

---

[137] IBID.

are valid. The rest is questionable. Learning the original meaning of Scripture will break down the paradigms and allow the true meaning of Yeshua's word to break through.

Reflections

Children do not have the paradigms of what church must be as adults do who grew up in the church. Adults who come to know Yeshua and join the church are not saddled with the traditional church paradigms. These are the adults that the church desperately needs to listen to in order to reach people who have not come to know Yeshua. These adults can tell the church which paradigms they needed to break through to be able to develop a faith in Yeshua and to join a church. Unfortunately, many of these adults discover that the church is inflexible to change. The tombstone of a former local church should read, "We will never change." There are functional paradigms that the local churches have that are necessary and should remain intact. However, there are many paradigms that the local church needs to rid itself of. Church LISTEN to these newly baptized adults and learn from them. They are the best resource to discover the changes needed for the church's survival.

MARK 10:17-27

Language

New American Standard 1995	Koine Greek
[17] As He was setting out on a journey, a man ran up to Him and knelt before Him, and asked Him, "Good Teacher, what shall I do to inherit eternal life?" [18] And Jesus said to him, "Why do you call Me good? No one is good except God alone. [19] "You know the commandments, 'DO NOT MURDER, DO NOT COMMIT ADULTERY, DO NOT STEAL, DO NOT BEAR FALSE WITNESS, Do not defraud, HONOR YOUR FATHER AND MOTHER.'" [20] And he said to Him, "Teacher, I have kept all these things from my youth up." [21] Looking at him, Jesus felt a love for him and said to him, "One thing you lack: go and sell all you possess and give to the poor, and you will have treasure in heaven; and come, follow Me." [22] But at these words he was saddened, and he went away grieving, for he was one who owned much property. [23] And Jesus, looking around, said to His disciples, "How hard it will be for those who are wealthy to enter the kingdom of God!" [24] The disciples were amazed at His words. But Jesus answered again and said to them, "Children, how hard it is to enter the kingdom of God! [25] "It is easier for a camel to go through the eye of a needle than for a rich man to enter the kingdom of God." [26] They were even more astonished and said to Him, "Then who can be saved?" [27] Looking at them, Jesus said, "'With people it is impossible, but not with God; for all things are possible with God."	[23] Καὶ περιβλεψάμενος ὁ Ἰησοῦς λέγει τοῖς μαθηταῖς αὐτοῦ, Πῶς δυσκόλως οἱ τὰ χρήματα ἔχοντες εἰς τὴν βασιλείαν τοῦ θεοῦ εἰσελεύσονται. [24] Οἱ δὲ μαθηταὶ ἐθαμβοῦντο ἐπὶ τοῖς λόγοις αὐτοῦ. Ὁ δὲ Ἰησοῦς πάλιν ἀποκριθεὶς λέγει αὐτοῖς, Τέκνα, πῶς δύσκολόν ἐστιν τοὺς πεποιθότας ἐπὶ χρήμασιν εἰς τὴν βασιλείαν τοῦ θεοῦ εἰσελθεῖν. [25] Εὐκοπώτερον ἐστιν κάμηλον διὰ τῆς τρυμαλιᾶς τῆς ῥαφίδος εἰσελθεῖν, ἢ πλούσιον εἰς τὴν βασιλείαν τοῦ θεοῦ εἰσελθεῖν. [26] Οἱ δὲ περισσῶς ἐξεπλήσσοντο, λέγοντες πρὸς ἑαυτούς, Καὶ τίς δύναται σωθῆναι; [27] Ἐμβλέψας δὲ αὐτοῖς ὁ Ἰησοῦς λέγει, Παρὰ ἀνθρώποις ἀδύνατον, ἀλλ᾽ οὐ παρὰ θεῷ· πάντα γὰρ δυνατά ἐστιν παρὰ τῷ θεῷ.

Process of Discovery

  Linguistics Section

   Linguistic Structure

[Question] [17] *a*As He was setting out on a journey, a man ran up to Him and knelt before Him, and asked Him, "Good Teacher, what shall I do to inherit eternal life?"

[Answer] [18] And Jesus said to him, "Why do you call Me good? No one is good except God alone. [19] "You know the commandments, *a*DO NOT MURDER, DO NOT COMMIT ADULTERY, DO NOT STEAL, DO NOT BEAR FALSE WITNESS, Do not defraud, HONOR YOUR FATHER AND MOTHER."'

[Question] [20] And he said to Him, "Teacher, I have kept all these things from my youth up."

[Answer] [21] Looking at him, Jesus felt a love for him and said to him, "One thing you lack: go and sell all you possess and give to the poor, and you will have *a*treasure in heaven; and come, follow Me."

[Result] [22] But at these words he was saddened, and he went away grieving, for he was one who owned much property.

[Yeshua's words] [23] And Jesus, looking around, said to His disciples, "*a*How hard it will be for those who are wealthy to enter the kingdom of God!"

[Parable] [24] The disciples were amazed at His words. But Jesus answered again and said to them, "Children, how hard it is to enter the kingdom of God! [25] "*a*It is easier for a camel to go through the eye of a needle than for a rich man to enter the kingdom of God."

[Disciples question] [26] They were even more astonished and said to Him, "*a*Then who can be saved?" [27] Looking at them, Jesus said, "*a*With people it is impossible, but not with God; for all things are possible with God."

Discussion

A man comes to Yeshua and discusses the means of entering Heaven. Why did Yeshua tell him to give up his wealth? Perhaps it is because when the need for money envelops a person, they tend to forget about other obligations. Money becomes a god, and that is idolatry.

Questioning the Passage

1. What does the parable mean in verse 25?

    The Aramaic word for camel is *gamla,* but it can also mean "rope" or "beam." The context of the sentence is what determines the usage of the word. When the sentence is referring to riding a camel or the burden of carrying objects, then the word means "camel." When the phrase "eye of a needle" is in the sentence, then *gamla* more correctly means "rope."[138]

    The problem is that Yeshua spoke Aramaic, not Greek. Therefore, someone had to translate the Aramaic into Greek. When that translation was done, the nuances of the word *gamla* were not taken into account. This same type of translation can be found in the Septuagint, Isaiah 7:14. The Hebrew says young maiden while the Greek translation says virgin. Therefore, using the Aramaic, the verse reads, "It is easier for a rope to go through the eye of a needle, than for a rich man to enter into the kingdom of God."

    People kept ropes in their homes for different purposes. The unused ropes were hung on the wall or placed in the corner of the house. Yeshua likes to use familiar objects when creating His parables. He could have pointed to the ropes to illustrate what he was saying. Needles came in several different sizes, like today. There were little needles for elegant embroidery, standard sewing needles, and enormous needles. Large needles were used for large bags, rugs, and tents. These needles were five to seven inches in length. A large rope would be used with the huge needle. The large rope could pass through the eye of the needle.

---

[138] Rocco A. Errico and George M. Lamsa, Aramaic Light on the Gospel of Matthew: a Commentary on the Teachings of Jesus from the Aramaic and Unchanged Near Eastern Customs (Santa Fe, NM: Noohra Foundation, 2000).

Many Christian scholars believe that Yeshua was referring to the needle's eye, which was a name for a little gate in a city wall. There are no known instances of any Near Eastern city having needle's eye gates where camels could bow down and pass through.[139]

This understanding is an incorrect interpretation of the phrase. However, suppose the translation of the Aramaic words of Yeshua into Greek combined with the Greek interpretation of the word occurred. In that case, it can be seen how this misinterpretation occurred.

Rich men can enter the Kingdom of Heaven if they share the wealth that the LORD has given them with people who are in need. The world's wealth was created by the LORD to be used by all of the LORD's children.

2. Is Yeshua telling us to give all our wealth away and that being rich is bad? (v. 17)
This verse is misinterpreted by the mainline churches today. If everyone gave away everything they had, the poor would be better off, but there would be a new class of poor people. Yeshua was saying that just following the book of Laws was not enough to enter the kingdom of Heaven. Yeshua said that one must work for the kingdom of Heaven!

Wealth and riches are a blessing from the LORD. People are stewards of the blessings and riches. It is how one attends to their wealth that matters. It is difficult to near impossible to attend to one's wealth and serve the Kingdom of Heaven at the same time. In today's world, that may be possible, but in Yeshua's day, it certainly was not. How can a man attend to his farm and serve the Kingdom of Heaven at the same time? The man could not do both.

"Sell everything and give to the poor" is interpreted literally by the church today (a Western/Greek way of interpretation). Yeshua did not intend this statement to apply to all people. Yeshua was telling the rich man who wanted to become an active member of

---

[139] IBID.

the Kingdom of Heaven that he had to sell all he had so that he could concentrate only on the Kingdom of Heaven. Yeshua never intended this statement to be a general command.

When a rope was passed into the eye of a needle small amounts of the rope would fray. Yeshua is using this example to say that if one has extra resources that they should be shared. The rich man must have had a large excess. He was unwilling to give more away then the biblically required tithe.

Culture Section

Questioning the passage

1. What was the culture of rich men in Yeshua's day? (v. 22)
   Greedy and wicked rich people were hated and despised in the Near East. They were the targets of preachers, prophets, and politicians. These types of wealthy people oppressed the poor in order to amass their wealth. They used the wrong ways to obtain wealth, for example, bribery, extortion, and confiscation.

   A strange custom of the time was that rich men became government officials and were promoted and demoted depending on their accumulated wealth. Usually, a rich greedy man would have certain privileges. Their property was not taxed. They were often appointed as tax collectors. In that role, they could extort the people in the name of the government. The oppression created by the greedy rich people resulted in discontent and bitterness among the people.

   When a government official entered a town, the wicked rich man would entertain the government official. The entertainment was done at the people's expense. Sheep and cattle were confiscated and killed by the wealthy to feed their important guests. Government visitors were given rugs, money, and other valuable articles from the oppressed people, not the rich man.

If the wealth of a greedy rich man decreased, he would lose his government position. During times of famine, rich men collected sheep and wheat from their subjects so that their wealth might not diminish.

People would say: "God blesses rich men." Unfortunately, many men did not wait until God blessed them. Instead, they amassed their wealth through injustice. These are the greedy rich men that Yeshua was condemning. Yeshua was not attacking the rich men who became rich via the blessing of the LORD but rather the ones who become wealthy at the cost of the poor.[140]

Culture and Linguistics Section

Discussion

Verse twenty-four is the example of culture and linguistics intersecting. The "camel" is probably not what Yeshua said. Yeshua used examples from His culture. Poor Galileans did not have the money to own camels. They would not have been familiar with camels. Ropes they knew all about and kept many in their homes. *Gamal* from Aramaic can be translated as "camel" or "rope." The context of the passage indicates that the translation "rope" is appropriated. That one error in the Greek translation gave rise to a saying of Yeshua that is considered difficult to understand. In order for the Greek minded church to make sense of it, the theologians had to develop some fascinating explanations. Using the translation of "rope," the parable comes to life and make sense.

---

[140] IBID.

Thoughts

Have you ever tried to thread a needle for clothing repair? It is a difficult task for young eyes and extremely difficult for old eyes. When *gamla* from the Aramaic is translated into "rope" instead of "camel," the parable about the needle makes perfect sense. It is difficult to thread a needle with a rope, even a big needle. It will be even more difficult for a rich man to enter the kingdom of heaven if, and that is huge if, the rich man does not use his God-given wealth to help the poor or if the rich man obtains his wealth at the cost of other people. A tithe goes to the church. After that, the LORD expects Almsgiving. When one has wealth that can be used for Almsgiving and does not, Yeshua says that person will not enter heaven.

Reflections

The church has abused this passage for centuries. First, it is a conversation between Yeshua and a man. Yeshua's answer to the question of eternal life was correct for the man He was speaking with. It is not an answer that is supposed to be universal. However, the church uses it universally. The church likes to say that money is a bad thing. Wait a minute, how much is the Catholic church worth, not just Vatican City?

Bankers estimate that the Vatican alone is worth between ten and fifteen billion dollars, and probably, even more, that does not include the buildings in the Vatican. The Vatican has enormous investments in Italy and other places in the world. If the local churches are added, this number will skyrocket. Who knows what the actual value of the Catholic church is because there are holdings of the church outside the Vatican.

How can the church say that wealth is bad for the individual, but church wealth is good? This is a hypocritical position. Does the Vatican accept the western view of Yeshua about rich men while being rich itself? Sure appears that way? The wealth that comes from the LORD and is used to help people is good wealth. The wealth that oppresses and extorts people and is not used to help the poor is terrible. How you obtain your wealth and what you do with it either angers or pleases the LORD. The best thing to do is to satisfy the LORD.

Additional Thoughts

The LORD created wealth by creating this world and everything in it. Yeshua said that the poor will always be with us. The Talmud says that the LORD created poor people so that more affluent people could help impoverished people. The church has used this passage to tell its members to give more money to the church. During the stewardship campaigns that usually land in the fall of every year, this story is used to shame members into giving more money to the church.

Sadly while the church tells its members to give more money, the church also says Yeshua does not like rich people. But the church accumulates wealth and pays big salaries to its Bishops and other high-ranking officials. As it turns out, the original meaning of this passage is about the abuse of money and obtaining wealth by hurting other people. The bottom line of all of the analysis is:

YESHUA LIKES RICH PEOPLE WHO OBTAIN THEIR WEALTH FROM THE LORD AND USES PART OF THAT WEALTH TO HELP THE POOR

This statement is the original meaning of the Rich Man story in the Gospels. There is nothing wrong with being wealthy. Yeshua DID NOT tell rich people to give all their wealth away. Instead, Yeshua said, USE YOUR WEALTH to help others. The Torah says that a tithe, 10%, goes to the LORD (for Christians today, that is the church). Almsgiving follows and can go up to 35%. Almsgiving is what you can spare after the tithe and paying your bills.

So do not feel bad when you accumulate wealth because the LORD has blessed you with talents and skills. The LORD creates people who can accumulate wealth. Do not let the church tell you anything different. If the LORD gave you this talent and you obtain wealth, then be proud that you are using your God-given talents the way the LORD wants you to by taking care of your family and helping others.

May you continue to grow in your understanding of the Gospel.

MARK 10:28-31

Language

New American Standard 1995	Koine Greek
[28] Peter began to say to Him, "Behold, we have left everything and followed You." [29] Jesus said, "Truly I say to you, there is no one who has left house or brothers or sisters or mother or father or children or farms, for My sake and for the Gospel's sake, [30] but that he will receive a hundred times as much now in the present age, houses and brothers and sisters and mothers and children and farms, along with persecutions; and in the age to come, eternal life. [31] "But many *who are* first will be last, and the last, first."	[28] Ἤρξατο ὁ Πέτρος λέγειν αὐτῷ, Ἰδού, ἡμεῖς ἀφήκαμεν πάντα, καὶ ἠκολουθήσαμέν σοι. [29] Ἀποκριθεὶς ὁ Ἰησοῦς εἶπεν, Ἀμὴν λέγω ὑμῖν, οὐδείς ἐστιν ὃς ἀφῆκεν οἰκίαν, ἢ ἀδελφούς, ἢ ἀδελφάς, ἢ πατέρα, ἢ μητέρα, ἢ γυναῖκα, ἢ τέκνα, ἢ ἀγρούς, ἕνεκεν ἐμοῦ καὶ ἕνεκεν τοῦ εὐαγγελίου, [30] ἐὰν μὴ λάβῃ ἑκατονταπλασίονα νῦν ἐν τῷ καιρῷ τούτῳ, οἰκίας καὶ ἀδελφοὺς καὶ ἀδελφὰς καὶ μητέρας καὶ τέκνα καὶ ἀγρούς, μετὰ διωγμῶν, καὶ ἐν τῷ αἰῶνι τῷ ἐρχομένῳ ζωὴν αἰώνιον. [31] Πολλοὶ δὲ ἔσονται πρῶτοι ἔσχατοι, καὶ ἔσχατοι πρῶτοι.

Process of Discovery

Linguistics Section

Linguistic Structure

[Disciples' statement] [28]   Peter began to say to Him, "Behold, we have left everything and followed You."

[Yeshua's response] [29] Jesus said, "Truly I say to you, there is no one who has left house or brothers or sisters or mother or father or children or farms, for My sake and for the Gospel's sake, [30] but that he will receive a hundred times as much now in the present age, houses and brothers and sisters and mothers and children and farms, along with persecutions; and in *a*the age to come, eternal life. [31] "But *a*many *who are* first will be last, and the last, first."

Discussion

This passage is a simple statement by the disciples and Yeshua's response. It is a fair question from Yeshua's disciples about what they will receive from giving up everything they had to spread His message. Note that the message of the Gospel is not theirs at this point.

Questioning the Passage

1. What is the implication of the Peshitta having the word "not" in verse thirty?
   The Peshitta reads, "who will not receive a hundredfold." The NASB and Koine Greek do not have the "not" in this verse. The difference is enormous. Since Yeshua spoke Aramaic, He told His disciples that they should not expect to receive a material payment for following Him. The culture said that the owner would give a worker on a farm a reward if the worker was asked to go to war with him. Taking up the task of spreading the Gospel was equivalent to asking the disciples to go to war. They probably thought that Yeshua would double, or more, their material possessions. Yeshua said they would receive huge rewards for spreading the Gospel message, not on Earth but in Heaven. Yeshua spoke about storing treasures in Heaven, and this was more important than storing material treasures on Earth.

Why would the Greek translators of Yeshua's words change what He said? The conditions for the early Yeshua movement met quite a bit of resistance from the ruling Jewish class and eventually from the Roman government. Why would people join the community to be persecuted? It is a strong possibility that the "not" was removed so that the Christian community would say that following Yeshua, thus changing religion, would result in material gains in this world. Today, this offer is still used by the Church to attract people to the Christian faith. The offer from Yeshua is for future gains in Heaven.

2. Why did the Greek translators use "persecutions" instead of "pursued" in verse thirty? Considering the removal of the word "not" in verse thirty coupled with the persecutions of the early Christian communities, the leadership had to explain why that was happening to them. The people who joined these communities did not experience one hundredfold gains in material possessions and were not protected from outside attacks. Therefore, the early Church used the translation of "persecution." Then the Church could say that Yeshua's promise of materialism was being hampered by the outside attacks of Jews and Romans. The Aramaic word used in the Peshitta is *rdopyah*. This word means "pursue, follow, and persecute." The English version of the Peshitta, like the NASB 1995, uses the translation "persecutions." The translation could be "along with other pursuits." There is so much more than disciples of Yeshua will receive in Heaven that can be pursued while on Earth. Again, this verse is a reference to storing Heavenly treasures instead of storing treasures on Earth.[141]

Culture Section

Discussion

Yeshua's day people did not have regular working hours instead of work schedules and factory shifts like today. Laborers worked from sunrise to sunset while shepherds and servants worked when necessary. Shepherds and servants rarely had the time to visit their families. Servants were required to be on call at the master of the house's desires.

---

[141] Rocco A. Errico, George M. Lamsa, *Aramaic Light on the Gospels of Mark and Luke: a Commentary on the Teachings of Jesus from the Aramaic and Unchanged Near Eastern Customs* (Smyrna, GA: Noohra Foundation, 2001).

Servants would live at their master's house and rarely visited their houses. They needed their master's permission to do so. The family of a servant became secondary to serving the master. They were not slaves. However, they might as well be called slaves because they were treated as such.

When a young man desired to learn a trade, he would leave his family and home to live at his master's house. He would eat, sleep and learn at the master's home. He did this to earn the master's trust so that the secrets of the trade would be passed down to him. Apprentices who lived in their own homes did not find favor with their masters. The masters viewed these apprentices as potential competition and did not invest them with all the trade knowledge. The apprentices who lived at their master's home would often be rewarded with marriage to a daughter of the master, inheriting the business and other property of the master.[142]

Questioning the passage

1. What did Yeshua mean by leaving your family?

    Yeshua was not literally telling His disciples to leave their families nor to forsake them. They were to remain close to their families. What Yeshua meant was that the disciples were to become as closely attached to him as was possible. For the disciples to learn the Gospel and to follow in the footsteps of Yeshua, they needed to become apprentices.

    Yeshua indeed asked them to forget about their wives, children, and their material concerns for a time. This time was their training period, where they learned the secrets of Yeshua's teaching. This act is within the confines of the culture of Yeshua's day. A faithful apprentice was not to have any worldly concerns while they concentrated on their trade. Becoming a Yeshua disciple was just like any trade. A disciple needed (and needs) to learn about the trade of spreading the Gospel message.

---

[142] IBID.

2. What does the reference to one hundred times mean? (v. 30)

   In Yeshua's day, if a man had ten sheep and the lord of the land he was shepherding asked him to go to war, the lord would promise to give the man twenty or more sheep in addition to his ten. Another example is a man who left twenty bushels of wheat in the field to go to war. When he returned, he would have received double that amount.[143] Yeshua promised His disciples that they would receive more than they left behind. When the Peshitta is examined, and the word "not" is understood as being what Yeshua said, the hundredfold is a Heavenly treasure and not an earthly treasure.

Thoughts

The early Church used the idea of "free" stuff when a person came to be a follower of Yeshua. It is documented that early followers of Yeshua had to give up everything that they owned to the general community. This passage has Yeshua telling them to do this. The result of giving everything to the community is to be rewarded with a larger amount of possessions. This made Christianity attractive, especially to peasants who owned very little. The Church still uses the idea of rewards in the present age (on Earth). One will not receive a sizeable materialistic gift because they come to know and love the Gospel. They will receive treasures in Heaven because they will start to act following the Gospel.

Reflections

The idea of persecutions because one became a member of a Yeshua community was well known. When 325CE came, and Emperor Constantine declared Christianity the religion of the Empire, the Church received huge material possessions. The Church received power, money, buildings, and protection. In addition, the Church received millions of new members that could be taxed (for the tithe). 325 CE was a hay day for the Church. Throughout the centuries, the Church held onto the power that Constantine gave it. Today its power is deteriorating because the Church refuses to change with the times. There is one exception, and that is the independent Church. They are flourishing because they understand that culture changes and that they must adapt.

---

[143] IBID.

MARK 10:32-34

Language

New American Standard 1995	Koine Greek
³² They were on the road going up to Jerusalem, and Jesus was walking on ahead of them; and they were amazed, and those who followed were fearful. And again He took the twelve aside and began to tell them what was going to happen to Him, ³³ *saying,* "Behold, we are going up to Jerusalem, and the Son of Man will be delivered to the chief priests and the scribes; and they will condemn Him to death and will hand Him over to the Gentiles. ³⁴ "They will mock Him and spit on Him, and scourge Him and kill *Him,* and three days later He will rise again."	³² Ἦσαν δὲ ἐν τῇ ὁδῷ ἀναβαίνοντες εἰς Ἱεροσόλυμα καὶ ἦν προάγων αὐτοὺς ὁ Ἰησοῦς, καὶ ἐθαμβοῦντο, καὶ ἀκολουθοῦντες ἐφοβοῦντο. Καὶ παραλαβὼν πάλιν τοὺς δώδεκα, ἤρξατο αὐτοῖς λέγειν τὰ μέλλοντα αὐτῷ συμβαίνειν ³³ ὅτι Ἰδού, ἀναβαίνομεν εἰς Ἱεροσόλυμα, καὶ ὁ υἱὸς τοῦ ἀνθρώπου παραδοθήσεται τοῖς ἀρχιερεῦσιν καὶ γραμματεῦσιν, καὶ κατακρινοῦσιν αὐτὸν θανάτω, καὶ παραδώσουσιν αὐτὸν τοῖς ἔθνεσιν, ³⁴ καὶ ἐμπαίξουσιν αὐτῷ, καὶ μαστιγώσουσιν αὐτόν, καὶ ἐμπτύσουσιν αὐτῷ, καὶ ἀποκτενοῦσιν αὐτὸν καὶ τῇ τρίτῃ ἡμέρᾳ ἀναστήσεται.

Process of Discovery

Linguistics Section

Linguistic Structure

[Movement] [32] They were on the road going up to Jerusalem, and Jesus was walking on ahead of them; and they were amazed, and those who followed were fearful. And again He took the twelve aside and began to tell them what was going to happen to Him, [33] *saying,*

[Prediction] "Behold, we are going up to Jerusalem, and the Son of Man will be delivered to the chief priests and the scribes; and they will condemn Him to death and will hand Him over to the Gentiles. [34] "They will mock Him and spit on Him, and scourge Him and kill *Him,* and three days later He will rise again."

Discussion

This passage is the third time that Yeshua has predicted His death. Three times is an indication that this is a divine event that occurred. There are several theological views of the atonement. How and when does one receives forgiveness of sin? No matter which theology is correct, this passage says that Yeshua's death in the manner tells us it was of divine origin, not unlike the prophets that came before Yeshua.

Questioning the Passage

1. What is the significance of going to Jerusalem? (v. 32)

    Jerusalem was the center of Judaism in Yeshua's day. It was considered the place for prophets to die. The reason was that prophets brought messages from the LORD that Kings and Temple Priests usually did not like. Prophets were sent by the LORD generally because the leaders of Israel were leading the people astray. It is the responsibility of leaders to ensure that the people serve the LORD.

2. What does it mean to go up to Jerusalem? (v. 32)

    The city of Jerusalem is on the top of Mount Zion. It is approximately 2,500 feet above sea level. Yeshua left Jericho, which is 900 feet below sea level, to go to Jerusalem. Today people who immigrate to Israel say that they are going up to Jerusalem even if they live on the coast of the country. Going up to Jerusalem has a spiritual dimension. Even if one was on Mount Everest, one still goes up to Jerusalem. The spiritual climb up the mountain can be viewed as increasing one's spiritual knowledge and awareness of the LORD.[144]

The concept of going up to Jerusalem is in the Kabbalah. One starts in the tenth emanation of Malkhut, and it is a spiritual climb to reach Chesed. While reading the Gospel of Matthew from this point, one should think about their spiritual climb to get closer to the LORD.

3. Why are the Gentiles mentioned? (v. 33)

Verse thirty-three is the first time that the Gentiles are mentioned concerning Yeshua's upcoming death. Yeshua is saying that the priests of the Temple will condemn Him to death, but it will be the Gentiles who perform the execution. In Yeshua's day, capital punishment was restricted to the Roman government. The priests could not execute Yeshua. However, they could condemn him to death.

For centuries the Church has condemned and punished Jews in the name of Yeshua because they caused His death. The Church's position was that the Gentiles had no part in Yeshua's execution. This passage says the opposite. The Gentiles had the opportunity to exonerate Yeshua and prevent His execution. The Gentiles did not stop Yeshua's execution. The Gentiles did the execution.

The Church's position throughout the centuries is not correct. It cannot hide behind the statement that it was only the Jews that wanted Yeshua dead. The Gentiles who had the power to stop the execution and scourging of Yeshua could have stopped it. Suppose the Church is looking to assign the responsibility for Yeshua's execution to someone. In that case, it has to assign it to all the people who were a part of it.

---

[144] David H. Stern, *Jewish New Testament Commentary: a Companion Volume to the Jewish New Testament* (Clarksville, MD: Jewish New Testament Publications, 1999).

Yeshua had his disciples, and a group of loyal followers understood Yeshua as the spiritual Messiah. This group was mainly composed of Jews, and it contained a small number of Gentile believers. They did not want Yeshua's execution. However, Yeshua went against the Temple leaders as all the LORD's prophets had done. At the same time, the Roman leaders wanted peace. Yeshua's entry into Jerusalem awoke the priests and Roman leaders. Therefore, it can be said that Jews and Gentiles wanted Him dead.

Thoughts

Are you traveling up to Jerusalem? The question is asking about your spirituality. What is your spiritual life? There are many ways in which to increase your spiritual awareness and blend it into your life. The Holy Spirit is always with us. Thus, the Divine is in us. The LORD breathed life into Adam, and his breath brought each of us to life. Our spiritual quest throughout our lives should be to strive to learn everything possible about the LORD and to come as close as possible to our Messiah, Jesus Christ. Spiritual life is manifested in physical life as long as one is alive. It is possible and desirable to integrate the two. One's words and actions should emulate the love and grace the LORD gives to us through Jesus Christ.

Reflections

How does a disciple of Jesus Christ grow spiritually? One way is to start with the Bible. The Bible offers a view of the LORD. The grace and love of the LORD are found in the pages of the Bible. Biblical passages dealing with punishment are a learning tool for us to digest and absorb so that we can avoid the mistakes of people in the past. It is said that people either learn from history or become destined to repeat it. Spiritual growth occurs by moving away from sin and towards acceptance of the lessons of the Scriptures. Everything in the Bible is there for our spiritual growth. As you grow spiritually, you will be confronted with new understandings of the Bible. Sometimes it will be frightening because what you discover in your spiritual growth may contradict what you were taught to believe. Do not let that possibility concern you. The LORD knows that transformations in understanding occur as each person grows spiritually. It is essential to be open to new possibilities and new learnings.

MARK 10:35-45

Language

New American Standard 1995	Koine Greek
[35] James and John, the two sons of Zebedee, came up to Jesus, saying, "Teacher, we want You to do for us whatever we ask of You." [36] And He said to them, "What do you want Me to do for you?" [37] They said to Him, "Grant that we [a]may sit, one on Your right and one on *Your* left, in Your glory." [38] But Jesus said to them, "You do not know what you are asking. Are you able to drink the cup that I drink, or to be baptized with the baptism with which I am baptized?" [39] They said to Him, "We are able." And Jesus said to them, "The cup that I drink [a]you shall drink; and you shall be baptized with the baptism with which I am baptized. [40] "But to sit on My right or on *My* left, this is not Mine to give; but it is for those for whom it has been prepared." [41] Hearing *this,* the ten began to feel indignant with James and John. [42] Calling them to Himself, Jesus said to them, "You know that those who are recognized as rulers of the Gentiles lord it over them; and their great men exercise authority over them. [43] "But it is not this way among you, but whoever wishes to become great among you shall be your servant; [44] and whoever wishes to be first among you shall be slave of all. [45] "For even the Son of Man did not come to be served, but to serve, and to give His life a ransom for many."	[35] Καὶ προσπορεύονται αὐτῷ Ἰάκωβος καὶ Ἰωάννης οἱ υἱοὶ Ζεβεδαίου, λέγοντες, Διδάσκαλε, θέλομεν ἵνα ὃ ἐὰν αἰτήσωμεν, ποιήσῃς ἡμῖν. [36] Ὁ δὲ εἶπεν αὐτοῖς, Τί θέλετε ποιῆσαί με ὑμῖν; [37] Οἱ δὲ εἶπον αὐτῷ, Δὸς ἡμῖν, ἵνα εἷς ἐκ δεξιῶν σου καὶ εἷς ἐξ εὐωνύμων σου καθίσωμεν ἐν τῇ δόξῃ σου. [38] Ὁ δὲ Ἰησοῦς εἶπεν αὐτοῖς, Οὐκ οἴδατε τί αἰτεῖσθε. Δύνασθε πιεῖν τὸ ποτήριον ὃ ἐγὼ πίνω, καὶ τὸ βάπτισμα ὃ ἐγὼ βαπτίζομαι βαπτισθῆναι; [39] Οἱ δὲ εἶπον αὐτῷ, Δυνάμεθα. Ὁ δὲ Ἰησοῦς εἶπεν αὐτοῖς, Τὸ μὲν ποτήριον ὃ ἐγὼ πίνω πίεσθε καὶ τὸ βάπτισμα ὃ ἐγὼ βαπτίζομαι βαπτισθήσεσθε· [40] τὸ δὲ καθίσαι ἐκ δεξιῶν μου καὶ ἐξ εὐωνύμων οὐκ ἔστιν ἐμὸν δοῦναι, ἀλλ' οἷς ἡτοίμασται. [41] Καὶ ἀκούσαντες οἱ δέκα ἤρξαντο ἀγανακτεῖν περὶ Ἰακώβου καὶ Ἰωάννου. [42] Ὁ δὲ Ἰησοῦς προσκαλεσάμενος αὐτοὺς λέγει αὐτοῖς, Οἴδατε ὅτι οἱ δοκοῦντες ἄρχειν τῶν ἐθνῶν κατακυριεύουσιν αὐτῶν καὶ οἱ μεγάλοι αὐτῶν κατεξουσιάζουσιν αὐτῶν. [43] Οὐχ οὕτω δὲ ἔσται ἐν ὑμῖν ἀλλ' ὃς ἐὰν θέλῃ γενέσθαι μέγας ἐν ὑμῖν, ἔσται ὑμῶν διάκονος [44] καὶ ὃς ἐὰν θέλῃ ὑμῶν γενέσθαι πρῶτος, ἔσται πάντων δοῦλος. [45] Καὶ γὰρ ὁ υἱὸς τοῦ ἀνθρώπου οὐκ ἦλθεν διακονηθῆναι, ἀλλὰ διακονῆσαι, καὶ δοῦναι τὴν ψυχὴν αὐτοῦ λύτρον ἀντὶ πολλῶν.

Process of Discovery

Linguistics Section

Linguistic Structure

[Dialogue] [35] James and John, the two sons of Zebedee, came up to Jesus, saying, "Teacher, we want You to do for us whatever we ask of You."

[Dialogue] [36] And He said to them, "What do you want Me to do for you?"

[Dialogue] [37] They said to Him, "Grant that we *a*may sit, one on Your right and one on *Your* left, in Your glory."

[Dialogue] [38] But Jesus said to them, "You do not know what you are asking. Are you able to drink the cup that I drink, or to be baptized with the baptism with which I am baptized?"

[Dialogue] [39] They said to Him, "We are able."

[Dialogue] And Jesus said to them, "The cup that I drink *a*you shall drink; and you shall be baptized with the baptism with which I am baptized. [40] "But to sit on My right or on *My* left, this is not Mine to give; but it is for those for whom it has been prepared."

[Action] [41] Hearing *this,* the ten began to feel indignant with James and John.

[Result] [42] Calling them to Himself, Jesus said to them, "You know that those who are recognized as rulers of the Gentiles lord it over them; and their great men exercise authority over them. [43] "But it is not this way among you, but whoever wishes to become great among you shall be your servant; [44] and whoever wishes to be first among you shall be slave of all. [45] "For even the Son of Man did not come to be served, but to serve, and to give His life a ransom for many."

Discussion

This narrative is a series of questions and answers. Interestingly, the sons of Zebedee are asking Yeshua to exalts them. Yeshua offered more information about the Kingdom of Heaven.

Questioning the passage

1. Is Yeshua offering a prophecy in verse thirty-nine?

    When the two brothers say that they were willing to drink from the Cup of Death (see the cultural section), they accepted Yeshua's prophecy. That prophecy was that His disciples would be executed for their discipleship, just like Yeshua.

2. What does the reaction of the ten disciples say? (v. 41)

    Politics! Even in the small circle of thirteen people, politics was happening. A hierarchy was trying to be formed. Yeshua was clear that this was not supposed to happen. After Yeshua's death, the human desire for control created a political system within the apostles. When Paul challenged Peter in the 48 CE Jerusalem Council Paul made it clear that he rejected the authority of Peter and the original apostles. The first split in the church had occurred. Over the years, the church split into denominations has always had a basis in politics, money, and control. It is said that the church did not heed the words of Yeshua. It is an obvious flaw in humanity.

3. What does Yeshua mean in verses forty-two through forty-five?

    The material world in Yeshua's day and today, in fact, in all of human recorded history, as had one thing in common. The system humans developed was for men (today women) to fight one another for positions of power. In Yeshua's day, it was to become the King or Emperor. Men wanted to rule others not for the betterment of the people but rather for their wealth. They taxed the people, built palaces, and created fortunes for themselves and their children.

    Yeshua wanted a different system on Earth where people cared and respected each other. On Earth, that would be considered a utopian idea. However, in the Kingdom of Heaven, it was to be a reality. Yeshua taught His disciples to be humble, lowly, meek, and just in their behavior and relationships.[145]

---

[145] Rocco A. Errico and George M. Lamsa, *Aramaic Light on the Gospel of Matthew: a Commentary on the Teachings of Jesus from the Aramaic and Unchanged Near Eastern Customs* (Santa Fe, NM: Noohra Foundation, 2000).

Even the Hebrew people had become corrupted. They were in the grip of corrupt politics, false prophets, and a horrible system of priests. The people had strayed from the ideology of the LORD that they received at Mount Sinai after the Exodus. Everything is from the LORD, and only the LORD should receive honor, praise, and glory. Unfortunately, today the church expects honor, praise, and glory to be given to its leaders.

Culture Section

Discussion

The Cup of Death is a cup with poison that a host of the banquet had put into the wine cup of a guest that he wanted dead. The poison cup was a custom in the Near East.

Questioning the passage

1. What does it mean to sit on the right and left hand of Yeshua? (v. 39)

    This statement means that one would have to relinquish all temporal joys and honors that the world has to offer.[146] Yeshua understood that James and John did not understand what their mother was asking for. They thought that the Kingdom of Heaven was going to be an earthly kingdom. The idea that the Messiah was going to remove the Roman oppression and reestablish the Kingdom of Israel was still in their minds. If this is what happened, then Yeshua, being the King, could decide who was on his left and right. This position indicated the second and third persons in power in the Kingdom.

2. What is the cup that is mentioned in verse twenty-two?

    The cup is the cup of poison usually given to a guest whom the host had marked for death. When a person was marked for death, the person wanting him dead held a banquet. The marked for death person was invited. During the banquet, that person would be given a cup of wine with poison in it. That is why Kings, princes, and noblemen usually employed a cupbearer who drank from the cup first and tasted the food.

---

[146] IBID.

Thoughts

There are a couple of items in this narrative that deserve attention. Here I will address the hierarchy. Churches develop a hierarchy no matter what size they are. A part of my doctor of ministry project was the analysis of church hierarchy. Church modeling says that churches of specific sizes develop the same hierarchy model. My research in this area proved that. The bigger the church, the bigger the hierarchy. Unfortunately, it is clear from this passage that Yeshua was against this. Unfortunately, it is a human flaw that folks want to control others when a group of people comes together to form an organization. This leadership structure has been discussed by Yeshua several times. Outside of the local church, there is a hierarchy of the universal church. The catholic church has the most massive hierarchical structure. It would be interesting to calculate what percentage of the clergy in the catholic church pastor a church. I believe it would be a meager percentage compared to the hierarchy above the local priest.

Reflections

In the United States today, becoming a Christian will not get you a death sentence. Religion is an institution that is continuing its downward spiral; there will be a time that being a Christian will not be a good thing. Hopefully, in this country, being a Christian will not come with the death penalty. It may, in time, limit what a person can do career-wise and financially. That would put us back to Yeshua's time when being a believer meant a certain death penalty. This movement can be seen in the newly elected persons in the House of Representatives. These persons downplay religion, especially Christianity and Judaism. The way to stop this is to educate our children and grandchildren about Yeshua and God. We must also stop voting anti-God people into office. The time for an evangelical movement in this country is now.

MARK 10:46-52

Language

New American Standard 1995	Koine Greek
[46] Then they came to Jericho. And as He was leaving Jericho with His disciples and a large crowd, a blind beggar *named* Bartimaeus, the son of Timaeus, was sitting by the road. [47] When he heard that it was Jesus the Nazarene, he began to cry out and say, "Jesus, Son of David, have mercy on me!" [48] Many were sternly telling him to be quiet, but he kept crying out all the more, "Son of David, have mercy on me!" [49] And Jesus stopped and said, "Call him *here.*" So they called the blind man, saying to him, "*ᵃ*Take courage, stand up! He is calling for you." [50] Throwing aside his cloak, he jumped up and came to Jesus. [51] And answering him, Jesus said, "What do you want Me to do for you?" And the blind man said to Him, "Rabboni, *I want* to regain my sight!" [52] And Jesus said to him, "Go; your faith has made you well." Immediately he regained his sight and *began* following Him on the road.	Καὶ ἔρχονται εἰς Ἰεριχώ καὶ ἐκπορευομένου αὐτοῦ ἀπὸ Ἰεριχώ καὶ τῶν μαθητῶν αὐτοῦ, καὶ ὄχλου ἱκανοῦ, υἱὸς Τιμαίου Βαρτίμαιος ὁ τυφλὸς ἐκάθητο παρὰ τὴν ὁδὸν προσαιτῶν. [47] Καὶ ἀκούσας ὅτι Ἰησοῦς ὁ Ναζωραῖὸς ἐστιν, ἤρξατο κράζειν καὶ λέγειν, Ὁ υἱὸς Δαυίδ, Ἰησοῦ, ἐλέησόν με. [48] Καὶ ἐπετίμων αὐτῷ πολλοὶ ἵνα σιωπήσῃ ὁ δὲ πολλῷ μᾶλλον ἔκραζεν, Υἱὲ Δαυίδ, ἐλέησόν με. [49] Καὶ στὰς ὁ Ἰησοῦς εἶπεν αὐτὸν φωνηθῆναι καὶ φωνοῦσιν τὸν τυφλόν, λέγοντες αὐτῷ, Θάρσει ἔγειραι, φωνεῖ σε. [50] Ὁ δὲ ἀποβαλὼν τὸ ἱμάτιον αὐτοῦ ἀναστὰς ἦλθεν πρὸς τὸν Ἰησοῦν. [51] Καὶ ἀποκριθεὶς λέγει αὐτῷ ὁ Ἰησοῦς, Τί θέλεις ποιήσω σοί; Ὁ δὲ τυφλὸς εἶπεν αὐτῷ, Ῥαββουνί, ἵνα ἀναβλέψω. [52] Ὁ δὲ Ἰησοῦς εἶπεν αὐτῷ, Ὕπαγε ἡ πίστις σου σέσωκέν σε. Καὶ εὐθέως ἀνέβλεψεν, καὶ ἠκολούθει τῷ Ἰησοῦ ἐν τῇ ὁδῷ.

Process of Discovery

Linguistics Section

Linguistic Structure

A [46] Then they came to Jericho. And as He was leaving Jericho with His disciples and a large crowd, a blind beggar *named* Bartimaeus, the son of Timaeus, was sitting by the road.

> **B** [47] When he heard that it was Jesus the Nazarene, he began to cry out and say, "Jesus, Son of David, have mercy on me!" [48] Many were sternly telling him to be quiet, but he kept crying out all the more, "Son of David, have mercy on me!"

> > **C** [49] And Jesus stopped and said, "Call him *here*." So they called the blind man, saying to him, "'Take courage, stand up! He is calling for you."

> > > **D** [50] Throwing aside his cloak, he jumped up and came to Jesus.

> > **C'** [51] And answering him, Jesus said, "What do you want Me to do for you?" And the blind man said to Him, "Rabboni, *I want* to regain my sight!"

> **B'** [52] And Jesus said to him, "Go; your faith has made you well."

A' Immediately he regained his sight and *began* following Him on the road.

A: Sitting / on the way. B: Faith. C: Dialogue with Jesus. D: Coming to Jesus.[147]

Discussion

This passage is a deep chiasm. A blind beggar heard that Yeshua was passing by and decided to call Him to help. Yeshua, in his usual compassion, restores the man's sight.

Questioning the Passage

1. Why is it significant that a large crowd followed Yeshua? (v. 46)

---

[147] Hajime Murai, "Literary Structure (Chiasm, Chiasmus) of Gospel of Mark," Literary structure (chiasm, chiasmus) of each pericopes of Gospel of Mark, accessed October 12, 2021, http://www.bible.literarystructure.info/bible/41_Mark_pericope_e.html.

The author is saying that the number of people who believed in Yeshua as the Messiah was growing. Yeshua's words and actions demonstrated the LORD's love for all His people. In a time of oppression Yeshua also gave hope to the people. The people then and now need to place their trust in the ways of the LORD. By following Yeshua by becoming Yeshua-like, the practices of the LORD come to Earth.

2. What does the title "son of David" mean? (v. 48)
    In Yeshua's day, the title "son of David" was used as a token of respect and admiration. It did not necessarily signify that Yeshua was a descendant of King David. It was also used to talk about a " David-like person." This practice was used in the Near East. In Luke 13:16, Yeshua calls a woman a "daughter of Abraham." Abraham lived 2000 years before the woman was born. In this case, Yeshua was saying that the woman was a Hebrew.

King David was a warrior. The people were waiting for the son of David to return, who would lead the revolt against the Romans. If the people kept calling Yeshua the son of David, then it stands to reason that they expected Yeshua to lead the fight. An example of this is when Peter pulled out a sword in the Garden of Gethsemane when Yeshua was arrested. However, Yeshua told him that violence was not His way. Was Yeshua telling us that He was not the son of David they expected?

King David is usually thought of as a warrior. Several of the Psalms in the book of Psalms are attributed to King David. There was a spiritual side of King David, which is usually not mentioned when talking about the Messiah. Yeshua was not the David-like warrior. If anything, he was the David-like prophet, as described by David's psalms.

2Sam. 7:12 "When your days are complete and you lie down with your fathers, I will raise up your descendant after you, who will come forth from you, and I will establish his kingdom. **13** "He shall build a house for My name, and I will establish the throne of his kingdom forever.

This verse is used by Christianity to justify calling Yeshua the son of David. The Hebrew word עוֹלָם is translated as "forever." However, this word is used in the Scripture to imply an extended period. Using this perspective, the LORD promised David that the Temple would be built by one of his sons. The Kingdom, with a descendant of David on the throne, would last a long time. If the Kingdom was promised forever, then the Babylonians would not have invaded and destroyed the Kingdom of David (Judea). Future events are based on current events. When the Judeans turned away from the LORD because of their leaders, the LORD had to punish them. If the translation of "forever" is used in 2 Sam 7:13, then the LORD would be reversing a covenant He made with David. Since the LORD does not do that, the translation of "for a long while" is more appropriate for עוֹלָם.

Therefore, the Kingdom of Judea, under a descendant of King David, does not apply. The messianic belief that a revolt would occur started about two hundred years before Yeshua's birth. The Messiah is a promise from the LORD. The theologians of that period created the imagery of the Messiah.

Yeshua was the Messiah who was sent to initiate the Kingdom of Heaven. The Kabbalah says that there will be two messiahs. Zechariah 9:9 is the basis of this theological position.

Zech. 9:9 Rejoice greatly, O daughter of Zion! Shout *in triumph,* O daughter of Jerusalem! Behold, your king is coming to you; He is just and endowed with salvation, Humble, and mounted on a donkey, Even on a colt, the foal of a donkey.

The Messiah does not have to be a descendant of King David! This statement probably sent shockwaves through Christians. Christianity has drilled into its followers that

Yeshua must be a descendant of King David. In Yeshua's day, for a religion to be accepted by the people, it had to have its roots in the past.

The new religious movement of Christianity was started when Paul converted several Mithras house churches. Paul had to establish Yeshua's connection to the past. The belief that the Messiah is a descendant of King David was known throughout the Roman Empire. Thus, when the Mithras church ejected Mithras and accepted Yeshua, they also accepted Yeshua's origins in the Hebrew Scriptures. The Hebrew Scriptures were well known and respected. The conversion of the Mithras church was straightforward, with Yeshua being a descendant of King David. The conversions explain why the Hebrew Scriptures were prominent in the development and growth of Christianity. The necessity of Yeshua being connected to a religion of the past was imperative. Paul made the connection for the new Yeshua churches. The Proto-orthodox church kept the Hebrew Scriptures as its basis for understanding the messiahship.

A group of people called Montanists established their faith in Yeshua without the Hebrew Scriptures in the second century CE. This group believed in the God of the Hebrew Scriptures, not the God of Yeshua. Unfortunately, the Proto-Orthodox church squashed this movement and destroyed their sacred writings. Today, this group is known because of the letters Bishops of the Proto-Orthodox church wrote to their churches, warning them about the Montanists.

Since Yeshua never refers to himself as the son of David, the question is, does it matter if Yeshua was a descendant of King David. The answer is no for the purity of Yeshua's messianic message of the Kingdom of Heaven. The two messiah theology says the first Messiah came to restore the spirituality of the people. The purpose of the Kingdom of Heaven on Earth is to return the people's spirituality to the LORD. Yeshua's actions and words point to this.

The son of David's title may have been attributed to him because of the reason explained earlier. Thus, the Gospels have to say that Yeshua was an actual descendant of King David. Since Mark and John do not have any information about Yeshua's birth but call him David's son, the authors were not concerned about that aspect. All four Gospels use the son of David quite a bit.

The Hebrew Scriptures are necessary for the understanding of Yeshua as the Messiah. In the Hebrew Scriptures, the LORD reveals the coming of the Messiah. This person was a particular prophet of the LORD. Yeshua is that special prophet, the LORD's Messiah. His words and actions were done for the benefit of all people.

Yeshua gave us the secret Torah that Moses had received on Mount Sinai and was lost. The secret of how to obtain eternal life with the LORD. Simply put, it is a loving neighbor and loving the LORD. Yeshua's life, as described in the Gospels, shows us how to accomplish these two things.

This view is a bit gnostic. Its value is to strip away all the unnecessary church's beliefs to reveal the true nature of Yeshua the Messiah. All the fanfare is nice, but the bottom line is how one loves their neighbor and the LORD that matters. Yeshua shows the way by demonstration.

3. Why did Yeshua cure the blind man? (v. 52)

Throughout the Gospels, Yeshua does two things consistently. Yeshua said that the way to Heaven and salvation is to follow the two great commandments, love neighbor and love the LORD. Yeshua said that every human being is a neighbor. It does not matter what nation or race a person belongs to. All people are neighbors. Yeshua demonstrated this fact. The blind man on the road was there to beg for help. Begging was a profession that was acceptable in Yeshua's time. However, the blind man did not ask for money. He asked to be cured. Once he was cured of blindness, they would have to leave their begging profession and go to work. He would become productive persons who could contribute to society and help other people. Yeshua did not hesitate nor ask any questions of them once He knew what he wanted. The blind man was cured.

Additional Discussion - this narrative as an allegory

If this narrative is viewed allegorically, the blind man is not physically blind but spiritually blind. They did not understand the ways of the LORD. They may have been taught the wrong interpretation of the LORD's word. This understanding was happening in Yeshua's time as the different sects of Judaism were interpreting the Torah. For example, the Pharisees and Sadducees interpreted the Torah differently. Which one was correct? By examining Yeshua's words and actions, one will discover that both groups got things right and got things wrong. Spiritual blindness is cured when one follows the interpretation of the Scripture in a way that pleases the LORD.

Nevertheless, how is one to know what is right? The simple answer is to learn how Yeshua interpreted the Scripture and follow His way. Yeshua is the Messiah. The Messiah has the proper interpretation of the Torah. The prophets that the LORD sent before Yeshua had the answers, but many people did not listen to them. Some people are spiritually blind today because they are not following the ways of Yeshua. The supreme spiritual doctor, Yeshua, can cure spiritual blindness.

Thoughts

The less window dressing a person has surrounded their faith in Yeshua, the closer they come to an understanding of the true meaning of Yeshua's life. When all the fanfare is removed, when all the extraneous ideas are gone, what is left is a true belief. Yeshua is the Messiah that the LORD promised. This statement comes from the words of the LORD's prophets. The understanding of what pleased the LORD had been lost over the centuries. Israel was blessed by the LORD and prospered until its leaders began to forget about the LORD and placed their own needs first. The prophet Samuel warned the people that this could happen. Unfortunately, the people did not listen. The LORD sent Yeshua the Messiah to restore the spiritual fabric of the Universe. That fabric was created when the Universe was created. Corruption had torn it. Yeshua, the Messiah, came to attempt to repair it. The fanfare that Christianity places on Yeshua as the son of David is not what is essential. It is Yeshua's message to us, which is demonstrated by His life, that matters. Love neighbor and love God is what Yeshua always did. Yeshua went to the cross because He believed this was the way the LORD wanted things. The LORD raised Him from the dead because of Yeshua's 100% commitment to the LORD.

Reflections

Yeshua is the supreme doctor. The first thing people think of is a medical doctor. Yeshua did cure a lot of people of diseases and infirmities in His day. How about today? There are many questions about physical healing. Science has shown that when a sick person prays for Yeshua to heal them, it bolsters their immune system. So, in a way, Yeshua is healing the body. The most important aspect of Yeshua's healing is not of the body but of the spirit. Yeshua is concerned that every human spirit can return to Heaven when life on Earth is over. Yeshua's mission was to give people the way to return by teaching people what they needed to do. The LORD expects us to love our neighbors and love the LORD. Yeshua demonstrated this during his life. The illness that so many of us suffer from, then get cured, and it can (and usually does) return, is spiritual blindness. Only Yeshua can cure spiritual blindness. Spiritual blindness is the ultimate disease. By learning about Yeshua's life and following His words and actions, one can be cured of spiritual blindness.

MARK 11:1-11

Language

New American Standard 1995	Koine Greek
[1] As they approached Jerusalem, at Bethphage and Bethany, near the Mount of Olives, He sent two of His disciples, [2] and said to them, "Go into the village opposite you, and immediately as you enter it, you will find a colt tied *there,* on which no one yet has ever sat; untie it and bring it *here.* [3] "If anyone says to you, 'Why are you doing this?' you say, 'The Lord has need of it'; and immediately he will send it back here." [4] They went away and found a colt tied at the door, outside in the street; and they untied it. [5] Some of the bystanders were saying to them, "What are you doing, untying the colt?" [6] They spoke to them just as Jesus had told *them,* and they gave them permission. [7] They brought the colt to Jesus and put their coats on it; and He sat on it. [8] And many spread their coats in the road, and others *spread* leafy branches which they had cut from the fields. [9] Those who went in front and those who followed were shouting: "Hosanna! BLESSED IS HE WHO COMES IN THE NAME OF THE LORD; [10] Blessed *is* the coming kingdom of our father David; Hosanna in the highest!" [11] Jesus entered Jerusalem *and came* into the temple; and after looking around at everything, He left for Bethany with the twelve, since it was already late.	[1] Καὶ ὅτε ἐγγίζουσιν εἰς Ἱερουσαλήμ, εἰς Βηθσφαγὴ καὶ Βηθανίαν, πρὸς τὸ ὄρος τῶν Ἐλαιῶν, ἀποστέλλει δύο τῶν μαθητῶν αὐτοῦ, [2] καὶ λέγει αὐτοῖς, Ὑπάγετε εἰς τὴν κώμην τὴν κατέναντι ὑμῶν καὶ εὐθέως εἰσπορευόμενοι εἰς αὐτὴν εὑρήσετε πῶλον δεδεμένον, ἐφ' ὃν οὐδεὶς ἀνθρώπων κεκάθικεν λύσαντες αὐτὸν ἀγάγετε. [3] Καὶ ἐάν τις ὑμῖν εἴπῃ, Τί ποιεῖτε τοῦτο; Εἴπατε ὅτι Ὁ κύριος αὐτοῦ χρείαν ἔχει καὶ εὐθέως αὐτὸν ἀποστελλεῖ ὧδε. [4] Ἀπῆλθον δὲ καὶ εὗρον πῶλον δεδεμένον πρὸς τὴν θύραν ἔξω ἐπὶ τοῦ ἀμφόδου, καὶ λύουσιν αὐτόν. [5] Καί τινες τῶν ἐκεῖ ἑστηκότων ἔλεγον αὐτοῖς, Τί ποιεῖτε λύοντες τὸν πῶλον; [6] Οἱ δὲ εἶπον αὐτοῖς καθὼς ἐνετείλατο ὁ Ἰησοῦς καὶ ἀφῆκαν αὐτούς. [7] Καὶ ἤγαγον τὸν πῶλον πρὸς τὸν Ἰησοῦν, καὶ ἐπέβαλον αὐτῷ τὰ ἱμάτια αὐτῶν, καὶ ἐκάθισεν ἐπ' αὐτῷ. [8] Πολλοὶ δὲ τὰ ἱμάτια αὐτῶν ἔστρωσαν εἰς τὴν ὁδόν ἄλλοι δὲ στοιβάδας ἔκοπτον ἐκ τῶν δένδρων, καὶ ἐστρώννυον εἰς τὴν ὁδόν. [9] Καὶ οἱ προάγοντες καὶ οἱ ἀκολουθοῦντες ἔκραζον, λέγοντες, Ὡσαννά εὐλογημένος ὁ ἐρχόμενος ἐν ὀνόματι κυρίου [10] Εὐλογημένη ἡ ἐρχομένη βασιλεία ἐν ὀνόματι κυρίου τοῦ πατρὸς ἡμῶν Δαυὶδ Ὡσαννὰ ἐν τοῖς ὑψίστοις. [11] Καὶ εἰσῆλθεν εἰς Ἱεροσόλυμα ὁ Ἰησοῦς, καὶ εἰς τὸ ἱερὸν καὶ περιβλεψάμενος πάντα, ὀψίας ἤδη οὔσης τῆς ὥρας, ἐξῆλθεν εἰς Βηθανίαν μετὰ τῶν δώδεκα.

Process of Discovery

Linguistics Section

Linguistic Structure

A [1] As they approached Jerusalem, at Bethphage and Bethany, near the Mount of Olives, He sent two of His disciples,

> **B** [2] and said to them, "Go into the village opposite you, and immediately as you enter it, you will find a colt tied *there,* on which no one yet has ever sat; untie it and bring it *here.* [3] "If anyone says to you, 'Why are you doing this?' you say, 'The Lord has need of it'; and immediately he will send it back here." [4] They went away and found a colt tied at the door, outside in the street; and they untied it. [5] Some of the bystanders were saying to them, "What are you doing, untying the colt?" [6] They spoke to them just as Jesus had told *them,* and they gave them permission.

> > **C** [7] They brought the colt to Jesus and put their coats on it;

> > > **D** and He sat on it.

> > **C'** [8] And many spread their coats in the road, and others *spread* leafy branches which they had cut from the fields.

> **B'** [9] Those who went in front and those who followed were shouting: "Hosanna! BLESSED IS HE WHO COMES IN THE NAME OF THE LORD; [10] Blessed *is* the coming kingdom of our father David; Hosanna in the highest!"

A' [11] Jesus entered Jerusalem *and came* into the temple; and after looking around at everything, He left for Bethany with the twelve, since it was already late.

Discussion

This narrative is a A-B-C-D chiasm.

Questioning the Passage

1. What is the significance of Yeshua starting at the Mount of Olives? (v. 1)

    [4] In that day His feet will stand on the Mount of Olives, which is in front of Jerusalem on the east; and the Mount of Olives will be split in its middle from east to west by a very large valley, so that half of the mountain will move toward the north and the other half toward the south. Zechariah 14:4

    "The LORD is describing what is considered the final battle before the return of the LORD, the Day of the LORD. The nations of the world will be brought together to fight against the Hebrew people in Judea and Jerusalem. At this final war, the city of Jerusalem will be captured, and half of the people will be exiled. Jerusalem's capture the LORD will come to Earth and will fight against the nations who banded together against Jerusalem. Since Jerusalem is on a fault line, the land will separate on the fault line."[148]

    Since the apocalyptic event did not occur when Yeshua entered the city, Matthew's author is saying what the people were looking for but did not happen. Yeshua brought the Kingdom of Heaven and not the apocalypse. Zechariah's prophecy was about a meek king who would not enter the city on a warhorse but instead on a donkey. This passage indicates two Messiahs. Yeshua was the Messiah who brought the Kingdom of Heaven.

2. Why did Yeshua send two disciples to the village (why not one or three)? (v. 1)

    People did not travel alone in ancient days. Therefore, Yeshua sent two of His disciples.

3. What village did the two disciples go to? (v. 2)

    Tradition says that Yeshua stopped at Bethany before moving to Bethphage. If so, then Bethany was the village Yeshua sent His disciples to get the animals. Mary, Martha, and Lazarus lived in that city. Most of the town knew Yeshua because he visited His friends there.

---

[148] Koplitz, Michael Harvey. *Understanding Zechariah*. CreateSpace, n.d. 2019.

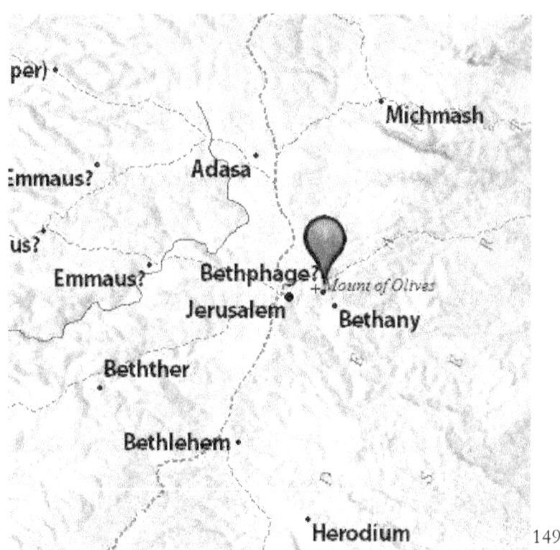

4. What day did Yeshua enter Jerusalem?

Mark places Yeshua's entry on Sunday.

"From John's account of Jesus' last week, there had arisen two thoughts on when he rode into Jerusalem to the accolades of the people and with palm branches of victory strewn along the road: Sunday, Nisan 9 and Monday, Nisan 10.

On Nisan 10, Israel was to select a lamb for Passover. On Nisan 14, the Passover lambs and Jesus died (Exodus 12:3, 6-10). In AD 33, Nisan 10 would have been Monday, and the Jews ate the Passover lambs on Friday evening (April 3, Julian calendar).

Jesus, therefore six days before the passover came to Bethany, where Lazarus was ... On the morrow the great multitude that had come to the feast, when they heard that Jesus was coming to Jerusalem, took the branches of the palm trees, and went forth to meet him, and cried out, Hosanna: Blessed is he that cometh in the name of the Lord, even the King of Israel" (John 12:1, 12-13)."[150]

---

[149] 149 "Bethphage Map." Bible Map: Bethphage. Accessed October 19. 2021. https://bibleatlas.org/bethphage.htm.

[150] Parkinson, James. "When Did Jesus Enter Jerusalem?" When Did Jesus Enter Jerusalem? Accessed April 10, 2019. http://www.heraldmag.org/2012/12ma_3.htm.

If Yeshua is considered the Passover lamb, then Nissan 10 is a better date for His entry. Nissan 10 was a Monday. Yeshua's entry into Jerusalem raised quite a stir. It alerted the Temple and Roman authorities that He entered the city. It was probably this event that triggered the week's events that led to Yeshua's death.

For our worship and understanding of Passion week, it does not matter whether Yeshua entered the city on Sunday or Monday. The result is the same.

Verse Comparison of citations or proof text

1. BLESSED IS HE WHO COMES IN THE NAME OF THE LORD; (v. 9)

    Verse nine is a citation from Psalm 118:26. "Blessed is he" means that Yeshua came with the power of the LORD behind Him. It is a verse that described people who came to Jerusalem to worship God at the Temple.[151]

Biblical Locations

1. Βηθφαγή *Bethphage* Meaning: 'house of unripe figs,' *Bethphage*, a village on the Mt. of Olives
2. Mount of Olives – located near Jerusalem.

Culture Section

Questioning the passage

1. Why would the owner of the donkeys hand them over without payment or any other kind of compensation? (v. 5-6)
    It was quite an honor to let a holy man use a family donkey so that he could ride upon it. Yeshua wanted to enter Jerusalem quietly. The donkey symbolized meekness and humility. Kings, princes, and rules would never have seen riding a donkey.

---

[151] *The New Interpreter's Bible. General Articles on the New Testament, the Gospel of Matthew, the Gospel of Mark.* Nashville, TN: Abingdon, 1995.

2. Why did the people spread coats on the ground? (v. 8)

   When Near Eastern kings or princes came to a town, the people would clean up the streets, repair roads, hang their tapestries from the windows or rooftops of the buildings, and spread rugs on the streets. The people who came out to see Yeshua enter the city were traveling with Him and were from Galilee. Many Galileans did not have carpets, so they took off their cloaks to cover the road. Verse 11 indicates that the people in the city did not know who Yeshua was. Therefore, the crowd described had to be those who traveled with Yeshua.

   Usually, a delegation from the city would leave the town to greet and escort royal guests. The city would offer a token of welcome from the city. Usually, the city provided a handsome horse saddled with an expensive livery. Hebraic people gave mules on such occasions. The mule was a symbol of strength.

   The political leadership of Jerusalem ignored Yeshua's entry into the city. From a political point of view, the entry into Jerusalem was a political failure.

   Yeshua did not want a big fanfare event because of the attention is placed upon him. The people could not hold back and made it a celebration.

3. Why did some of the people cut branches off the trees? (v. 8)

   The trees were palm-type trees that grow in the Middle East. The people waved their palms as Yeshua passed. This custom was done when a King or when an army General returned from winning an impressive battle. It was a sign of respect and reverence for the person entering the city. It also demonstrated that the city was happy to receive the person.

4. What does Hosanna mean? (v. 9)

   Shouting the word "Hosanna" was a celebration cry for a great leader. Today people would shout "bravo" and place their lives in the hands of the person entering the city. Those who shouted Hosanna to Yeshua wanted Him to perform the tasks of the Messiah as they understood them.

Thoughts

Yeshua had decided that He would enter Jerusalem, which stirred up trouble. By riding into the city on a donkey, He was fulfilling an ancient prophecy about the Messiah. A question for Yeshua would be, why this time? So, why cause all this trouble. There is some speculation that the year Yeshua died was a Jubilee year. If this is true, then His death in that year becomes significant. Dying at the time of the Passover would allow for the theology of the Paschal Lamb sacrifice. This line of thought fuels the Substitution atonement theory. Perhaps it was just bad timing that the week's events developed as they did. By Yeshua challenging the religious and government authorities, his destination became crucifixion. Passover was a time of unrest in Jerusalem. The new governor, Pilate, had strict orders not to allow any incidents to arise in Jerusalem. His hands were tied when Yeshua caused a disturbance. Pilate had to get involved.

The people cheering were waiting for the Messiah who would expel the Romans and re-establish the Kingdom of Israel. However, that would be restoring a temporary kingdom. When the Maccabees defeated the Greeks, the country was rebuilt only to be conquered by the Romans. Yeshua knew that an independent Israel would be short-lived. Israel was too weak to survive as an independent state.

Instead, Yeshua came to create the permanent kingdom of God. The Kingdom of God is a kingdom that will last an eternity. God uses miracles for long-term gains, not short-term gains. The Kingdom of God is a worthy mission.

Reflections

The Liturgy of the Palms calls us to communal faith. The foundation of Christianity occurs in Passion week. Jesus had to die on Good Friday so that the gift of God could be seen and felt on Easter morning. Instead of all the believers coming together to worship God for the gift of atonement and to Jesus for bringing the message, most Christians will not be found in church worship this week. The Christmas-Easter Christians will come out on Easter morning. They want to celebrate Jesus' conquering death and open the pathway for us to return to Heaven. But they will not acknowledge what it took; that is what Jesus had to endure, to get to Easter morning. How sad for the C & E Christians because they may be standing before God alone on judgment day. We need to feel the pain that Jesus endured. It is a sin of the world that placed Him on that cross. It was not a "simple" death. Instead, it was excruciating. Even though He could have avoided it, He did not. Everything Jesus did in His life was for our benefit. To honor His selfless act, we must remember all the events of Holy Week. Then the actual celebration of salvation can be celebrated on Easter morning.

MARK 11:12-14

Language

New American Standard 1995	Koine Greek
[12] On the next day, when they had left Bethany, He became hungry. [13] Seeing at a distance a fig tree in leaf, He went *to see* if perhaps He would find anything on it; and when He came to it, He found nothing but leaves, for it was not the season for figs. [14] He said to it, "May no one ever eat fruit from you again!" And His disciples were listening.	[12] Καὶ τῇ ἐπαύριον ἐξελθόντων αὐτῶν ἀπὸ Βηθανίας, ἐπείνασεν. [13] Καὶ ἰδὼν συκῆν μακρόθεν, ἐχουσαν φύλλα, ἦλθεν εἰ ἄρα εὑρήσει τι ἐν αὐτῇ καὶ ελθὼν ἐπ' αὐτήν, οὐδὲν εὗρεν εἰ μὴ φύλλα οὐ γὰρ ἦν καιρὸς σύκων. [14] Καὶ ἀποκριθεὶς ὁ Ἰησοῦς εἶπεν αὐτῇ, Μηκέτι ἐκ σοῦ εἰς τὸν αἰῶνα μηδεὶς καρπὸν φάγοι. Καὶ ἤκουον οἱ μαθηταὶ αὐτοῦ.

Process of Discovery

Linguistics Section

Linguistic Structure

[The Fig Tree] [12] On the next day, when they had left Bethany, He became hungry. [13] Seeing at a distance a fig tree in leaf, He went *to see* if perhaps He would find anything on it; and when He came to it, He found nothing but leaves, for it was not the season for figs. [14] He said to it, "May no one ever eat fruit from you again!" And His disciples were listening.

Discussion

The problem many people have interpreting this narrative is because they read it literally. If it is read this way, the customs and language emphasis is missed.

Questioning the Passage

1. What is the symbolic meaning of the fig tree?

    The fig tree can be examined as a symbol of the LORD's work in the world. A fig tree that is full of fruit can symbolize the blessings of the LORD upon the people. The fruitless tree would symbolize the LORD's judgment of destruction.[152] Yeshua was about to reenter Jerusalem to discover the corruption that was happening in the LORD's Temple. The destruction of the Temple, which Yeshua will predict, in 70 CE can be viewed as the LORD's judgment upon the Hebrews who had strayed from the faith.

Culture Section

Discussion

Fruit trees that grew along the roadside in the Near East were owned by travelers and the poor. The trees were public property. Therefore, any traveler could pick its fruit. Usually, a fruit tree

---

[152] Ched Myers, *Binding the Strong Man a Political Reading of Mark's Story of Jesus* (Maryknoll, NY: Orbis Books, 1988).

belonged to the person who planted it. Over time if the owner became unknown, then the tree became public property. Travelers would look for fruit trees when they got hungry. Semitic people did not eat early meals, i.e., breakfast. They would leave their homes fasting. This passage says that Yeshua became hungry. He saw a fig tree and walked over to it. Yeshua knew that it was the season for fruit. When He reached the fig tree, He was angered that there was no fruit on it. Other travelers probably picked the tree clean.[153]

Questioning the passage

1. Why did Yeshua curse the fig tree? (v. 14)

Yeshua did not curse the fig tree. In reading the narrative literally, it appears that He did. Near Eastern men who are searching for food and not finding it will make a negative remark. Yeshua was hungry and went up to a fig tree looking to have its fruit. The fig tree did not have any figs. Yeshua's remark about the tree is a typical remark of disappointment. Yeshua was not cursing the tree but rather displaying His disappointment that the figs were gone. Other travelers may have picked the tree clean. It is also possible that the tree was not able to produce fruit that season.[154]

Thoughts

Using the view of the symbolism of the fig tree, one is left to wonder how the LORD is working in the world. The tree full of fruit would be the LORD's blessings being bestowed upon the people. The travelers would be able to fill their hunger with the fig tree's fruit. The tree's fig would give the traveler the strength to continue their journey. If the journey is pleasing to the LORD, then the traveler would find fruit trees along the path. The fruitless tree symbolizes the LORD's punishment. In this case, the LORD's punishment is not destruction but rather a removal of blessings. Each of us will have to determine which direction to go in. Ask yourself, "How important are the blessings of the LORD to you?"

---

[153] Rocco A. Errico, George M. Lamsa, and George M. Lamsa, *Aramaic Light on the Gospels of Mark and Luke: a Commentary on the Teachings of Jesus from the Aramaic and Unchanged Near Eastern Customs* (Smyrna, GA: Noohra Foundation, 2001).
[154] IBID.

Reflections

The LORD's judgment does not have to be catastrophic. It can be as simple as the LORD taking His blessings away. The Ten Commandments clearly say that the LORD will bless the children of Israel as long as they follow the commandments given to them. The commandments can be found in the Torah (Genesis through Deuteronomy). As long as the people followed the LORD's law, the blessings came down from Heaven. The fig tree was full of fruit. The tree Yeshua went to was barren of fruit. This was an indication that the LORD was not happy with the people and removed His blessings.

MARK 11:15-19

Language

New American Standard 1995	Koine Greek
[15] Then they came to Jerusalem. And He entered the Temple and began to drive out those who were buying and selling in the Temple, and overturned the tables of the money changers and the seats of those who were selling doves; [16] and He would not permit anyone to carry merchandise through the Temple. [17] And He *began* to teach and say to them, "Is it not written, 'MY HOUSE SHALL BE CALLED A HOUSE OF PRAYER FOR ALL THE NATIONS'? But you have made it a ROBBERS' DEN." [18] The chief priests and the scribes heard *this,* and *began* seeking how to destroy Him; for they were afraid of Him, for the whole crowd was astonished at His teaching. [19] When evening came, they would go out of the city.	[15] Καὶ ἔρχονται εἰς Ἱεροσόλυμα· καὶ εἰσελθὼν ὁ Ἰησοῦς εἰς τὸ ἱερὸν ἤρξατο ἐκβάλλειν τοὺς πωλοῦντας καὶ ἀγοράζοντας ἐν τῷ ἱερῷ καὶ τὰς τραπέζας τῶν κολλυβιστῶν, καὶ τὰς καθέδρας τῶν πωλούντων τὰς περιστερὰς κατέστρεψεν· [16] καὶ οὐκ ἤφιεν ἵνα τις διενέγκῃ σκεῦος διὰ τοῦ ἱεροῦ. [17] Καὶ ἐδίδασκεν, λέγων αὐτοῖς, Οὐ γέγραπται ὅτι Ὁ οἶκός μου οἶκος προσευχῆς κληθήσεται πᾶσιν τοῖς ἔθνεσιν; Ὑμεῖς δὲ ἐποιήσατε αὐτὸν σπήλαιον λῃστῶν. [18] Καὶ ἤκουσαν οἱ γραμματεῖς καὶ οἱ ἀρχιερεῖς, καὶ ἐζήτουν πῶς αὐτὸν ἀπολέσωσιν· ἐφοβοῦντο γὰρ αὐτόν, ὅτι πᾶς ὁ ὄχλος ἐξεπλήσσετο ἐπὶ τῇ διδαχῇ αὐτοῦ. Καὶ ὅτε ὀψὲ ἐγένετο, ἐξεπορεύετο ἔξω τῆς πόλεως.

Process of Discovery

Linguistics Section

Linguistic Structure

[Transition] [15] Then they came to Jerusalem.

[Yeshua's actions] And He entered the Temple and began to drive out those who were buying and selling in the Temple, and overturned the tables of the money changers and the seats of those who were selling doves; [16] and He would not permit anyone to carry merchandise through the Temple. [17] And He *began* to teach and say to them, "Is it not written, 'MY HOUSE SHALL BE CALLED A HOUSE OF PRAYER FOR ALL THE NATIONS'? But you have made it a ROBBERS' DEN.'"

[Reaction] [18] The chief priests and the scribes heard *this,* and *began* seeking how to destroy Him; for they were afraid of Him, for the whole crowd was astonished at His teaching.

[Transition] [19] When evening came, they would go out of the city.

Questioning the Passage

1. Why was there a need for money changers in the Temple?

   The need for money changers was because the currency accepted by the Temple for the tithe and offerings was different than the Roman currency. Roman currency had a depiction of the ruling Emperor on one face of the coin. Since the Romans considered Caesar to be a god the usage of such coins was considered unclean. It violated the law about grave images and because the Roman emperor was not a god. So, the Temple could not accept the Roman currency. However, people who traveled to Jerusalem would have had Roman money. Therefore, there was a need for money exchangers.

   The problem with the money exchangers was that they wanted to make a profit by exchanging money. The way to make money by exchanging money was to give the person less Temple currency than their Roman currency was worth. It would have been expected that there would be a charge to exchange money. However, the money changers were charging outrageous exchange rates.

A modern-day example would be if a US citizen traveled to Canada. Once there, he would have to exchange his US dollars for Canadian dollars. Let us say that the exchange rate, for this example, is $1 US is worth $1.25 Canadian. Let us say that a fair exchange rate is $1 US for $1 Canadian. However, the money changer gave 0.50 Canadian dollars for each $1 US. That would be overcharging. That is what was happening in the Temple when Jesus overturned the money tables.

He was angry because the exchange rates were outrageous and that the money changers were cheating the people. The people had no choice but to accept the exchange rate no matter how bad it was. They needed the Temple currency and had no other choice. Therefore, it was not that the money changers were in the Temple but rather their greed in cheating the people on the exchange that angered Jesus.

Verse Comparison of citations or proof text

1. [13] And He said to them, "It is written, 'MY HOUSE SHALL BE CALLED A HOUSE OF PRAYER'; but you are making it a ROBBERS' DEN."

    [7] Even those I will bring to My holy mountain And make them joyful in My house of prayer. Their burnt offerings and their sacrifices will be acceptable on My altar; For My house will be called a house of prayer for all the peoples." (Isa. 56:7 NAU)

    [11] "Has this house, which is called by My name, become a den of robbers in your sight? Behold, I, even I, have seen *it*," declares the LORD. (Jer. 7:11 NAU)

    Jesus combined the Isaiah and Jeremiah passages to make His point. The Temple of the LORD is a place for prayer and the study of the Torah. The money changers turned it into a robbers' den.

When King Solomon dedicated the Temple, he called it a "House of Prayer."

Thoughts

The Temple leaders allowed vendors to set up inside the Temple. A good question for that time would have been why did the Temple authorities allow the money changers and vendors into the outer court. The merchants could have easily set up their tables outside the Temple. A thought is that the Temple was getting a kickback from the vendors. It reminds me of going to a baseball game and seeing the different vendors selling concessions inside the park. There were also vendors set up outside of the park selling concessions. Of course, the baseball team did not get a percentage of the sales outside the park. They certainly did inside the park. Well, the animal sacrifice system created the need for money changers and vendors, just like the need for beer and peanuts (and more) are needed for a baseball game. The requirement was fulfilled by these vendors then and now.

Reflections

This narrative always reminds me of a story that my candidacy and ordination mentor Brad told me. It is not a perfect match but similar at the same time. Brad was appointed to a church in the York, PA area. Appointments in the United Methodist Church start on July 1. So, Brad went to his new church appointment. Everything was going well until the first weekend in November. A church member came into his office and told him that he was to report to the church's kitchen at 5:00 AM the following day. Why Brad asked? He said the man looked shocked. He did respond, "to cook the chili for the bazaar." Brad immediately said, "no." He explained to the parishioner that cooking chili and the bazaar does not make disciples for Jesus Christ. Therefore, it should not be done. The church had held the bazaar for decades, and the leadership never understood why Brad did not help them cook the chili. The question is, what does the church do that does not make disciples for Christ? Also, why are they doing it?

MARK 11:20-26

Language

New American Standard 1995	Koine Greek
[20] As they were passing by in the morning, they saw the fig tree withered from the roots *up*. [21] Being reminded, Peter said to Him, Rabbi, look, the fig tree which You cursed has withered." [22] And Jesus answered saying to them, "Have faith in God. [23] "Truly I say to you, whoever says to this mountain, 'Be taken up and cast into the sea,' and does not doubt in his heart, but believes that what he says is going to happen, it will be *granted* him. [24] "Therefore I say to you, all things for which you pray and ask, believe that you have received them, and they will be *granted* you. [25] "Whenever you *stand praying, forgive, if you have anything against anyone, so that your Father who is in heaven will also forgive you your transgressions. [26] ["But if you do not forgive, neither will your Father who is in heaven forgive your transgressions."]	[20] Καὶ πρωῒ παραπορευόμενοι, ειδον τὴν συκῆν εξηραμμένην ἐκ ῥίζῶν. [21] Καὶ ἀναμνησθεὶς ὁ Πέτρος λέγει αυτῷ, Ῥαββί, ἰδε, ἡ συκῆ ἦν κατηράσω εξήρανται. [22] Καὶ ἀποκριθεὶς ὁ Ἰησοῦς λέγει αυτοῖς, Ἐχετε πιστιν θεοῦ. [23] Ἀμὴν γὰρ λέγω ὑμῖν ὅτι ὃς ἀν εἴπῃ τῷ ὄρει τουτω, Ἀρθητι, καὶ βλήθητι εἰς τὴν θάλασσαν, καὶ μὴ διακριθῇ ἐν τῇ καρδίᾳ αὑτοῦ, ἀλλὰ πιστεύσῃ ὅτι ἀ λέγει γίνεται εσται αυτῷ ὁ ἐὰν εἴπῃ. [24] Διὰ τοῦτο λέγω ὑμῖν, Πάντα ὁσα ἀν προσευχόμενοι ⸀ αἰτῆσθε ⸀, πιστεύετε ὅτι λαμβάνετε, καὶ ἐσται ὑμῖν. [25] Καὶ ὅταν στήκητε προσευχόμενοι, ἀφίετε εἴ τι ἐχετε κατά τινος ἱνα καὶ ὁ πατὴρ ὑμῶν ὁ ἐν τοῖς ουρανοῖς ἀφῇ ὑμῖν τὰ παραπτώματα ὑμῶν. [26] Εἰ δὲ ὑμεῖς ουκ ἀφίετε, ουδὲ ὁ πατὴρ ὑμῶν ὁ ἐν τοῖς ουρανοῖς ἀφήσει τὰ παραπτώματα ὑμῶν.

Process of Discovery

Linguistics Section

Linguistic Structure

[Transition] [20] As they were passing by in the morning, they saw the fig tree withered from the roots *up*. [21] Being reminded, Peter said to Him, Rabbi, look, the fig tree which You cursed has withered."

[Followup to the fig tree narrative] [22] And Jesus answered saying to them, "Have faith in God. [23] "Truly I say to you, whoever says to this mountain, 'Be taken up and cast into the sea,' and does not doubt in his heart, but believes that what he says is going to happen, it will be *granted* him. [24] "Therefore I say to you, all things for which you pray and ask, believe that you have received them, and they will be *granted* you. [25] "Whenever you *a*stand praying, forgive, if you have anything against anyone, so that your Father who is in heaven will also forgive you your transgressions. [26] [*a*But if you do not forgive, neither will your Father who is in heaven forgive your transgressions."]

Discussion

The problem many people have interpreting this narrative is that they read it literally. If it is read this way, the customs and language emphasis is missed.

Questioning the Passage

1. Why did the fig tree wither so quickly? (v. 21)

    The fig tree is symbolic of faith. When a prayer is not answered in the way the person wishes, does the person lose faith in the LORD? Not every prayer is going to be answered in the way desired. How many people develop faith when they are in trouble? If their prayers work out, their faith will multiply. However, if the prayer is not answered, they tend to do walk away from the LORD. Faith in the LORD ignites prayer.

This could be a foreshadowing of what was going to happen to His disciples during the week. Their faith withered like the tree after Yeshua's death. They were told that Yeshua would rise from death. For a moment, they lost faith.

Phrase Study

1. πίστις, εως, ἡ. (v. 23) Meaning: that which evokes trust and faith. The Aramaic word that Yeshua used would have been *heymanutha*. *Pistis* is a good transliteration. The emphasis in Christian commentaries is that *pistis* means "faith." The tendency is to ignore the trust part. Trust and faith in the LORD can be viewed as the same thing. By not using both words, trust and faith, people tend to forget that trusting in the LORD is equivalent to having faith in the LORD.

Culture Section

Discussion

In Yeshua's day, the moving of mountains and tree-uprooting images were found in legal, legendary, thaumaturgic (miracle worker), and eschatological contexts and employed in connection with the Rabbi, the king, the hero, the thaumaturge, or the Messianic follower. The Temple at Jerusalem was known as the "mountain of the house" or "this mountain."[155] In chapter thirteen, Yeshua said that the Temple would be torn down in three days. He did not mean it literally. The tearing down of the Temple is directly related to the movement of the mountain. It means that the Temple leadership with its manufactured traditions and rules would be destroyed and replaced by what the LORD initially gave the Jewish people at Sinai. The disciples are told that they have the power to effect massive changes in the Temple. Suppose the Yeshua movement did not become a Gentile movement. In that case, the Jewish followers of Yeshua's teaching might have been able to make the reforms to Judaism that Yeshua was attempting to do.

Questioning the passage

1. Why did Yeshua curse the fig tree? (v. 21)

---

[155] Ched Myers, *Binding the Strong Man a Political Reading of Mark's Story of Jesus* (Maryknoll, NY: Orbis Books, 1988).

Yeshua did not curse the fig tree. In reading the narrative literally, it appears that He did. Near Eastern men who are searching for food and not finding it will make a negative remark. Yeshua was hungry and went up to a fig tree looking to have its fruit. The fig tree did not have any figs. Yeshua's remark about the tree is a typical remark of disappointment. Yeshua was not cursing the tree but rather displaying His disappointment that the figs were gone. Other travelers may have picked the tree clean. It is also possible that the tree was not able to produce fruit that season.[156]

2. Can a person of faith remove a mountain? (v. 23)

By reading the narrative literally, the original meaning of its content is lost. Yeshua is not saying that a person can remove or move a mountain. Near Eastern people often exaggerated and used sweeping statements. The Scriptures are filled with exaggerated statements. It is the meaning of the exaggeration that is important. Yeshua was talking about the level of faith a person has.

Thoughts

Faith and trust should be going hand in hand. When a prayer is not answered, does the person continue to have trust in the LORD? Suppose one is going to follow the LORD. In that case, one must understand that there are times where the LORD's direction is different from the person's direction. Following the life of Abraham in Genesis, one finds that there were ten tests for him. The LORD was testing Abraham's faith and trust. The LORD may test a person's faith and trust when a prayer is not answered. Faith and trust are two things that always go together.

Reflections

If I have faith and trust in the LORD as strong as Yeshua says it should be, why are there prayers that seem to go unanswered? Richard Foster's book titled <u>Prayer</u> is an excellent resource for learning about prayer. Not every prayer that a person offers to the LORD is a prayer that the LORD will

---

[156] Rocco A. Errico and George M. Lamsa, *Aramaic Light on the Gospel of Matthew: a Commentary on the Teachings of Jesus from the Aramaic and Unchanged Near Eastern Customs* (Santa Fe, NM: Noohra Foundation, 2000).

answer. Foster said that if one prays for something material, it will not happen through divine intervention. Why? Because the LORD is spiritual, not material. However, prayer changes us. Therefore, the prayer might open the person's mind to how they can obtain the material item. Prayer changes us. In this narrative, Yeshua is telling us to have faith and trust always in the LORD, knowing that the LORD will do what is best.

MARK 11:27-33

Language

New American Standard 1995	Koine Greek
²⁷ They came again to Jerusalem. And as He was walking in the temple, the chief priests and the scribes and the elders came to Him, ²⁸ and *began* saying to Him, "By what authority are You doing these things, or who gave You this authority to do these things?" ²⁹ And Jesus said to them, "I will ask you one question, and you answer Me, and *then* I will tell you by what authority I do these things. ³⁰ "Was the baptism of John from heaven, or from men? Answer Me." ³¹ They *began* reasoning among themselves, saying, "If we say, 'From heaven,' He will say, 'Then why did you not believe him?' ³² "But shall we say, 'From men'?" — they were afraid of the people, for everyone considered John to have been a real prophet. ³³ Answering Jesus, they said, "We do not know." And Jesus said to them, "Nor will I tell you by what authority I do these things."	²⁷ Καὶ ἔρχονται πάλιν εἰς Ἱεροσόλυμα καὶ ἐν τῷ ἱερῷ περιπατοῦντος αυτοῦ, ἔρχονται πρὸς αυτὸν οἱ ἀρχιερεῖς καὶ οἱ γραμματεῖς καὶ οἱ πρεσβύτεροι, ²⁸ καὶ λέγουσιν αὐτῷ, Ἐν ποίᾳ εξουσίᾳ ταῦτα ποιεῖς; Καὶ τίς σοι τὴν εξουσίαν ταύτην ἔδωκεν ἵνα ταῦτα ποιῇς; ²⁹ Ὁ δὲ Ἰησοῦς ἀποκριθεὶς εἶπεν αὐτοῖς, Ἐπερωτήσω ὑμᾶς καὶ ἐγὼ ἕνα λόγον, καὶ ἀποκρίθητέ μοι, καὶ ἐρῶ ὑμῖν ἐν ποίᾳ εξουσίᾳ ταῦτα ποιω. ³⁰ Τὸ βάπτισμα Ἰωάννου ἐξ οὐρανοῦ ἦν, ἢ ἐξ ἀνθρώπων; Ἀποκρίθητέ μοι. ³¹ Καὶ ελογίζοντο πρὸς ἑαυτούς, λέγοντες, Ἐὰν εἴπωμεν, Ἐξ οὐρανου, ἐρεῖ, Διὰ τί οὖν οὐκ ἐπιστεύσατε αὐτῷ; ³² Ἀλλ' εἴπωμεν, Ἐξ ἀνθρώπων, εφοβοῦντο τὸν λαόν ἅπαντες γαρ εἶχον τὸν Ἰωάννην, ὅτι ὄντως προφήτης ἦν. ³³ Καὶ ἀποκριθέντες λέγουσιν τῷ Ἰησοῦ, Οὐκ οἴδαμεν. Καὶ ὁ Ἰησοῦς ἀποκριθεὶς λέγει αὐτοῖς, Οὐδὲ ἐγὼ λέγω ὑμῖν ἐν ποίᾳ εξουσίᾳ ταῦτα ποιω.

Process of Discovery

Linguistics Section

Linguistic Structure

A [27] They came again to Jerusalem. And as He was walking in the temple, the chief priests and the scribes and the elders came to Him, [28] and *began* saying to Him, "By what authority are You doing these things, or who gave You this authority to do these things?"

> **B** [29] And Jesus said to them, "I will ask you one question, and you answer Me, and *then* I will tell you by what authority I do these things. [30] "Was the baptism of John from heaven, or from men? Answer Me."

> > **C** [31] They *began* reasoning among themselves, saying, "If we say, 'From heaven,' He will say, 'Then why did you not believe him?' [32] "But shall we say, 'From men'?" — they were afraid of the people, for everyone considered John to have been a real prophet.

> **B'** [33] Answering Jesus, they said, "We do not know."

A' And Jesus said to them, "Nor will I tell you by what authority I do these things."

Discussion

Yeshua's authority to interpret Scripture and to offer new interpretations was challenged. The passage is an ABC chiasm.

Questioning the Passage

1. Why is ἀρχιερεῖς translated as chief priests (plural)? (v. 27)

    This verse implies that the High Priest and the President of the Sanhedrin were present with the elders (members of the Sanhedrin) when they approached Yeshua. The events of Passion week got Yeshua noticed. The leaders of the Temple were now involved.

2. What were the rivals of Yeshua looking for?

The Sanhedrin, along with the High Priest of the Temple, was looking for what honor Yeshua had to offer His new teachings.[157] The honor-shame system of Yeshua's day was connected to the LORD. The honor was bestowed upon people who stood for the LORD, i.e., prophets. Shame was brought upon anyone who turned out to be a false prophet. The conversation was about the religious leaders attempt to shame Yeshua for saying that His authority was from the LORD. Yeshua turned the tables on them so that they left Him with the same information they had before confronting Him, which was nothing. The confrontation probably resulted in more Jews believing in Yeshua. He stood up to the most powerful humans in the religious structure and won.

Phrase Study

1. ἀρχιερεύς, έως, ὁ [158] (v. 27)

    1. one who serves as head priest, *high priest*

    a. gentile MPol 21=Ἀσιάρχης (q.v.) 12:2.

    b. Israelite

    α. president of the Sanhedrin

    2. a priest of high rank, *chief priest*

Culture Section

Discussion

In Yeshua's time, religious teachers would turn the tables and ask their rivals to answer a question of their own first when having to answer a difficult question. Yeshua answered the question put to Him by asking his question. Since they could not answer the question, Yeshua told them that He would not answer their question.

---

[157] Brandon J. O'Brien and E. Randolph. Richards, *Misreading Scripture with Western Eyes* (IVP Books, 2012).
[158] BDAG from Accordance Bible Software

1. By what authority did Yeshua have to do what He was doing? (v. 28)

   The transliteration of the word "authority," ἐξουσία in the Greek, in Hebrew is s'mikhah. This word means "leaning" or "laying" on of hands in the ordination ceremony for a judge, elder, or a rabbi. The practice of ordination started when Moses ordained Joshua to take his place. Ordination was considered a transfer of duties and privileges to perform the LORD's work.

   Ordination allowed the person to decide on points of Halakhah (law). A board of three elders, one having been ordained, were able to ordain new rabbis. Yeshua was approached by the leaders of the Temple, wanting to know who was the board of three elders who ordained Him. They wanted to interrogate the board as to why they gave Yeshua His ordination.[159]

Thoughts

By what authority is a question that the church has used throughout its 2000-year history. The proto-orthodox church that Paul established became the dominant faction of early Christianity. Instead of working with other forms of Christianity to form a greater understanding of the life of Yeshua, they decided that they were the only ones who had the authority to be the church. For centuries the catholic-orthodox church had been destroying any movement, not conforming to their understanding of Christianity. To question the church was not accepted.

A great example is the movie "Luther," which was released in 2006. Martin Luther asked his theology professor how the catholic church could condemn the saints from before the catholic-orthodox separation as false saints. The professor's answer was, "are you challenging the church's decision." Luther was not challenging the church's authority but instead asking about the inconsistencies of the decisions of the church. History says that Luther saw the problems in the church and started the

---

[159] David H. Stern, *Jewish New Testament Commentary: a Companion Volume to the Jewish New Testament* (Clarksville, MD: Jewish New Testament Publications, 1999).

Reformation. The authority of the church became supreme, even surpassing the Bible. The Bible must be the supreme authority of the world, not the church. Five hundred years later, the mainline protestant churches have returned to a "catholic state" because they use their rule books as the supreme authority. They need to return to having the Bible as their supreme authority.

Reflections

Who would agree that "we do not know" is a valid religious response? The Temple leaders approached Yeshua with that question, "we do not know by what authority you have?" They left with the question unanswered. Numerous aspects of the world are not understandable, nor are they explainable. There is nothing wrong with the answer, "we do not know." It is better to say that something is not known rather than trying to create an explanation. For example, how can the bread and wine used at a communion celebration be turned into the body and blood of Yeshua? Many theologians have tried to answer this question. There is nothing wrong with saying, "we do not know." It is one of the mysteries of the LORD that we may never fully understand. Even in today's world, some things happen in nature and physics that cannot be explained. To accept Yeshua on faith means that there are things that are believed in without explanation.

MARK 12:1-11

Language

New American Standard 1995	Koine Greek
[1] And He began to speak to them in parables: "[cb]A man PLANTED A VINEYARD AND PUT A WALL AROUND IT, AND DUG A VAT UNDER THE WINE PRESS AND BUILT A TOWER, and rented it out to vine-growers and went on a journey. [2] "At the *harvest* time he sent a slave to the vine-growers, in order to receive *some* of the produce of the vineyard from the vine-growers. [3] "They took him, and beat him and sent him away empty-handed. [4] "Again he sent them another slave, and they wounded him in the head, and treated him shamefully. [5] "And he sent another, and that one they killed; and *so with* many others, beating some and killing others. [6] "He had one more *to send,* a beloved son; he sent him last *of all* to them, saying, 'They will respect my son.' [7] "But those vine-growers said to one another, 'This is the heir; come, let us kill him, and the inheritance will be ours!' [8] "They took him, and killed him and threw him out of the vineyard. [9] "What will the owner of the vineyard do? He will come and destroy the vine-growers, and will give the vineyard to others. [10] "Have you not even read this Scripture: 'THE STONE WHICH THE BUILDERS REJECTED, THIS BECAME THE CHIEF CORNER *stone;* [11] THIS CAME ABOUT FROM THE LORD, AND IT IS MARVELOUS IN OUR EYES'?"	[12] Καὶ ἤρξατο αὐτοῖς ἐν παραβολαῖς λέγειν, Ἀμπελῶνα ἐφύτευσεν ἄνθρωπος, καὶ περιέθηκεν φραγμόν, καὶ ὤρυξεν ὑπολήνιον, καὶ ᾠκοδόμησεν πύργον, καὶ ἐξέδοτο αὐτὸν γεωργοῖς, καὶ ἀπεδήμησεν. [2] Καὶ ἀπέστειλεν πρὸς τοὺς γεωργοὺς τῷ καιρῷ δοῦλον, ἵνα παρὰ τῶν γεωργῶν λάβῃ ἀπὸ τοῦ καρποῦ τοῦ ἀμπελῶνος. [3] Οἱ δὲ λαβόντες αὐτὸν ἔδειραν, καὶ ἀπέστειλαν κενόν. [4] Καὶ πάλιν ἀπέστειλεν πρὸς αὐτοὺς ἄλλον δοῦλον κἀκεῖνον λιθοβολήσαντες ἐκεφαλαίωσαν, καὶ ἀπέστειλαν ἠτιμωμένον. [5] Καὶ πάλιν ἄλλον ἀπέστειλεν κἀκεῖνον ἀπέκτειναν καὶ πολλοὺς ἄλλους, τοὺς μὲν δέροντες, τοὺς δὲ ἀποκτένοντες. [6] Ἔτι οὖν ἕνα υἱὸν ἔχων ἀγαπητὸν αὐτοῦ, ἀπέστειλεν καὶ αὐτὸν πρὸς αὐτοὺς ἔσχατον, λέγων ὅτι Ἐντραπήσονται τὸν υἱόν μου. [7] Ἐκεῖνοι δὲ οἱ γεωργοὶ εἶπον πρὸς ἑαυτοὺς ὅτι Οὗτός ἐστιν ὁ κληρονόμος δεῦτε, ἀποκτείνωμεν αὐτόν, καὶ ἡμῶν ἔσται ἡ κληρονομία. [8] Καὶ λαβόντες αὐτὸν ἀπέκτειναν, καὶ ἐξέβαλον ἔξω τοῦ ἀμπελῶνος. [9] Τί οὖν ποιήσει ὁ κύριος τοῦ ἀμπελῶνος; Ἐλεύσεται καὶ ἀπολέσει τοὺς γεωργούς, καὶ δώσει τὸν ἀμπελῶνα ἄλλοις. [10] Οὐδὲ τὴν γραφὴν ταύτην ἀνέγνωτε, Λίθον ὃν ἀπεδοκίμασαν οἱ οἰκοδομοῦντες, οὗτος ἐγενήθη εἰς κεφαλὴν γωνίας [11] παρὰ κυρίου ἐγένετο αὕτη, καὶ ἔστιν θαυμαστὴ ἐν ὀφθαλμοῖς ἡμῶν; [12] Καὶ ἐζήτουν αὐτὸν κρατῆσαι, καὶ ἐφοβήθησαν τὸν ὄχλον· ἔγνωσαν γὰρ ὅτι πρὸς αὐτοὺς τὴν παραβολὴν εἶπεν καὶ ἀφέντες αὐτὸν ἀπῆλθον.

Process of Discovery

Linguistics Section

Linguistic Structure

[1] And He began to speak to them in parables: "[b]A man PLANTED A VINEYARD AND PUT A WALL AROUND IT, AND DUG A VAT UNDER THE WINE PRESS AND BUILT A TOWER, and rented it out to vine-growers and went on a journey. [2] "At the *harvest* time he sent a slave to the vine-growers, in order to receive *some* of the produce of the vineyard from the vine-growers. [3] "They took him, and beat him and sent him away empty-handed. [4] "Again he sent them another slave, and they wounded him in the head, and treated him shamefully. [5] "And he sent another, and that one they killed; and *so with* many others, beating some and killing others. [6] "He had one more *to send,* a beloved son; he sent him last *of all* to them, saying, 'They will respect my son.' [7] "But those vine-growers said to one another, 'This is the heir; come, let us kill him, and the inheritance will be ours!' [8] "They took him, and killed him and threw him out of the vineyard. [9] "What will the owner of the vineyard do? He will come and destroy the vine-growers, and will give the vineyard to others. [10] "Have you not even read this Scripture: 'THE STONE WHICH THE BUILDERS REJECTED, THIS BECAME THE CHIEF CORNER *stone;* [11] THIS CAME ABOUT FROM THE LORD, AND IT IS MARVELOUS IN OUR EYES'?"

Discussion

This is a complex parable that Yeshua offered. It uses the culture of the day to make the point. In addition, it also uses two Hebrew Scripture citations.

Questioning the passage

1. What was the going rate to rent a vineyard? (v. 1)

   "Vineyards that are large are often rented out to one or more families. When this is done, the peasant who rents the vineyard agrees to give half or more of the products of the grapes. When harvest-time comes, the owner will send his servant to secure his share of the grapes, raisins, wine, or dibs."[160]

2. Why did the landowner send a slave to get the proceeds? (v. 2)

---

[160] Wight, Fred. "Vineyard." In *Manners and Customs of Bible Lands.* Minneapolis: Billy Graham Evangelistic Association, 1994.

The landowner probably sent a steward of his household. The Master Steward would have been the accountant of the family. He would have sent a servant of his to collect the proceeds.

3. Why the distinction between the two killed slaves – one was stoned? (v. 5)

   The parable speaks about the way prophets were killed. Sometimes it was a quick death, while other times, it was a slow death (like stoning).

4. Why did the landowner think that his son would be respected? (v. 7)

   This is a twist in the parable. The landowner knew that his son would be mistreated. However, he sent him anyway.

5. Why did the renters believe they would receive the son's inheritance if they killed him? (v. 7)

   If the vineyard owner did not have any sons to inherit the land, then the land would become available for purchase and transfer from the old family owner to the new family owner. Again, a twist in the culture because there will almost always be a legitimate heir to the property.

6. Why the extra verbiage "threw him out of the vineyard?" (v. 8)

   This excess verbiage Christianizes the parable. It is the foreshadowing that Yeshua was to be executed outside the city of Jerusalem. The parable holds together if that jargon is removed. The prophets were killed in Jerusalem, and then their bodies were tossed out of the city.

Verse Comparison on citations or proof text

1. PLANTED A VINEYARD AND PUT A WALL AROUND IT, AND DUG A VAT UNDER THE WINE PRESS AND BUILT A TOWER (v. 1)

[1] Let me sing now for my well-beloved A song of my beloved concerning His vineyard. My well-beloved had a vineyard on a fertile hill. [2] He dug it all around, removed its stones, And planted it with the choicest vine. And He built a tower in the middle of it And also hewed out

a wine vat in it; Then He expected *it* to produce *good* grapes, But it produced *only* worthless ones. (Isa. 5:1-2 NAU)

2. 'THE STONE WHICH THE BUILDERS REJECTED, THIS BECAME THE CHIEF CORNER *stone;* [11] THIS CAME ABOUT FROM THE LORD, AND IT IS MARVELOUS IN OUR EYES'?"

[22] The stone which the builders rejected Has become the chief corner *stone.* (Ps. 118:22 NAU)

Linguistic Echoes

This parable is echoed in the book of Isaiah, chapter five. Therefore, the imagery backdrop for Yeshua's parable is the Hebrew parable in Isaiah 5. In the Isaiah parable, the vineyard was believed to be the Hebrew people. Some envisioned the vineyard as the city of Jerusalem. The LORD desired to see justice and righteousness from his people, but he did not see that. All he saw was bloodshed and heard the anguished cry of the oppressed.

The LORD sent His servants, the prophets, to warn the people about their sins. The LORD told them that they needed to change their actions and beliefs or else one day the LORD's anger would be upon them. But the people did not change. God kept his promise, and the Temple and city of Jerusalem were destroyed. Only the tribes of Judah and Benjamin survived.

The people listening to Yeshua knew this history. They would have seen Yeshua's parable as a repetition of the Isaiah parable with some additional warnings from the LORD. Yeshua simply updated the original parable to their time. Yeshua would not have taken pleasure in making these pronouncements. He wanted to save the city and the Temple of the LORD.

The vineyard owner sent one set of servants to collect the money due. The people responded by beatings and murder. These persons represent the biblical prophets. The second set of servants were the contemporary prophets of Yeshua's day.

The son was sent. The LORD sent Yeshua to give a final warning. The people did not listen to Him. Therefore, the owner of the vineyard, the LORD, punished the renters by removing them and giving the vineyard to another set of tenants. This was the destruction of Jerusalem and the Temple by the Romans in 66 CE.

Yeshua's actual death should not be connected to this parable. Prophets were generally killed in Jerusalem because the King and Sanhedrin did not want to hear the words of the LORD when it came to condemning them. They were wicked leaders living in a wicked world. Along came a prophet filled with love and hope who condemned a wicked world. The wicked world killed the prophet.[161]

Culture Section

Discussion

The Cornerstone

When a person in the Near East decided to build a home, he would start by gathering together the needed supplies. He would gather stones, cut beams, and other materials required. There would be large and small stones that were used for the foundation. The home builders would generally reject the huge stones because they were hard to fit into the foundation. However, an owner could insist that they be used. If so, the largest stone would be placed in the corner of the foundation wall and covered with dirt so its size would not be seen. Yeshua saw himself as a cornerstone for a universal movement that the LORD wanted to start. Yeshua was the prophet from Galilee that was rejected by the religious leadership in Jerusalem, like all the others. "Usually what men would select, God rejects. And what God selects, men frequently reject."[162]

---

[161] Stern, Frank. *A Rabbi Looks at Jesus' Parables*. Lanham, Md: Rowman & Littlefield, 2006. 120-25.**Invalid source specified.**

[162] Errico, Rocco A., and George M. Lamsa. "Chapter 21." In *Aramaic Light on the Gospel of Matthew: A Commentary on the Teachings of Jesus from the Aramaic and Unchanged Near Eastern Customs*. Santa Fe, NM: Noohra Foundation, 2000.

Since sending the prophets did not work, the LORD decided to start over, but this time, the start was sending the Messiah Yeshua. Therefore, He became the cornerstone of the new movement.

Large and Small stones – Eternal truth

The religious leaders did not take care of the Kingdom of God correctly. Therefore, Yeshua told them that God would transfer this guardianship to people who would take better care. In the case of the emerging church, the Gentiles took it over from the Hebrews. I am not sure that I could say today that the Gentiles are doing a better job attending to God's Kingdom.

The stone in verse 44 is a metaphor meaning "truth." The truth is sometimes hard and strong. Thus, Near Eastern people call the truth "a stone." "And he who falls on this stone" signifies that anyone attacking the truth of God's kingdom will be destroyed (a metaphor for defeat). Therefore, verse 44 can read, replacing the metaphors:

"And he who goes against the truth of the Kingdom of God will be defeated and will be destroyed."

Questioning the passage

1. What was the typical size of a vineyard? (v. 31)
   There is no "typical" size for a vineyard.

2. Why was a wall built around the vineyard? (v. 33)
   The wall was built to secure the vineyard and guard it against animals and thieves.

Thoughts

Yeshua came to tell the people of Judah and the Galilee that they needed to follow the calling to repentance that the prophets of old and the prophets of then brought. The prophet of then was John the Baptist and his contemporaries. What happened to each of these previous prophets? The prophets of old were killed when they brought their message from the LORD. John the Baptist was killed when he told Herod Antipas that he stole his brother's wife against the LORD's Laws. Kings and rulers did not like prophets telling them when they sinned. The typical response was to kill them. So, Yeshua was not killed by the Jews. Instead, He was killed by the ruling class, who did not like the message that He brought. Even the Son of God was not going to be listened to. Today we have rabbis, ministers, and priests who interpret the Bible. People attend worship settings and hear the Word of the LORD, listen to the interpretation offered, and then leave the worship time and either forget what they heard or say to themselves, "he/she does not know what they are talking about." People go to the medical doctor or lawyer and follow them implicitly. Then why do they not listen to their spiritual leaders? It is true that before following a spiritual leader, the education level and knowledge of the spiritual leader need to be verified. Once this is done, then one should have confidence in the leader the LORD has sent.

Reflections

This parable has always been viewed by Christians as the rejection of Jesus as the Messiah and the beginning of the end for Jesus. Modern Christians should be sensitive to this interpretation because it has sparked centuries of anti-Semitism. Even today, anti-Semitism exists, with many Christians being taught that the Jews of Jesus' day wanted Him dead. How can the followers of the Messiah of Peace use His words to condemn another ethnic group to death? Anti-Semitism exists in today's churches. Even Jews who have come to know and follow the Lord Jesus Christ find anti-Semitism in the church. The church should rejoice when a Hebrew comes to know the true Messiah. In fact, that rejoicing should be for anyone.

MARK 12:12-17

Language

New American Standard 1995	Koine Greek
[12] And they were seeking to seize Him, and *yet* they feared the people, for they understood that He spoke the parable against them. And *so* they left Him and went away. [13] Then they sent some of the Pharisees and Herodians to Him in order to trap Him in a statement. [14] They came and said to Him, "Teacher, we know that You are truthful and defer to no one; for You are not partial to any, but teach the way of God in truth. Is it lawful to pay a poll-tax to Caesar, or not? [15] "Shall we pay or shall we not pay?" But He, knowing their hypocrisy, said to them, "Why are you testing Me? Bring Me a [1]denarius to look at." [16] They brought *one*. And He said to them, "Whose likeness and inscription is this?" And they said to Him, "Caesar's." [17] And Jesus said to them, "Render to Caesar the things that are Caesar's, and to God the things that are God's." And they were amazed at Him.	[12] Καὶ ἐζήτουν αὐτὸν κρατῆσαι, καὶ ἐφοβήθησαν τὸν ὄχλον ἔγνωσαν γὰρ ὅτι πρὸς αὐτοὺς τὴν παραβολὴν εἶπεν· καὶ ἀφέντες αὐτὸν ἀπῆλθον. [13] Καὶ ἀποστέλλουσιν πρὸς αὐτόν τινας τῶν Φαρισαίων καὶ τῶν Ἡρωδιανῶν, ἵνα αὐτὸν ἀγρεύσωσιν λόγῳ. [14] Οἱ δὲ ἐλθόντες λέγουσιν αὐτῷ, Διδάσκαλε, οἴδαμεν ὅτι ἀληθὴς εἶ, καὶ οὐ μέλει σοι περὶ οὐδενός· οὐ γὰρ βλέπεις εἰς πρόσωπον ἀνθρώπων, ἀλλ᾽ ἐπ᾽ ἀληθείας τὴν ὁδὸν τοῦ θεοῦ διδάσκεις· ἔξεστιν κῆνσον Καίσαρι δοῦναι ἢ οὔ; [15] Δῶμεν, ἢ μὴ δῶμεν; Ὁ δὲ εἰδὼς αὐτῶν τὴν ὑπόκρισιν εἶπεν αὐτοῖς, Τί με πειράζετε; φέρετέ μοι δηνάριον, ἵνα ἴδω. [16] Οἱ δὲ ἤνεγκαν. Καὶ λέγει αὐτοῖς, Τίνος ἡ εἰκὼν αὕτη καὶ ἡ ἐπιγραφή; Οἱ δὲ εἶπον αὐτῷ, Καίσαρος. [17] Καὶ ἀποκριθεὶς ὁ Ἰησοῦς εἶπεν αὐτοῖς, Ἀπόδοτε τὰ Καίσαρος Καίσαρι, καὶ τὰ τοῦ θεοῦ τῷ θεῷ. Καὶ ἐθαύμασαν ἐπ᾽ αὐτῷ.

Process of Discovery

Linguistics Section

Linguistic Structure

[Transition] [12] And they were seeking to seize Him, and *yet* they feared the people, for they understood that He spoke the parable against them. And *so* they left Him and went away.

A [13] Then they sent some of the Pharisees and Herodians to Him in order to trap Him in a statement.

> **B** [14] They came and said to Him, "Teacher, we know that You are truthful and defer to no one; for You are not partial to any, but teach the way of God in truth. Is it lawful to pay a poll-tax to Caesar, or not? [15] "Shall we pay or shall we not pay?"
>
>> **C** But He, knowing their hypocrisy, said to them, "Why are you testing Me? Bring Me a denarius to look at." [16] They brought *one*. And He said to them, "Whose likeness and inscription is this?" And they said to Him, "Caesar's."
>
> **B'** [17] And Jesus said to them, "'Render to Caesar the things that are Caesar's, and to God the things that are God's."

A' And they were amazed at Him.

Discussion

The structure of this parable is a question from the Pharisees and the answer that Yeshua offers. It is a simple A-B-C chiasm. Yeshua does not answer their question but turns the table on them by offering a different problem.

Questioning the Passage

1. Who were the Herodians? (v. 13)

    The Herodians in this narrative would have been guards from Herod Antipas, the ruler of the territory.

2. Why did the Pharisees send Herodians to see Yeshua? (v. 13)

    If the purpose was to trap Yeshua, then the Pharisees needed the Herodian guards there to arrest Yeshua. The question that was posed, if answered, would have condemned Yeshua either as a traitor to His people or a traitor to Rome. Either way, an answer would cause the Herodian guards to arrest him.

3. What was the malice in asking the question? (v. 14)

From Yeshua's dialogue, He believed that their question was not about discovering his political views but rather about convicting Him of a crime he had not committed.

4. Why were the questioners amazed? (v. 17)

Yeshua did not answer the question. He turned it back upon the questioners. That was amazing to the bystanders.

Main/Center Point

Perhaps this passage is about loyalty to the LORD. Those Hebrews who had Roman coins, and used them, were committing idolatry. Since the Roman coin had the image of the Emperor and the Emperor thought he was a god, the coins were considered idols. Yeshua did recognize that the tax had to be paid as citizens of the Roman empire. Therefore, he said to pay the tax because you must but do not mix your earthly obligations with your spiritual obligations.

For example: pay your government taxes because you are a citizen of the government. You pay these taxes because the penalty for not paying them is imprisonment. Pay your tithe to the LORD because you want to please the LORD and receive His blessings. As Paul said, "God loves a joyful giver." Complaining about the government requirement for taxes is acceptable. Complaining about God's requirement to tithe is not. If one does not contribute to the LORD's work, the consequences are not material; rather they are spiritual. Perhaps one's place in Heaven will be determined by how one responds to the LORD's calling.

Culture Section

Discussion

The circumstances concerning why the tax was being collect are not offered. Also, the reasons the Hebrews objected to paying such a tax is not recorded. Was the tax a poll tax or a tribute tax? Poll taxes were levied on an individual as a head tax is today. A tribute tax was paid by states in the Roman Empire, which were protectorates and retained their own independence. In the Hebrew

Scriptures, it is written that Hezekiah, King of Judah, paid tribute to Sennacherib, King of Assyria.[163]

Hebrews did not resent the taxes on the property, but they did vigorously object to paying a personal head tax, especially since the head taxes were paid on their sheep and cattle. The tax was religiously unlawful because a temporal power exacted it. The people felt their allegiance to the LORD as the supreme ruler of the State meant that they paid a tax to the LORD cheerfully. A two-shekel payment was made to the Temple treasury during Yeshua's day.

Jewish kings were considered the servants of the LORD. The Roman Emperors were worshiped as gods, thus paying a head tax to Rome was considered idolatry.

The shekel coin did not have an image nor an inscription on it. Since the imperial coin had an image of the Emperor on it, the coin was not acceptable and not considered legal tender to pay the Temple tax. Gentile money was exchanged for acceptable Temple money for the Temple. The Hebrews could not offer God a coin with a human god on it. The coins collected for the tax were placed on the altar of the Temple and consecrated to the LORD.[164]

Questioning the passage

1. What was a poll-tax? (v. 14)

    The poll-tax was a tax on everyone in the Empire. It is also called a head tax.

Culture and Linguistics Section

Discussion

The idea is that the parable revolves around idolatry. Since the imperial coin of Rome was considered an idol because of the figure of the Emperor on it, then using such a coin would be

---

[163] 2 Kings 18:14

[164] Errico, Rocco A., and George M. Lamsa. "Chapter 22." In *Aramaic Light on the Gospel of Matthew: A Commentary on the Teachings of Jesus from the Aramaic and Unchanged Near Eastern Customs*. Santa Fe, NM: Noohra Foundation, 2000.

considered idolatry. Therefore, such a coin could never be used for the LORD. Perhaps a lesson here is that a disciple of Yeshua should never do anything that is idolatrous.

"Several forms of idolatry have been distinguished. Gross or overt, idolatry consists of explicit acts of reverence addressed to a person or an object—the sun, the king, an animal, a statue. This may exist alongside the acknowledgment of a supreme being; *e.g.,* Israel worshiped the golden calf at the foot of Mount Sinai, where it had encamped to receive the Law and the covenant of the one true God.

A person becomes guilty of a subtler idolatry, however, when, although overt acts of adoration are avoided, he attaches to a creature the confidence, loyalty, and devotion that properly belongs only to the Creator. Thus, the nation is a good creature of God, but it is to be loved and served with an affection appropriate to it, not with the ultimate devotion that must be reserved for the Lord of all nations. Even true doctrine (*e.g.,* true doctrine about idolatry) may become an idol if it fails to point beyond itself to God alone."[165]

After the Empire absorbed Christianity, several Roman and Byzantine coins were produced with a "likeness" of Yeshua. Are these coins a form of idolatry? Yeshua would say yes. When the church broke away from its Jewish roots, it must have decided to relax a lot of the Jewish beliefs, in this case, idolatry.

So, is this parable about idolatry? This is one possible theme.

Thoughts

Considering the reason that using a Roman coin was considered idolatry, a view of this parable is that there are obligations that we must follow because of the government in which we live, and there are obligations to God. The obligations to the government may not be godly. The Roman government of Yeshua's day believed in idolatry. The Emperor considered himself to be a god. Even

---

[165] The Editors of Encyclopædia Britannica. "Idolatry." Encyclopædia Britannica. June 07, 2013. Accessed October 18, 2017. https://www.britannica.com/topic/idolatry.

though the Hebrew people would not give the Emperor that reverence, they still lived under his rule. The people of Judea and the Galilee were not happy to be under pagan rule. They learned to accept the oppression of Rome. In 66 CE and 135 CE, the Hebrew people attempted a revolt against Roman rule and suffered. Yeshua knew that a revolt would fail. The Roman Empire was too mighty, and they were experienced in dealing with revolts. Therefore, by Yeshua saying, "give to Caesar what is Caesar," he said that the people needed to acquiesce to their situation.

However, they also needed to remember to give to the LORD what the LORD expected of them. Whether it be the tithe or service to the LORD, it also needed to be done. Today we serve Yeshua, and we serve the country in which we live. The government has fines and penalties that make us follow the laws of the land. The LORD's law must also be followed. There may be no penalty for not following the LORD's law while living on Earth, but there will be a penalty to pay or repent for when the day of judgment occurs.

Suppose you are not following the Laws of the LORD through Yeshua's teaching. In that case, you must consider asking for forgiveness for your decisions and start following the ways of God.

Reflections

Some things belong to the Emperor, and some to God is a misnomer. Everything belongs to God. So, the Emperor did not understand that fact. Psalm 24 reminds us that the Earth was created by God and belongs to God. We are simply stewards of the planet and its resources. We owe everything to God. While on Earth, we must show allegiance to the human powers, but our ultimate and deeper allegiance is to God. It sometimes may be confusing throughout our lives as to which allegiance to follow. A way to determine this is to ask, does your allegiance follow the Laws of God. An overused example is kids' sports on Sunday morning. When a parent decides that Sunday sports is more important than worshiping God, they send a signal to their children and God that their allegiance is to earthly manners first. Each of us must make the decision as to where our loyalties are. Which side of the coin are you on? God's side or an earthly side.

MARK 12:18-27

Language

New American Standard 1995	Koine Greek
[18] *Some* Sadducees (who say that there is no resurrection) came to Jesus, and *began* questioning Him, saying, [19] "Teacher, Moses wrote for us that IF A MAN'S BROTHER DIES and leaves behind a wife AND LEAVES NO CHILD, HIS BROTHER SHOULD MARRY THE WIFE AND RAISE UP CHILDREN TO HIS BROTHER. [20] "There were seven brothers; and the first took a wife, and died leaving no children. [21] "The second one married her, and died leaving behind no children; and the third likewise; [22] and *so* all seven left no children. Last of all the woman died also. [23] "In the resurrection, when they rise again, which one's wife will she be? For all seven had married her." [24] Jesus said to them, "Is this not the reason you are mistaken, that you do not understand the Scriptures or the power of God? [25] "For when they rise from the dead, they neither marry nor are given in marriage, but are like angels in heaven. [26] "But regarding the fact that the dead rise again, have you not read in the book of Moses, in the *passage* about *the burning* bush, how God spoke to him, saying, 'I AM THE GOD OF ABRAHAM, AND THE GOD OF ISAAC, AND THE GOD OF JACOB'? [27] "*ᵃ*He is not the God of the dead, but of the living; you are greatly mistaken."	[18] Καὶ ἔρχονται Σαδδουκαῖοι πρὸς αὐτόν, οἵτινες λέγουσιν ἀνάστασιν μὴ εἶναι καὶ ἐπηρώτησαν αὐτόν, λέγοντες, [19] Διδάσκαλε, Μωσῆς ἔγραψεν ἡμῖν, ὅτι ἐάν τινος ἀδελφὸς ἀποθάνῃ, καὶ καταλίπῃ γυναῖκα, καὶ τέκνα μὴ ἀφῇ, ἵνα λάβῃ ὁ ἀδελφὸς αὐτοῦ τὴν γυναῖκα αὐτοῦ, καὶ ἐξαναστήσῃ σπέρμα τῷ ἀδελφῷ αὐτοῦ [20] ἑπτὰ ἀδελφοὶ ἦσαν καὶ ὁ πρῶτος ἔλαβεν γυναῖκα, καὶ ἀποθνήσκων οὐκ ἀφῆκεν σπέρμα [21] καὶ ὁ δεύτερος ἔλαβεν αὐτήν, καὶ ἀπέθανεν, καὶ οὐδὲ αὐτὸς ἀφῆκεν σπέρμα καὶ ὁ τρίτος ὡσαύτως. [22] Καὶ ἔλαβον αὐτὴν οἱ ἑπτά, καὶ οὐκ ἀφῆκαν σπέρμα. Ἐσχάτη πάντων ἀπέθανεν καὶ ἡ γυνή. [23] Ἐν τῇ ἀναστάσει, ὅταν ἀναστῶσιν, τίνος αὐτῶν ἔσται γυνή; Οἱ γὰρ ἑπτὰ ἔσχον αὐτὴν γυναῖκα. [24] Καὶ ἀποκριθεὶς ὁ Ἰησοῦς εἶπεν αὐτοῖς, Οὐ διὰ τοῦτο πλανᾶσθε, μὴ εἰδότες τὰς γραφάς, μηδὲ τὴν δύναμιν τοῦ θεοῦ; [25] Ὅταν γὰρ ἐκ νεκρῶν ἀναστῶσιν, οὔτε γαμοῦσιν, οὔτε γαμίσκονται, ἀλλ' εἰσὶν ὡς ἄγγελοι οἱ ἐν τοῖς οὐρανοῖς. [26] Περὶ δὲ τῶν νεκρῶν, ὅτι ἐγείρονται, οὐκ ἀνέγνωτε ἐν τῇ βίβλῳ Μωσέως, ἐπὶ τοῦ βάτου, ὡς εἶπεν αὐτῷ ὁ θεός, λέγων, Ἐγὼ ὁ θεὸς Ἀβραάμ, καὶ ὁ θεὸς Ἰσαάκ, καὶ ὁ θεὸς Ἰακώβ; [27] οὐκ ἔστιν ὁ θεὸς νεκρῶν, ἀλλὰ θεὸς ζώντων ὑμεῖς οὖν πολὺ πλανᾶσθε.

Process of Discovery

Linguistics Section

Linguistic Structure

A [18] *Some* Sadducees (who say that there is no resurrection) came to Jesus, and *began* questioning Him, saying,

> **B** [19] "Teacher, Moses wrote for us that IF A MAN'S BROTHER DIES and leaves behind a wife AND LEAVES NO CHILD, HIS BROTHER SHOULD MARRY THE WIFE AND RAISE UP CHILDREN TO HIS BROTHER.

>> **C** [20] "There were seven brothers; and the first took a wife, and died leaving no children. [21] "The second one married her, and died leaving behind no children; and the third likewise; [22] and *so* all seven left no children. Last of all the woman died also. [23] "In the resurrection, when they rise again, which one's wife will she be? For all seven had married her."

>>> **D** [24] Jesus said to them, "Is this not the reason you are mistaken, that you do not understand the Scriptures or the power of God?

>> **C'** [25] "For when they rise from the dead, they neither marry nor are given in marriage, but are like angels in heaven.

> **B'** [26] "But regarding the fact that the dead rise again, have you not read in the book of Moses, in the *passage* about *the burning* bush, how God spoke to him, saying, 'I AM THE GOD OF ABRAHAM, AND THE GOD OF ISAAC, AND THE GOD OF JACOB'?

A' [27] "'He is not the God of the dead, but of the living; you are greatly mistaken."

Discussion

This encounter between Yeshua and the Sadducees brings up a fascinating question about the purpose of the question.

Questioning the Passage

1. What did the Sadducees believe? (v. 18)

   The Sadducees believed in the purity of life. They discounted the dogmatic theology and traditions of the Jewish religion. This group was not interested in rituals for ceremonies. The Sadducees wanted peace and prosperity and were content with the Roman rule in Judea.[166]

   The commentary from the author of the Gospel "(who say there is no resurrection)" was probably added because the readers of the Gospel were not aware of who this group was. It is interesting that Sadducees would question Yeshua about resurrection when they did not believe in it. Therefore, it raises the question, why did they ask Yeshua a question about the resurrection.

2. What does "but are like the angels in heaven" mean? (v. 25)
   This is a Semitic phrase meaning "Godlike innocence." The LORD is the Eternal Spirit, and human spirits are created in His image. That means that human spirits are like the LORD; they are good, eternal, and indestructible. The LORD ordained marriage on the Earth for the Nephesh (the physical body) to populate the Earth. In Heaven, there is no need for the Nephesh; therefore, the need for sexual reproduction does not exist.[167]

3. What does the reference to the God of Abraham, the God of Isaac, and the God of Jacob mean? (v. 26)

   Yeshua is saying that the God of Abraham, Isaac, and Jacob is the God of the living. The patriarchs are living spiritual beings. In the Kabbalah, these three Ruach (spirit) live in the Sephirot, Chesed, Geburah, and Tiferet. Since human Ruachim (spirits) are in the image of the LORD, then these Ruachim are also eternal. The LORD is the God of the living. Therefore, after the Nephesh dies, the Ruach lives on. The Zohar says that the

---

[166] Rocco A. Errico and George M. Lamsa, *Aramaic Light on the Gospel of Matthew: a Commentary on the Teachings of Jesus from the Aramaic and Unchanged Near Eastern Customs* (Santa Fe, NM: Noohra Foundation, 2000).
[167] IBID.

Ruach returns to Yesod in the Lower Waters of Heaven. Death is not a finality but rather a doorway into the World to Come.

Verse Comparison of citations or proof text

1. [26] "But regarding the fact that the dead rise again, have you not read in the book of Moses, in the *passage* about *the burning* bush, how God spoke to him, saying, [b]I AM THE GOD OF ABRAHAM, AND THE GOD OF ISAAC, AND THE GOD OF JACOB'?

   Ex. 3:6 He said also, "I am the God of your father, the God of Abraham, the God of Isaac, and the God of Jacob." Then Moses hid his face, for he was afraid to look at God.

   Yeshua quotes Exodus 3:6. It is of interest that the Sadducees did not believe in the resurrection of the Ruach. However, they did understand that the LORD was the God of the living.

Culture Section

Discussion

The question arises from the Levirate marriage law. "Levirate marriage is the obligation of a surviving brother to marry the widow of his brother if he died without having sired children (Deuteronomy 25:5-6). The corollary is that the widow must marry a brother-in-law rather than anyone outside the family. The oldest of the surviving brothers had the first obligation to perform this commandment, which also allowed him to inherit all of his dead brother's property."[168]

---

[168] Ronald L. Eisenberg, "Levirate Marriage and Halitzah," My Jewish Learning, accessed May 20, 2020, https://www.myjewishlearning.com/article/levirate-marriage-and-halitzah/.

Culture and Linguistics Section

Discussion

Two questions arise: why is this narrative in the Gospel, and did it happen? The questioning from the Sadduccees to Yeshua about resurrection could have been used to determine if Yeshua was a Sadducee in his thinking or was He a Pharisee?

Yeshua was not in line with the Sadducees thinking about resurrection. From Yeshua's answer, it can be derived that He saw the human Ruach as internal as the LORD's Ruach was. Therefore, death was not the end of the Ruach but rather the end of the Nephesh. When the Nephesh dies, the Ruach returns to Heaven. Follow-up questions could have been: when does the Ruach return to Heaven, and do all Ruachim return? There is no follow-up from the Sadducees after Yeshua's answer, but there are many questions.

The other purpose of this narrative is to ask Yeshua if all of the Mitzvot of the Torah have to be followed. For a Hebrew community, the answer is clear the Mitzvot of the Torah must be followed. However, for a Pauline church, which is based on Mithras, the question of having to follow the Mitzvot would be a natural question. Paul could not have left any of his established churches with the answers to all of the regulations of the Torah, nor could he leave a copy of the Torah. Therefore, this encounter is the question from the community about following all the Torah laws. Yeshua is saying, "no." The situation posed by the Sadducees would not have happened. When Tamar married Judah's oldest son, he died, leaving no children. The brother married Tamar, and he died, leaving no heirs. Judah decided that his third and last son was not going to marry Tamar. When Tamar found out, she set a trap for Judah. From that encounter, Tamar became pregnant with Judah's child. Since the Messiah came from the line of Judah, the LORD was not displeased. Therefore, does the Levirate Marriage law have to be obeyed?

Today Christians and Jews would say that the law is obsolete and must be abandoned. However, if the people are allowed to choose the Mitzvot and Halacha (laws) they are wise to follow, then why not abandon them? At that point, Christians could ask why the rules and regulations that

Paul established in his letter follow? This is the underlying tone of the narrative because Judah did not follow the Levarite law but became the ancestor of Yeshua, the Messiah.

Paul's laws were given to the churches because there were many acts that the Mithras churches had done for centuries in direct contrast to the general Hebraic beliefs. Paul did not eliminate all of Mithra's ethics and behaviors. He did attempt to eliminate the ones that he felt needed to be eliminated. So, today how many of the Bible laws and Mitzvot do Christians have to follow? That question is one of many that popes and bishops have struggled with for centuries. The more laws the Church imposes on the people, the more control it has. In the latter 20th and now in the 21st century, church rule is being challenged. The Church imposes the biblical rules that it wants to so that it can maintain control over people. The people are revolting, even in Protestant churches, which can be seen in the rise of so many independent churches. These churches established their rules and regulations and told prospective members that they must believe in the way established by the independent Church or worship elsewhere.

There are archaic laws and regulations in the Scripture. Levirate marriage is one of them. When this law was enacted, it made good sense. The inheritance of portions of the Holy Land needed to remain in the clans of the tribes. When the Babylonian Exile occurred, all ancient claims were gone. The marriage law was no longer necessary. The Hebrews owned no lands. The Mitzvot and Laws in the Torah about the animal sacrifice system are null and void because there is not a Temple in Jerusalem.

So, who determines which laws and Mitzvot of the entire Bible does one live by?

Thoughts

The situation that the Sadducees brought to Yeshua would probably have never happened. Indeed, in Yeshua's day, this problem would not have occurred. The need to have children for land was long gone. The encounter could have been as simple as the Sadducees wanting to know if Yeshua thought like them. After all, Yeshua broke many traditions and rituals that the Pharisees had established. The Sadducees could have been doing a final check on Yeshua. The Sadducees also liked the traditional ways under the Roman government. They were prospering, and life was good for them. They did not want some rouge teaching changing the way the Romans interacted with them.

Reflections

The narrative could be used to show an underlining statement that not all the Torah Laws have to be followed. The question is, does following the Torah Law lead to a time in Heaven? The answer from this encounter is, "no, it does not have any effect." If marriage is viewed as a metaphor representing the Torah law, then Yeshua said that not following a Torah law does not affect the entry into the Kingdom of Heaven. That is what the Gentiles wanted and needed to hear as they began to accept Yeshua instead of Mithras as their God. Therefore, the Pauline churches could toss the kosher laws out and not have to worry about them. The Church has disposed of many of the Torah laws over the years. In the day of accepting sexual attitudes by society, which could be considered antibiblical, whether one has to follow the Torah laws is the real question. A church denomination that says that homosexuality is against the Bible cannot say that kosher laws can be ignored (one of many examples that the Church determined a believer does not have to follow). Using the Church's examples from its past, homosexuality should not be dividing the Church. It should not matter what a person's sexual orientation is. Marriage has no meaning in Heaven.

MARK 12:28-37

Language

New American Standard 1995	Koine Greek
[28] One of the scribes came and heard them arguing, and recognizing that He had answered them well, asked Him, "What commandment is the foremost of all?" [29] Jesus answered, "The foremost is, 'HEAR, O ISRAEL! THE LORD OUR GOD IS ONE LORD; [30] *a*AND YOU SHALL LOVE THE LORD YOUR GOD WITH ALL YOUR HEART, AND WITH ALL YOUR SOUL, AND WITH ALL YOUR MIND, AND WITH ALL YOUR STRENGTH.' [31] "The second is this, *a*'YOU SHALL LOVE YOUR NEIGHBOR AS YOURSELF.' There is no other commandment greater than these." [32] The scribe said to Him, "Right, Teacher; You have truly stated that HE IS ONE, AND THERE IS NO ONE ELSE BESIDES HIM; [33] AND TO LOVE HIM WITH ALL THE HEART AND WITH ALL THE UNDERSTANDING AND WITH ALL THE STRENGTH, AND TO LOVE ONE'S NEIGHBOR AS HIMSELF, is much more than all burnt offerings and sacrifices." [34] When Jesus saw that he had answered intelligently, He said to him, "You are not far from the kingdom of God." After that, no one would venture to ask Him any more questions. [35] And Jesus *began* to say, as He taught in the temple, "How *is it that* the scribes say that the Christ is the son of David? [36] "David himself said in the Holy Spirit, 'THE LORD SAID TO MY LORD, SIT AT MY RIGHT HAND, UNTIL I PUT YOUR ENEMIES BENEATH YOUR FEET.' [37] "David himself calls Him 'Lord'; so in what sense is He his son?" And the large crowd enjoyed listening to Him.	[28] Καὶ προσελθὼν εἷς τῶν γραμματέων, ἀκούσας αὐτῶν συζητούντων, εἰδὼς ὅτι καλῶς αὐτοῖς ἀπεκρίθη, ἐπηρώτησεν αὐτόν. Ποία ἐστὶν πρώτη πάντων ἐντολή; [29] Ὁ δὲ Ἰησοῦς ἀπεκρίθη αὐτῷ ὅτι Πρώτη πάντων τῶν ἐντολῶν, Ἄκουε, Ἰσραήλ κύριος ὁ θεὸς ἡμῶν, κύριος εἷς ἐστιν [30] καὶ ἀγαπήσεις κύριον τὸν θεόν σου ἐξ ὅλης τῆς καρδίας σου, καὶ ἐξ ὅλης τῆς ψυχῆς σου, καὶ ἐξ ὅλης τῆς διανοίας σου, καὶ ἐξ ὅλης τῆς ἰσχύος σου. Αὕτη πρώτη ἐντολή. [31] Καὶ δευτέρα ὁμοία αὕτη, Ἀγαπήσεις τὸν πλησίον σου ὡς σεαυτόν. Μείζων τούτων ἄλλη ἐντολή οὐκ ἔστιν. [32] Καὶ εἶπεν αὐτῷ ὁ γραμματεύς, Καλῶς, διδάσκαλε, ἐπ' ἀληθείας εἶπας ὅτι εἷς ἐστιν, καὶ οὐκ ἔστιν ἄλλος πλὴν αὐτοῦ [33] καὶ τὸ ἀγαπᾶν αὐτὸν ἐξ ὅλης τῆς καρδίας, καὶ ἐξ ὅλης τῆς συνέσεως, καὶ ἐξ ὅλης τῆς ψυχῆς, καὶ ἐξ ὅλης τῆς ἰσχύος, καὶ τὸ ἀγαπᾶν τὸν πλησίον ὡς ἑαυτόν, πλεῖόν ἐστιν πάντων τῶν ὁλοκαυτωμάτων καὶ θυσιῶν. [34] Καὶ ὁ Ἰησοῦς ἰδὼν αὐτὸν ὅτι νουνεχῶς ἀπεκρίθη, εἶπεν αὐτῷ, Οὐ μακρὰν εἶ ἀπὸ τῆς βασιλείας τοῦ θεοῦ. Καὶ οὐδεὶς οὐκέτι ἐτόλμα αὐτὸν ἐπερωτῆσαι. [35] Καὶ ἀποκριθεὶς ὁ Ἰησοῦς ἔλεγεν, διδάσκων ἐν τῷ ἱερῷ, Πῶς λέγουσιν οἱ γραμματεῖς ὅτι ὁ χριστὸς υἱός ἐστιν Δαυίδ; [36] Αὐτὸς γὰρ Δαυὶδ εἶπεν ἐν πνεύματι ἁγίῳ, Λέγει ὁ κύριος τῷ κυρίῳ μου, Κάθου ἐκ δεξιῶν μου, ἕως ἂν θῶ τοὺς ἐχθρούς σου ὑποπόδιον τῶν ποδῶν σου. [37] Αὐτὸς οὖν Δαυὶδ λέγει αὐτὸν κύριον καὶ πόθεν υἱὸς αὐτοῦ ἐστιν; Καὶ ὁ πολὺς ὄχλος ἤκουεν αὐτοῦ ἡδέως.

Process of Discovery

Linguistics Section

Linguistic Structure

[Foremost commandment] [28]   One of the scribes came and heard them arguing, and recognizing that He had answered them well, asked Him, "What commandment is the foremost of all?" [29] Jesus answered, "The foremost is, 'HEAR, O ISRAEL! THE LORD OUR GOD IS ONE LORD; [30] *a*AND YOU SHALL LOVE THE LORD YOUR GOD WITH ALL YOUR HEART, AND WITH ALL YOUR SOUL, AND WITH ALL YOUR MIND, AND WITH ALL YOUR STRENGTH.' [31] "The second is this, '"YOU SHALL LOVE YOUR NEIGHBOR AS YOURSELF.' There is no other commandment greater than these."

[Scribe response] [32] The scribe said to Him, "Right, Teacher; You have truly stated that HE IS ONE, AND THERE IS NO ONE ELSE BESIDES HIM; [33] AND TO LOVE HIM WITH ALL THE HEART AND WITH ALL THE UNDERSTANDING AND WITH ALL THE STRENGTH, AND TO LOVE ONE'S NEIGHBOR AS HIMSELF, is much more than all burnt offerings and sacrifices."

[Yeshua's response][34] When Jesus saw that he had answered intelligently, He said to him, "You are not far from the kingdom of God." After that, no one would venture to ask Him any more questions. [35]   And Jesus *began* to say, as He taught in the temple, "How *is it that* the scribes say that the Christ is the son of David? [36] "David himself said in the Holy Spirit, 'THE LORD SAID TO MY LORD, SIT AT MY RIGHT HAND, UNTIL I PUT YOUR ENEMIES BENEATH YOUR FEET." [37] "David himself calls Him 'Lord'; so in what sense is He his son?" And the large crowd enjoyed listening to Him.

Discussion

This passage consists of two short chiasms. The first chiasm deals with the two great commandments. The second deals with the title "son of David."

Questioning the Passage

1. Why did the scribe ask Yeshua about the greatest commandment? (v. 28)

   The "scribe" is a person who was very versed in Mosaic Law. By asking Yeshua about the

   Torah, he attempted to discover which House of learning Yeshua belonged. There were two main houses of study in Yeshua's time. One was the House of Hillel. This house was more relaxed about the Torah. The other was the House of Shammai. This house was more strict about the written letter of the Torah.

2. Why did they ask Yeshua about the messiah? (v. 35)

   Even for the early church, the understanding of the Messiah was in flux. In Hebraic tradition, the Messiah is not God incarnate. This is an idea that the early church added. There are two good resources available that deal with this topic:

   How Jesus Became God: The Exaltation of a Jewish Preacher from Galilee by Bart D. Ehrman

   How on Earth Did Jesus Become a God?: Historical Questions about Earliest Devotion to Jesus - by Larry W. Hurtado

   So, when did the LORD reveal that Yeshua was the Messiah? A possible answer is that the revelation was made on Easter morning when the Father raised the Son from the grave. Yeshua's resurrection can be viewed as God is revealing His Messiah to the world, as demonstrated in Mark's Gospel.

Verse Comparison of citations or proof text

1. ⁴³ He said to them, "Then how does David in the Spirit call Him 'Lord,' saying ⁴⁴ 'THE LORD SAID TO MY LORD, "SIT AT MY RIGHT HAND, UNTIL I PUT YOUR ENEMIES BENEATH YOUR FEET "'? (Matt. 22:43-44 NAU)

   ^{WTT} **Psalm 110:1** לְדָוִד מִזְמוֹר נְאֻם יְהוָה לַאדֹנִי שֵׁב לִימִינִי עַד־אָשִׁית אֹיְבֶיךָ הֲדֹם לְרַגְלֶיךָ

Mark 12:36-37 is one of the most misunderstood verses in the Gospels. The misunderstanding from the church through the centuries occurred when the church broke away from its Jewish roots. The church left behind several of the most important tools to discover the meaning of the Hebrew Scriptures. One of those tools is the Targum. The Targums are a collection of rabbinic translations with commentary included. After the Diaspora occurred, the rabbis became concerned that the Hebrew people would not stay connected to the LORD through the Torah because they were not speaking Hebrew. The people were speaking Aramaic. Therefore, the Targums were written by translating the Hebrew into Aramaic. A bonus for us today is that the rabbis included commentary to help explain some of the verses of the Scripture. Psalm 110:1 is a beautiful example. The question from the lawyer about this verse shows that the Christian Church did not understand the true nature of this verse. "Then how does David in the Spirit call him 'Lord.' By examining the Targums, the true meaning is revealed. The lawyer did not know the Scriptures as well as he thought. Remember that the Gospel of Mark was written at least 30 years after the Resurrection. The Gentile influence was dominated in the churches by then.

[NAU] **Psalm 110:1** A Psalm of David. The LORD says to my Lord: "Sit at My right hand Until I make Your enemies a footstool for Your feet."

[PST] **Psalm 110:1** *Composed* by David, a psalm. The LORD said *in his decree to make me lord of all Israel, but he said to me, "Wait still for Saul of the tribe of Benjamin to die, for one reign must not encroach on another; and afterwards* I will make your enemies a prop for your feet."[169]

ANOTHER TARGUM: The LORD *spoke by his decree to give me the dominion in exchange for sitting in study of Torah. "Wait* at my right hand until I make your enemies a prop for your feet."

ANOTHER TARGUM: The LORD *said in his decree to appoint me ruler over Israel, but the LORD said to me, "Wait for Saul of the tribe of Benjamin to pass away from the world; and afterwards you will inherit the kingship, and* I will make your enemies a prop for your feet." (Ps. 110:1 PST)

If King David was the psalmist, which he appears to be, he is acknowledging a commandment from the LORD that he must wait until the death of King Saul before he becomes king. David

---

[169] PST – Psalms Targum in English

was not to execute a coup or revolt of any kind. The LORD was going to take care of Saul in His time, and then after that event, the LORD was going to put David on the throne. Humans have a tendency of not wanting to wait (delayed gratification). Therefore, the LORD intervened because the change in the kingship of Israel was to be done by the LORD in His time and not in David's time.

So, Yeshua's answer to the question about the messiah and the messiah's relationship with David was answered. The answer was that they needed to wait until the LORD revealed the Messiah. In the same manner that David had to wait to become the King when the LORD was ready for it to happen, they needed to wait until the LORD was ready to reveal the messiah. When did the LORD reveal this information to the church? This becomes an interesting question as the early church develops and tries to answer who was Jesus of Nazareth.

Perhaps Yeshua is telling us that the plan for us is with the LORD. We have the micro-control while the LORD has the macro control. Knowing that we have free will, the LORD may have to adjust the macro plan as the micro plan may shift things around.

Another approach is that the LORD knows what the best plan is. When you develop plans for your future, do you consult with the LORD about them? The LORD may want you to go in a different direction. How will you know if you never consult the LORD? We must be ready for the LORD to say no to our ideas when we do this. That does not mean you cannot move forward with your expectations. What is does mean is that your path may not be the best path forward. Since we are guided by the Holy Spirit, we need to ask for guidance.

Some biblical references about the LORD's guidance:

Psalm 25:4-5 - "Show me your ways, LORD, teach me your paths. Guide me in your truth and teach me, for you are God my Savior, and my hope is in you all day long."

Psalm 16:7-8 - "I will praise the LORD, who counsels me; even at night my heart instructs me. I keep my eyes always on the LORD. With him at my right hand, I will not be shaken."

Proverbs 3:5-6 - "Trust in the LORD with all your heart and lean not on your own understanding; in all your ways submit to him, and he will make your paths straight."

Psalm 32:8-9 - "I will instruct you and teach you in the way you should go; I will counsel you with my loving eye on you.

Main/Center Point

Since this event was during passion week, it is appropriate to say that the religious leaders were trying to get Yeshua arrested because of the troubles He was causing. During the Passover week, the Zealots in Jerusalem would try to spark revolt. During these revolts, many innocent people died. Therefore, it was essential to stop these aggressions against Rome. The governor of the province, Pontius Pilate, was specifically sent to Judea to stop the revolts. Pilate was ruthless and would stop at nothing to restore order to the Empire. In the common Christian commentary used by the church, the reason given for the religious leaders' desire to arrest Yeshua is that they did not want to lose their power or have the people flock to the new teacher. That is a distinct possibility. Also, one must consider that since Judea was allowed to have its own government under the umbrella of the Roman government that the leadership was not ready to let that privilege go. Therefore, they would do anything they could to maintain their relationship with Rome. After the 66 CE revolt, the relationship would be altered forever.

Culture Section

Discussion

Many teachers of the laws of the LORD did not understand that breaking one law was equivalent to breaking all of the Laws. Therefore, to call for punishment for breaking one law while they were breaking other laws made them hypocrites. For example, to tell a lie is on the "same level" as committing adultery. That is not the way the Pharisees saw the Law in Yeshua's day. Yes, a different sacrifice was offered, depending on the sin. However, this did not mean that it was acceptable to break one law over another. The problems that occur between humans is generally caused by people committing injustices against one another. The lesson of loving one another goes back to the days of Cain and Abel.[170]

Questioning the passage

1. What does "son of David" mean?

    According to Hebraic tradition, the Messiah was thought to be a physical descendant of King David. This son of David was going to restore the glory of the Kingdom of Israel as was seen during the reign of David. It was during the reign of David that the nation of Israel received full recognition as a national power. When the Kingdom split into two kingdoms, each became weak and was eventually overrun by the larger Empires to the north. During the years of oppression, the people tried to get away from their yoke through political means but to no avail. For a century, the Maccabees were able to free Israel from Greek domination. Then the Romans came into the area, and Judea was no match for Rome. So, the people of Yeshua's day were waiting for the Messiah to come and overthrow the aggressive Roman government.

    Yeshua believed that the term "son of David" meant that the Messiah was to be like David in courage, zeal, and greatness. The "son of David" was not necessarily to be a direct descendant of the ancient King. Yeshua could perform some grand miracles and obtained the title of "son of David." Therefore, it did not matter to Yeshua whether he was biologically from the line of David. What did matter is that He had the courage, zeal, and greatness of David inside of Him?[171]

Thoughts

A Hebraic view of this passage can be understood when a correct interpretation of Psalm 110:1 is done. The words "The LORD said to my Lord," is a phrase that is misunderstood today. The

---

[170] Errico, Rocco A., and George M. Lamsa. "Chapter 22." In *Aramaic Light on the Gospel of Matthew: A Commentary on the Teachings of Jesus from the Aramaic and Unchanged Near Eastern Customs*. Santa Fe, NM: Noohra Foundation, 2000.
[171] IBID.

Targums on the Psalms clean up the verse by offering the verse with the rabbinic understanding of it. Since the Targums were written only slightly prior to Yeshua's life, we can use them as a resource. Yeshua would have read the Targums and knew of the correct usage of Psalm 110. Psalm 110:1 tells us that King David, the Lord (a title for the King), was told by Yahweh, the LORD, that he needed to wait to assume the throne of Israel. The LORD needed to deal with King Saul before the change could take place. So, David waited. How long did King David have to wait? Psalm 110 does not tell us. However, the Scripture does tell us that David did indeed wait until the LORD removed King Saul from power. Then King David could assume the throne with the full power of the LORD behind him. In the same way, Yeshua is telling us that it is the LORD who will inform us about His Son, the Messiah. When a person's heart is prepared for the truth, the LORD sends the truth.

Reflections

The question tossed back to the Pharisees is a question that should be tossed to every person who claims to be a disciple or follower of Jesus Christ. This question is, "who is Jesus, and why do you follow Him?" So many Christians really cannot answer that question beyond, "He is the Messiah" or "He died for my sins." So many Christians today cannot give an answer to who Jesus is a question beyond the basic statement of "he is the savior." What does it mean that Jesus is the savior of the world? How does Jesus save the world from its sins? This was a fundamental question that I asked. How can a man who died 2000 years ago on a cross save me from my sins? I never received an adequate answer from church folks. For me, the answer to this question has evolved over the years as I studied the Scriptures and traditions of the church. Perhaps a decline in church relevance in our society today revolves around how many people sitting in the pews on Sunday cannot answer the basic question about Jesus. If they could answer the question, then their behaviors and attitudes would certainly reflect it.

MARK 12:38-40

Language

New American Standard 1995	Koine Greek
[38] In His teaching He was saying: "Beware of the scribes who like to walk around in long robes, and *like* respectful greetings in the market places, [39] and chief seats in the synagogues and places of honor at banquets, [40] who devour widows' houses, and for appearance's sake offer long prayers; these will receive greater condemnation."	[38] Καὶ ἔλεγεν αὐτοῖς ἐν τῇ διδαχῇ αὐτοῦ, Βλέπετε ἀπὸ τῶν γραμματέων, τῶν θελόντων ἐν στολαῖς περιπατεῖν, καὶ ἀσπασμοὺς ἐν ταῖς ἀγοραῖς, [39] καὶ πρωτοκαθεδρίας ἐν ταῖς συναγωγαῖς, καὶ πρωτοκλισίας ἐν τοῖς δείπνοις [40] οἱ κατεσθίοντες τὰς οἰκίας τῶν χηρῶν, καὶ προφάσει μακρὰ προσευχόμενοι οὗτοι λήψονται περισσότερον κρίμα.

Process of Discovery

Linguistics Section

Linguistic Structure

[Yeshua's teaching] [38] In His teaching He was saying: "Beware of the scribes who like to walk around in long robes, and *like* respectful greetings in the market places, [39] and chief seats in the synagogues and places of honor at banquets, [40] who devour widows' houses, and for appearance's sake offer long prayers; these will receive greater condemnation."

Discussion

This is a simple saying of Yeshua.

Questioning the Passage

1. What does the reference to "long robes" mean? (v. 38)

   The "long robes" refer to the tallit. A tallit is a rectangular cloth that is worn around the shoulders. In Yeshua's day, all Jewish men would have worn a tallit. The tassels are called the tzitzit. There was a tzitzit on each corner of the tallis. This is still done today and conforms with the LORD's commandment.

   > [38] "Speak to the sons of Israel, and tell them that they shall make for themselves tassels on the corners of their garments throughout their generations, and that they shall put on the tassel of each corner a cord of blue. (Num. 15:38 NAU)

   Pious people who wished to demonstrate their piety lengthened their tzitzit. The scribes made their tzitzit long, showing the public their piety when in reality, behind closed doors, they were not following the Laws of the Torah.

Culture Section

Discussion

In Yeshua's day, a transparent methodology for seating at banquets was also applied to the synagogue. Banquets were held in the largest room of a home. Semitic etiquette was that honorable guests, such as priests, politicians, and rich men, took the top places at the banquets. The principal places had plentiful food. These places were the furthest from the door to the room.

The rest of the guests' seating was arranged according to their social standing in the community. The least essential guests, such as musicians and beggars, were sitting at the door. If a distinguished person came late to the banquet, a guest would be moved from their seat and was told to take a lower place, that is, a seat closer to the door.[172]

Questioning the passage

1. Why did Yeshua tell His disciples to sit at the lower seats? (v. 39)

    Yeshua told His disciples to observe how the scribes conducted themselves thinking that they were better than everyone else and never to act that way. Instead of thinking that they were influential men who took the higher seats, they took the lower seats. They were to attend banquets but not as dignitaries.

2. What does it mean to devour widows' homes? (v. 40)

    A practice in Yeshua's day was for a scribe to take over the conservatorship of an estate of a widow. This practice was generally done when a widow was considered unable or untrustworthy to manage the estate. A scribe would be assigned to deal with the estate. Many times, in Yeshua's day, the assigned scribe might embezzle more than they were assigned to receive. A percentage of the estate would be given to the scribe for his work. This action violated the Torah Law concerning the care of widows and orphans.[173]

Thoughts

The first thought is about people who come to church and do things that make them look good. I have known people who do tasks for the church and demand colossal praise. When they do not get their praise, they start a movement to eliminate the pastor or church leaders who are not pouring

---

[172] Rocco A. Errico, George M. Lamsa, and George M. Lamsa, *Aramaic Light on the Gospels of Mark and Luke: a Commentary on the Teachings of Jesus from the Aramaic and Unchanged Near Eastern Customs* (Smyrna, GA: Noohra Foundation, 2001).
[173] Ched Myers, *Binding the Strong Man a Political Reading of Mark's Story of Jesus* (Maryknoll, NY: Orbis Books, 1988).

public praise on them. Yeshua said in this narrative that what is done for the LORD is done for the LORD and not to impress anyone.

Reflections

Not only should we do things for the good of the church community and not for our own recognition but not create a hierarchy in the community. Everyone in the church community is equal. Yeshua has said this more than once. There should not be any hierarchy in the church community. When a hierarchy is created, then there will be persons in the community who want to have the power to control other persons. A power grab will occur. This action is something that should be avoided.

MARK 12:41-44

Language

New American Standard 1995	Koine Greek
[41] And He sat down opposite the treasury, and *began* observing how the people were putting money into the treasury; and many rich people were putting in large sums. [42] A poor widow came and put in two small copper coins, which amount to a cent. [43] Calling His disciples to Him, He said to them, "Truly I say to you, this poor widow put in more than all the contributors to the treasury; [44] for they all put in out of their surplus, but she, out of her poverty, put in all she owned, all she had to live on."	[41] Καὶ καθίσας ὁ Ἰησοῦς κατέναντι τοῦ γαζοφυλακίου ἐθεώρει πῶς ὁ ὄχλος βάλλει χαλκὸν εἰς τὸ γαζοφυλάκιον καὶ πολλοὶ πλούσιοι ἔβαλλον πολλά. [42] Καὶ ἐλθοῦσα μία χήρα πτωχὴ ἔβαλεν λεπτὰ δύο, ὅ ἐστιν κοδράντης. [43] Καὶ προσκαλεσάμενος τοὺς μαθητὰς αὐτοῦ, λέγει αὐτοῖς, Ἀμὴν λέγω ὑμῖν ὅτι ἡ χήρα αὕτη ἡ πτωχὴ πλεῖον πάντων βέβληκεν τῶν ⌐ βαλλόντων ⌐ εἰς τὸ γαζοφυλάκιον [44] πάντες γὰρ ἐκ τοῦ περισσεύοντος αὐτοῖς ἔβαλον αὕτη δὲ ἐκ τῆς ὑστερήσεως αὐτῆς πάντα ὅσα εἶχεν ἔβαλεν, ὅλον τὸν βίον αὐτῆς.

Process of Discovery

Linguistics Section

Linguistic Structure

[Narrative] [41] And He sat down opposite the treasury, and *began* observing how the people were putting money into the treasury; and many rich people were putting in large sums. [42] A poor widow came and put in two small copper coins, which amount to a cent. [43] Calling His disciples to Him, He said to them, "Truly I say to you, this poor widow put in more than all the contributors to the treasury; [44] for they all put in out of their surplus, but she, out of her poverty, put in all she owned, all she had to live on."

Discussion

This narrative is a singular story about a widow who gave her last coin to the work of the Temple.

Questioning the Passage

1. What was the Temple treasury? (v. 41)

   In his writing "The Jewish War 5.5.2" Josephus said that the treasury referred to receptacles for collecting the Temple taxes and freewill offerings.[174]

Linguistic Echoes

1. There are linguistic echoes about giving tithes to the LORD and the mistreatment of widows. The book of Amos has two echoes: Amos 4:4-5, 5:11-12.
2. The image of the impoverished widow can be found in 1 Kings 17:8-16.

---

[174] *The New Interpreter's Bible: General Articles & Introduction, Commentary, & Reflections for Each Book of the Bible, Including the Apocryphal/Deuterocanonical Books* (Nashville: Abingdon Press, 1994).

Culture Section

Discussion

The coins the widow gave to the Temple were a "mite."

This coin would be equivalent to a penny today. This narrative it is usually not discussed how the widow became poor. This could happen in a couple of circumstances. In the Hebraic culture of Yeshua's day, a widow would have been taken in by one of the sons. This would not have happened if the woman had no male children. Taking care of one's mother after the father dies is a moral obligation in the Torah.

The LORD commanded His people to take care of widows and orphans. This woman was not being cared for in the manner prescribed by the Torah. By examining the culture of Yeshua's day, a new interpretation of the narrative is drawn. Yeshua is telling us that we need to attend to our obligations to the LORD.

Yeshua's understanding of obligations is further explained if this narrative is connected to the previous one. Yeshua spoke about the scribes who robbed widows by embezzlement in the previous narrative. It was the obligation of men to help widows, not rip them off.

Thoughts

Today, the church uses this passage to shame people into giving money to the church. If a poor widow can give her last two coins to the LORD, why cannot our well-off parishioners give more than 1.8% of their income to the church? The financial problems in most churches can be solved by an easy 1% increase in giving. However, saying this in the church can land the preacher into many difficulties. People do not like to be told what to give. Wait, reader, the preacher, is not saying this, but rather the Scripture is saying to do this. Shaming people usually does not work.

Reflections

This narrative has a different meaning when the culture of Yeshua's day is known. The care of widows and orphans is well defined in the Scripture. There is an obligation on the community to take care of the widow and orphan. Why did the community allow a widow to become so poor that she only had two mites left to her name. What happened to the family obligation? Perhaps Yeshua was talking about our obligations to our neighbor?

MARK 13:1-13

Language

New American Standard 1995	Koine Greek
[1] As He was going out of the temple, one of His disciples said to Him, "Teacher, behold [1]what wonderful stones and [1]what wonderful buildings!" [2] And Jesus said to him, "Do you see these great buildings? Not one stone will be left upon another which will not be torn down." [3] As He was sitting on the Mount of Olives opposite the temple, Peter and James and John and Andrew were questioning Him privately, [4] "Tell us, when will these things be, and what *will be* the sign when all these things are going to be fulfilled?" [5] And Jesus began to say to them, "See to it that no one misleads you. [6] "Many will come in My name, saying, *"I am He!'* and will mislead many. [7] "When you hear of wars and rumors of wars, do not be frightened; *those things* must take place; but *that is* not yet the end. [8] "For nation will rise up against nation, and kingdom against kingdom; there will be earthquakes in various places; there will *also* be famines. These things are *merely* the beginning of birth pangs. [9] "But be on your guard; for they will deliver you to *the* courts, and you will be flogged in *the* synagogues, and you will stand before governors and kings for My sake, as a testimony to them. [10] "The gospel must first be preached to all the nations. [11] ""When they arrest you and hand you over, do not worry beforehand about what you are to say, but say whatever is given you in that hour; for it is not you who speak, but *it is* the Holy Spirit. [12] "Brother will betray brother to death, and a father *his* child; and children will rise up against parents and have them put to death. [13] "You will be hated by all because of My name, but the one who endures to the end, he will be saved.	[1] Καὶ ἐκπορευομένου αὐτοῦ ἐκ τοῦ ἱεροῦ, λέγει αὐτῷ εἷς τῶν μαθητῶν αὐτοῦ, Διδάσκαλε, ἴδε, ποταποὶ λίθοι καὶ ποταπαὶ οἰκοδομαί. [2] Καὶ ὁ Ἰησοῦς ἀποκριθεὶς εἶπεν αὐτῷ, Βλέπεις ταύτας τὰς μεγάλας οἰκοδομάς; Οὐ μὴ ἀφεθῇ λίθος ἐπὶ λίθῳ, ὃς οὐ μὴ καταλυθῇ. [3] Καὶ καθημένου αὐτοῦ εἰς τὸ ὄρος τῶν ἐλαιῶν κατέναντι τοῦ ἱεροῦ, ἐπηρώτων αὐτὸν κατ' ἰδίαν Πέτρος καὶ Ἰάκωβος καὶ Ἰωάννης καὶ Ἀνδρέας, [4] Εἰπὲ ἡμῖν, πότε ταῦτα ἔσται; Καὶ τι τὸ σημεῖον ὅταν μέλλῃ πάντα ταῦτα συντελεῖσθαι; [5] Ὁ δὲ Ἰησοῦς ἀποκριθεὶς αὐτοῖς ἤρξατο λέγειν, Βλέπετε μή τις ὑμᾶς πλανήσῃ. [6] Πολλοὶ γὰρ ἐλεύσονται ἐπὶ τῷ ὀνόματί μου, λέγοντες ὅτι Ἐγώ εἰμι καὶ πολλοὺς πλανήσουσιν. [7] Ὅταν δὲ ἀκούσητε πολέμους καὶ ἀκοὰς πολέμων, μὴ θροεῖσθε δεῖ γὰρ γενέσθαι ἀλλ' οὔπω τὸ τέλος. [8] Ἐγερθήσεται γὰρ ἔθνος ἐπὶ ἔθνος, καὶ βασιλεία ἐπὶ βασιλείαν καὶ ἔσονται σεισμοὶ κατὰ τόπους, καὶ ἔσονται λιμοὶ καὶ ταραχαί ἀρχαὶ ὠδίνων ταῦτα. [9] Βλέπετε δὲ ὑμεῖς ἑαυτοὺς παραδώσουσιν γὰρ ὑμᾶς εἰς συνέδρια, καὶ εἰς συναγωγὰς δαρήσεσθε, καὶ ἐπὶ ἡγεμόνων καὶ βασιλέων σταθήσεσθε ἕνεκεν ἐμοῦ, εἰς μαρτύριον αὐτοῖς. [10] Καὶ εἰς πάντα τὰ ἔθνη δεῖ πρῶτον κηρυχθῆναι τὸ εὐαγγέλιον. [11] Ὅταν δὲ ἀγάγωσιν ὑμᾶς παραδιδόντες, μὴ προμεριμνᾶτε τί λαλήσητε, μηδὲ μελετᾶτε ἀλλ' ὃ ἐὰν δοθῇ ὑμῖν ἐν ἐκείνῃ τῇ ὥρᾳ, τοῦτο λαλεῖτε οὐ γὰρ ἐστε ὑμεῖς οἱ λαλοῦντες, ἀλλὰ τὸ πνεῦμα τὸ ἅγιον. [12] Παραδώσει δὲ ἀδελφὸς ἀδελφὸν εἰς θάνατον, καὶ πατὴρ τέκνον καὶ ἐπαναστήσονται τέκνα ἐπὶ γονεῖς, καὶ θανατώσουσιν αὐτούς [13] καὶ ἔσεσθε μισούμενοι ὑπὸ πάντων διὰ τὸ ὄνομά μου. ὁ δὲ ὑπομείνας εἰς τέλος, οὗτος σωθήσεται.

Process of Discovery

   Linguistics Section

      Linguistic Structure

[Question] [1] As He was going out of the temple, one of His disciples said to Him, "Teacher, behold [1]what wonderful stones and [1]what wonderful buildings!"

[Answer] [2] And Jesus said to him, "Do you see these great buildings? Not one stone will be left upon another which will not be torn down."

[Question] [3] As He was sitting on the Mount of Olives opposite the temple, Peter and James and John and Andrew were questioning Him privately, [4] "Tell us, when will these things be, and what *will be* the sign when all these things are going to be fulfilled?"

[Answer] [5] And Jesus began to say to them, "See to it that no one misleads you. [6] "Many will come in My name, saying, *"I am He!"* and will mislead many. [7] "When you hear of wars and rumors of wars, do not be frightened; *those things* must take place; but *that is* not yet the end. [8] "For nation will rise up against nation, and kingdom against kingdom; there will be earthquakes in various places; there will *also* be famines. These things are *merely* the beginning of birth pangs. [9] "But be on your guard; for they will deliver you to *the* courts, and you will be flogged in *the* synagogues, and you will stand before governors and kings for My sake, as a testimony to them. [10] "The gospel must first be preached to all the nations. [11] ""When they arrest you and hand you over, do not worry beforehand about what you are to say, but say whatever is given you in that hour; for it is not you who speak, but *it is* the Holy Spirit. [12] "Brother will betray brother to death, and a father *his* child; and children will rise up against parents and have them put to death. [13] "You will be hated by all because of My name, but the one who endures to the end, he will be saved.

   Discussion

   This narrative is broken into two parts. The first part is a question about the Temple. The second is about the timing of the destruction of the Temple. The Temple can be viewed as a metaphor for the world. In this context, it is the apocalypse that was being questioned. A second possibility is that the Temple is a metaphor for the Roman government. The end of the Roman empire occurred when war broke out with the Visigoths..

Questioning the Passage

1. Was Yeshua's prophecy fulfilled? (v. 2)

   General Titus captured Jerusalem in 70 CE and destroyed the Temple at Jerusalem. The great pillars and stores of the Temple were removed and sent to a town in Lebanon called Baalbek. This town was about 160 miles north of Jerusalem. The Romans tried to build a temple there to either Zeus or Jupiter. However, something happened that prevented the temple from being completed. Theologians would say that the LORD was angry that the Romans would defile the stones from the Temple in Jerusalem because they tried to dedicate the stones to a false god.[175]

2. What "things" were Yeshua referring to in verse two?

   The things were the upcoming events. The disciples still thought that Yeshua would start the revolution and reinstate the nation. Yeshua understood the politics of His day and knew that was never going to happen. The forces of Evil (Romans and Jewish leaders) were not going to give up their power. It is foolish to start a revolution that cannot be won. History says this. The result of the Zealot movement was the destruction the Temple in 70 CE.

   The "things" were the realization that the Kingdom of Heaven was not going to be established by any kind of armed revolt. The Kingdom of Heaven was a spiritual understanding of the LORD's love for all people. The people of the Earth have to embrace the love for the Kingdom.

3. Is there significance to the Mount of Olives? (v. 3)

---

[175] Rocco A. Errico, George M. Lamsa, and George M. Lamsa, *Aramaic Light on the Gospels of Mark and Luke: a Commentary on the Teachings of Jesus from the Aramaic and Unchanged Near Eastern Customs* (Smyrna, GA: Noohra Foundation, 2001).

Ezekiel 11:23 says that the Shekinah, the glory of the LORD, left the Temple and went to the mountain east of Jerusalem. This place is the location of the Mount of Olives.

> [23] The glory of the LORD went up from the midst of the city and stood over the mountain which is east of the city.

Yeshua took His disciples to the Mount of Olives. This place is unique because the Shekinah left the Temple before its destruction when the Babylonians invaded. Yeshua's leaving the Temple symbolically was taking the Shekinah with Him. The LORD's Temple was no longer dedicated to the LORD when the Shekinah left. In a way, Yeshua decommissioned the Temple.

4. What were the rumors of war? (v.6)

   There were rumors in Yeshua's days, due to the Zealots, that a revolutionary war was about to occur. A possible reason for Yeshua's arrest and death was that Pilate was concerned that a revolt might occur. Each year at the Passover, the Zealots would stage a revolt inside the city of Jerusalem. Pilate's task was to stop the revolts so that the Legion in northern Galilee could be used in the war against the Parthians.

5. What does the symbol "birth pangs" mean? (v. 8)

   "Birth pangs" is a metaphor for the apocalypse.[176]

Biblical Locations

1. "Mount of Olives, Arabic Jabal al-Ṭūr, Hebrew Har ha-Zetim, multi-summit limestone ridge just east of the Old City of Jerusalem and separated from it by the Kidron Valley. Frequently mentioned in the Bible and later religious literature, it is holy to Judaism, Christianity, and Islam."[177]

---

[176] *The New Interpreter's Bible: General Articles & Introduction, Commentary, & Reflections for Each Book of the Bible, Including the Apocryphal/Deuterocanonical Books* (Nashville: Abingdon, 1996).

[177] The Editors of Encyclopaedia Britannica, "Mount of Olives," Encyclopædia Britannica (Encyclopædia Britannica, inc., July 8, 2019), https://www.britannica.com/place/Mount-of-Olives. Accessed June 10, 2020

Linguistic Echoes

1. The linguistic echo is to the Talmud, Sanhedrin 97a

"That is why the Messiah is called *bar nifli*. Rabbi Yitzḥak said to him that this is what Rabbi Yoḥanan says: During the generation in which the Messiah, son of David, comes, Torah scholars decrease; and as for the rest of the people, their eyes fail with sorrow and grief, and troubles increase. And the harsh decrees will be introduced; before the first passes the second quickly comes.

The Sages taught in a *baraita*: With regard to the seven-year period, i.e., the Sabbatical cycle, during which the Messiah, son of David, comes: During the first year, this verse will be fulfilled: "And I will cause it to rain upon one city and cause it not to rain upon another city" (Amos 4:7). During the second year of that period, arrows of famine will be shot, indicating that there will be famine only in certain places. During the third year there will be a great famine, and men, women, children, the pious, and men of action will die, and the Torah is forgotten by those who study it. During the fourth year there will be plenty but not great plenty. During the fifth year there will be great plenty and they will eat, and drink, and rejoice, and the Torah will return to those who study it. During the sixth year, heavenly voices will be heard. During the Sabbatical Year, wars, e.g., the war of Gog and Magog, will be waged involving the Jewish people. During the year after the conclusion of the Sabbatical Year, the son of David will come. Rav Yosef said: Haven't there been several Sabbatical cycles during which events transpired in that manner and nevertheless, the Messiah did not come? Abaye said: Have the phenomena: During the sixth year, heavenly voices, and during the Sabbatical Year, wars, transpired? And furthermore, have all these phenomena transpired in the order in which they were listed in the *baraita*? The verse states: "That Your enemies taunted, Lord, that they have taunted the footsteps of Your anointed" (Psalms 89:52). It is taught in a *baraita* that Rabbi Yehuda says: During the generation that the son of David comes, the hall of the assembly of the Sages will be designated for prostitution, and the Galilee will be destroyed, and the Gavlan, i.e., Bashan, will be desolate, and the residents of the border who flee the neighboring gentiles will circulate from city to city and will receive no sympathy. The wisdom of scholars will diminish, and sin-fearing people will be despised. And the face of the generation will be like the face of a dog in its impudence and shamelessness. And the truth will be lacking, as it is stated: "And the truth is lacking [*ne' ederet*], and he who departs from evil is negated" (Isaiah 59:15). What is the meaning of the phrase: And the truth is lacking [*ne' ederet*]? The Sages of the study hall of Rav said: This teaches that truth will become like so many flocks [*adarim*] and walk away. What is the meaning of the phrase: "And he that departs from evil is negated"? The Sages of the study hall of Rabbi Sheila said: Anyone who deviates from evil is deemed insane by the people. Concerning the lack of truth, Rava says: Initially I would say that there is no truth anywhere in the world. There was a certain one of the Sages, and Rav Tavut is his name, and some say Rav Tavyomei is his name, who was so honest that if they were to give him the entire world, he would not deviate from the truth in his statement. He said to me: One time I happened to come to a certain place, and Truth is its name, and its residents would not deviate from the truth in their statements, and no person from there would die prematurely. I married a woman from among them, and I had two sons from her. One day his wife was sitting and washing the hair on her head. Her neighbor came and knocked on the door. He thought: It is not proper conduct to tell the neighbor that his wife is bathing. He said to her: She is not here. Since he deviated from the truth his two sons died. The people residing in that place came before him and said to him: What is the meaning of this? He said to them: This was the nature of the incident, and told them what happened. They said to him: Please leave our place and do not provoke premature death upon these people. The Gemara resumes its discussion of the messianic period. It is taught in a *baraita* that Rabbi Nehorai says: During the generation in which the son of David comes, youths will humiliate elders and elders will stand in deference before youths, and a daughter will rebel against her mother, and a bride against her mother-in-law, and the face of the generation will be like the face of a dog, and a son will not be ashamed before his father. It is taught in a *baraita* that Rabbi Neḥemya says: During the generation that the son of David comes, arrogance will proliferate and the cost of living will corrupt people so they will engage in deceit. The vine will produce its fruit, and nevertheless, the wine will be costly. And the entire gentile monarchy will be converted to the heresy of Christianity, and there will be no inclination among the people to accept rebuke. This *baraita* supports the opinion of Rabbi Yitzḥak, as Rabbi Yitzḥak says: The son of David will not come until the entire kingdom will be converted to heresy. Rava says: What is the verse from which this statement is derived? It is the verse: "It is all turned white; he is ritually pure" (Leviticus 13:13). One is a leper and ritually impure only if he has a leprous mark, however small, but not if his skin is completely leprous. Similarly, the world will be redeemed only when the Jewish people reach their lowest point. The Sages taught in a *baraita*: The verse states: "For the Lord shall judge His people and atone for His servants, when He sees that their power is gone and there is none shut up or left" (Deuteronomy 32:36). From the phrase "their power is gone" it is derived that the son of David will not come until informers will proliferate. Alternatively, the Messiah will not come until the number of students of Torah diminishes. Alternatively, the Messiah will not come until the *peruta* will cease from the purse. Alternatively, the Messiah will not come until they despair from the redemption, as it is stated: "And there is none shut up or left," as though there were no supporter or helper for the Jewish people. This is as in that practice of Rabbi Zeira, who, when he would find Sages who were engaging in discussions about the coming of the Messiah, said to them: Please, I ask of you, do not delay his coming by calculating the end of days. As we learn in a *baraita*: There are three matters that come only by means of diversion of attention from those matters, and these are they: The Messiah, a lost item, and a scorpion. Rav Ketina says: Six thousand years is the duration of the world, and it is in ruins for one thousand years. The duration of the period during which the world is in ruins is derived from a verse, as it is stated: "And the Lord alone shall be exalted on that day" (Isaiah 2:11), and the day of God lasts one thousand years. Abaye says: It is in ruins for two thousand years, as it is stated: "After two days He will revive us; in the third day

He will revive us, and we shall live in His presence" (Hosea 6:2). It is taught in a *baraita* in accordance with the opinion of Rav Ketina: Just as the Sabbatical Year abrogates debts once in seven years, so too, the world abrogates its typical existence for one thousand years in every seven thousand years, as it is stated: "And the Lord alone shall be exalted on that day," and it states: "A psalm, a song for the Shabbat day" (Psalms 92:1), meaning a day, i.e., one thousand years, that is entirely Shabbat. And it says in explanation of the equation between one day and one thousand years: "For a thousand years in Your eyes are but like yesterday when it is past, and like a watch in the night" (Psalms 90:4). The school of Eliyahu taught: Six thousand years is the duration of the world. Two thousand of the six thousand years are characterized by chaos; two thousand years are characterized by Torah, from the era of the Patriarchs until the end of the mishnaic period; and two thousand years are the period of the coming of the Messiah."

Culture Section

Discussion

King Herod had enlarged the Temple of Solomon in Jerusalem to please the Hebrew people so that they would accept him as their sovereign. The Temple had transformed from worshiping and praising the LORD into a marketplace. Yeshua had overturned the money-changing tables in the Temple to expose further the evil that had entered the LORD's home. Yeshua prophesized about the destruction of the Temple and the city. It was evident in His day that the fever of revolt was growing. Yeshua understood that the Zealots and their followers would not defeat the Roman legions. It was clear that the confrontation would happen in the near future. In 66 CE, the first Jewish revolt occurred. In 70 CE Jerusalem and the Temple were destroyed. In 72 CE, the fortress at Masada fell, and the revolt was over.

The phrase "the end of the world" and "end of the age" refers to the reconstitution of the word following the highest ethical standards that the Hebrew prophets had predicted.[178] Humanity had to go through a reconstitution by a change of heart and mind.

---

[178] Rocco A. Errico and George M. Lamsa, *Aramaic Light on the Gospel of Matthew: a Commentary on the Teachings of Jesus from the Aramaic and Unchanged Near Eastern Customs* (Santa Fe, NM: Noohra Foundation, 2000).

Yeshua understood the politics of His day. He knew that after His death, the political situation in Judea would worsen. The Romans demanded more taxes and tribute from the people. Many people could not comply and were oppressed, persecuted, and put to death. The last days Yeshua was referring to was the situation in Judea. He prophesized that uprising, and famines would occur. Yeshua warned His followers that false Messiahs would continue to appear and must be avoided. Many of these false Messiahs had Zealot ideas of retaking the Judea. They would cause the first Jewish Revolt. A second revolt occurred in 135 CE, which had devasting results

The destruction of the Temple in 70 CE changed the face of Judaism. Not only was it gone, the religious leaders had to figure out how to recreate the religion. The idea of animal sacrifices for the forgiveness of sin was gone. They needed to develop a new way and get the people to accept it.

Yeshua offered a new way. He spoke about the Kingdom of Heaven. The LORD must become a part of everything. That fact was lost to the people over the centuries of oppression. The LORD must be involved in human affairs of there is to be harmony and peace in the world. Yeshua spoke about the end of the war, famine, poverty, and the lust of having power over people. If the Gospel is accepted and practiced everywhere, and the love of the LORD is given to all people, then the result would be the full implementation of the Kingdom of Heaven. Military weapons and soldiers would no longer be necessary. These resources could go into eliminating famine and poverty. There would be plenty for all people to share.

The world has never come to a state nearing the Kingdom of Heaven. It is unclear if it ever will. Yeshua waits for us to understand the errors of our ways.

Questioning the passage

1. What did Yeshua's advice mean from verse eleven?

Lawyers did not exist in the Near East until the 1920s. Rich and noble persons were urged to make peace and resolve their disputes. The authorities forced the poor to settle their differences or pay heavy fines. When a person was brought in front of authorities and charged with a crime, that person would have to defend him/herself. The tribunal was oral arguments because written records were rarely available. The outcome depended on the defendant's words and the honesty of the judge. Many times a defendant would be coached by experienced men familiar with the unwritten law and the demeanor of the judges. They told the defendant how to answer questions. Yeshua wanted His disciples to be truthful and be led by the Holy Spirit.[179]

2. Why would a brother betray his brother? (v. 12)

In the Near East, if a person decides to change religion, he/she would be renounced by the family. All family ties are broken. The family becomes ready to avenge the disgrace brought upon the family by killing the person who left the family. Yeshua knew that this could happen to people who left their religion to join the Yeshua movement.

The disciples would have known that this would happen. Yeshua did not need to talk about it. Therefore, it is possible that Mark's author added it in for the new converts who were not from the Near East. This narrative could have been used to explain why the government was persecuting the community.

Thoughts

Unfortunately for us today, the world's people do not seem to want to work together. Strife and tension seem to have become a part of society. Even within countries, the signs of strife are evident. Sometimes it is difficult to see the LORD's love among His people. The Holy Spirit works in the world to bring us together. This method seems not to be working. Of course, since we were given free will, humanity can do whatever it wants to do. People of differing views used to be able to

---

[179] Rocco A. Errico, George M. Lamsa, and George M. Lamsa, *Aramaic Light on the Gospels of Mark and Luke: a Commentary on the Teachings of Jesus from the Aramaic and Unchanged Near Eastern Customs* (Smyrna, GA: Noohra Foundation, 2001).

discuss their differences and work out compromises. Now people view people with different opinions as an enemy and, in some cases, a combative enemy. The message of the Gospel is being lost. A good question for the church to tackle is "will the Gospel survive?" The church needs to stand up and preach the original Gospel.

Reflections

Saying that the church must stand up and preach the Gospel is problematic. First is the problem that the church is divided within itself. How can the church preach the Gospel of Jesus Christ when the church does not agree on what that message is. The result of over one thousand separate Christian denominations makes that clear. The world will probably never come together as one through the Gospel of Jesus Christ until the church of Jesus Christ does the same thing. The church has to come to grips with its original mission. She needs to return to spreading the Gospel of Jesus Christ in its original form.

MARK 13:14-23

Language

New American Standard 1995	Koine Greek
[14] "But when you see the ABOMINATION OF DESOLATION standing where it should not be (let the reader understand), then those who are in Judea must flee to the mountains. [15] ""The one who is on the housetop must not go down, or go in to get anything out of his house; [16] and the one who is in the field must not turn back to get his coat. [17] "But woe to those who are pregnant and to those who are nursing babies in those days! [18] "But pray that it may not happen in the winter. [19] "For those days will be a *time of tribulation* such as has not occurred since the beginning of the creation which God created until now, and never will. [20] "Unless the Lord had shortened *those* days, no life would have been saved; but for the sake of the elect, whom He chose, He shortened the days. [21] "And then if anyone says to you, 'Behold, here is the Christ'; or, 'Behold, *He is* there'; do not believe *him;* [22] for false Christs and false prophets will arise, and will show signs and wonders, in order to lead astray, if possible, the elect. [23] "But take heed; behold, I have told you everything in advance.	[14] Ὅταν δὲ ἴδητε τὸ βδέλυγμα τῆς ἐρημώσεως, τὸ ῥηθὲν ὑπὸ Δανιὴλ τοῦ προφήτου, ἑστὼς ὅπου οὐ δεῖ_ ὁ ἀναγινώσκων νοείτω _ τότε οἱ ἐν τῇ Ἰουδαίᾳ φευγέτωσαν εἰς τὰ ὄρη [15] ὁ δὲ ἐπὶ τοῦ δώματος μὴ καταβάτω εἰς τὴν οἰκίαν, μηδὲ εἰσελθέτω ἆραί τι ἐκ τῆς οἰκίας αυτοῦ [16] καὶ ὁ εἰς τὸν ἀγρὸν ὢν μὴ ἐπιστρεψάτω εἰς τὰ ὀπίσω, ἆραι τὸ ἱμάτιον αυτοῦ. [17] Οὐαὶ δὲ ταῖς ἐν γαστρὶ ἐχούσαις καὶ ταῖς θηλαζούσαις ἐν ἐκείναις ταῖς ἡμέραις. [18] Προσεύχεσθε δὲ ἵνα μὴ γένηται ἡ φυγὴ ὑμῶν χειμῶνος. [19] Ἔσονται γὰρ αἱ ἡμέραι ἐκεῖναι θλῖψις, οἵα οὐ γέγονεν τοιαύτη ἀπ' ἀρχῆς κτίσεως ἧς ἔκτισεν ὁ θεὸς ἕως τοῦ νῦν, καὶ οὐ μὴ γένηται. [20] Καὶ εἰ μὴ κύριος ἐκολόβωσεν τὰς ἡμέρας, οὐκ ἂν ἐσώθη πᾶσα σὰρξ ἀλλὰ διὰ τοὺς ἐκλεκτούς, οὓς ἐξελέξατο, ἐκολόβωσεν τὰς ἡμέρας. [21] ⸀ Τότε ⸀ ἐάν τις ὑμῖν εἴπῃ, Ἰδού, ὧδε ὁ χριστός, ἢ Ἰδού, ἐκεῖ, μὴ πιστεύετε. [22] Ἐγερθήσονται γὰρ ψευδόχριστοι καὶ ψευδοπροφῆται, καὶ δώσουσιν σημεῖα καὶ τέρατα, πρὸς τὸ ἀποπλανᾶν, εἰ δυνατόν, καὶ τοὺς ἐκλεκτούς. [23] Ὑμεῖς δὲ βλέπετε ἰδού, προείρηκα ὑμῖν πάντα.

Process of Discovery

Linguistics Section

Linguistic Structure

[14] "But when you see the ABOMINATION OF DESOLATION standing where it should not be (let the reader understand), then those who are in Judea must flee to the mountains. [15] "'The one who is on the housetop must not go down, or go in to get anything out of his house; [16] and the one who is in the field must not turn back to get his coat. [17] "But woe to those who are pregnant and to those who are nursing babies in those days! [18] "But pray that it may not happen in the winter. [19] "For those days will be a *time of* tribulation such as has not occurred since the beginning of the creation which God created until now, and never will. [20] "Unless the Lord had shortened *those* days, no life would have been saved; but for the sake of the elect, whom He chose, He shortened the days. [21] "And then if anyone says to you, 'Behold, here is the Christ'; or, 'Behold, *He is* there'; do not believe *him;* [22] for false Christs and false prophets will arise, and will show signs and wonders, in order to lead astray, if possible, the elect. [23] "But take heed; behold, I have told you everything in advance.

Discussion

The Christian church has taught that this passage is about the end of time and the return of Yeshua. However, this passage is the continuation of the previous narrative about the destruction of Jerusalem and the Temple. Yeshua prophesized about the destruction of the city. It continues in this passage with the signs that mark a siege and destruction of a city.

Questioning the Passage

1. What does the Daniel reference (abomination of desolation) mean in verse fourteen?
   [27] "And he will make a firm covenant with the many for one week, but in the middle of the week he will put a stop to sacrifice and grain offering; and on the wing of abominations *will come* one who makes desolate, even until a complete destruction, one that is decreed, is poured out on the one who [2]makes desolate." (Daniel 9:27)

Daniel prophesized the abomination of a pagan statue in the Temple in Jerusalem. Antiochus IV conquered Jerusalem in 167 BCE. He erected a statue of Zeus in the Temple in Jerusalem. 1 Maccabees 6:7 refers to this statue as a fulfillment of Daniel's prophecy.[180]

1 Maccabees 6:7 that they had torn down the abomination that he had erected on the altar in Jerusalem; and that they had surrounded the sanctuary with high walls as before, and also Beth-zur, his town.

Yeshua said that something like this would happen again

Culture Section

Questioning the passage

1. What is the abomination of desolation? (v. 14)

When the Roman army besieged Jerusalem, the inhabitants of the city took refuge in the city's citadel and holy places (the Temple). The citadel and sacred places offered the best protection for the people from their enemy. The Romans cut off the city's water supply. The situation forced the people to dig wells in the hope of discovering water. Food became scarce as the siege continued. There was an accumulation of waste and refuse, which filled the streets and every place where the people took refuge. Refuse was regularly taken from the streets and used as fertilizer for the local fields. When the siege occurred, this cleaning could not be done. Therefore, it piled up on the roads. This situation resulted in disease and plague.

The abomination of desolation refers to the piling up of refuse because of the siege. The Temple and other sacred shrines in the city became polluted by the people. When the Romans entered the walls, they brought swine into the holy places in Jerusalem, which was another abomination.

---

[180] David H. Stern, *Jewish New Testament Commentary: a Companion Volume to the Jewish New Testament* (Clarksville, MD: Jewish New Testament Publications, 1999).

Yeshua referred to Daniel because Daniel offered the same description when the Babylonians seized Jerusalem.[181]

2. What are the sudden calamities?

The disaster of the fall of the city came quickly. The following was prophesized by Yeshua when the Romans attacked:[182]

a. People from the outlining areas of the city would flee from the Roman army by going up the mountains. They found caves in the mountains so that they could hide from the Roman soldiers.

b. The people who slept on the housetops did not have the time to come into the house to gather their belongings. They would have enough time to get away.

c. The people working in the fields would not be able to go home to gather clothes or belongings. They would be cut off from the family members who were in the house at the time of the invasion.

d. Pregnant women and women with infants had a problematic time escaping from the invaders because they could not move quickly. Generally, the invading army raped and killed women.

e. If the invasion occurred on the Sabbath, the Sabbath restrictions would cause many to die. Traveling was very limited on the Sabbath.

f. Pregnant women would wish they were not pregnant. Pregnant women are slow making it difficult for them to run away.

g. Nursing women would wish that their babies were never born. Women with children were slow.

h. The "elect" is not in the Aramaic versions of Matthew's Gospel. According to the Peshitta, the "pious" (which is an equivalent to the elect) would not suffer long. The destruction of the Temple by the Romans was the worst in Jewish history. There was a large amount of slaughtering of the people. The pious who stayed at the Temple did not suffer long.

---

[181] Rocco A. Errico and George M. Lamsa, *Aramaic Light on the Gospel of Matthew: a Commentary on the Teachings of Jesus from the Aramaic and Unchanged Near Eastern Customs* (Santa Fe, NM: Noohra Foundation, 2000).

[182] IBID.

3. What did Yeshua say about the false Messiahs and prophets? (v. 22 – 23)

    When the Roman invasion commenced, there were plenty of men who stood up and proclaimed that they were the Messiah. Some people took advantage of their fellow Jews during the attack in an attempt to exploit them. Yeshua knew that after His death, that false prophets would come. These false prophets were not interested in the people but rather how they could dominate their fellow Jews.

Thoughts

This passage is considered apocalyptic because the church has said so for two thousand years. This passage is more descriptive of what did happen when the Roman army invaded Jerusalem and destroyed the Temple. Each of the verses, each of the events, describes what happened in the Near East when a city was invaded. Some scholars believe that Matthew's Gospel was a wartime document. If it was written in the mid to late 60s CE, then the war influenced the Gospel. The Temple was destroyed in 70 CE, and the results of the Roman invasion of the city did occur. This narrative purpose was added to the Gospel to prove that Yeshua predicted the Temple's destruction. In this way, it was the LORD's Will.

Reflections

The Gospels were written during a time of war in Judea and Galilee. From the Jewish point of view, their world was about to end. When the Temple in Jerusalem was destroyed in 70 CE, it meant the end of a way of life for the Hebrew people. How were they going to continue as the LORD's people when the LORD's Temple was gone. Their survival became rabbinic Judaism. This meant that prayer and other methods had to be developed for the forgiveness of sins. The rabbinical leaders of the day did figure out how to revamp Judaism.

MARK 13:24-27

Language

New American Standard 1995	Koine Greek
[24] "But in those days, after that tribulation, THE SUN WILL BE DARKENED AND THE MOON WILL NOT GIVE ITS LIGHT, [25] AND THE STARS WILL BE FALLING from heaven, and the powers that are in the heavens will be shaken. [26] "Then they will see THE SON OF MAN COMING IN CLOUDS with great power and glory. [27] "And then He will send forth the angels, and will gather together His elect from the four winds, [b]from the farthest end of the earth to the farthest end of heaven.	[24] Ἀλλ' ἐν ἐκείναις ταῖς ἡμέραις, μετὰ τὴν θλῖψιν ἐκείνην, ὁ ἥλιος σκοτισθήσεται, καὶ ἡ σελήνη οὐ δώσει τὸ φέγγος αὐτῆς, [25] καὶ οἱ ἀστέρες τοῦ οὐρανοῦ ἔσονται ἐκπίπτοντες, καὶ αἱ δυνάμεις αἱ ἐν τοῖς οὐρανοῖς σαλευθήσονται. [26] Καὶ τότε ὄψονται τὸν υἱὸν τοῦ ἀνθρώπου ἐρχόμενον ἐν νεφέλαις μετὰ δυνάμεως πολλῆς καὶ δόξης. [27] Καὶ τότε ἀποστελεῖ τοὺς ἀγγέλους αὐτοῦ, καὶ ἐπισυνάξει τοὺς ἐκλεκτοὺς αὐτοῦ ἐκ τῶν τεσσάρων ἀνέμων, ἀπ' ἄκρου γῆς ἕως ἄκρου οὐρανοῦ.

Process of Discovery

Linguistics Section

Linguistic Structure

[The Second Coming] [24] "But in those days, after that tribulation, THE SUN WILL BE DARKENED AND THE MOON WILL NOT GIVE ITS LIGHT, [25] AND THE STARS WILL BE FALLING from heaven, and the powers that are in the heavens will be shaken. [26] "Then they will see THE SON OF MAN COMING IN CLOUDS with great power and glory. [27] "And then He will send forth the angels, and will gather together His elect from the four winds, [b]from the farthest end of the earth to the farthest end of heaven.

Discussion

This is a self contained narrative about Yeshua's second coming.

Questioning the Passage

1. What does verse twenty-six and twenty-seven mean?

    These two verses must not be taken literally. The Semitic figures of speech are listed:[183]

    1. "coming" – a revelation of universal presence

    2. "send forth the angels" – Yeshua's messengers will announce His return so that his followers may be ready to greet Him.

    3. "four winds" – signified the four corners of the earth. Yeshua's disciples will come from all parts of the Earth.

    4. "heaven" – indicates the universe (note that the NAU translated οὐρανῶν as sky, a better translation is "heaven").

    5. "from one end of heaven to the other" – a universal gathering.

    6. "clouds" – symbolic of God's presence.

    7. "to come on a cloud" – means "to succeed in a mission."

---

[183] Errico, Rocco A., and George M. Lamsa. Aramaic Light on the Gospel of Matthew: A Commentary on the Teachings of Jesus from the Aramaic and Unchanged Near Eastern Customs. Santa Fe, NM: Noohra Foundation, 2000.

Yeshua is saying that when it is time for His return, things will be very different then it was on His appearance. There will be an announcement that the time has come for Yeshua's return. When the angels announce His return, the disciples will be gathered from all corners of the Earth in one location. The presence of the LORD will be with Yeshua when He returns. Yeshua will be bringing us an important message that every disciple will need to hear.

Rewording these two verses replacing the figurative language could give us:

A sign will appear to alert the Earth that Yeshua is about to return. The true disciples will mourn that Yeshua had to die for their sins. The disciples will see Yeshua returning from Heaven. Yeshua will send angels to make the important announcement that He is about to return. The angels will also gather together all His disciples in one location on the earth. They will come from all corners of the world because His disciples have spread his Gospel message. When Yeshua returns, His gathered disciples will offer Him extreme honor and praise. Yeshua's mission of the creation of the Kingdom of Heaven will be complete.

Verse Comparison of citations or proof text

1. Mark 13:24   "But in those days, after that tribulation, THE SUN WILL BE DARKENED AND THE MOON WILL NOT GIVE ITS LIGHT

   Isaiah 13:10 For the stars of heaven and their constellations will not flash forth their light; The sun will be dark when it rises snd the moon will not shed its light. [11]Thus I will [a]punish the world for its evil

2. [25] AND THE STARS WILL BE FALLING from heaven, and the powers that are in the heavens will be shaken.

   Isaiah 34:4 And all the host of heaven will wear away, and the sky will be rolled up like a scroll; All their hosts will also wither away as a leaf withers from the vine, or as *one* withers from the fig tree.

Both of the citation passages are from the apocalyptic sections of Isaiah. Yeshua was connecting Himself to the prophet Isaiah.

Phrase Study

1. τοὺς ἐκλεκτοὺς (v. 27)

   This phrase is translated as "his elect." The BDAG lexicon translation indicates that this phrase is about a select or chosen group of people. There have been centuries of discussion about "the elect." In modern days perhaps, it is a simple process of separating those who say they are disciples of Yeshua verses those who truly are disciples. There are many Christians in the world who are not disciples of Yeshua. Anyone can say that they are Christians, very few people can prove that they are true disciples. Discipleship is more than just saying "I believe." Discipleship is something that one demonstrates to Yeshua. Therefore, many will say they are disciples, but they are not. Upon Yeshua's return, He will separate the Christians into two groups. One group will be the true disciples who showed Yeshua their hearts. The other group of false disciples will be punished.

Culture Section

Questioning the passage

1. What do the figures of speech in verse twenty-nine mean?

   The sun and moon shall not give off light, and the stars will fall from Heaven are Semitic figures of speech. They are not to be taken literally. The western church has taken them literally because they do not understand how Semitic people spoke and wrote in Yeshua's day. When Yeshua died, the sun turned black. When Alexander the Great died, Semitic writers said that the sun, moon, and stars refused to shine. When Yeshua died, a great light was removed from the world, and the Gospels say that the sun darkened. That great light was the spiritual being of Yeshua. Also, "stars" refer to "great men, emperors, and princes who control the world."[184]

---

[184] Errico, Rocco A., and George M. Lamsa. Aramaic Light on the Gospel of Matthew: A Commentary on the Teachings of Jesus from the Aramaic and Unchanged Near Eastern Customs. Santa Fe, NM: Noohra Foundation, 2000.

Thoughts

The second coming of Yeshua has been a part of the Christian tradition since the inception of the church. Perhaps it developed because Yeshua did not complete the mission that the people were looking for. The Roman occupation continued long after Yeshua's ascension, which was a key to the messianic revolt. In the sense that Yeshua was to implement the Kingdom of Heaven, a spiritual kingdom, then He did accomplish His mission. A second thought is to integrate the two Messiah theology from Zechariah 9:9 and the Zohar. The first appearance of the Messiah was to be Messiah ben Joseph. The Messiah's first appearance was to "repair" the spirituality of the people. Thus, Yeshua initiating the Kingdom of Heaven on Earth fit the description of the first Messiah. The second Messiah will be Messiah ben David, who will restore the physical kingdom of Israel. He will separate the good people from the evil and purify the Earth by initiating the new Earth and new Heaven that Isaiah spoke of. There is a theological belief that the two appearances of the Messiah can be one person. If Yeshua saw himself as the first Messiah, then He would have uttered these words. If He did not, then it is a mechanism that early Christianity created to explain to would-be disciples why the Messiah came and did not appear to do what everyone thought. Since the second coming narrative was written thirty years after Yeshua, this possibility is plausible.

Reflections

Do Christians today care about the second coming of Yeshua? Probably not since so many who call themselves disciples do not attend church nor follow the commandments of the Bible. The people in Paul's day, 40 to 65 CE or so, believed that Yeshua was going to return in their lifetime. Paul was convinced of this, and this idea can be found in his letters to the churches. But it did not happen. Paul died, Peter died, the rest of the disciples died, and no return of Yeshua. It is almost 2000 years later, and Yeshua has not returned. Will He return? If Yeshua said the words about His return, then we have to believe that He will. If Yeshua did not say these words, then we are waiting for something that is not going to occur.

"Preterists believe that most or all of Bible Prophecy (especially the big three events) has already been fulfilled in Christ and the on-going expansion of His Eternal Kingdom."[185] Preterists believe that the Second coming of Yeshua occurred in 70 CE when the Temple of Jerusalem was destroyed. From the Jewish people's point of view, the end of their religion had occurred (chapter 24 begins with this event). Now they had to rebuild their response to the forgiveness from sin. The animal sacrifice system was gone and was replaced by a prayer system. Thus, the spiritual Kingdom of Heaven is fully established. Therefore, Yeshua came to see the Temple destroyed, the second coming, and left.

Which is correct? Did Yeshua not say that He would return? Did He return in 70 CE? Is He going to return at some later date?

---

[185] "What Is the Preterist View?" International Preterist Association. October 04, 2014. Accessed November 28, 2018. http://www.preterist.org/about-us/what-is-preterist-view/.

MARK 13:28-32

Language

New American Standard 1995	Koine Greek
[28] "Now learn the parable from the fig tree: when its branch has already become tender and puts forth its leaves, you know that summer is near. [29] "Even so, you too, when you see these things happening, recognize that [2]He is near, *right* at the door. [30] "Truly I say to you, this generation will not pass away until all these things take place. [31] "Heaven and earth will pass away, but My words will not pass away. [32] "But of that day or hour no one knows, not even the angels in heaven, nor the Son, but the Father *alone*.	[28] Ἀπὸ δὲ τῆς συκῆς μάθετε τὴν παραβολὴν ὅταν αὐτῆς ἤδη ὁ κλάδος ἁπαλὸς γένηται καὶ ἐκφύῃ τὰ φύλλα, γινώσκετε ὅτι ἐγγὺς τὸ θέρος ἐστίν· [29] οὕτως καὶ ὑμεῖς, ὅταν ταῦτα ἴδητε γινόμενα, γινώσκετε ὅτι ἐγγύς ἐστιν ἐπὶ θύραις. [30] Ἀμὴν λέγω ὑμῖν ὅτι οὐ μὴ παρέλθῃ ἡ γενεὰ αὕτη, μέχρι οὗ πάντα ταῦτα γένηται. [31] Ὁ οὐρανὸς καὶ ἡ γῆ ⸂ παρελεύσεται ⸃ οἱ δὲ λόγοι μου οὐ μὴ παρέλθωσιν.

Process of Discovery

Linguistics Section

Linguistic Structure

[Parable of the fig tree explained] [28] "Now learn the parable from the fig tree: when its branch has already become tender and puts forth its leaves, you know that summer is near. [29] "Even so, you too, when you see these things happening, recognize that He is near, *right* at the door. [30] "Truly I say to you, this generation will not pass away until all these things take place. [31] "Heaven and earth will pass away, but My words will not pass away. [32] "But of that day or hour no one knows, not even the angels in heaven, nor the Son, but the Father *alone*.

Discussion

This is a continuation of the preceding narrative.

Questioning the Passage

1. What does it mean in verse thirty-four that this generation shall not pass? (v. 30)

   In the Peshitta, the Aramaic word is *sharbtha*. This word means "a family, tribe, race, nation, generation, or genealogy." In this verse, the best translation is "race." Yeshua said that the Hebrew race would survive until the end of time.[186] History has proven that the Hebrew people can be attacked, but the LORD always ensures that a remanent of the Hebrew people survives. Yeshua is reminding His disciples about this. It would have behooved the church over the centuries to understand what Yeshua meant. It would have stopped the massive amounts of murder the church did to the Hebrew people.

Linguistic Echoes

1. Micah 4:1-7

   And it will come about in the last days that the mountain of the house of the LORD will be established as the chief of the mountains. It will be raised above the hills, and the peoples will stream to it. Many nations will come and say, "Come and let us go up to the

---

[186] Errico, Rocco A., and George M. Lamsa. *Aramaic Light on the Gospel of Matthew: a Commentary on the Teachings of Jesus from the Aramaic and Unchanged Near Eastern Customs*. Santa Fe, NM: Noohra Foundation, 2000.

mountain of the LORD and to the house of the God of Jacob, that He may teach us about His ways and that we may walk in His paths." For from Zion will go forth the law, Even the word of the LORD from Jerusalem. And He will judge between many peoples and render decisions for mighty, distant nations. Then they will hammer their swords into plowshares and their spears into pruning hooks; Nation will not lift up sword against nation, and never again will they train for war. Each of them will sit under his vine and under his fig tree, with no one to make them afraid, of or the mouth of the LORD of hosts has spoken. Though all the peoples walk each in the name of his god, As for us, we will walk in the name of the LORD our God forever and ever. In that day," declares the LORD, "I will assemble the lame and gather the outcasts, even those whom I have afflicted. "I will make the lame a remnant and the outcasts a strong nation, and the LORD will reign over them in Mount Zion from now on and forever.

Micah used the example of the fig tree to describe the apocalypse. Since Yeshua used a fig tree, a connection can be made between these two pieces of Scripture.

2. Isaiah 34:4

> [4] And all the host of heaven will [1]wear away, and the sky will be rolled up like a scroll; all their hosts will also wither away as a leaf withers from the vine, or as *one* withers from the fig tree.

> Isaiah's use of the fig tree says that there is a beginning to the world and there is an end.

Culture Section

Questioning the passage

1. What is the significance of the fig tree? (v. 28)

   In the ancient world, people used trees as calendars. The fig tree grows embryonic buds in April and May. By June, the tree is filled with leaves and figs. Farmers knew when to plant their crops by watching their trees. Yeshua used the symbolism of the fig tree to talk about the coming of the Kingdom of Heaven. Micah 4:1-7 echoes his narrative. Micah used the example of a fig tree to talk about the end of time.[187]

2. What does "even heaven and earth will pass away, but my words will not pass away?" (v. 31)

This phrase is an Aramaic figure of speech, which means "What I say must come true." Semitic people believe that Heaven and Earth are everlasting. When this phrase is used, it expresses surety of what is said. A prophet's reputation is staked on the truth of his words. This figure of speech conveys the truth of what the prophet (or Messiah) was saying.

3. When will these things happen? (v. 32)

Yeshua told His disciples that it was unknown when the tribulation would occur. If this statement is connected to the destruction of the Temple in Jerusalem, then Yeshua told His disciples that He did not know when the destruction would occur. The atmosphere was ripe for rebellion. The Romans placed heavy occupational burdens on the people. Eventually, the Zealots started a revolt. The Zealots needed time to gather men and swords. When would they have enough? Even the Zealots were not sure. What would be the final straw in Yeshua's time that caused the revolt? No one knew.

Thoughts

This narrative follows the second coming event. Therefore, it must be considered from that perspective. A big question about the return of Yeshua is when it will happen? Perhaps the idea of Yeshua's return is because His work was not finished in His lifetime. Yeshua introduced the Kingdom of Heaven. However, its institution and growth still need to happen. A problem with this idea is that Yeshua did not tell us when He would return. There are no indications of what event or events have to occur for His return. Christianity should not be concerned about this event but rather about how it continues to demonstrate the love and grace of Yeshua to the world.

---

[187] Stern, Frank. *A Rabbi Looks at Jesus' Parables*. Lanham (Md.): Rowman & Littlefield, 2006.

Reflections

Another theory about the return of Yeshua is based on the Mithras religion. Mithras died, was resurrected, and told his disciples that he would return. When Paul converted the Mithras churches, these concepts about Mithras became associated with Yeshua. I am not saying that Yeshua's return is a myth. The people of the first century believed it. When the end of the first century came, the Mithras conversion was well underway. The new proto-orthodox church was asked the question about Yeshua's return. The apostles were dead, and the Roman oppression was only getting stronger. Where was Yeshua? When was he going to liberate the followers? The book of Revelation is the answer to these questions. In that book, the author placed Yeshua's return about 2000 years after the resurrection. Putting the event so far into the future calmed down the church. Well, two thousand years have either passed or are about to pass. Will Yeshua return? Only God knows.

MARK 13:33-37

Language

New American Standard 1995	Koine Greek
33 "Take heed, keep on the alert; for you do not know when the *appointed* time will come. 34 *"It is* like a man away on a journey, *who* upon leaving his house and putting his slaves in charge, *assigning* to each one his task, also commanded the doorkeeper to stay on the alert. 35 "Therefore, be on the alert — for you do not know when the master of the house is coming, whether in the evening, at midnight, or when the rooster crows, or in the morning — 36 in case he should come suddenly and find you asleep. 37 "What I say to you I say to all, *"Be on the alert!"'*	33 Βλέπετε, ἀγρυπνεῖτε καὶ προσεύχεσθε οὐκ οἴδατε γὰρ πότε ὁ καιρός ἐστιν. 34 Ὡς ἄνθρωπος ἀπόδημος ἀφεὶς τὴν οἰκίαν αὐτοῦ, καὶ δοὺς τοῖς δούλοις αὐτοῦ τὴν ἐξουσίαν, καὶ ἑκάστῳ τὸ ἔργον αὐτοῦ, καὶ τῷ θυρωρῷ ἐνετείλατο ἵνα γρηγορῇ. 35 Γρηγορεῖτε οὖν οὐκ οἴδατε γὰρ πότε ὁ κύριος τῆς οἰκίας ἔρχεται, ὀψέ, ἢ μεσονυκτίου, ἢ ἀλεκτοροφωνίας, ἢ πρωΐ 36 μὴ ἐλθὼν ἐξαίφνης εὕρη ὑμᾶς καθεύδοντας. 37 Ἃ δὲ ὑμῖν λέγω πᾶσιν λέγω, Γρηγορεῖτε.

Process of Discovery

Linguistics Section

Linguistic Structure

A [33] "Take heed, keep on the alert; for you do not know when the *appointed* time will come.

> **B** [34] "*It is* like a man away on a journey, *who* upon leaving his house and putting his slaves in charge, *assigning* to each one his task, also commanded the doorkeeper to stay on the alert.

> **B'** [35] "Therefore, be on the alert — for you do not know when the master of the house is coming, whether in the evening, at midnight, or when the rooster crows, or in the morning — [36] in case he should come suddenly and find you asleep.

A' [37] "What I say to you I say to all, "Be on the alert!""

Discussion

Chapter thirteen of Mark's Gospel continues with the subject of the apocalypse. This material enhances the previous statements about the apocalypse.

Thoughts

Several passages in this chapter demonstrate the need to be ready for the apocalypse. Christian scholars like to say that the LORD had not yet selected a time for the end of time. They say this because if Yeshua is considered a part of God, the Trinity Doctrine, He would undoubtedly have known when the end was to come. Clearly, the idea of Yeshua knowing the end of time is that He had no clue.

What does that leave us with? We are directed to stay alert. What should we be doing? Every one of us should be ready to meet the LORD. That means that we have to be ready for the day of judgment.

Reflections

What happens if we examine this last apocalyptic passage in its time period? What that means is Yeshua was talking about the end of the Jewish age of animal sacrifices to cover sin. The destruction of the Temple at Jerusalem in 70 CE was the end of an era. How would sins be forgiven without the animal sacrifice system? A whole new system had to be built. In 90 CE, there was a rabbinical conference where the rabbis decided what would happen. There are Jews who eagerly await the rebuilding of the Temple at Jerusalem. They want the old ways back. It is also a prediction that when the Temple at Jerusalem is rebuilt, Israel's nation will prosper again.

MARK 14:1-2

Language

New American Standard 1995	Koine Greek
[1] Now the Passover and Unleavened Bread were two days away; and the chief priests and the scribes were seeking how to seize Him by stealth and kill *Him;* [2] for they were saying, "Not during the festival, otherwise there might be a riot of the people."	[1] Ἦν δὲ τὸ Πάσχα καὶ τὰ ἄζυμα μετὰ δύο ἡμέρας καὶ ἐζήτουν οἱ ἀρχιερεῖς καὶ οἱ γραμματεῖς πῶς αὐτὸν ἐν δόλῳ κρατήσαντες ἀποκτείνωσιν [2] ἔλεγον δέ, Μὴ ἐν τῇ ἑορτῇ, μήποτε θόρυβος ἔσται τοῦ λαοῦ.

Process of Discovery

Linguistics Section

Linguistic Structure

[Narrative] [1] Now the Passover and Unleavened Bread were two days away; and the chief priests and the scribes were seeking how to seize Him by stealth and kill *Him;* [2] for they were saying, "Not during the festival, otherwise there might be a riot of the people."

Discussion

The stage is set for the crucifixion.

Questioning the Passage

1. What is the significance of Yeshua saying that the Passover was two days away? (v. 2) The Passover is a celebration of the LORD's salvation for Israel when they were in bondage in Egypt. By Yeshua's time, it was a spiritual celebration and a reminder of the Spiritual World. The Material World of the Sanhedrin was about to come into conflict with the Spiritual World. The events from this point until Easter morning reflect the conflict. On Easter morning, the proof of the Spiritual World and its victory was shown to the world.[188]

Culture Section

Discussion

Yeshua had been warned many times not to go to Jerusalem, especially during the Passover. Every year since the Roman occupation, there was rioting in Jerusalem as the Hebrew people demanded their freedom from Roman oppression. There was usually a clash between Roman soldiers and the people. It was a volatile time. Yeshua decided to enter Jerusalem. After Yeshua's triumphant entry into Jerusalem, He became a threat to the stability of the city. The church has

---

[188] *The New Interpreter's Bible: General Articles & Introduction, Commentary, & Reflections for Each Book of the Bible, Including the Apocryphal/Deuterocanonical Books*. Nashville: Abingdon, 1996.

offered the desire for the Sanhedrin to have Yeshua eliminated as a political threat. That is one way to view it.

Another way to view it is that Yeshua wanted the freedom of the Hebrew people but through peaceful measures. However, the Zealots saw the turmoil as an opportunity to stir up trouble. Yeshua became the focus of the Zealots-based riot. Therefore, the Sanhedrin had to stop Yeshua. Several members of the Sanhedrin spoke to yeshua. Yeshua did not change His mind about His being in Jerusalem. He probably would not have been executed if Yeshua had left the city. However, Yeshua did not leave. The Sanhedrin felt that they had no choice but to offer Yeshua's life to prevent the Roman army's destruction in the city.

Questioning the passage

1. What is the significance of the Passover? (v. 2)

   In Yeshua's time, the Hebrew people held a fast on Nissan 14, the day before the Passover, to remember that Israel's first-born children were spared from the tenth plague. This tradition faded during the years that followed Yeshua. The central event of the Pesach is the selection of a lamb that was without any blemishes or spots. The lamb was sacrificed to the LORD in the afternoon. At the original Passover, the lamb's blood was painted onto the doorposts of the Hebrew home. The angel of death then passed over their homes. Yeshua added significance to the Passover at the church's "Last Supper."

   Was the banquet an actual Sedar, or was it a celebration banquet? When a rabbi and his students completed a study of a tractate of the Talmud, they celebrated with a *se'udat mitzvah* (a "banquet of completion"). In Yeshua's day, rabbis would try to end a study by Nissan 14 so that they could hold the banquet of completion and avoid the fast. The banquet took precedence over the fast of Nissan 14. This was not considered cheating the fast but rather a custom of the people.

   By Yeshua saying that there were two days to the Passover, He could have been implying that there were two more days left for Him to teach His disciples about the Kingdom of

Heaven. The banquet of Nissan 14 would then be the celebration of the completion of their training. The disciples would have to take over Yeshua's mission.

Since this custom of completion has not been celebrated for years and because the church broke away from its Hebraic roots, it is not aware today of this custom. Therefore, the descriptions in the synoptic Gospels are of a Passover celebration. John's Gospel accurately describes the "Last Supper" as a banquet of completion, not a Passover seder.[189]

Continuing with John's Gospel, it is the only Gospel that recorded that Yeshua's blood was spilled at the crucifixion. The Gospel says that a Roman soldier ensured that He was dead by stabbing Him in His side with a spear. Blood and water rushed out of His body. The church established a doctrine that states that Yeshua's blood was spilled to wash away the sins of people. However, only John's Gospel says that Yeshua's blood was actually spilled. Also, if the Last Supper was a Passover seder, then Yeshua could not have died on the Day of Preparation. That day is Nissan 14. The Feast of the Unleavened Bread is Nissan 15. Today the Feast of the Unleavened Bread is combined with Passover. The sacrifice of the lamb for its blood was made on the afternoon of Nissan 14. For Yeshua to become the cosmic sacrifice, thus replacing the lamb of the Passover, His death had to be on Nissan 14.

The church's doctrine about atonement is built on the bleeding death of Yeshua, as described in John's Gospel. However, it maintains that the Last Supper was a Passover seder, which John's Gospel does not say. The conflict is unmistakable. For the blood doctrine to work, John's Gospel must be used for the timeline of Yeshua's death. At 6:00 PM, Nissan 14, at the beginning of the day, Yeshua gathered His disciples together to have a banquet of celebration. The celebration could have been the conclusion of the training that He was giving them. They would learn a lot more from the Risen Yeshua and the

---

[189] Stern, David H. *Jewish New Testament Commentary: a Companion Volume to the Jewish New Testament.* Clarksville, MD: Jewish New Testament Publications, 1999.

Holy Spirit but nothing else from the earthly bound Yeshua. He died in the afternoon on Nissan 14, the day of preparation.

Thoughts

Yeshua starts the day by reminding His disciples that His death was upon them. Perhaps Yeshua did this to allow the disciples to ask any last questions. Their understanding of the Kingdom of Heaven was shallow. They would have to understand Yeshua's mission, which was to initiate the Kingdom of Heaven, if they were going to be successful students. Their training was about to end. They had two days left to talk to Yeshua about divine subjects.

Reflections

Living in the Materialistic World, the conflict between that world and the Spiritual World is everyday. Yeshua made sure that His disciples were ready to bring the Spiritual World into the Materialistic world. Ask yourself, are you ready to be a true disciple of Yeshua? Can you say the words that will convince people to join the Kingdom of Heaven?. In the end, Yeshua will commission His followers to teach the ways of the Spiritual World, the Kingdom of Heaven, to everyone on Earth. So, are you ready to take up the cross and teach the Kingdom of Heaven? If not, what do you believe that you need to work for Yeshua?

MARK 14:3-9

Language

New American Standard 1995	Koine Greek
³While He was in Bethany at the home of Simon the leper, and reclining *at the table,* there came a woman with an alabaster vial of very costly perfume of pure nard; *and* she broke the vial and poured it over His head. ⁴ But some were indignantly *remarking* to one another, "Why has this perfume been wasted? ⁵ "For this perfume might have been sold for over three hundred denarii, and *the money* given to the poor." And they were scolding her. ⁶ But Jesus said, "Let her alone; why do you bother her? She has done a good deed to Me. ⁷ "For you always have the poor with you, and whenever you wish you can do good to them; but you do not always have Me. ⁸ "She has done what she could; she has anointed My body beforehand for the burial. ⁹ "Truly I say to you, wherever the gospel is preached in the whole world, what this woman has done will also be spoken of in memory of her."	**Mark 14:3** Καὶ ὄντος αὐτοῦ ἐν Βηθανίᾳ, ἐν τῇ οἰκίᾳ Σίμωνος τοῦ λεπροῦ, κατακειμένου αὐτοῦ, ἦλθεν γυνὴ ἔχουσα ἀλάβαστρον μύρου νάρδου πιστικῆς πολυτελοῦς καὶ συντρίψασα ⸀ τὸ ⸀ ἀλάβαστρον, κατέχεεν αὐτοῦ κατὰ τῆς κεφαλῆς. ⁴ Ἦσαν δέ τινες ἀγανακτοῦντες πρὸς ἑαυτούς, καὶ λέγοντες, Εἰς τί ἡ ἀπώλεια αὕτη τοῦ μύρου γέγονεν; ⁵ Ἠδύνατο γὰρ τοῦτο πραθῆναι ἐπάνω τριακοσίων δηναρίων, καὶ δοθῆναι τοῖς πτωχοῖς. Καὶ ἐνεβριμῶντο αὐτῇ. ⁶ Ὁ δὲ Ἰησοῦς εἶπεν, Ἄφετε αὐτήν τί αὐτῇ κόπους παρέχετε; Καλὸν ἔργον εἰργάσατο ἐν ἐμοί. ⁷ Πάντοτε γὰρ τοὺς πτωχοὺς ἔχετε μεθ᾽ ἑαυτῶν, καὶ ὅταν θέλητε δύνασθε αὐτοὺς εὖ ποιῆσαι ἐμὲ δὲ οὐ πάντοτε ἔχετε. ⁸ Ὃ ἔσχεν αὕτη ἐποίησεν προέλαβεν μυρίσαι μου τὸ σῶμα εἰς τὸν ἐνταφιασμόν. ⁹ Ἀμὴν ⸀ λέγω ⸀ ὑμῖν, ὅπου ἐὰν κηρυχθῇ τὸ εὐαγγέλιον τοῦτο εἰς ὅλον τὸν κόσμον, καὶ ὃ ἐποίησεν αὕτη λαληθήσεται εἰς μνημόσυνον αὐτῆς.

Process of Discovery

Linguistics Section

Linguistic Structure

[Introduction] ³While He was in Bethany at the home of Simon the leper, and reclining *at the table,* there came a woman with an alabaster vial of very costly perfume of pure nard; *and* she broke the vial and poured it over His head.

[Action] ⁴ But some were indignantly *remarking* to one another, "Why has this perfume been wasted? ⁵ "For this perfume might have been sold for over three hundred denarii, and *the money* given to the poor." And they were scolding her.

[Reaction] ⁶ But Jesus said, "Let her alone; why do you bother her? She has done a good deed to Me. ⁷ "For you always have the poor with you, and whenever you wish you can do good to them; but you do not always have Me. ⁸ "She has done what she could; she has anointed My body beforehand for the burial.

[Conclusion] ⁹ "Truly I say to you, wherever the gospel is preached in the whole world, what this woman has done will also be spoken of in memory of her."

Discussion

This is a narrative about what does a person value

Questioning the Passage

1. What is the significance of Yeshua being in Bethany? (v. 3)
    Bethany was a village on the Mount of Olives. Yeshua used the Mount of Olives as His place to retire each evening.

2. Why did Yeshua go to Simon the Leper's home? (v. 3)
    Yeshua either knew Simon or was invited by him. Since Yeshua retired to the Mount of Olives every evening during Passion week, it makes sense that He would visit a friend's home or stay with a person who gave Him an invitation.

3. Was the Leper at home? (v. 3)

   If Simon were suffering from leprosy, he would not have been at home when Yeshua arrived. People who suffered from leprosy were forced to live outside the community. It is possible that Simon had leprosy and was cured. That would allow him to be at his home. By calling Simon a leper, it takes the emphasis of the narrative away from Simon. Even knowing that it was his home is not necessary for the narrative. Matthew's author could have said that Yeshua was at anyone's home. It is not essential to know. It is also possible that Yeshua had healed him, and he was repaying the blessing.

4. Why was Yeshua reclining at the table? (v. 4)

   Free people reclined at a table during a meal. During the Passover seder, the participants recline and lean at the table. This act represents that the people were free and not slaves.

5. What was the value of the perfume? (v. 5)

   It is not known how much alabaster was poured on Yeshua. Therefore, it is unknown what the economic value was. Many commentators say that the alabaster cost was about one year's salary, which would have made it around 300 denari. Since the narrative says that the perfume could have been sold at a high price, the 300 denari is a good guess.

6. Why did the disciples talk about the poor? (v. 5)

   Their statement could have been a reaction that a strange woman came to Yeshua. The disciples would have been surprised that this happened. Instead of the men denouncing the woman for breaking the custom of the day, the author of Matthew's Gospel has them denouncing her for a different reason. Yeshua was known for breaking from cultural customs. If the disciples had condemned the woman on Hebraic customs of the day, Yeshua would have quickly denounced them. Instead, they used a "giving to the poor" argument for the woman's actions. They were probably startled by Yeshua's condemnation of them.

7. Why is anointing Yeshua a good deed? (v. 8)

In Matthew's Gospel, the reason for the women going to the tomb on the third day after Yeshua's death is not because the body needed to be anointed; instead, it was for them to say their final good-byes. Since Yeshua said that the woman anointed Him that evening for death, it did not have to occur a second time. So the good deed is that woman prepared Yeshua for death, and she accepted that it was the LORD's plan for this to happen.[190] This event is a foreshadowing of what is to come.

8. Why is it important to remember this woman? (v. 9)

The use of wealth and money was important to Yeshua. The woman was to be remembered because she shared her wealth with Yeshua. Her action was considered a mitzvah. Remembering to follow the mitzvot of the Torah is vital to staying on the path to righteousness.

Biblical Personalities

1. Simon the Leper – "Simon the Leper is sometimes identified with Simon the Pharisee (see Shimon ben Gamliel), who is mentioned in the Gospel of Luke as the host of a meal during which the feet of Jesus are anointed by a penitent woman. Because of some similarities, efforts have been made to reconcile the events and characters, but some scholars have pointed out differences between the two events. For example, the Lucan account is considerably longer than the other gospel narratives, and the woman fills the void created by the host, Simon the Pharisee, when he neglects the usual or expected acts of hospitality such as the anointing of the head with oil, a kiss for the cheek, and water for the feet. Further, the anonymous woman is identified as a "sinner" and welcomes Jesus in the most profligate manner. An alternative explanation for the similarities is that the Luke 7 anointing and the anointing at Bethany happened with some of the same participants, but several years apart.

---

[190] *The New Interpreter's Bible: General Articles & Introduction, Commentary, & Reflections for Each Book of the Bible, Including the Apocryphal/Deuterocanonical Books.* Nashville: Abingdon, 1996.

Simon the Leper is also sometimes identified as the same person as Lazarus of Bethany, or identified as his father or brother. This is because Matthew and Mark mention Simon, while John mentions Lazarus, but all four gospels assume one lodging at Bethany during the last week. Abbé Drioux identified all three as one: Lazarus of Bethany, Simon the Leper of Bethany, and the Lazarus of the parable, on the basis that in the parable Lazarus is depicted as a leper, and due to a perceived coincidence between Luke 22:2 and John 12:10—where after the raising of Lazarus, Caiaphas and Annas tried to have him killed."[191]

Biblical Locations

1. Bethany – "1) A village, 15 furlongs from Jerusalem (John 11:18), on the road to Jericho, at the Mount of Olives (Mark 11:1 Luke 19:29), where lived "Simon the leper" (Mark 14:3) and Mary, Martha and Lazarus (John 11:18 f). This village may justifiably be called the Judean home of Jesus, as He appears to have preferred to lodge there rather than in Jerusalem itself (Matthew 21:17 Mark 11:11). Here occurred the incident of the raising of Lazarus (John 11) and the feast at the house of Simon (Matthew 26:1-13 Mark 14:3-9 Luke 7:36-50 John 1:2:1-8). The Ascension as recorded in Luke 24:50-51 is thus described: "He led them out until they were over against Bethany: and he lifted up his hands, and blessed them. And it came to pass, while he blessed them, he parted from them, and was carried up into heaven."

---

[191] "Simon the Leper." Wikipedia. Wikimedia Foundation, March 31, 2020. Accessed August 4, 2020 https://en.wikipedia.org/wiki/Simon_the_Leper.

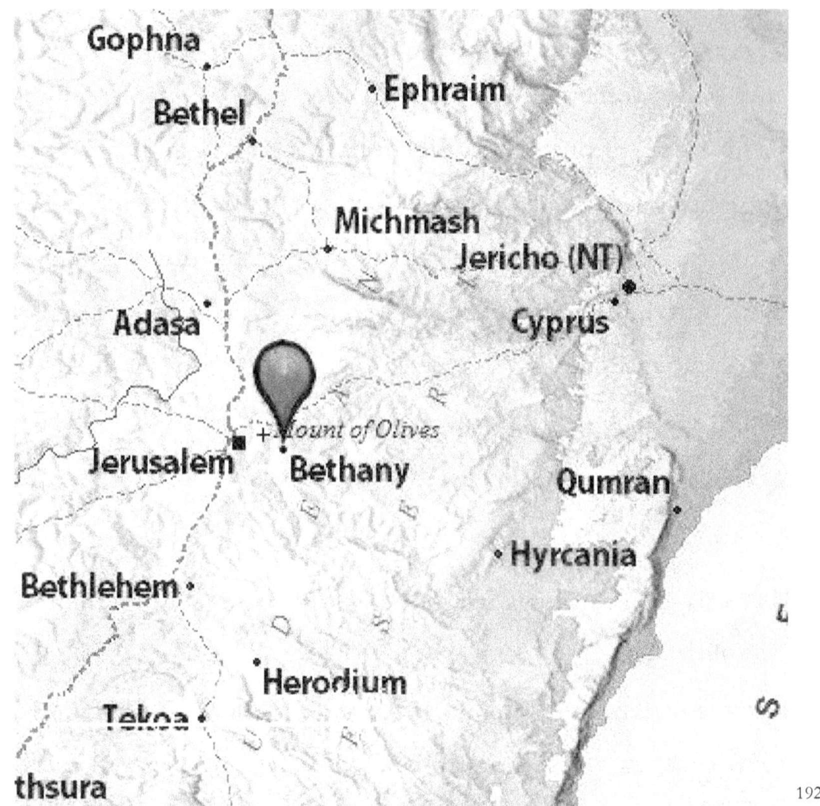

Culture Section

Discussion

In a zero-growth economy, like in Yeshua's time, for a person to accumulate wealth meant that wealth had to be taken from someone else. Money is a topic that Yeshua often spoke about. Wealth and money are not a problem. The problem is the use of wealth and money. When obtaining wealth, it must be done without hurting someone else. In today's economy, one can obtain wealth without cheating on other people. That is what Yeshua was referring to. As far as poor people, there will always be poor people. There are many reasons for poor people. The Torah teaches that giving help to poor people is a mitzvah. There are midrashim about poor people that say the LORD created poor people so that the mitzvot of giving to the poor is

---

192 Bible Map: Bethany. Accessed August 4, 2020. https://bibleatlas.org/bethany.htm.

available for righteousness. Another area to consider is what does one value? The woman valued Yeshua, and she demonstrated it.

Questioning the passage

1. What was the custom of a woman interacting with a man? (v. 3)

    A woman who did not know a man would not have approached him openly unless she was a harlot looking to offer her services. Since the narrative says that a woman came to Him in Simon's home, unannounced and unknown, she must have been a harlot or a sinner. So this church interpretation of the woman came from the custom of the separation of men and women. Why would an unknown woman stroll into Simon's home? Who let the woman in?[193]

2. Could this narrative be about money?

    Homes in Bethany were generally not huge. If she could sneak in without being noticed until she came up to Yeshua, it could be indicating that Simon was wealthy because the house must have been large enough that she was not noticed. If one assumes that Simon was wealthy, then the question of money fits the narrative. Perhaps it was a lesson to Simon, and wealthy people, that they should be openly willing to share their wealth with poor people as instructed in the Torah. The Gospel has the message of using wealth to help people in need. Yeshua and his disciples would have been considered poor. They depended on supporters for their food and shelter. They did not work. They sat with Yeshua to learn about the Kingdom of Heaven.

    Therefore, this narrative could be viewed as a final lesson about wealth—the lesson being that it is a mitzvah to help poor people whenever possible.

---

[193] Errico, Rocco A., and George M. Lamsa. *Aramaic Light on the Gospel of Matthew: a Commentary on the Teachings of Jesus from the Aramaic and Unchanged Near Eastern Customs*. Santa Fe, NM: Noohra Foundation, 2000.

Thoughts

This narrative is a bit difficult because of church interpretation. There are several holes in the narrative that cannot be explained. A strange woman walked into a house and was able to get to Yeshua to anoint him. That sounds very strange. Even the twelve disciples did not stop her. With tensions running high during that week, it seems improbable that the disciples were not surrounding Yeshua like a wall, thus not letting anyone enter the inner circle without permission. Also, would a strange woman pour an entire year's worth of money on Yeshua? She was either married to a wealthy man or was a harlot who saved up her money. The church decided that the woman must have been a sinner. The narrative is missing much information, which allows for a tremendous about of speculation.

Reflections

The concentration of the narrative throughout the years has been on the woman's love for Yeshua that she would spend her wealth for alabaster to anoint Yeshua. Using Ancient Bible study methods, it is seen that this narrative also talks about the use of money, wealth, and about what one values. The final teachings of Yeshua were given to the disciples and us. The final lessons included some reviews. The usage of wealth and money is the topic of this lesson, which reflects what a person values. Beware of how you earn your wealth and money. Also, remember it is a mitzvah to help the poor. The LORD gave us poor people so that through the disciples of Yeshua, the LORD's love for them will shine through.

MARK 14:10-21

Language

New American Standard 1995	Koine Greek
[10] Then Judas Iscariot, who was one of the twelve, went off to the chief priests in order to betray Him to them. [11] They were glad when they heard *this,* and promised to give him money. And he *began* seeking how to betray Him at an opportune time.	[10] Καὶ ὁ Ἰούδας ὁ Ἰσκαριώτης, εἷς τῶν δώδεκα, ἀπῆλθεν πρὸς τοὺς ἀρχιερεῖς, ἵνα παραδῷ αὐτὸν αὐτοῖς. [11] Οἱ δὲ ἀκούσαντες ἐχάρησαν, καὶ ἐπηγγείλαντο αὐτῷ ἀργύριον δοῦναι καὶ ἐζήτει πῶς εὐκαίρως αὐτὸν παραδῷ.
[12] On the first day of Unleavened Bread, when the Passover *lamb* was being sacrificed, His disciples said to Him, "Where do You want us to go and prepare for You to eat the Passover?" [13] And He sent two of His disciples and said to them, "Go into the city, and a man will meet you carrying a pitcher of water; follow him; [14] and wherever he enters, say to the owner of the house, The Teacher says, "Where is My guest room in which I may eat the Passover with My disciples?"' [15] "And he himself will show you a large upper room furnished *and* ready; prepare for us there." [16] The disciples went out and came to the city, and found *it* just as He had told them; and they prepared the Passover.	[12] Καὶ τῇ πρώτῃ ἡμέρᾳ τῶν ἀζύμων, ὅτε τὸ Πάσχα ἔθυον, λέγουσιν αὐτῷ οἱ μαθηταὶ αὐτοῦ, Ποῦ θέλεις ἀπελθόντες ⸂ ἑτοιμάσωμεν ⸃ ἵνα φάγῃς τὸ Πάσχα; [13] Καὶ ἀποστέλλει δύο τῶν μαθητῶν αὐτοῦ, καὶ λέγει αὐτοῖς, Ὑπάγετε εἰς τὴν πόλιν, καὶ ἀπαντήσει ὑμῖν ἄνθρωπος κεράμιον ὕδατος βαστάζων ἀκολουθήσατε αὐτῷ, [14] καὶ ὅπου ἐὰν εἰσέλθῃ, εἴπατε τῷ οἰκοδεσπότῃ ὅτι Ὁ διδάσκαλος λέγει, Ποῦ ἐστιν τὸ κατάλυμα, ὅπου τὸ Πάσχα μετὰ τῶν μαθητῶν μου φάγω; [15] Καὶ αὐτὸς ὑμῖν δείξει ⸂ ἀνώγεον ⸃ μέγα ἐστρωμένον ἕτοιμον ἐκεῖ ἑτοιμάσατε ἡμῖν. [16] Καὶ ἐξῆλθον οἱ μαθηταὶ αὐτοῦ, καὶ ἦλθον εἰς τὴν πόλιν, καὶ εὗρον καθὼς εἶπεν αὐτοῖς, καὶ ἡτοίμασαν τὸ Πάσχα.
[17] When it was evening He came with the twelve. [18] As they were reclining *at the table* and eating, Jesus said, "Truly I say to you that one of you will betray Me — one who is eating with Me." [19] They began to be grieved and to say to Him one by one, "Surely not I?" [20] And He said to them, "*It is* one of the twelve, one who dips with Me in the bowl. [21] "For the Son of Man *is to* go just as it is written of Him; but woe to that man by whom the Son of Man is betrayed! *It would have been* good for that man if he had not been born."	[17] Καὶ ὀψίας γενομένης ἔρχεται μετὰ τῶν δώδεκα. [18] Καὶ ἀνακειμένων αὐτῶν καὶ ἐσθιόντων, εἶπεν ὁ Ἰησοῦς, Ἀμὴν λέγω ὑμῖν, ὅτι εἷς ἐξ ὑμῶν παραδώσει με, ὁ ἐσθίων μετ' ἐμοῦ. [19] Οἱ δὲ ἤρξαντο λυπεῖσθαι, καὶ λέγειν αὐτῷ εἷς καθ' εἷς, Μήτι ἐγώ; Καὶ ἄλλος, Μήτι ἐγώ; [20] Ὁ δὲ ἀποκριθεὶς εἶπεν αὐτοῖς, Εἷς ἐκ τῶν δώδεκα, ὁ ἐμβαπτόμενος μετ' ἐμοῦ εἰς τὸ τρύβλιον. [21] Ὁ μὲν υἱὸς τοῦ ἀνθρώπου ὑπάγει, καθὼς γέγραπται περὶ αὐτοῦ οὐαὶ δὲ τῷ ἀνθρώπῳ ἐκείνῳ δι' οὗ ὁ υἱὸς τοῦ ἀνθρώπου παραδίδοται καλὸν ἦν αὐτῷ εἰ οὐκ ἐγεννήθη ὁ ἄνθρωπος ἐκεῖνος.

Process of Discovery

   Linguistics Section

    Linguistic Structure

[Judas' betrayal] [10]   Then Judas Iscariot, who was one of the twelve, went off to the chief priests in order to betray Him to them. [11] They were glad when they heard *this,* and promised to give him money. And he *began* seeking how to betray Him at an opportune time.

[Passover preparation] [12]   On the first day of Unleavened Bread, when the Passover *lamb* was being sacrificed, His disciples said to Him, "Where do You want us to go and prepare for You to eat the Passover?" [13] And He sent two of His disciples and said to them, "Go into the city, and a man will meet you carrying a pitcher of water; follow him; [14] and wherever he enters, say to the owner of the house, The Teacher says, "Where is My guest room in which I may eat the Passover with My disciples?"" [15] "And he himself will show you a large upper room furnished *and* ready; prepare for us there." [16] The disciples went out and came to the city, and found *it* just as He had told them; and they prepared the Passover.

[The Passover] [17]   When it was evening He came with the twelve. [18] As they were reclining *at the table* and eating, Jesus said, "Truly I say to you that one of you will betray Me — one who is eating with Me." [19] They began to be grieved and to say to Him one by one, "Surely not I?" [20] And He said to them, "*It is* one of the twelve, one who dips with Me in the bowl. [21] "For the Son of Man *is to* go just as it is written of Him; but woe to that man by whom the Son of Man is betrayed! *It would have been* good for that man if he had not been born."

   Discussion

   This narrative sets the stage for the Last Supper.

Questioning the Passage

1. Why did Judas turn Yeshua over to the High Priest?

    An interesting note is that the High Priest and members of the Sanhedrin needed Judas to turn Yeshua over to them. That indicates that they had never seen Yeshua face to face. This probability suggests that they only heard rumors and gossip about Him. They based their fears and anxiety on a person whom they never spoke with. There is no doubt that there were priests of the Temple staff who did speak with Yeshua. They must have reported back to the leaders, telling them about Yeshua.

    There are several possible answers to why Judas turned Yeshua over to the Temple leaders.

    a. Judas was greedy.

        Matthew's Gospel says that Judas was the treasurer of the group. There are several passages where Judas shows concern for money. In the preceding narrative, the women with the perfume, church interpreters of the Scripture have written that it was Judas who complained about the "waste" of the perfume. They continue by saying that Judas was not concerned about the poor, but instead, he wanted to sell the perfume and take part in the sale price for himself. This type of greed was never proven in the Gospel. However, it is plausible that Judas was greedy. Thirty pieces of silver is a small price to betray Yeshua. A greedy person would have demanded a lot more money.

    b. Judas wanted the Messianic age to commence.

        If the disciples believed that Yeshua was the Messiah described in the Hebrew Scriptures, then why did Yeshua not start the revolution? A traditional belief was that the Messiah would initiate the battle between Israel and their oppressors. Israel would win the final war and would place a descendant of David on the throne of Israel. This would fulfill the LORD's covenant to David that a descendant of David would always sit upon the throne of Israel.

        For three years, Judas Iscariot waited. It is believed that Judas was a Zealot. The Zealot movement was created to overthrow the Roman oppressors. Judas became impatient, waiting for Yeshua to do something. Therefore, Judas took it upon himself to start the

Messianic age and the revolt. He believed that when the Temple Guard came to take Yeshua and arrest Him that Yeshua would start the Messianic age war. Judas witnessed what happened when Peter started the armed revolt. Yeshua said that the Kingdom of Heaven was not to come by war but rather by peace. Judas then realized that Yeshua was not the traditional Messiah that he was taught but rather a spiritual Messiah. This error caused Judas to commit suicide.

c. The "betrayal" and subsequent events are allegorical. The events from the "betrayal" to the Resurrection represent a movement from the material world to the spiritual world.

The allegory is that Judas' actions were to release the human Christ into becoming the spiritual Christ. Judas was given thirty pieces of silver to turn over Yeshua. The thirty pieces represent the cost of a slave, as found in the book of Exodus. Yeshua was a slave to the material world into which the Christ Spirit was born. It was time to release the Christ Spirit from its flesh prison so that the Kingdom of Heaven could commence. The Kingdom of Heaven is a spiritual concept. Yeshua, while in the flesh, lived in the material world. Yeshua's message of repenting for the Kingdom of Heaven is near is a call for people to change their thinking and concentration from the material world to the spiritual world.

How was the spiritual Christ going to be released from the prison of the flesh? Yeshua had to die for that to happen. In fact, on Easter morning, it was the spiritual Christ that the people experienced. The flesh was shed, and the true spiritual nature of the Messiah was revealed. Therefore, Judas purchased Yeshua's freedom from the material world.

Yeshua offers His followers the same deal. The cost of leaving the slavery of the material world was paid to Judas. The Christ Spirit was no longer a slave to the material world. Following the ways of the Christ Spirit, Yeshua, one is released from the hold that the material world has on a person. It is more important to know the LORD than it is to bask in the riches of the material world.

So this narrative is the beginning of the move of Yeshua from the material world to the spiritual world. The pathway to Heaven was initiated by Judas purchasing Yeshua's slavery and releasing Him.

2. What is Passover?

In Aramaic, *pesakh* means "rejoicing." It is a festival that is celebrated every year since the time of the first Passover, the Exodus of the Jewish people from the slavery of Egypt. It occurs on the fifteenth day of the month of Nisan. According to the book of the Exodus, the Passover must occur in the springtime. Today lamb and unleavened bread are eaten at the Passover seder (dinner). The lamb is to remind the people that lamb's blood was spread on the doorposts and lentils so that the Angel of Death passed over the homes of the Hebrew people. The unleavened bread is to commemorate the hast of the people who left Egypt. They could not wait for the bread to rise.

3. What is the feast of the unleavened bread?

Today the feast of the unleavened bread has become a part of the Passover.

4. What was the situation with the followers of Yeshua during Passion week?

The church declares that Yeshua's entry into Jerusalem was a triumphal entry. Indeed it says that there was fanfare and that people came out to see Him. Historically the people that lined the streets were mainly the people who came from Galilee with Yeshua. Rocco Errico, an Aramaic scholar, called Yeshua's entry into Jerusalem a humiliating experience. He said that Yeshua's followers became doubtful about His messiahship. The Messiah was supposed to become the King of Israel. The faith of his inner circle, the disciples, was weakened because He was not greeted that way.

Why was this event a humiliation? The disciples and followers of Yeshua believed that a large delegation of priests, scribes, Pharisees, and government officials would come to greet Yeshua with a white horse and with salt and bread. These gifts were an ancient custom to greet the new king to the city. There was no warm reception for Yeshua and His followers. This disappointment weakened their ranks considerably.

The disciples were looking forward to a successful mission in Jerusalem where Yeshua would become King of Israel. They did not expect Him to die, but instead, He would be exalted. It is possible that Judas decided that he wanted to separate himself from Yeshua and thus claim immunity from the Sanhedrin's judgment by helping them to capture Yeshua.

Judas was the treasurer of the group and felt that he was in a higher position than the others. Therefore, he sat next to Yeshua at the Passover seder so that he could dip into Yeshua's dish. He thought by doing so; he would show Yeshua that he loved him and remained loyal. However, Yeshua could tell that this was a lie and called Judas out. Yeshua said to the group that one of them would betray Him, which was a shock and a surprise. This act was a severe breach of Semitic trust.

Yeshua said this because He wanted to have His disciples and future followers to participate in the Passover feast to memorialize Him at the same time when they celebrated the Passover. Yeshua became the slain lamb for the salvation of all people, and He told them this through the Passover feast ritual. The church determined that Yeshua died as a sacrifice for salvation because of narratives like this one where Yeshua equated himself to the Passover lamb.

Biblical Personalities
1. Iscariot – "surname of Judas, betrayer of Jesus, in New Testament, from Latin *Iscariota*, from Greek *Iskariotes*, said to be from Hebrew *ishq'riyoth* "man of Kerioth" (a place in Palestine). In English from 1640s as a noun meaning "traitor.""[194]

---

[194] "Iscariot," Index, accessed August 19, 2020, https://www.etymonline.com/word/iscariot.

Culture Section

Questioning the passage

1. Customs about lodging in the Near East

    a. Some places provided lodging for men only.

    b. People were reluctant to invite large groups into their homes, especially a party of men with no women accompanying them.

    c. Inns existed just for unmarried strangers, foreigners, and gentiles.

    d. Women were not permitted to work at inns with gentiles.

    e. Women were not permitted to draw water for foreigners or strangers.

    f. Men worked at the lodges for the gentiles and brought water to them in sheepskin containers.

    g. Women brought water to their families at homes and other places using earthen vessels, which could be carried on their heads.

2. Customs about meals and the sharing of food

    a. Near Eastern Semitic men usually expressed their emotions openly, whether of sorrow, joy, or deep disappointment.

    b. Good friends exchange sop (bread soaked in gravy), by sharing and dipping into each other's food.

    c. It was a token of friendship and loyalty to share food.

    d. The choice of food was always placed before the honored guest.

    e. The honored guest would share that food with whomever he wished.

    f. Two dishes and two spoons were sufficient for twelve guests, especially during a wedding or festival.

    g. Men often took food from the dish of another man sitting near them.

    h. Often a man would eat half a sop and hand it to another man. This act was considered a token of love between two friends.

    i. A man bestowed a great honor on another man by eating the other half of the sop or eating from his friend's dish.

3. Why were the men reclining at the table? (v. 18)

During the Passover, it is emphasized that the Jewish people become free from the tyranny of Egypt. Freemen recline when they are at a table for a meal. This is a reminder that the LORD saved His people from slavery and made them freemen.

Thoughts

It is too easy to accept the long-standing interpretation that Judas Iscariot was greedy. Thirty shekels of silver is not much money. If Judas was greedy, then he would have demanded a much higher price. However, he did not. He would not have been able to spend any sum that he was paid to betray Yeshua until he separated himself from Yeshua and the rest of the disciples. This interpretation has been around for centuries and clouds people from seeing the act in any other manner.

Reflections

Freedom from the slavery of the flesh is a paramount move when a person wants to enter the spiritual world. The Kingdom of Heaven is the spiritual world that Yeshua spoke about. To enter that world, a person must release themselves to what ties the spirit down in the material world. The needs and wants of the flesh must be overcome. Since a person has to live in the material world, some needs must be fulfilled. It is the wants of the flesh that have to be overcome. Once that occurs, a person can concentrate on the needs of the spiritual world. The allegorical message of Judas' acts is that he freed Yeshua from the slavery of the flesh so that Yeshua could usher in the Kingdom of Heaven.

MARK 14:22-25

Language

New American Standard 1995	Koine Greek
[22] While they were eating, He took *some* bread, and after a blessing He broke *it,* and gave *it* to them, and said, "Take *it;* this is My body." [23] And when He had taken a cup *and* given thanks, He gave *it* to them, and they all drank from it. [24] And He said to them, "This is My blood of the covenant, which is poured out for many. [25] "Truly I say to you, I will never again drink of the fruit of the vine until that day when I drink it new in the kingdom of God."	[22] Καὶ ἐσθιόντων αὐτῶν, λαβὼν ὁ Ἰησοῦς ἄρτον εὐλογήσας ἔκλασεν, καὶ ἔδωκεν αὐτοῖς, καὶ εἶπεν, Λάβετε, φάγετε τοῦτό ἐστιν τὸ σῶμά μου. [23] Καὶ λαβὼν τὸ ποτήριον εὐχαριστήσας ἔδωκεν αὐτοῖς καὶ ἔπιον ἐξ αὐτοῦ πάντες. [24] Καὶ εἶπεν αὐτοῖς, Τοῦτό ἐστιν τὸ αἷμά μου, τὸ τῆς καινῆς διαθήκης, τὸ περὶ πολλῶν ἐκχυνόμενον. [25] Ἀμὴν λέγω ὑμῖν ὅτι οὐκέτι οὐ μὴ πίω ἐκ τοῦ γενήματος τῆς ἀμπέλου, ἕως τῆς ἡμέρας ἐκείνης ὅταν αὐτὸ πίνω καινὸν ἐν τῇ βασιλείᾳ τοῦ θεοῦ.

Process of Discovery

Linguistics Section

Linguistic Structure

[Communion] [22] While they were eating, He took *some* bread, and after a blessing He broke *it,* and gave *it* to them, and said, "Take *it;* this is My body." [23] And when He had taken a cup *and* given thanks, He gave *it* to them, and they all drank from it. [24] And He said to them, "This is My blood of the covenant, which is poured out for many. [25] "Truly I say to you, I will never again drink of the fruit of the vine until that day when I drink it new in the kingdom of God."

Discussion

This passage is the introduction of the Communion Sacrament.

Culture Section

Discussion

During the Passover meal, Yeshua and His disciples would have removed their shoes. It was considered an insult to the host of the dinner to be wearing shoes. They kept their hats on while eating because it was the etiquette of that day.

Questioning the passage

1. What is the significance of the cup?

   Families in Yeshua's time had one cup for the entire family. Even rich people seldomly used two cups when eating. The same cup was used for water and wine. The cup was passed between guests and family members to take a drink and then to pass the cup to the next person.

   At the Passover seder, there were four cups of wine drunk. Each cup represents an act of redemption.

2. What does "I will not drink of this fruit of the vine from now on until that day when I drink it new with you in My Father's kingdom" mean? (v. 25)

    This Semitic expression of speech means, "I will not be fully joyful again till we are all together once more." "Wine" in Aramaic is a metaphor representing "joy, teaching, and inspiration."[195]

    The blood covenant that Yeshua established is connected with the rite of circumcision, the Passover, and the promise to Abraham that the LORD would one day walk in His blood.

3. What is the significance of the bread?

    The bread was considered sacred in the Near East. The bread was something more than just food. People thought that bread possessed a mystic sacred significance. The bread was grown from the sacred earth that the LORD created in Genesis chapter one. Therefore, bread was treated differently than other food.

    Semitic people did not tell a lie when bread was before them. It was wrong to mistreat bread. Among Semitic people, bread has always been eaten with a deep sense of sacredness.

4. What does "eat my body and drink my blood" mean?

    To eat from the body of one's teacher is to say that the student would carry out the teacher's mission. Drinking the blood of the teacher meant that one accepted the mission, knowing that there were dangers and sacrifices with the acceptance of the mission.

---

[195] Errico, Rocco A., and George M. Lamsa. *Aramaic Light on the Gospel of Matthew: a Commentary on the Teachings of Jesus from the Aramaic and Unchanged Near Eastern Customs*. Santa Fe, NM: Noohra Foundation, 2000.

What is Missing?

The Mark Communion description does not have Yeshua saying, "remember me." Indeed only the Gospel of Luke does Yeshua say "do this in remembrance of me" at the Communion meal. Paul wrote to the church at Corinth:

> 1Corinthians 11:24 (NAS95S) and when He had given thanks, He broke it and said, "This is My body, which is for you; do this in remembrance of Me." [25] In the same way *He took* the cup also after supper, saying, "This cup is the "ew covenant in My blood; do this, as often as you drink *it,* in remembrance of Me."

Paul said this because he was converting Mithras churches into Jesus' churches. The idea of a communion sacrament came from the Mithras religion. For centuries followers of Mithras had a sacrament where they ate the body of Mithras and drank his blood. The original meaning of Communion was lost to the emerging proto-orthodox church because they were based on Mithras and severed their relationship with Judaism. Since Mithras liturgy said that the followers must remember him, Paul had to introduce this concept to the new proto-orthodox churches.

How did Paul connect the consumption of the blood of Jesus to Judaism? Paul did attempt to connect the Mithras rituals to Jewish rituals. The drinking of blood was abhorrent and still is to Jews today. Paul could have used the blood covenants from the Hebrew Scriptures to justify his position. The story of Abraham and the smoking pot is a perfect example. The LORD told Abraham to cut three animals in half and to place them on the banks of a wadi (dry stream bed). Abraham was told to walk through the blood. Then he fell asleep and saw a smoking pot on a rod move through the blood. The LORD told him that one day He would walk through the blood. That story could easily be used to demonstrate that Yeshua had to walk in His own blood.

Thoughts

The time had come for Yeshua's disciples to decide. Were they going to follow the teaching of their Master and continue the mission of preaching repentance to the world? They had three years of instruction and an understanding of how Yeshua wanted the mission to be accomplished. However, they had not committed to the mission. At this Passover, Yeshua asked directly, "will you take on my mission?" He also told them that there would be a danger. By taking the bread and drinking from the cup, each disciple agreed to carry on the work of the mission. Unfortunately, there was one person there who was not going to follow the mission. Judas had the opportunity to lie to Yeshua one more time.

Reflections

The communion sacrament that the church developed centers around a person saying to Yeshua that he/she believes in the words and actions of Yeshua, even accepting Yeshua as God. The communion ritual is a restatement of one's beliefs. The true meaning of the event has been clouded by the church not understanding what the words and actions meant to the men in that room. Suppose the church emphasized that the Communion was an act of doing Yeshua's work, then perhaps the churches would be filled and prosperous. The mission is to tell people to repent for the Kingdom of Heaven is near. Once a person has repented, the blessings of the Kingdom of Heaven will become available.

MARK 14:26-31

Language

New American Standard 1995	Koine Greek
[26]After singing a hymn, they went out to the Mount of Olives. [27] And Jesus said to them, "You will all fall away, because it is written, 'I WILL STRIKE DOWN THE SHEPHERD, AND THE SHEEP SHALL BE SCATTERED.' [28] "But after I have been raised, I will go ahead of you to Galilee." [29] But Peter said to Him, "*Even* though all may fall away, yet I will not." [30] And Jesus said to him, "Truly I say to you, that this very night, before a rooster crows twice, you yourself will deny Me three times." [31] But *Peter* kept saying insistently, "*Even* if I have to die with You, I will not deny You!" And they all were saying the same thing also.	[26] Καὶ ὑμνήσαντες ἐξῆλθον εἰς τὸ ὄρος τῶν Ἐλαιῶν. [27] Καὶ λέγει αὐτοῖς ὁ Ἰησοῦς ὅτι Πάντες σκανδαλισθήσεσθε ἐν ἐμοὶ ἐν τῇ νυκτὶ ταύτῃ ὅτι γέγραπται, Πατάξω τὸν ποιμένα, καὶ διασκορπισθήσεται τὰ πρόβατα. [28] Ἀλλὰ μετὰ τὸ ἐγερθῆναί με, προάξω ὑμᾶς εἰς τὴν Γαλιλαίαν. [29] Ὁ δὲ Πέτρος ἔφη αὐτῷ, Καὶ εἰ πάντες σκανδαλισθήσονται, ἀλλ' οὐκ ἐγώ. [30] Καὶ λέγει αὐτῷ ὁ Ἰησοῦς, Ἀμὴν λέγω σοι, ὅτι σὺ σήμερον ἐν τῇ νυκτὶ ταύτῃ, πρὶν ἢ δὶς ἀλέκτορα φωνῆσαι, τρὶς ἀπαρνήσῃ με. [31] Ὁ δὲ ἐκπερισσοῦ ἔλεγεν μᾶλλον, Ἐάν με δέῃ συναποθανεῖν σοι, οὐ μή σε ἀπαρνήσωμαι. Ὡσαύτως δὲ καὶ πάντες ἔλεγον.

Process of Discovery

  Linguistics Section

   Linguistic Structure

[Transition] [26]After singing a hymn, they went out to the Mount of Olives

[Yeshua's Words] [27] And Jesus said to them, "You will all fall away, because it is written, 'I WILL STRIKE DOWN THE SHEPHERD, AND THE SHEEP SHALL BE SCATTERED.' [28] "But after I have been raised, I will go ahead of you to Galilee."

[Peter's Words] [29] But Peter said to Him, "*Even* though all may fall away, yet I will not."

[Yeshua's Words] [30] And Jesus said to him, "Truly I say to you, that this very night, before a rooster crows twice, you yourself will deny Me three times."

[Peter's Words] [31] But *Peter* kept saying insistently, "*Even* if I have to die with You, I will not deny You!" And they all were saying the same thing also.

Discussion

  This is a conversation between Yeshua and Peter.

Questioning the Passage

1. What do verses twenty-seven and twenty-eight mean?

Yeshua knew that the end of His life was coming. He showed His love for His disciples because He knew that their lives were in jeopardy. He decided to use the Scripture about the smitten shepherd (from Zech 13:7). When robbers slay a shepherd, the sheep scatter. The sheep need someone to lead them. Sheep can sense danger. Also, sheep can smell blood, and that agitates them. If their shepherd is killed and his blood spilled, they know they might be next. The sheep are at ease when they see the shepherd and his staff are in his hands. They need a leader.

Sheep are timid. They are easier frightened, especially when a stranger is present. The voice of their shepherd calms them, but the voice of a stranger terrifies them.[196]

When Yeshua was arrested, his disciples saw the danger to them and scattered. They did not want to be arrested and killed. After Yeshua was arrested, they scattered like sheep without a shepherd.

2. Why did Yeshua talk about a rooster crowing? (v. 35)

Clocks did not exist in Yeshua's time. How did people know when it was time to arise? When the sun rose in the east, the people knew it was morning. The stars at night told them when it was evening. The start of the day occurred when the rooster crowed. Roosters were in nearly every home. Chickens lived in the same room as people did. When the rooster crowed, people knew to wake up and go to work. In the Near East, when a priest failed to appear in the temple and laborers did not get to work immediately, like Americans blamed a faulty clock, Near Eastern people blamed the rooster.

Yeshua had no method to tell Peter exactly when his denials would occur. Therefore, Yeshua could not tell Peter exactly when his denials would be. Therefore, Yeshua used a generic time, the morning.

Thoughts

Yeshua told his disciples in the Garden of Gethsemane what would happen at His death. They were going to scatter. When Yeshua was arrested, they scattered. Yeshua makes it sound like a bad thing. However, when one contemplates the situation, is it not evident that they too would have been arrested and killed. If that happened, who would have brought us the Gospel message today? Perhaps it is necessary to scatter. The disciples did regroup after Yeshua's crucifixion. They gathered together in Jerusalem and pondered what was next. Then they saw the risen Christ, and they

---

[196] Rocco A. Errico and George M. Lamsa, *Aramaic Light on the Gospel of Matthew: a Commentary on the Teachings of Jesus from the Aramaic and Unchanged Near Eastern Customs* (Santa Fe, NM: Noohra Foundation, 2000).

reformed. The general feeling of the church today is that the disciples were cowards and should never have left Yeshua's side.

Reflections

There are times when an army fighting in a war has to retreat and regroup rather than be annihilated on the battlefield. How about I talk about something that does not entail death. There are times when a chess player knows that they must retreat their pieces to be placed on better squares or repel an attack from their opponent. It is better to retreat and keep the piece on the board than to sacrifice unnecessarily. Defensive play is essential to learn as much as offensive play. This narrative talks about defensive play. The plan of the Messiah had been disrupted. Perhaps the disciples knew that it would happen, and perhaps they did not. In either case, they retreated and regrouped.

MARK 14:32-42

Language

New American Standard 1995	Koine Greek
[32] They came to a place named Gethsemane; and He said to His disciples, "Sit here until I have prayed." [33] And He took with Him Peter and James and John, and began to be very distressed and troubled. [34] And He *said to them, "*My soul is deeply grieved to the point of death; remain here and keep watch." [35] And He went a little beyond *them,* and fell to the ground and *began* to pray that if it were possible, the hour might pass Him by. [36] And He was saying, "Abba! Father! All things are possible for You; remove this cup from Me; yet not what I will, but what You will." [37] And He came and found them sleeping, and said to Peter, "Simon, are you asleep? Could you not keep watch for one hour? [38] "Keep watching and praying that you may not come into temptation; the spirit is willing, but the flesh is weak." [39] Again He went away and prayed, saying the same words. [40] And again He came and found them sleeping, for their eyes were very heavy; and they did not know what to answer Him. [41] And He came the third time, and said to them, "*1*Are you still sleeping and resting? It is enough; *a*the hour has come; behold, the Son of Man is being betrayed into the hands of sinners. [42] "Get up, let us be going; behold, the one who betrays Me is at hand!"	[32] Καὶ ἔρχονται εἰς χωρίον οὗ τὸ ὄνομα Γεθσημανῆ καὶ λέγει τοῖς μαθηταῖς αὐτοῦ, Καθίσατε ὧδε, ἕως προσεύξωμαι. [33] Καὶ παραλαμβάνει τὸν Πέτρον καὶ Ἰάκωβον καὶ Ἰωάννην μεθ' ἑαυτοῦ, καὶ ἤρξατο ἐκθαμβεῖσθαι καὶ ἀδημονεῖν. [34] Καὶ λέγει αὐτοῖς, Περίλυπός ἐστιν ἡ ψυχή μου ἕως θανάτου μείνατε ὧδε καὶ γρηγορεῖτε. [35] Καὶ προσελθὼν μικρόν, ἔπεσεν ἐπὶ τῆς γῆς, καὶ προσηύχετο ἵνα, εἰ δυνατόν ἐστιν, παρέλθῃ ἀπ' αὐτοῦ ἡ ὥρα. [36] Καὶ ἔλεγεν, Ἀββᾶ, ὁ πατήρ, πάντα δυνατά σοι. Παρένεγκε τὸ ποτήριον ἀπ' ἐμοῦ τοῦτο ἀλλ' οὐ τί ἐγὼ θέλω, ἀλλὰ τί σύ. [37] Καὶ ἔρχεται καὶ εὑρίσκει αὐτοὺς καθεύδοντας, καὶ λέγει τῷ Πέτρῳ, Σίμων, καθεύδεις; Οὐκ ἴσχυσας μίαν ὥραν γρηγορῆσαι; [38] Γρηγορεῖτε καὶ προσεύχεσθε, ἵνα μὴ εἰσέλθητε εἰς πειρασμόν. Τὸ μὲν πνεῦμα πρόθυμον, ἡ δὲ σὰρξ ἀσθενής. [39] Καὶ πάλιν ἀπελθὼν προσηύξατο, τὸν αὐτὸν λόγον εἰπών. [40] Καὶ ὑποστρέψας εὗρεν αὐτοὺς πάλιν καθεύδοντας ἦσαν γὰρ οἱ ὀφθαλμοὶ αὐτῶν βεβαρημένοι, καὶ οὐκ ᾔδεισαν τί αὐτῷ ἀποκριθῶσιν. [41] Καὶ ἔρχεται τὸ τρίτον, καὶ λέγει αὐτοῖς, Καθεύδετε λοιπὸν καὶ ἀναπαύεσθε. Ἀπέχει ἦλθεν ἡ ὥρα ἰδού, παραδίδοται ὁ υἱὸς τοῦ ἀνθρώπου εἰς τὰς χεῖρας τῶν ἁμαρτωλῶν. [42] Ἐγείρεσθε, ἄγωμεν ἰδού, ὁ παραδιδούς με ἤγγικεν.

Process of Discovery

Linguistics Section

Linguistic Structure

A [32] They came to a place named Gethsemane; and He said to His disciples, "Sit here until I have prayed."

B [33] And He took with Him Peter and James and John, and began to be very distressed and troubled. [34] And He *said to them, ""My soul is deeply grieved to the point of death; remain here and keep watch."

C [35] And He went a little beyond *them,* and fell to the ground and *began* to pray that if it were possible, the hour might pass Him by. [36] And He was saying, "Abba! Father! All things are possible for You; remove this cup from Me; yet not what I will, but what You will."

D [37] And He came and found them sleeping, and said to Peter, "Simon, are you asleep? Could you not keep watch for one hour? [38] "Keep watching and praying that you may not come into temptation; the spirit is willing, but the flesh is weak."

C' [39] Again He went away and prayed, saying the same words. [40] And again He came and found them sleeping, for their eyes were very heavy; and they did not know what to answer Him.

B' [41] And He came the third time, and said to them, "'Are you still sleeping and resting? It is enough; "the hour has come; behold, the Son of Man is being betrayed into the hands of sinners.

A' [42] "Get up, let us be going; behold, the one who betrays Me is at hand!"

Discussion

This narrative has an A-B-C-D chiasm. The chiasm revolves around the center point of the flesh being weak. Yeshua was about to show how much the flesh could suffer for the LORD.

Questioning the Passage

1. What happened in the Garden of Gethsemane? (v. 32-42)

    Yeshua and His eleven disciples arrived in the garden. Yeshua decided to go deeper into the garden with Peter, James, and John. Yeshua agonized over what was about to happen. Yeshua's flesh (Nefesh) was protesting the thought of leaving this world. His Spirit (Ruach) knew what had to be done and that the LORD would raise him. There was a desire to live and not die. This decision was tough for Yeshua, whether to stay or flee.

    Prayer was the only consolation for such a time. Was Yeshua going to allow His body or his Spirit to win the fight? That is why he was in agony in the garden. His disciples were tired and exhausted from the work they did during the week and the physical climb from Jerusalem to the garden. It seems appropriate that they wanted to sleep. As Matthew tells the narrative, they did fall asleep during Yeshua's prayer time. It is not written why they needed to be awake for Yeshua beyond His requesting it.[197]

    Yeshua referred to drinking from a cup. It is a long-established custom that when one wishes to kill an enemy that he gives the enemy a banquet and a cup of poisoned wine. The guest to be killed is given the honor of the banquet. Once the victim appears to trust the host, the host gives him a cup of wine with poison. When wine is served, it is expected that everyone drinks. If the victim becomes suspicious of the chance of poisoning, he must kill his host or die.

---

[197] IBID.

Yeshua had the opportunity to either go with the authorities who were about to arrest Him and execute Him or flee quickly. Yeshua admonished His disciples to pray that they would not enter into temptation. They did not pray for the LORD to take the temptation away, but rather that they would conquer it. They needed the protection and strength of the LORD more than ever. Yeshua did not want to see them become like Judas.

The disciples' faith in Yeshua as their leader had been damaged. The grand entrance into Jerusalem did not happen. They believed that the Messiah would not die, and now Yeshua was talking about His death. In Yeshua's time, like today, many people hold onto their lives and consider it more precious than their religion. Yeshua wanted them to keep watch so that they might overcome their fear and come to understand what their leader was doing.

Yeshua's prayer in the garden was another temptation between life and death. The Ruach (Spirit) was ready to move on, but the Nefesh (flesh) was not. The Nefesh fought for its survival. Yeshua, as a human, wanted to live. Yeshua, as the Messiah Spirit, knew it was time to demonstrate the glory of the LORD.

Yeshua's Ruach believed that the cross was the only way to awaken humankind to end violence and learn to live in peace with each other. Humankind needed then and now to change their hearts to focus on the principles of the Kingdom of Heaven. It was difficult for Yeshua to surrender his life force because life is the most precious thing in this world. Yeshua knew that since he challenged the authorities of His day that He was to suffer the same fate that the prophets of the LORD faced centuries before Him.

2. Why did Yeshua accept that Judas was coming with guards to arrest Him? (v. 42) Yeshua had two choices, (1) Stay, (2) Run. He could have run off with the eleven disciples. The answer is in Yeshua's statement, which is verse forty-six. The agonizing between the Nefesh and Ruach was over. The Ruach won that internal battle. Therefore, it was time to let events happen.

Biblical Locations

1. Gethsemane

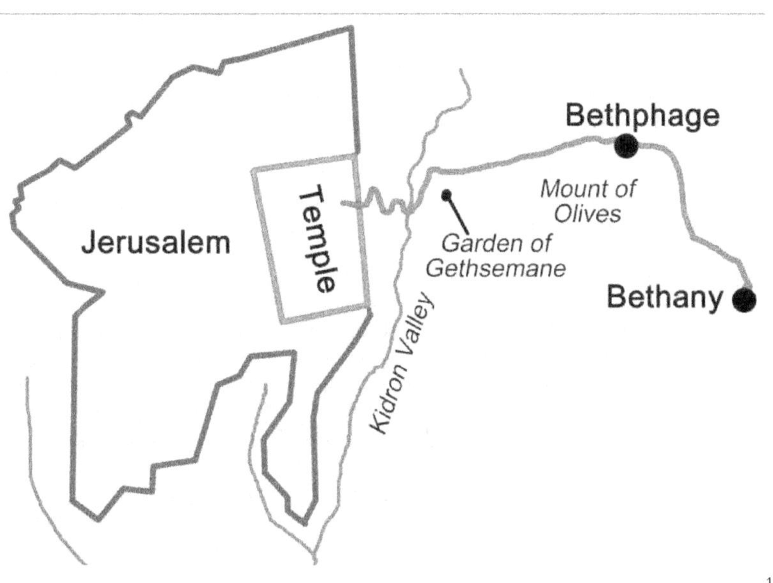

198

Culture Section

Discussion

When Yeshua came back to Peter, James and John, he caught them asleep. Yeshua addressed Peter as Simon, which was his name before his being commissioned by Yeshua. In verse thirty-one, Peter told Yeshua that he would never forsake him. Yeshua told him that he would. This screen is a foreshadowing of what was to happen.[199] Peter did forsake Yeshua. The flesh is weak and can overtake the desires of the soul. A problem for disciples even today is when the needs and wants of the flesh take over the soul.

---

[198] "Gethsemane," Gethsemane, accessed March 22, 2022, https://2.bp.blogspot.com/-RFYxRW5VQh0/Wq5Q3VRAfsI/AAAAAAAAAg8/J8kD6Zp3rkokbxsfo_IMzSiNkr7HpoOHQCLcBGAs/s1600/city%2Bof%2Bjerusalem%2Bmap.jpg.

[199] Ched Myers, *Binding the Strong Man a Political Reading of Mark's Story of Jesus* (Maryknoll, NY: Orbis Books, 1988).

Thoughts

The final struggle for Yeshua was between life and death. The body did not want to let go of life. That is normal for everyone who is alive. A person rarely wishes to die. There may be reasons for a person wanting death, but it is rare. In Yeshua's case, His body wanted to live. His Spirit knew that it was time to return to the LORD. It looked toward Easter morning. It caused pain to Yeshua. He prayed about the situation three times until He gave into the direction of the LORD.

Reflections

Yeshua gave up His very life for the LORD's plans. Ask yourself, what are you willing to give up for Yeshua. One area that church people do not want to hear about is a sermon about tithing. People like to keep their money as much as they like keeping their lives. Since Yeshua gave His life to bring us the message of how to attain eternal life in Heaven, should not His followers be willing to give something back to the LORD without complaining or trying to cheat it? The money situation is an example of what Yeshua went through, except that Yeshua gave up what He wanted, his life, to stay true to the LORD. Next time you contemplate your tithing, is your giving to the LORD what He asks for, thus emulating what Yeshua did.

MARK 14:43-52

Language

New American Standard 1995	Koine Greek
[43] Immediately while He was still speaking, Judas, one of the twelve, came up accompanied by a crowd with swords and clubs, *who were* from the chief priests and the scribes and the elders. [44] Now he who was betraying Him had given them a signal, saying, "Whomever I kiss, He is the one; seize Him and lead Him away under guard." [45] After coming, Judas immediately went to Him, saying, "*"Rabbi!"* and kissed Him. [46] They laid hands on Him and seized Him. [47] But one of those who stood by drew his sword, and struck the slave of the high priest and cut off his ear. [48] And Jesus said to them, "Have you come out with swords and clubs to arrest Me, as *you would* against a robber? [49] "Every day I was with you *a*in the temple teaching, and you did not seize Me; but *this has taken place* to fulfill the Scriptures." [50] And they all left Him and fled. [51] A young man was following Him, wearing *nothing but* a linen sheet over *his* naked *body;* and they seized him. [52] But he pulled free of the linen sheet and escaped naked.	[43] Καὶ εὐθέως, ἔτι αὐτοῦ λαλοῦντος, παραγίνεται Ἰούδας, εἷς ὢν τῶν δώδεκα, καὶ μετ' αὐτοῦ ὄχλος πολὺς μετὰ μαχαιρῶν καὶ ξύλων, παρὰ τῶν ἀρχιερέων καὶ τῶν γραμματέων καὶ τῶν πρεσβυτέρων. [44] Δεδώκει δὲ ὁ παραδιδοὺς αὐτὸν σύσσημον αὐτοῖς, λέγων, Ὃν ἂν φιλήσω, αὐτός ἐστιν κρατήσατε αὐτόν, καὶ ἀπαγάγετε ἀσφαλῶς. [45] Καὶ ἐλθών, εὐθέως προσελθὼν αὐτῷ λέγει αὐτῷ, Ραββί, ῥαββὶ καὶ κατεφίλησεν αὐτόν. [46] Οἱ δὲ ἐπέβαλον ἐπ' αὐτὸν τὰς χεῖρας αὐτῶν, καὶ ἐκράτησαν αὐτόν. [47] Εἷς δέ τις τῶν παρεστηκότων σπασάμενος τὴν μάχαιραν ἔπαισεν τὸν δοῦλον τοῦ ἀρχιερέως, καὶ ἀφεῖλεν αὐτοῦ τὸ ὠτίον. [48] Καὶ ἀποκριθεὶς ὁ Ἰησοῦς εἶπεν αὐτοῖς, Ὡς ἐπὶ λῃστὴν ἐξήλθετε μετὰ μαχαιρῶν καὶ ξύλων συλλαβεῖν με; [49] Καθ' ἡμέραν ἤμην πρὸς ὑμᾶς ἐν τῷ ἱερῷ διδάσκων, καὶ οὐκ ἐκρατήσατέ με ἀλλ' ἵνα πληρωθῶσιν αἱ γραφαί. [50] Καὶ ἀφέντες αὐτὸν πάντες ἔφυγον. [51] Καὶ εἷς τις νεανίσκος ἠκολούθησεν αὐτῷ, περιβεβλημένος σινδόνα ἐπὶ γυμνοῦ. Καὶ κρατοῦσιν αὐτὸν οἱ νεανίσκοι [52] ὁ δὲ καταλιπὼν τὴν σινδόνα γυμνὸς ἔφυγεν ἀπ' αὐτῶν.

Process of Discovery

Linguistics Section

Linguistic Structure

[The betrayal] [43] Immediately while He was still speaking, Judas, one of the twelve, came up accompanied by a crowd with swords and clubs, *who were* from the chief priests and the scribes and the elders.

[Judas' betrayal] [44] Now he who was betraying Him had given them a signal, saying, "Whomever I kiss, He is the one; seize Him and lead Him away under guard." [45] After coming, Judas immediately went to Him, saying, "*"Rabbi!*" and kissed Him. [46] They laid hands on Him and seized Him.

[Reaction to the betrayal] [47] But one of those who stood by drew his sword, and struck the slave of the high priest and cut off his ear.

[Jesus' words] [48] And Jesus said to them, "Have you come out with swords and clubs to arrest Me, as *you would* against a robber? [49] "Every day I was with you *"in the temple teaching, and you did not seize Me; but *this has taken place* to fulfill the Scriptures."

[Disciples' reaction] [50] And they all left Him and fled.

[Cameo] [51] A young man was following Him, wearing *nothing but* a linen sheet over *his* naked *body;* and they seized him. [52] But he pulled free of the linen sheet and escaped naked.

Discussion

Yeshua's arrest turns Passion Week from lessons about the Messiah to lessons about the world's evil. On Easter Sunday, the Messiah proves that His words were divine truths, and the teaching about the Spiritual world continued.

Questioning the Passage

1. Why did Yeshua stop the disciple who pulled out his sword? (v. 47)

   It can be considered an axiom from the Hebrew Scriptures that when a person uses a sword, they die by the sword. Using force is a double-edged sword. For the moment, using the sword may bring victory, but in the long run, it brings death.

2. What did Yeshua teach in Gethsemane? (v. 43-51)

   Yeshua taught:

   a. The way of non-violence, non-retaliation, and love for enemies is to be pursued to the end.

   b. Yeshua did not put up a struggle when arrested. He kept calm and did not react negatively.

   c. The Scripture must be fulfilled even though it meant that He had to die.

3. Who was the young man in verses fifty to fifty-two?

   There are several interpretations of this cameo appearance. One idea is that Gethsemane was a public park. Poor people who do not have housing, like travelers to Jerusalem, would sleep in the park. This person fleed from the guards because he did not want to be implicated with Yeshua and his men. Since Mark's author did not identify the young man, it is difficult to determine an exact purpose for this cameo.

   However, there is a possible connection between the young man in the Garden and the young man at Yeshua's tomb. Ched Meyers, in his book "Binding the strong Man," offers the following idea. The young man in the Garden symbolizes the discipleship community who fled from Yeshua. His nake escape is indicative of shame. The linen cloth foretells the linen cloth that covered Yeshua's body when he died. The first young man symbolizes "saving life and losing it." The second one is "losing life to save it."[200]

---

[200] Ched Myers, *Binding the Strong Man a Political Reading of Mark's Story of Jesus* (Maryknoll, NY: Orbis Books, 1988).

Culture Section

Questioning the passage

1. What was the custom of Yeshua's day about a kiss? (v. 50)

   The custom of men kissing each other was a natural act in the Near East. When two men greeted each other, the one of lower social status would kiss his superior's hand. The superior man kissed his friend on the cheek. Judas employed this ancient custom to point out Yeshua to the guards. Judas degraded the custom because he used the custom of friendship to betray Yeshua. In verse fifty, Yeshua said, "friend…" He used this language because the kiss was only used between male friends. Judas was not only betraying Yeshua; he betrayed the customs of his day.[201]

2. What was the custom of carrying a sword? (v. 47)

   In Matthew's Gospel, it is not identified who drew the sword. What was drawn was a long knife that was used to chop up wood and to prepare food. Each of the disciples would have had such a blade with them.

3. Why did Yeshua not want resistance to his arrest?

   Yeshua's prayers convinced his Nefesh (flesh) that the Will of the LORD must be fulfilled. He knew that it was important for the Messiah to die on the cross so that He could reveal the hidden truths in the Jewish religion to the world. By Yeshua dying on the cross, He proved to the world that his words and methods were of a divine nature.[202]

Thoughts

How many times have you contemplated striking someone? When you are driving and another car cuts you off, do you feel like getting even? It is challenging to be wronged and not want some kind of restitution, especially when the person who did the act will not apologize. The call to violence

---

[201] Rocco A. Errico and George M. Lamsa, *Aramaic Light on the Gospel of Matthew: a Commentary on the Teachings of Jesus from the Aramaic and Unchanged Near Eastern Customs* (Santa Fe, NM: Noohra Foundation, 2000).
[202] IBID.

seems to be a part of our nature. In the wild, animals survive by their fight or flee instinct. Humans still have this instinct. So when provoked, a person either fights or flees. Yeshua showed a third option. That option was to go along with the will of the people who came to get him. He did not react to the situation. The next time you have a fight or flee the situation, contemplate what would happen if you did nothing.

Reflections

The disciple who pulled out his knife wanted to protect His Rabbi. The eleven disciples in the Garden with Yeshua knew what was happening. Judas led the group in order to point out Yeshua. Messianic tradition says that the Messiah is not supposed to die. The group that was approaching them was interested in grabbing Yeshua so that he could be killed. The reaction of pulling out the knife makes perfect sense. Yeshua must have surprised them when he said that an insurrection was not going to happen. It should have shocked the guards that grabbed Yeshua. The supposed leader of the insurrection told his disciples that an armed revolution was not going to occur. However, the guards were under orders and obeyed them to bring Yeshua in.

MARK 14:53-72

Language

New American Standard 1995	Koine Greek
53 They led Jesus away to the high priest; and all the chief priests and the elders and the scribes gathered together. **54** Peter had followed Him at a distance, right into the courtyard of the high priest; and he was sitting with the officers and warming himself at the fire. **55** Now the chief priests and the whole Council kept trying to obtain testimony against Jesus to put Him to death, and they were not finding any. **56** For many were giving false testimony against Him, but their testimony was not consistent. **57** Some stood up and *began* to give false testimony against Him, saying, **58** "We heard Him say, 'I will destroy this temple made with hands, and in three days I will build another made without hands.'" **59** Not even in this respect was their testimony consistent. **60** The high priest stood up *and came* forward and questioned Jesus, saying, "Do You not answer? ¹What is it that these men are testifying against You?" **61** But He kept silent and did not answer. Again the high priest was questioning Him, and saying to Him, "Are You the Christ, the Son of the Blessed *One?*" **62** And Jesus said, "I am; and you shall see THE SON OF MAN SITTING AT THE RIGHT HAND OF POWER, and COMING WITH THE CLOUDS OF HEAVEN." **63** Tearing his clothes, the high priest said, "What further need do we have of witnesses? **64** "You have heard the blasphemy; how does it seem to you?" And they all condemned Him to be deserving of death. **65** Some began to spit at Him, and to blindfold Him, and to beat Him with their fists, and to say to Him, "Prophesy!" And the officers received Him with slaps *in the face.* **66** As Peter was below in the courtyard, one of the servant-girls of the high priest came, **67** and seeing Peter warming himself, she looked at him and said, "You also were with Jesus the Nazarene." **68** But he denied	**53** Καὶ ἀπήγαγον τὸν Ἰησοῦν πρὸς τὸν ἀρχιερέα καὶ συνέρχονται αὐτῷ πάντες οἱ ἀρχιερεῖς καὶ οἱ πρεσβύτεροι καὶ οἱ γραμματεῖς. **54** Καὶ ὁ Πέτρος ἀπὸ μακρόθεν ἠκολούθησεν αὐτῷ ἕως ἔσω εἰς τὴν αὐλὴν τοῦ ἀρχιερέως καὶ ἦν συγκαθήμενος μετὰ τῶν ὑπηρετῶν, καὶ θερμαινόμενος πρὸς τὸ φῶς. **55** Οἱ δὲ ἀρχιερεῖς καὶ ὅλον τὸ συνέδριον ἐζήτουν κατὰ τοῦ Ἰησοῦ μαρτυρίαν, εἰς τὸ θανατῶσαι αὐτόν καὶ οὐχ εὕρισκον. **56** Πολλοὶ γὰρ ἐψευδομαρτύρουν κατ' αὐτοῦ, καὶ ἴσαι αἱ μαρτυρίαι οὐκ ἦσαν. **57** Καὶ τινες ἀναστάντες ἐψευδομαρτύρουν κατ' αὐτοῦ, λέγοντες **58** ὅτι Ἡμεῖς ἠκούσαμεν αὐτοῦ λέγοντος ὅτι Ἐγὼ καταλύσω τὸν ναὸν τοῦτον τὸν χειροποίητον, καὶ διὰ τριῶν ἡμερῶν ἄλλον ἀχειροποίητον οἰκοδομήσω. **59** Καὶ οὐδὲ οὕτως ἴση ἦν ἡ μαρτυρία αὐτῶν. **60** Καὶ ἀναστὰς ὁ ἀρχιερευς εἰς μέσον ἐπηρώτησεν τὸν Ἰησοῦν, λέγων, Οὐκ ἀποκρίνῃ οὐδέν; Τί οὗτοί σου καταμαρτυροῦσιν; **61** Ὁ δὲ ἐσιώπα, καὶ οὐδὲν ἀπεκρίνατο. Πάλιν ὁ ἀρχιερευς ἐπηρώτα αὐτόν, καὶ λέγει αὐτῷ, Σὺ εἶ ὁ χριστός; Ὁ υἱὸς τοῦ εὐλογητοῦ; **62** Ὁ δὲ Ἰησοῦς εἶπεν, Ἐγώ εἰμι. Καὶ ὄψεσθε τὸν υἱὸν τοῦ ἀνθρώπου ἐκ δεξιῶν καθήμενον τῆς δυνάμεως, καὶ ἐρχόμενον μετὰ τῶν νεφελῶν τοῦ οὐρανοῦ. **63** Ὁ δὲ ἀρχιερευς διαρρήξας τοὺς χιτῶνας αὐτοῦ λέγει, Τί ἔτι χρειαν ἔχομεν μαρτυρων; **64** Ἠκούσατε τῆς βλασφημίας τί ὑμῖν φαίνεται; Οἱ δὲ πάντες κατέκριναν αὐτὸν εἶναι ἔνοχον θανάτου. **65** Καὶ ἤρξαντο τινες ἐμπτύειν αὐτῷ, καὶ περικαλύπτειν τὸ πρόσωπον αὐτοῦ, καὶ κολαφίζειν αὐτόν, καὶ λέγειν αὐτῷ, Προφήτευσον καὶ οἱ ὑπηρέται ῥαπίσμασιν αὐτὸν ⸆ ἔβαλλον. ⸆ **66** Καὶ ὄντος τοῦ Πέτρου ἐν τῇ αὐλῇ κάτω, ἔρχεται μία τῶν παιδισκῶν τοῦ ἀρχιερέως, **67** καὶ ἰδοῦσα τὸν Πέτρον θερμαινόμενον, ἐμβλέψασα αὐτῷ λέγει, Καὶ σὺ μετὰ τοῦ Ναζαρηνοῦ Ἰησοῦ ἦσθα. **68**

it, saying, "I neither know nor understand what you are talking about." And he went out onto the porch.[2] 69 The servant-girl saw him, and began once more to say to the bystanders, "This is *one* of them!" 70 But again he denied it. And after a little while the bystanders were again saying to Peter, "Surely you are *one* of them, for you are a Galilean too." 71 But he began to curse and swear, "I do not know this man you are talking about!" 72 Immediately a rooster crowed a second time. And Peter remembered how Jesus had made the remark to him, "Before a rooster crows twice, you will deny Me three times." And he began to weep.	Ὁ δὲ ἠρνήσατο, λέγων, Οὐκ οἶδα, ⸀ οὐδὲ ⸀ ἐπίσταμαι τι σὺ λέγεις. Καὶ ἐξῆλθεν ἔξω εἰς τὸ προαύλιον καὶ ἀλέκτωρ ἐφώνησεν. 69 Καὶ ἡ παιδίσκη ἰδοῦσα αὐτὸν πάλιν ἤρξατο λέγειν τοῖς παρεστηκόσιν ὅτι Οὗτος ἐξ αὐτῶν ἐστίν. 70 Ὁ δὲ πάλιν ἠρνεῖτο. Καὶ μετὰ μικρὸν πάλιν οἱ παρεστῶτες ἔλεγον τῷ Πέτρῳ, Ἀληθῶς ἐξ αὐτῶν εἶ· καὶ γὰρ Γαλιλαῖος εἶ, καὶ ἡ λαλιά σου ὁμοιάζει. 71 Ὁ δὲ ἤρξατο ἀναθεματίζειν καὶ ὀμνύναι ὅτι Οὐκ οἶδα τὸν ἄνθρωπον τοῦτον ὃν λέγετε. 72 Καὶ ἐκ δευτέρου ἀλέκτωρ ἐφώνησεν. Καὶ ἀνεμνήσθη ὁ Πέτρος τὸ ῥῆμα ὃ εἶπεν αὐτῷ ὁ Ἰησοῦς ὅτι Πρὶν ἀλέκτορα φωνῆσαι δίς, ἀπαρνήσῃ με τρίς. Καὶ ἐπιβαλὼν ἔκλαιεν.

Process of Discovery

Linguistics Section

Linguistic Structure

A [53] They led Jesus away to the high priest; and all the chief priests and the elders and the scribes gathered together. [54] Peter had followed Him at a distance, right into the courtyard of the high priest; and he was sitting with the officers and warming himself at the fire.

> **B** [55] Now the chief priests and the whole Council kept trying to obtain testimony against Jesus to put Him to death, and they were not finding any. [56] For many were giving false testimony against Him, but their testimony was not consistent.

> > **C** [57] Some stood up and *began* to give false testimony against Him, saying, [58] "We heard Him say, 'I will destroy this temple made with hands, and in three days I will build another made without hands.'" [59] Not even in this respect was their testimony consistent.

> > > **D** [60] The high priest stood up *and came* forward and questioned Jesus, saying, "Do You not answer? ¹What is it that these men are testifying against You?"

> > > > **E** [61] But He kept silent and did not answer.

> > > **D'** Again the high priest was questioning Him, and saying to Him, "Are You the Christ, the Son of the Blessed *One?*"

> > **C'** [62] And Jesus said, "I am; and you shall see THE SON OF MAN SITTING AT THE RIGHT HAND OF POWER, and COMING WITH THE CLOUDS OF HEAVEN."

> **B'** [63] Tearing his clothes, the high priest said, "What further need do we have of witnesses? [64] "You have heard the blasphemy; how does it seem to you?" And they all condemned Him to be deserving of death.

A' [65] Some began to spit at Him, and to blindfold Him, and to beat Him with their fists, and to say to Him, "Prophesy!" And the officers received Him with slaps *in the face.*

[Peter's Denial] [66] As Peter was below in the courtyard, one of the servant-girls of the high priest came, [67] and seeing Peter warming himself, she looked at him and said, "You also were with Jesus the Nazarene." [68] But he denied *it,* saying, "I neither know nor understand what you are talking about." And he went out onto the porch.[2]

[Peter's Second Denial] [69] The servant-girl saw him, and began once more to say to the bystanders, "This is *one* of them!" [70] But again he denied it.

[Peter's Third Denial] And after a little while the bystanders were again saying to Peter, "Surely you are *one* of them, for you are a Galilean too." [71] But he began to curse and swear, "I do not know this man you are talking about!"

[Rooster] [72] Immediately a rooster crowed a second time. And Peter remembered how Jesus had made the remark to him, "Before a rooster crows twice, you will deny Me three times." And he began to weep.

Discussion

This narrative consists of a deep chiasm followed by Peter's three denials of Yeshua.

Questioning the Passage
1. Why did the Sanhedrin not find any testimony that would convict Yeshua? (v. 55)
   Yeshua was arrested as a revolutionary, as demonstrated in the previous passage's analysis. The witnesses that came before the Sanhedrin did not offer any information that proved this. The testimony that was offered did not coincide with each other.

2. What is the difference in the testimony of the "two" who came forward? (v. 58-59)
   The two persons who came forward did not offer a witness that Yeshua was a revolutionary. However, they did offer testimony that Yeshua could have been blaspheming. That offense was punishable under the death penalty. If the Sanhedrin's main objective was to dispose of Yeshua's influence by His death, the offense had to be sufficient enough for the death penalty.

3. Why was Yeshua silent when the High Priest spoke to Him? (v. 62)

    Yeshua took on the same attitude that He held in the Garden when He was arrested. He was a man of peace and refused to instigate any adverse reactions.

4. What did it mean that Caiaphas tore his clothing? (v. 63)

    A witness told the Sanhedrin that Yeshua spoke about destroying the Temple in Jerusalem and rebuilding it in three days. The people in Jerusalem took Yeshua's words literally. His statement was not literal but figurative. The tearing of clothing is a response to death; thus, it was an expression of sorrow. Modern Jews still do this today. However, in Yeshua's day, the tearing of clothing also was done as a ritualistic expression of indignation against the words of a blasphemer. Caiaphas decided that Yeshua's words about the Temple was blasphemy and tore his clothing.

    In Leviticus 10:6 it is written:

    > [6] Then Moses said to Aaron and to his sons Eleazar and Ithamar, "Do not uncover your heads nor tear your clothes, so that you will not die and that He will not become wrathful against all the congregation.

    And in Leviticus 11:10 it is written:

    > [10] The priest who is the highest among his brothers, on whose head the anointing oil has been poured and who has been consecrated to wear the garments, shall not uncover his head nor tear his clothes;

    The author of Mark's Gospel has the High Priest violating the Torah when he condemned Yeshua to death. Why would the author do this? The author must have wanted to show the reader that Yeshua's death sentence was against the Laws of the LORD. Therefore, Yeshua was killed for purely political reasons. The High Priest did the same thing that the Kings of Israel and Judea and done for centuries. They killed the messengers from the LORD because they did not like the message that the LORD sent them.[203]

---

[203] Rocco A. Errico and George M. Lamsa, *Aramaic Light on the Gospel of Matthew: a Commentary on the Teachings of Jesus from the Aramaic and Unchanged Near Eastern Customs* (Santa Fe, NM: Noohra Foundation, 2000).

5. Why did people spit in Yeshua's face? (v. 65)

   This act was a sign of mockery.

6. Why was Yeshua asked who hit Him? (v. 65)

   The theory is that Mark's Gospel is based on Mark's Gospel. In Mark's Gospel, Yeshua is blindfolded when He was struck. In that situation, the question of who is striking makes sense. In Mark's narrative, Yeshua is not blindfolded. Therefore, verse 67 does not belong in the narrative. The author and editors never caught this contradiction, or they would have removed the verse. The statement about prophecy does say that the members of the Sanhedrin did not believe that Yeshua had prophetic powers.[204]

7. Why did Peter deny knowing Yeshua three times?

   The author of Mark's Gospel liked writing events in triads. Peter's denial of Yeshua is in a triad – he did it three times. Yeshua prayed three times in Gethsemane. Peter fell asleep three times in Gethsemane. Yeshua stood firm before Ciaphas three times. Did Peter deny knowing Yeshua three times? It is possible, but since the author likes triads, Peter could have denied Yeshua once. However, it was written three times to maintain the structure of the entire Gospel.

8. If there a significance to Peter's denial of two servant girls and one unknown person?

   According to the Jesus Seminar, the denial of Peter was added to the Gospels because of a dispute over who was the true leader of the new Christian movement. In Paul's letter to the Galatians, he wrote that he and Peter were at odds over who was the real leader of the movement. In the Gospel of Thomas (12:2), we learn that James the Just was the leader of the Jerusalem movement, not Peter.

   Having the denial before two servant girls and one unknown person demonstrated Peter's inability to lead. The leader of the Christian movement had to be a person of firm conviction. Having this narrative of Peter's three denials shows that he should not be the

---

[204] Leander K. Keck, *The NEW INTERPRETER'S BIBLE VOLUME VIII* (Nashville, TN: ABINGDON, 1995).

leader. A true leader of the new movement would have stood firm in his resolution that he was the leader. Instead, Peter shirked that responsibility. The church had a narrative placed into the Gospels that proved that Paul and James were the true leaders of the church. Politics at work as the new movement commenced.[205]

9. What was the Sanhedrin?

"Sanhedrin, also spelled Sanhedrin, any of several official Jewish councils in Palestine under Roman rule, to which various political, religious, and judicial functions have been attributed. Taken from the Greek word for council (synedrion), the term was apparently applied to various bodies but became especially the designation for the supreme Jewish legislative and judicial court—the Great Sanhedrin, or simply the Sanhedrin, in Jerusalem. There were also local or provincial sanhedrins of lesser jurisdiction and authority. A council of elders, or senate, called the gerousia, which existed under Persian and Syrian rule (333–165 BC), is considered by some scholars the forerunner of the Great Sanhedrin."[206]

Verse Comparison of citations or proof text

1. [62] And Jesus said, "I am; and you shall see THE SON OF MAN SITTING AT THE RIGHT HAND OF POWER, and COMING WITH THE CLOUDS OF HEAVEN."

   Psalms 110:1 (NAS95S) The LORD says to my Lord: "Sit at My right hand until I make Your enemies a footstool for Your feet."

   Daniel 7:13 "I kept looking in the night visions, And behold, with the clouds of heaven One like a Son of Man was coming, And He came up to the Ancient of Days and was presented before Him

---

205 Robert Walter Funk and Roy W. Hoover, *The Five Gospels: the Search for the Authentic Words of Jesus: New Translation and Commentary* (San Francisco, CA: Harper San Francisco, 2007).
206 The Editors of Encyclopaedia Britannica, "Sanhedrin," Encyclopædia Britannica (Encyclopædia Britannica, inc., September 30, 2008), https://www.britannica.com/topic/sanhedrin. Accessed 9/22/2020.

This verse is an eschatological statement that Yeshua made before the Sanhedrin. He told them that they had the power at that point in time to falsely convict him of a crime that he did not commit. Nevertheless, on judgment day that He would return and judge them for their injustices.

Biblical Personalities

1. "CAIAPHAS, JOSEPH, high priest (18–36 C.E.) at the time of Jesus' activity and crucifixion. Caiaphas was mentioned by Josephus Flavius (Ant. 18:35:95) and in the New Testament (Matt. 26:3, 57; Luke 3:2; John 11:49; 18:13–14, 24, 28; Acts 4:6), Caiaphas was appointed by the procurator Valerius Gratus to succeed *Simeon b. Kimḥit. He served in office throughout the administration of Gratus' successor, *Pontius Pilate (26–36), and was deposed the same year as Pilate by Vitellius, governor of Syria. Jonathan b. Ḥanan was appointed to replace him. Historical sources indicate the influential priestly background of Joseph Caiaphas: he was the son-in-law of *Anan son of Seth, a member of a powerful and important priestly family in Jerusalem (John 18:13); the Mishnah (Par. 3:5) speaks of a high priest named Elioeneiai (*Elionaeus) b. ha-Kayyaf (ha-Kof), who may have been a son of Joseph Caiaphas; and the Tosefta (Yev. 1:10) mentions the House of Kaipha as a high-priestly family. Although Caiaphas was high priest at the time of Jesus' arrest, he does not seem to have played a major role in the matter. Jesus was first taken to the house of Anan b. Seth (John 18:12–13), only later being brought to Caiaphas (Matt. 26:57; John 18:24), who is reported as having said: "It is better for you that one man die for the nation than that the entire nation be lost" (John 11:49–51; 18:14; the quotation is adapted from a rabbinic statement, cf. Gen. R. 94:9). In 1990 a rockhewn burial chamber was uncovered by Z. Greenhut to the south of Jerusalem and within it was a stone box containing bones (ossuary) bearing the Aramaic inscription "Yehosef bar (son of) Qafa (Caiapha)." It is assumed that this tomb belonged to the family of the High Priest Caiaphas."[207]

---

[207] "Joseph Caiaphas," Caiaphas, Joseph, accessed September 22, 2020, https://www.jewishvirtuallibrary.org/caiaphas-joseph.

Culture Section

Discussion

The people of Jerusalem would have known very little about Yeshua and His teachings and doctrines. Yeshua spent His time in the Galilee and the lands surrounding that territory. The Sanhedrin did not have information about Yeshua, and that caused them to misinterpret and misunderstand what Yeshua's ministry was all about. They were sure that Yeshua was a revolutionary that wanted to start a revolt against Rome. That was a false understanding of Yeshua's purpose; however, it was the only one they had. Therefore, the Sanhedrin moved forward on that premise. They ran into a problem when the witnesses that initially came forward had differing stories. The next best conviction that required the death penalty was blasphemy.

The Galilee was close to the borders of Syria and the Decapolis. These areas were filled with pagan worshipers. Therefore, the Sanhedrin interpreted everything that Yeshua spoke about as a pagan influenced religion. History showed that pagan thoughts and ideas were continually bombarding the Hebrew people. The memory of King Ahab and Jezebel was fresh in their collective memories. They did not want that problem to emerge. Therefore, they were cautious and mistrusting anyone who offered a different interpretation or feelings about their religious institutions.

Questioning the passage

1. Why was Yeshua asked if he was the "Son of the blessed one?" (v. 61)

   The Son of the blessed one is Mark's author's way of saying "Son of God." The "Son of God" is a title of honor and distinction. When men of rank and nobility are addressed according to their social standing and status, they were addressed as "my lord." Religious men who were honored by the people were called "rabbi" or "father." The ordinary peasant on the street was called "a son of man." Yeshua used the term "son of man" to describe himself. This was the calling of a peasant. Yeshua was a Galilean and could not easily assert that he was royal or connected to a priestly lineage. The people of Judea, especially in Jerusalem, did not feel that the people from the Galilee amounted to much. The Judeans were snobbish toward the Jews in Galilee. Yeshua called Himself a son of man more times than a son of God. When Yeshua was asked if He was the Son of God, he did not answer.[208]

2. What does "coming in the clouds of heaven" mean? (v. 62)

    This phrase meant that the people would see Yeshua's mission succeed with great honor.

3. What does "sitting at the right hand of God mean? (v. 62)

    This phrase means that the people would see that the LORD was backing Yeshua in His mission and ministry.

Thoughts

The idea that the newly forming church could influence the authors of the Gospel may have been changed or added later is difficult to accept. However, scholars have demonstrated other places in the New Testament writings where this was done. What Peter's denial says is that politics entered the church even before it became known as the church. Whenever a group of people is brought together to form a great organization that politics will be there to tear it asunder. James was leading in Jerusalem while Paul was in Asia Minor. Peter was not leading anyone. Oddly, Peter becomes known as the first bishop, thus acknowledging Peter as the true leader of the church. The bottom line is a demonstration that the politics of the church will hurt the church. Oh my, is that not a problem today?

Reflections

Yeshua stood his ground and to His conviction. When He was arrested, He said nothing. He went willingly with the guards knowing that He was facing execution. In front of Caiaphas, he was quiet about His situation. Yeshua walked the walk and talked the talk. To the very end, He allowed the LORD's will to be "in charge" of Him. The Sanhedrin could not convict Him as a revolutionary, so

---

[208] Rocco A. Errico and George M. Lamsa, *Aramaic Light on the Gospel of Mark: a Commentary on the Teachings of Jesus from the Aramaic and Unchanged Near Eastern Customs* (Santa Fe, NM: Noohra Foundation, 2000).

they had to develop some other trumped upcharge. Blasphemy was no doubt the easiest to accuse Yeshua of and the one that needed the least amount of credible facts.

MARK 15:1-5

Language

New American Standard 1995	Koine Greek
[1] Early in the morning the chief priests with the elders and scribes and the whole Council, immediately held a consultation; and binding Jesus, they led Him away and delivered Him to Pilate. [2] Pilate questioned Him, "Are You the King of the Jews?" And He answered him, *"It is as you say."* [3] The chief priests *began* to accuse Him harshly. [4] Then Pilate questioned Him again, saying, "Do You not answer? See how many charges they bring against You!" [5] But Jesus made no further answer; so Pilate was amazed.	[1] Καὶ εὐθέως ἐπὶ τὸ πρωῒ συμβούλιον ποιήσαντες οἱ ἀρχιερεῖς μετὰ τῶν πρεσβυτέρων καὶ γραμματέων, καὶ ὅλον τὸ συνέδριον, δήσαντες τὸν Ἰησοῦν ἀπήνεγκαν καὶ παρέδωκαν τῷ Πιλάτῳ. [2] Καὶ ἐπηρώτησεν αὐτὸν ὁ Πιλάτος, Σὺ εἶ ὁ βασιλεὺς τῶν Ἰουδαίων; Ὁ δὲ ἀποκριθεὶς εἶπεν αὐτῷ, Σὺ λέγεις. [3] Καὶ κατηγόρουν αὐτοῦ οἱ ἀρχιερεῖς πολλά [4] ὁ δὲ Πιλάτος πάλιν ἐπηρώτησεν αὐτόν, λέγων, Οὐκ ἀποκρίνῃ οὐδέν; Ἴδε, πόσα σου καταμαρτυροῦσιν. [5] Ὁ δὲ Ἰησοῦς οὐκέτι οὐδὲν ἀπεκρίθη, ὥστε θαυμάζειν τὸν Πιλάτον.

Process of Discovery

Linguistics Section

Linguistic Structure

[Yeshua sent to Pilate] [1] Early in the morning the chief priests with the elders and scribes and the whole Council, immediately held a consultation; and binding Jesus, they led Him away and delivered Him to Pilate. [2] Pilate questioned Him, "Are You the King of the Jews?" And He answered him, "*It is as* you say." [3] The chief priests *began* to accuse Him harshly. [4] Then Pilate questioned Him again, saying, "Do You not answer? See how many charges they bring against You!" [5] But Jesus made no further answer; so Pilate was amazed.

Discussion

This narrative starts with the transition verse that Yeshua was taken to Pilate. It then focuses on Judas returning the silver and the purchase of the Potter's Field.

Questioning the Passage

1. Why was Yeshua taken to Pilate? (v. 1-2)

   The Romans gave ecclesiastical authority to the High Priest and the Sanhedrin. They condemned Yeshua to death for religious reasons. However, they could not execute Him. The death penalty could only be authorized by Pilate, the Roman governor of the province. Therefore, the Sanhedrin had to send Yeshua to Pilate.

Biblical Personalities

1. Pontius Pilate was the prefect of Judea from 18 to 36 CE. He was the judge at Yeshua's trial after the Sanhedrin condemned Him to death.

MARK 15:6-24

Language

New American Standard 1995	Koine Greek
[6] Now at *the* feast he used to release for them *any* one prisoner whom they requested. [7] The man named Barabbas had been imprisoned with the insurrectionists who had committed murder in the insurrection. [8] The crowd went up and began asking him *to do* as he had been accustomed to do for them. [9] Pilate answered them, saying, "Do you want me to release for you the King of the Jews?" [10] For he was aware that the chief priests had handed Him over because of envy. [11] But the chief priests stirred up the crowd *to ask* him to release Barabbas for them instead. [12] Answering again, Pilate said to them, "Then what shall I do with Him whom you call the King of the Jews?" [13] They shouted back, "Crucify Him!" [14] But Pilate said to them, "Why, what evil has He done?" But they shouted all the more, "Crucify Him!" [15] Wishing to satisfy the crowd, Pilate released Barabbas for them, and after having Jesus scourged, he handed Him over to be crucified.	[6] Κατὰ δὲ ἑορτὴν ἀπέλυεν αὐτοῖς ἕνα δέσμιον, ὅνπερ ἠτοῦντο. [7] Ἦν δὲ ὁ λεγόμενος Βαραββᾶς μετὰ τῶν συστασιαστῶν δεδεμένος, οἵτινες ἐν τῇ στάσει φόνον πεποιήκεισαν. [8] Καὶ ἀναβοήσας ὁ ὄχλος ἤρξατο αἰτεῖσθαι καθὼς ἀεὶ ἐποίει αὐτοῖς. [9] Ὁ δὲ Πιλᾶτος ἀπεκρίθη αὐτοῖς, λέγων, Θέλετε ἀπολύσω ὑμῖν τὸν βασιλέα τῶν Ἰουδαίων; [10] Ἐγίνωσκεν γὰρ ὅτι διὰ φθόνον παραδεδώκεισαν αὐτὸν οἱ ἀρχιερεῖς. [11] Οἱ δὲ ἀρχιερεῖς ἀνέσεισαν τὸν ὄχλον, ἵνα μᾶλλον τὸν Βαραββᾶν ἀπολύσῃ αὐτοῖς. [12] Ὁ δὲ Πιλᾶτος ἀποκριθεὶς πάλιν εἶπεν αὐτοῖς, Τί οὖν θέλετε ποιήσω ὃν λέγετε βασιλέα τῶν Ἰουδαίων; [13] Οἱ δὲ πάλιν ἔκραξαν, Σταύρωσον αὐτόν. [14] Ὁ δὲ Πιλᾶτος ἔλεγεν αὐτοῖς, Τί γὰρ κακὸν ἐποίησεν; Οἱ δὲ περισσοτέρως ἔκραξαν, Σταύρωσον αὐτόν. [15] Ὁ δὲ Πιλᾶτος βουλόμενος τῷ ὄχλῳ τὸ ἱκανὸν ποιῆσαι, ἀπέλυσεν αὐτοῖς τὸν Βαραββᾶν καὶ παρέδωκεν τὸν Ἰησοῦν, φραγελλώσας, ἵνα σταυρωθῇ.

Process of Discovery

Linguistics Section

Linguistic Structure

[Yeshua before the people] [6] Now at *the* feast he used to release for them *any* one prisoner whom they requested. [7] The man named Barabbas had been imprisoned with the insurrectionists who had committed murder in the insurrection. [8] The crowd went up and began asking him *to do* as he had been accustomed to do for them. [9] Pilate answered them, saying, "Do you want me to release for you the King of the Jews?" [10] For he was aware that the chief priests had handed Him over because of envy. [11] But the chief priests stirred up the crowd *to ask* him to release Barabbas for them instead. [12] Answering again, Pilate said to them, "Then what shall I do with Him whom you call the King of the Jews?" [13] They shouted back, "Crucify Him!" [14] But Pilate said to them, "Why, what evil has He done?" But they shouted all the more, "Crucify Him!" [15] Wishing to satisfy the crowd, Pilate released Barabbas for them, and after having Jesus scourged, he handed Him over to be crucified. [22] Pilate said to them, "Then what shall I do with Jesus who is called Christ?" They all said, "Let Him be crucified!" [23] And he said, "Why, what evil has He done?" But they kept shouting all the more, saying, "Let Him be crucified!" [24] And when Pilate saw that he was accomplishing nothing, but rather that a riot was starting, he took water and washed his hands in front of the multitude, saying, "I am innocent of this Man's blood; see *to that* yourselves." [25] And all the people answered and said, "His blood *be* on us and on our children!" [26] Then he released Barabbas for them; but after having Jesus scourged, he delivered Him to be crucified.

Discussion

Yeshua came before Pilate and offered no defense for the crimes he was accused of doing. During the Passover, Pilate released one prisoner from jail. It was a choice of Yeshua or Barabbas. The people called out for Barabbas.

Biblical Personalities

1. Barabbas – in Aramaic, this name is *bar abba*, which means "son of the father." The man brought out was a known criminal. His true identity is not known since his name is a generic statement about every man. His name is not as important as the actions of the people. It was the custom of the Judean governor to release a prisoner to the people. The people chose Barabbas. This astonished Pilate that the people wanted a known criminal released as opposed to Yeshua. The custom was to release whomever the people wanted; therefore, Pilate had no choice but to release Barabbas.

Culture Section

Discussion

Roman prefects had to learn the language of the local people. The conversation between Pilate and Yeshua would have been in Aramaic. When Pilate asked Yeshua if he was the king of the Jews, Yeshua's answer was *at amarat*. This Semitic phrase is subtle, and its meaning is based on facial expression, hand movement, and voice inflection. A direct translation to English is "You are saying this" or "That is what you say." Yeshua told Pilate that He never said those words and never thought of himself as a King. Yeshua's kingdom was the Kingdom of Heaven, not the Kingdom on Earth.[209]

No doubt, Pilate was surprised at the charges from the Sanhedrin. To Pilate, a simple Galilean peasant was standing before him. Pilate did not believe that Yeshua did anything wrong, especially something that required the death penalty. If Yeshua would have acknowledged His being the king of the Jews, then Pilate could have convicted Him immediately. Pilate wanted to be fair to Yeshua. He was always concerned about how his actions looked to Rome.

---

[209]Rocco A. Errico and George M. Lamsa, *Aramaic Light on the Gospel of Matthew: a Commentary on the Teachings of Jesus from the Aramaic and Unchanged Near Eastern Customs* (Santa Fe, NM: Noohra Foundation, 2000).

MARK 15:16-21

Language

New American Standard 1995	Koine Greek
[16] The soldiers took Him away into the palace (that is, the Praetorium), and they called together the whole *Roman* cohort. [17] They dressed Him up in purple, and after twisting a crown of thorns, they put it on Him; [18] and they began to acclaim Him, "Hail, King of the Jews!" [19] They kept beating His head with a reed, and spitting on Him, and kneeling and bowing before Him. [20] After they had mocked Him, they took the purple robe off Him and put His *own* garments on Him. And they led Him out to crucify Him. [21] They pressed into service a passer-by coming from the country, Simon of Cyrene (the father of Alexander and Rufus), to bear His cross.	[16] Οἱ δὲ στρατιῶται ἀπήγαγον αὐτὸν ἔσω τῆς αὐλῆς, ὅ ἐστιν πραιτώριον, καὶ συγκαλοῦσιν ὅλην τὴν σπεῖραν. [17] Καὶ ἐνδύουσιν αὐτὸν πορφύραν, καὶ περιτιθέασιν αὐτῷ πλέξαντες ἀκάνθινον στέφανον, [18] καὶ ἤρξαντο ἀσπάζεσθαι αὐτόν, Χαῖρε, ὁ βασιλεὺς τῶν Ἰουδαίων [19] καὶ ἔτυπτον αὐτοῦ τὴν κεφαλὴν καλάμῳ, καὶ ἐνέπτυον αὐτῷ, καὶ τιθέντες τὰ γόνατα προσεκύνουν αὐτῷ. [20] Καὶ ὅτε ἐνέπαιξαν αὐτῷ, ἐξέδυσαν αὐτὸν τὴν πορφύραν, καὶ ἐνέδυσαν αὐτὸν τὰ ἱμάτια τὰ ἴδια. Καὶ ἐξάγουσιν αὐτὸν ἵνα σταυρώσωσιν αὐτόν. [21] Καὶ ἀγγαρεύουσιν παράγοντά τινα Σίμωνα Κυρηναῖον, ἐρχόμενον ἀπ' ἀγροῦ, τὸν πατέρα Ἀλεξάνδρου καὶ Ῥούφου, ἵνα ἄρῃ τὸν σταυρὸν αὐτοῦ.

Process of Discovery

Linguistics Section

Linguistic Structure

[16] The soldiers took Him away into the palace (that is, the Praetorium), and they called together the whole *Roman* cohort. [17] They dressed Him up in purple, and after twisting a crown of thorns, they put it on Him; [18] and they began to acclaim Him, "Hail, King of the Jews!" [19] They kept beating His head with a reed, and spitting on Him, and kneeling and bowing before Him. [20] After they had mocked Him, they took the purple robe off Him and put His *own* garments on Him. And they led Him out to crucify Him. [21] They pressed into service a passer-by coming from the country, Simon of Cyrene (the father of Alexander and Rufus), to bear His cross.

Discussion

After Yeshua was flogged, He was humiliated by the Roman soldiers. After that, He was forced to carry His cross to the place of Golgotha.

Questioning the Passage

1. What does the crown of thorns represent? (v. 17)

   The crown represents a king's crown.

2. What does the reed represent? (v. 19)

   As a part of the mockery, the guards placed a reed in Yeshua's right hand to represent a king's scepter.

Biblical Locations

1. Where was Cyrene? (v. 21)

   Cyrene is the ancient name of Libya. The author of Matthew's Gospel wanted to have Gentile participate in the crucifixion. The author wanted to show that the Jews wanted Yeshua dead, and the Gentiles wanted Him alive. It is a false assumption that all Jews wanted Yeshua dead. Yeshua's disciples and the majority of followers were Jewish. This point is a sign of antisemitism added to the Gospel after establishing the Church and the results of the 66 CE revolt.

Culture Section

Questioning the passage

1. What is the significance of a purple (scarlet) robe? (v. 20)

   The cloth was made in Lebanon, and the color was derived from seashells. Only Kings could afford to wear a scarlet robe because it was a costly garment. A legend says that the scarlet robe belonged to a Maccabean King. Another legend says it was an old robe of Herod. Near Eastern people took great pride in dressing a man who claimed to be a king in royal clothing before he was put to death.[210]

   It was a common practice in Yeshua's day for kings and princes to confer royal garments upon their brave and distinguished men of valor. The scarlet robe was a symbol of authority, honor, and great acclaim. The color scarlet also stood for loyalty and a willingness to give one's life for others. For this reason, it is appropriate for Yeshua to have been dressed this way.

Cultural Echoes

1. Yeshua was dressed in a scarlet robe and mocked as the king of the Jews. The dressing of a person in a scarlet robe of honor is echoed in Esther 6:8-11.

   Esther 6:8-11 (NASB) [8] let them bring a royal robe which the king has worn, and *a* the horse on which the king has ridden, and on whose head *b* a royal crown has been placed; [9] and let the robe and the horse be handed over to one of the king's most noble princes and let them array the man whom the king desires to honor and lead him on horseback through the city

---

[210] Rocco A. Errico and George M. Lamsa, *Aramaic Light on the Gospel of Matthew: a Commentary on the Teachings of Jesus from the Aramaic and Unchanged Near Eastern Customs* (Santa Fe, NM: Noohra Foundation, 2000).

square, *a*and proclaim before him, 'Thus it shall be done to the man whom the king desires to honor.'"

[10]Then the king said to Haman, "Take quickly the robes and the horse as you have said, and do so for Mordecai the Jew, who is sitting at the king's gate; do not fall short in anything of all that you have said." [11] So Haman took the robe and the horse, and arrayed Mordecai, and led him *on horseback* through the city square, and proclaimed before him, "Thus it shall be done to the man whom the king desires to honor."

MARK 15:22-41

Language

New American Standard 1995	Koine Greek
[22] Then they brought Him to the place Golgotha, which is translated, Place of a Skull. [23] They tried to give Him wine mixed with myrrh; but He did not take it. [24] And they crucified Him, and divided up His garments among themselves, casting [1]lots for them *to decide* what each man should take. [25] It was the third hour [2]when they crucified Him. [26] The inscription of the charge against Him read, "THE KING OF THE JEWS." [27] They crucified two robbers with Him, one on His right and one on His left. [28] [And the Scripture was fulfilled which says, "And He was numbered with transgressors."] [29] Those passing by were hurling abuse at Him, wagging their heads, and saying, "Ha! You who *are going to* destroy the temple and rebuild it in three days, [30] save Yourself, and come down from the cross!" [31] In the same way the chief priests also, along with the scribes, were mocking *Him* among themselves and saying, "He saved others; He cannot save Himself. [32] "Let *this* Christ, the King of Israel, now come down from the cross, so that we may see and believe!" those who were crucified with Him were also insulting Him. [33] When the sixth hour came, darkness fell over the whole land until the ninth hour. [34] At the ninth hour Jesus cried out with a loud voice, "ELOI, ELOI, LAMA SABACHTHANI?" which is translated, "MY GOD, MY GOD, WHY HAVE YOU FORSAKEN ME?" [35] When some of the bystanders heard it, they *began* saying, "Behold, He is calling for Elijah." [36] Someone ran and filled a sponge with sour wine, put it on a reed, and gave Him a drink, saying, "[1]Let us see whether Elijah will come to take Him down." [37] And Jesus uttered a loud cry, and breathed His last. [38] And the veil of the temple was torn in two from top to bottom. [39] When the centurion, who was standing right in front of Him, saw the way He breathed His last, he said, "Truly this man was the Son of God!" [40] There were also *some* women looking on from a	[22] Καὶ φέρουσιν αὐτὸν ἐπὶ Γολγοθᾶ τόπον, ὅ ἐστιν μεθερμηνευόμενον, Κρανίου Τόπος. [23] Καὶ ἐδίδουν αὐτῷ πιεῖν ἐσμυρνισμένον οἶνον ὁ δὲ οὐκ ἔλαβεν. [24] Καὶ σταυρώσαντες αὐτόν, διεμερίζονται τὰ ἱμάτια αὐτοῦ, βάλλοντες κλῆρον ἐπ' αὐτά, τίς τί ἄρῃ. [25] Ἦν δὲ ὥρα τρίτη, καὶ ἐσταύρωσαν αὐτόν. [26] Καὶ ἦν ἡ ἐπιγραφὴ τῆς αἰτίας αὐτοῦ ἐπιγεγραμμένη, Ὁ βασιλεὺς τῶν Ἰουδαίων. [27] Καὶ σὺν αὐτῷ σταυροῦσιν δύο λῃστάς, ἕνα ἐκ δεξιῶν καὶ ἕνα ἐξ εὐωνύμων αὐτοῦ. [28] Καὶ ἐπληρώθη ἡ γραφὴ ἡ λέγουσα, Καὶ μετὰ ἀνόμων ἐλογίσθη. [29] Καὶ οἱ παραπορευόμενοι ἐβλασφήμουν αὐτόν, κινοῦντες τὰς κεφαλὰς αὐτῶν, καὶ λέγοντες, Οὐά, ὁ καταλύων τὸν ναόν, καὶ ἐν τρισὶν ἡμέραις οἰκοδομῶν, [30] σῶσον σεαυτόν, καὶ κατάβα ἀπὸ τοῦ σταυροῦ. [31] Ὁμοίως καὶ οἱ ἀρχιερεῖς ἐμπαίζοντες πρὸς ἀλλήλους μετὰ τῶν γραμματέων ἔλεγον, Ἄλλους ἔσωσεν, ἑαυτὸν οὐ δύναται σῶσαι. [32] Ὁ χριστὸς ὁ βασιλεὺς τοῦ Ἰσραὴλ καταβάτω νῦν ἀπὸ τοῦ σταυροῦ, ἵνα ἴδωμεν καὶ πιστεύσωμεν αὐτῷ. Καὶ οἱ συνεσταυρωμένοι αὐτῷ ὠνείδιζον αὐτόν. [33] Γενομένης δὲ ὥρας ἕκτης, σκότος ἐγένετο ἐφ' ὅλην τὴν γῆν ἕως ὥρας ἐνάτης. [34] Καὶ τῇ ὥρᾳ τῇ ἐνάτῃ ἐβόησεν ὁ Ἰησοῦς φωνῇ μεγάλῃ, λέγων, Ἐλωΐ, Ἐλωΐ, λιμὰ σαβαχθανί; Ὅ ἐστιν μεθερμηνευόμενον, Ὁ θεός μου, ὁ θεός μου, εἰς τί με ἐγκατέλιπες; [35] Καί τινες τῶν παρεστηκότων ἀκούσαντες ἔλεγον, Ἰδού, Ἡλίαν φωνεῖ. [36] Δραμὼν δὲ εἷς, καὶ γεμίσας σπόγγον ὄξους, περιθείς τε καλάμῳ, ἐπότιζεν αὐτόν, λέγων, Ἄφετε, ἴδωμεν εἰ ἔρχεται Ἡλίας καθελεῖν αὐτόν. [37] Ὁ δὲ Ἰησοῦς ἀφεὶς φωνὴν μεγάλην ἐξέπνευσεν. [38] Καὶ τὸ καταπέτασμα τοῦ ναοῦ ἐσχίσθη εἰς δύο ἀπὸ ἄνωθεν ἕως κάτω. [39] Ἰδὼν δὲ ὁ κεντυρίων ὁ παρεστηκὼς ἐξ ἐναντίας αὐτοῦ ὅτι οὕτως κράξας ἐξέπνευσεν, εἶπεν, Ἀληθῶς ὁ ἄνθρωπος οὗτος υἱὸς ἦν θεοῦ. [40] Ἦσαν δὲ καὶ γυναῖκες ἀπὸ μακρόθεν θεωροῦσαι, ἐν αἷς ἦν καὶ Μαρία ἡ Μαγδαληνή, καὶ Μαρία ἡ τοῦ Ἰακώβου τοῦ μικροῦ καὶ Ἰωσῆ

distance, among whom *were* Mary Magdalene, and Mary the mother of James the Less and Joses, and Salome. [41] When He was in Galilee, they used to follow Him and minister to Him; and *there were* many other women who came up with Him to Jerusalem.	μήτηρ, καὶ Σαλώμη, [41] αἱ καί, ὅτε ἦν ἐν τῇ Γαλιλαίᾳ, ἠκολούθουν αὐτῷ, καὶ διηκόνουν αὐτῷ, καὶ ἄλλαι πολλαὶ αἱ συναναβᾶσαι αὐτῷ εἰς Ἱεροσόλυμα.

Process of Discovery

Linguistics Section

Linguistic Structure

[Yeshua's crucifixion] [22] Then they brought Him to the place Golgotha, which is translated, Place of a Skull. [23] They tried to give Him wine mixed with myrrh; but He did not take it. [24] And they crucified Him, and divided up His garments among themselves, casting [1]lots for them *to decide* what each man should take. [25] It was the third hour when they crucified Him. [26] The inscription of the charge against Him read, "THE KING OF THE JEWS." [27] They crucified two robbers with Him, one on His right and one on His left. [28] [And the Scripture was fulfilled which says, "And He was numbered with transgressors."] [29] Those passing by were hurling abuse at Him, wagging their heads, and saying, "Ha! You who *are going to* destroy the temple and rebuild it in three days, [30] save Yourself, and come down from the cross!" [31] In the same way the chief priests also, along with the scribes, were mocking *Him* among themselves and saying, "He saved others; He cannot save Himself. [32] "Let *this* Christ, the King of Israel, now come down from the cross, so that we may see and believe!" Those who were crucified with Him were also insulting Him. [33] When the sixth hour came, darkness fell over the whole land until the ninth hour. [34] At the ninth hour Jesus cried out with a loud voice, "[b]ELOI, ELOI, LAMA SABACHTHANI?" which is translated, "MY GOD, MY GOD, WHY HAVE YOU FORSAKEN ME?" [35] When some of the bystanders heard it, they *began* saying, "Behold, He is calling for Elijah." [36] Someone ran and filled a sponge with sour wine, put it on a reed, and gave Him a drink, saying, "[1]Let us see whether Elijah will come to take Him down." [37] And Jesus uttered a loud cry, and breathed His last. [38] And the veil of the temple was torn in two from top to bottom. [39] When the centurion, who was standing right in front of Him, saw the way He breathed His last, he said, "Truly this man was the Son of God!" [40] There were also *some* women looking on from a distance, among whom *were* Mary Magdalene, and Mary the mother of James the Less and Joses, and Salome. [41] When He was in Galilee, they used to follow Him and minister to Him; and *there were* many other women who came up with Him to Jerusalem.

Discussion

This narrative is a description of the Crucifixion.

Questioning the Passage

1. Why were there two criminals crucified with Yeshua? (v. 27)

    It is not known why there would have been other men crucified with Yeshua. A note is

    that in Matthew's Gospel, neither of the criminals repented their sins and asked for

    Yeshua's forgiveness.

2. When was the sixth hour? (v. 33)

The sixth hour was noon. The ninth hour was 3:00 PM.

3. Why was Yeshua offered the wine and gall drink? (v. 36)

   This was a narcotic that was offered to a person being crucified because it deadened some of the pain that the person was about to endure. It was a merciful move by the Romans. Yeshua rejected the drink. He had to have been thirsty because He did not have water to drink since His arrest and after losing a lot of blood, His body would have desired water.

4. What is the significance of the veil in the Temple tearing? (v. 37)

   The author is noting that nature grieved when Yeshua died. Semitic people tear their clothing when a blood relative or a great hero dies in honor of them. Mark does not describe the darkness that came over the land, as the other authors did. Instead, he describes an earthquake that resulted in the veil in the Temple tearing.

   That veil was the one that separated the Ark of the Covenant from the public. The Holy of Holies was in the center of Solomon's Temple. Veils surrounded it. The tear is symbolic of the Word of the LORD becoming available to all people. Another symbolic view is that the LORD's love was now available to all the people of the Earth.[211]

Biblical Locations

1. Golgotha – its exact location is unknown. A church was built on a site near Jerusalem and declared the site of Yeshua's death by Emperor Constantine's mother.

Culture Section

Questioning the passage

1. What did Yeshua's cry from the cross mean? (V. 34)

---

[211] Rocco A. Errico and George M. Lamsa, *Aramaic Light on the Gospel of Matthew: a Commentary on the Teachings of Jesus from the Aramaic and Unchanged Near Eastern Customs* (Santa Fe, NM: Noohra Foundation, 2000).

Yeshua's cry has been misunderstood by the Church for centuries. Yeshua spoke Galilean Aramaic, not Koine Greek. If Yeshua cried out in the way the NASB says, then it would indicate that He did not understand what was happening to Him. It implies that the LORD did forsake Him. That is not the case. What Yeshua was crying out was his deep understanding of His reason to live and to die. His cry was a victory for the LORD. He was NOT abandoned at the cross.

Yeshua knew that His destiny was going to be death on a cross. He brought a message of peace and love into a sinful world. His death symbolizes the completion of His earthly task that the LORD gave to him. The cry was not a call for help. No Near Eastern martyr would have spoken of the LORD's desertion in the hour of their suffering.

The Galileans who were present at the cross knew that Yeshua means that His destiny was fulfilled. None of them mention it in their writings. Even Saint Paul, the apostle, never mentions Yeshua crying out at the cross. If the religious leaders at the cry had heard Yeshua crying out that the LORD had forsaken Him, they would have made an issue out of it and declared that Yeshua was definitely a sinner. The LORD abandons sinners because the sinners would be going to Sheol, and communication for them to the LORD would be cut off.

Semitic people believed that the manner of a man's death is predetermined. Therefore, they would not have believed that Yeshua said that the LORD forsook him. When death comes, Semitic people believed that the LORD was closer to the person than at any time in their lives. Therefore, Yeshua's cry was His declaration that He was fulfilling His destiny and was staying faithful to His teaching.

Yeshua would have said something like, "My LORD, my LORD, this is my destiny for which I was born." Yeshua would have forgiven the people for what they did to Him. It was all a part of the LORD's plan for His life. The Assyrian Church today teaches that the LORD was with Yeshua through His death on the cross to His ascension.

Why would the LORD abandon His beloved Son on the cross? From the culture of the day, it is clear that this would not have happened. So, why did the Church change the meaning of

Yeshua's last words? The words that the author of Mark's Gospel uses comes from Psalm 22. The casting of lots for Yeshua's clothing is derived from this Psalm.

Psalm 22 has been considered by the Church as a sign of the inclusion of Gentiles into the Kingdom of Heaven when Yeshua died. The Gospel writers probably added Psalm 22 to the crucifixion narrative. It would reinforce the idea that Yeshua came for the Gentiles since the Jews rejected Yeshua. Yeshua's mission was to include all the peoples of the Earth into the Kingdom of Heaven, first the Jews and then the Gentiles. Paul makes that clear in Romans 1:16. The inclusion of the Gentiles by having Psalm 22 as a part of the story reinforces Paul's statement that the Gospel is for Jews and Gentiles.

Based on the culture of Yeshua's day, His last words were changed by the authors of the Gospel, or the Church later on, to reflect the addition of the Gentiles into the Kingdom of Heaven.

MARK 15:42-47

Language

New American Standard 1995	Koine Greek
[42] When evening had already come, because it was the preparation day, that is, the day before the Sabbath, [43] Joseph of Arimathea came, a prominent member of the Council, who himself was waiting for the kingdom of God; and he gathered up courage and went in before Pilate, and asked for the body of Jesus. [44] Pilate wondered if He was dead by this time, and summoning the centurion, he questioned him as to whether He was already dead. [45] And ascertaining this from the centurion, he granted the body to Joseph. [46] Joseph bought a linen cloth, took Him down, wrapped Him in the linen cloth and laid Him in a tomb which had been hewn out in the rock; and he rolled a stone against the entrance of the tomb. [47] Mary Magdalene and Mary the *mother* of Joses were looking on *to see* where He was laid.	[42] Καὶ ἤδη ὀψίας γενομένης, ἐπεὶ ἦν Παρασκευή, ὅ ἐστιν προσάββατον, [43] ἦλθεν Ἰωσηφ ὁ ἀπὸ Ἀριμαθαίας, εὐσχήμων βουλευτής, ὃς καὶ αὐτὸς ἦν προσδεχόμενος τὴν βασιλείαν τοῦ θεοῦ· τολμήσας εἰσῆλθεν πρὸς Πιλᾶτον, καὶ ἠτήσατο τὸ σῶμα τοῦ Ἰησοῦ. [44] Ὁ δὲ Πιλᾶτος ἐθαύμασεν εἰ ἤδη τέθνηκεν καὶ προσκαλεσάμενος τὸν κεντυρίωνα, ἐπηρώτησεν αὐτὸν εἰ πάλαι ἀπέθανεν. [45] Καὶ γνοὺς ἀπὸ τοῦ κεντυρίωνος, ἐδωρήσατο τὸ σῶμα τῷ Ἰωσήφ. [46] Καὶ ἀγοράσας σινδόνα, καὶ καθελὼν αὐτόν, ἐνείλησεν τῇ σινδόνι, καὶ κατέθηκεν αὐτὸν ἐν μνημείῳ, ὃ ἦν λελατομημένον ἐκ πέτρας καὶ προσεκύλισεν λίθον ἐπὶ τὴν θύραν τοῦ μνημείου. [47] Ἡ δὲ Μαρία ἡ Μαγδαληνὴ καὶ Μαρια Ἰωσῆ ἐθεώρουν ποῦ τίθεται.

Process of Discovery

Linguistics Section

Linguistic Structure

[Yeshua's Burial] [42] When evening had already come, because it was the preparation day, that is, the day before the Sabbath, [43] Joseph of Arimathea came, a prominent member of the Council, who himself was waiting for the kingdom of God; and he gathered up courage and went in before Pilate, and asked for the body of Jesus. [44] Pilate wondered if He was dead by this time, and summoning the centurion, he questioned him as to whether He was already dead. [45] And ascertaining this from the centurion, he granted the body to Joseph. [46] Joseph bought a linen cloth, took Him down, wrapped Him in the linen cloth and laid Him in a tomb which had been hewn out in the rock; and he rolled a stone against the entrance of the tomb. [47] Mary Magdalene and Mary the *mother* of Joses were looking on *to see* where He was laid.

Discussion

This section of chapter twenty-seven describes Yeshua's burial.

Biblical Personalities

1. Joseph of Arimathea – "Joseph of Arimathea is venerated as a saint by the Roman Catholic, Eastern Orthodox, and some Protestant churches. The traditional Roman calendar marked his feast day on 17 March, but he is now listed, along with Saint Nicodemus, on 31 August in the Martyrologium Romanum. Eastern Orthodox churches commemorate him on the *Third Sunday of Pascha* (i.e., the second Sunday after Easter) and on 31 July, the date shared by Lutheran churches.[3] Although a series of legends developed during the Middle Ages (perhaps elaborations of early New Testament Apocrypha) tied this Joseph to Britain as well as the Holy Grail, he is not currently on the abbreviated liturgical calendar of the Church of England, although this Joseph is on the calendars of some churches of the Anglican communion, such as the Episcopal Church, which commemorates him on 1 August."[212]

---

[212] "Joseph of Arimathea," Wikipedia (Wikimedia Foundation, September 4, 2020), https://en.wikipedia.org/wiki/Joseph_of_Arimathea. Accessed September 29, 2020

Thoughts on Chapter 15

This chapter offers a conclusion of Yeshua's ministry in a way that shines a light on the Gentiles and condemns the Jews. Unfortunately, the author decided to write his Gospel in this manner. Yeshua, the Messiah, came for the Jews and the Gentiles. Not every Jew in Yeshua's time wanted Him to be eliminated. His disciples were twelve Jewish men. Most of the earliest followers of Yeshua's way were Jewish. The Gentile takeover of the early Church is demonstrated in the presentation of the chapter. Several steps of Yeshua's death correspond to Scripture, which implies Gentile inclusion. Unfortunately, this antisemitic attitude arose in the Church in its infancy.

Reflections on Chapter 15

How many people today would die for what they believed and preached? Not many. Yeshua's words and ways are from the LORD because He was willing to die to preach those words. The only way the leaders of the day shut Yeshua down was by their execution of Him. To their dismay, three days later, Yeshua rose from the grave and became even more popular than when He was alive. How can a religion based on peace and love, hate anybody? It should not, but antisemitism still runs rampant in the churches today. It is a sad commentary to write that the Church and some of its members do not always follow the teachings of their founder, Yeshua of Nazareth.

MARK 16:1-8

Language

New American Standard 1995	Koine Greek
¹ When the Sabbath was over, Mary Magdalene, and Mary the *mother* of James, and Salome, bought spices, so that they might come and anoint Him. ² Very early on the first day of the week, they came to the tomb when the sun had risen. ³ They were saying to one another, "Who will roll away the stone for us from the entrance of the tomb?" ⁴ Looking up, they saw that the stone had been rolled away, although it was extremely large. ⁵ Entering the tomb, they saw a young man sitting at the right, wearing a white robe; and they were amazed. ⁶ And he said to them, ""Do not be amazed; you are looking for Jesus the Nazarene, who has been crucified. He has risen; He is not here; behold, *here is* the place where they laid Him. ⁷ "But go, tell His disciples and Peter, ""He is going ahead of you to Galilee; there you will see Him, just as He told you."" ⁸ They went out and fled from the tomb, for trembling and astonishment had gripped them; and they said nothing to anyone, for they were afraid.	1 Καὶ διαγενομένου τοῦ σαββάτου, Μαρία ἡ Μαγδαληνὴ καὶ Μαρία ˹Ἰακώβου˺ καὶ Σαλώμη ἠγόρασαν ἀρώματα, ἵνα ἐλθοῦσαι ἀλείψωσιν αὐτόν. ² Καὶ λίαν πρωῒ τῆς μιᾶς σαββάτων ἔρχονται ἐπὶ τὸ μνημεῖον, ἀνατείλαντος τοῦ ἡλίου. ³ Καὶ ἔλεγον πρὸς ἑαυτάς, Τίς ἀποκυλίσει ἡμῖν τὸν λίθον ἐκ τῆς θύρας τοῦ μνημείου; ⁴ Καὶ ἀναβλέψασαι θεωροῦσιν ὅτι ἀποκεκύλισται ὁ λίθος· ἦν γὰρ μέγας σφόδρα. ⁵ Καὶ εἰσελθοῦσαι εἰς τὸ μνημεῖον, εἶδον νεανίσκον καθήμενον ἐν τοῖς δεξιοῖς, περιβεβλημένον στολὴν λευκήν· καὶ ἐξεθαμβήθησαν. ⁶ Ὁ δὲ λέγει αὐταῖς, Μὴ ἐκθαμβεῖσθε· Ἰησοῦν ζητεῖτε τὸν Ναζαρηνὸν τὸν ἐσταυρωμένον· ἠγέρθη, οὐκ ἔστιν ὧδε· ἴδε, ὁ τόπος ὅπου ἔθηκαν αὐτόν. ⁷ Ἀλλ' ὑπάγετε, εἴπατε τοῖς μαθηταῖς αὐτοῦ καὶ τῷ Πέτρῳ ὅτι Προάγει ὑμᾶς εἰς τὴν Γαλιλαίαν· ἐκεῖ αὐτὸν ὄψεσθε, καθὼς εἶπεν ὑμῖν. ⁸ Καὶ ἐξελθοῦσαι ἔφυγον ἀπὸ τοῦ μνημείου· εἶχεν δὲ αὐτὰς τρόμος καὶ ἔκστασις· καὶ οὐδενὶ οὐδὲν εἶπον, ἐφοβοῦντο γάρ.

Process of Discovery

Linguistics Section

Linguistic Structure

[The Resurrection] ¹ When the Sabbath was over, Mary Magdalene, and Mary the *mother* of James, and Salome, bought spices, so that they might come and anoint Him. ² Very early on the first day of the week, they came to the tomb when the sun had risen. ³ They were saying to one another, "Who will roll away the stone for us from the entrance of the tomb?" ⁴ Looking up, they saw that the stone had been rolled away, although it was extremely large. ⁵ Entering the tomb, they saw a young man sitting at the right, wearing a white robe; and they were amazed. ⁶ And he said to them, ""Do not be amazed; you are looking for Jesus the Nazarene, who has been crucified. He has risen; He is not here; behold, *here is* the place where they laid Him.

[The Commandment] ⁷ "But go, tell His disciples and Peter, "He is going ahead of you to Galilee; there you will see Him, just as He told you."" ⁸ They went out and fled from the tomb, for trembling and astonishment had gripped them; and they said nothing to anyone, for they were afraid.

Discussion

This is the story of Yeshua's resurrection.

Questioning the Passage

1. Why did the women decide to go to the tomb on Sunday morning (the first day of the week)? (v. 1)

    In the Near East, people believed that the living could communicate with the dead on the third day after death. Mourners thought that the person's spirit would be listening to them at the tomb. Therefore, the two women went to the tomb to say their goodbyes to Yeshua. They did not go to anoint the dead body as described in the other Gospels.

2. Who were the Marys? (v. 1)

    The Mary's of the Gospels are:²¹³

---

²¹³ Cole-Rous, Jim. "Home." Mary - The Other Mary. Accessed April 17, 2019. https://globalchristiancenter.com/christian-living/lesser-known-bible-people/31268-mary-the-other-mary.

- Mary Mother of Jesus: John

- Mary Magdalene: Matthew, Mark, Luke, John

- Mary, mother of James & Joses: Matthew, Mark, Luke,

- Mary, the wife of Clopas, (Luke calls him Alphaeus <u>Acts 1:13</u>) John.

- The other Mary.

- Salome, mother of James & John: Matthew, Mark, Luke

As shown in the list, the other Mary is distinguished from the list of known women named Mary. Mary's name was Miriam in Hebrew and Aramaic. It was a common name in Yeshua's day. There was another female follower of Yeshua called Mary, who did not receive any recognition beyond being named Mary.

3. Why did Yeshua pick Galilee to meet the disciples? (v. 7)
The Galilee is a logical place for Yeshua to meet His disciples. The Galilee was where His mission started. His mission did not end in the Galilee. Yeshua transferred His mission to His disciples and followers. The task has been passed down throughout the centuries to His current followers.

Culture Section

Questioning the passage

1. Why is it necessary that the three women saw the empty tomb? (v. 1)
According to the Torah, if two or three people observe a sin, then it is confirmed. This law also would apply to the viewing of a sign or miracle. Therefore, Mark has three women finding the empty tomb. Thus, the disciples and followers of Yeshua must have believed them. The disciples and followers gathered in the Galilee at the end of the gospel to see the risen Yeshua.

[15] "A single witness shall not rise up against a man on account of any iniquity or any sin which he has committed; on the evidence of two or three witnesses, a matter shall be confirmed. (Deut. 19:15 NAU)

Thoughts

By questioning the passage, I discovered a vast amount of information in this narrative. For example, there are connections in the narrative to biblical events in the book of Daniel. Matthew's decision that the Risen Yeshua was of flesh and blood comes forth by the women touching Him. The event was witnessed by two women who fulfill the Deuteronomy passage about the evidence of seeing an event. The foundation of the Christian faith is the Resurrection of Yeshua. The LORD demonstrated His love for us by sending Yeshua with the message of the Kingdom of Heaven and how we can resolve our sinful lives to the LORD's satisfaction. Yeshua died to bring us the message of salvation. Now all of Yeshua's followers need to follow His interpretation of the Torah and the Prophets so that we are pleasing to the LORD and will one day enter His Heaven.

Reflections

The resurrection event is a critical story of the Gospels that holds the faith together. For many Christians, every story in the Gospels must be historically accurate. But as one matures in the faith and comes to understand that the Scriptures were written using allegories and metaphors, the need to view every narrative as fact changes. However, this final story of the Resurrection of Yeshua is a factual story at its core. It is a fact that Yeshua rose that first Easter morning. The details of the story were not crucial to the Hebrew storytellers. The fact that Yeshua rose from the grave is what matters and is the truth of the narrative. Yeshua's Resurrection is a fact described by Josephus, Philo and even the Koran. His Resurrection is proof that everything Yeshua taught is the truth and what the LORD expects of us.

MARK 16:9-19

Language

New American Standard 1995	Koine Greek
[9] [Now after He had risen early on the first day of the week, He first appeared to Mary Magdalene, from whom He had cast out seven demons. [10] She went and reported to those who had been with Him, while they were mourning and weeping. [11] When they heard that He was alive and had been seen by her, they refused to believe it. [12] After that, He appeared in a different form to two of them while they were walking along on their way to the country. [13] They went away and reported it to the others, but they did not believe them either. [14] Afterward He appeared to the eleven themselves as they were reclining *at the table;* and He reproached them for their unbelief and hardness of heart, because they had not believed those who had seen Him after He had risen. [15] And He said to them, "Go into all the world and preach the Gospel to all creation. [16] "He who has believed and has been baptized shall be saved; but he who has disbelieved shall be condemned. [17] "These signs will accompany those who have believed: in My name they will cast out demons, they will speak with new tongues; [18] they will pick up serpents, and if they drink any deadly *poison,* it will not hurt them; they will lay hands on the sick, and they will recover." [19] So then, when the Lord Jesus had spoken to them, He was received up into heaven and sat down at the right hand of God. [20] And they went out and preached everywhere, while the Lord worked with them, and confirmed the word by the signs that followed.] [And they promptly reported all these instructions to Peter and his companions. And after that, Jesus Himself sent out through them from east to west the sacred and imperishable proclamation of eternal salvation.]	[9] Ἀναστὰς δὲ πρωῒ πρώτη σαββάτου ἐφάνη πρῶτον Μαρίᾳ τῇ Μαγδαληνῇ, ἀφ' ἧς ἐκβεβλήκει ἑπτὰ δαιμόνια. [10] Ἐκείνη πορευθεῖσα ἀπήγγειλεν τοῖς μετ' αὐτοῦ γενομένοις, πενθοῦσιν καὶ κλαίουσιν. [11] Κἀκεῖνοι ἀκούσαντες ὅτι ζῇ καὶ ἐθεάθη ὑπ' αὐτῆς ἠπίστησαν. [12] Μετὰ δὲ ταῦτα δυσὶν ἐξ αὐτῶν περιπατοῦσιν ἐφανερώθη ἐν ἑτέρᾳ μορφῇ, πορευομένοις εἰς ἀγρόν. [13] Κἀκεῖνοι ἀπελθόντες ἀπήγγειλαν τοῖς λοιποῖς οὐδὲ ἐκείνοις ἐπίστευσαν. [14] Ὕστερον ἀνακειμένοις αὐτοῖς τοῖς ἕνδεκα ἐφανερώθη, καὶ ὠνείδισεν τὴν ἀπιστίαν αὐτῶν καὶ σκληροκαρδίαν, ὅτι τοῖς θεασαμένοις αὐτὸν ἐγηγερμένον οὐκ ἐπίστευσαν. [15] Καὶ εἶπεν αὐτοῖς, Πορευθέντες εἰς τὸν κόσμον ἅπαντα, κηρύξατε τὸ εὐαγγέλιον πάσῃ τῇ κτίσει. [16] Ὁ πιστεύσας καὶ βαπτισθεὶς σωθήσεται ὁ δὲ ἀπιστήσας κατακριθήσεται. [17] Σημεῖα δὲ τοῖς πιστεύσασιν ταῦτα παρακολουθήσει ἐν τῷ ὀνόματί μου δαιμόνια ἐκβαλοῦσιν γλώσσαις λαλήσουσιν καιναῖς [18] ὄφεις ἀροῦσιν κἂν θανάσιμόν τι πίωσιν, οὐ μὴ αὐτοὺς βλάψῃ ἐπὶ ἀρρώστους χεῖρας ἐπιθήσουσιν, καὶ καλῶς ἕξουσιν. [19] Ὁ μὲν οὖν κύριος, μετὰ τὸ λαλῆσαι αὐτοῖς, ἀνελήφθη εἰς τὸν οὐρανόν, καὶ ἐκάθισεν ἐκ δεξιῶν τοῦ θεοῦ. [20] Ἐκεῖνοι δὲ ἐξελθόντες ἐκήρυξαν πανταχοῦ, τοῦ κυρίου συνεργοῦντος, καὶ τὸν λόγον βεβαιοῦντος διὰ τῶν ἐπακολουθούντων σημείων. Ἀμήν.

Process of Discovery

Linguistics Section

Linguistic Structure

[9] Now after He had risen early on the first day of the week, He first appeared to Mary Magdalene, from whom He had cast out seven demons. [10] She went and reported to those who had been with Him, while they were mourning and weeping. [11] When they heard that He was alive and had been seen by her, they refused to believe it. [12] After that, He appeared in a different form to two of them while they were walking along on their way to the country. [13] They went away and reported it to the others, but they did not believe them either. [14] Afterward He appeared to the eleven themselves as they were reclining *at the table;* and He reproached them for their unbelief and hardness of heart, because they had not believed those who had seen Him after He had risen. [15] And He said to them, "Go into all the world and preach the Gospel to all creation. [16] "He who has believed and has been baptized shall be saved; but he who has disbelieved shall be condemned. [17] "These signs will accompany those who have believed: in My name they will cast out demons, they will speak with new tongues; [18] they will pick up serpents, and if they drink any deadly *poison,* it will not hurt them; they will lay hands on the sick, and they will recover." [19] So then, when the Lord Jesus had spoken to them, He was received up into heaven and sat down at the right hand of God. [20] And they went out and preached everywhere, while the Lord worked with them, and confirmed the word by the signs that followed.

(this narrative was added later to the original Mark Gospel)

[And they promptly reported all these instructions to Peter and his companions. And after that, Jesus Himself sent out through them from east to west the sacred and imperishable proclamation of eternal salvation.]

(this narrative was added later to the original Mark Gospel)

Discussion

This narrative is not found in the earliest copies of Mark's Gospel. It was either not important to the author that Yeshua appeared to anyone after the resurrection or it was lost from the original.

Culture Section

Questioning the passage

1. What did baptism mean in Yeshua's day? (v. 16)

    Only true believers were to be baptized. To be a true believer, a person has to accept the belief and practices of Yeshua. One had to demonstrate that they believed in loving kindness, meekness, peacemaking, compassion, and inclusiveness of others into the Kingdom of Heaven. When a person is baptized in Yeshua's name, it means that he or she has become a participant in Yeshua's way of life. Baptism by water became a mark of initiation and identification of a believer in Yeshua.[214]

2. What does it mean that disbelievers will be condemned? (v. 16)

    Yeshua would have never threatened people. Therefore, modern scholars believe that this was added to Mark's Gospel by the church to maintain control over the people. People who are baptized and continue to practice evil will be condemned along with the world's sinners. The church probably used this addition to excommunicate people.

3. What kind of signs can believers perform? (v. 17)

    Signs and miracles were considered synonyms in Yeshua's day. The Aramaic word for miracle is *tedmorta*. The root word *damar* means "to be seized with astonishment or surprise." The phrase "it is a miracle" was very common. It does not mean that something supernatural had occurred. Anything that caused astonishment or surprise was considered a miracle. For

---

[214] Rocco A. Errico, George M. Lamsa, and George M. Lamsa, *Aramaic Light on the Gospels of Mark and Luke: a Commentary on the Teachings of Jesus from the Aramaic and Unchanged Near Eastern Customs* (Smyrna, GA: Noohra Foundation, 2001).

example, when a sick person recovers, Semites say, "it is a miracle." When a woman could economize her family budget and feed her family and guests well, it was called a miracle.[215]

4. What does "speaking with new tongues" mean? (v. 17)

This phrase means that the disciples of Yeshua were able to speak other languages. The Holy Spirit helped the missionaries to learn to speak a new language. Many times it was a language that they had never heard before. This ability allowed them to spread the Gospel to different parts of the world. The Holy Spirit guided them.

A "new tongue" also means that a new teaching is proclaimed. The Gospel of the LORD's kingdom of peace and hope was a "new tongue."

5. What does "pick up snakes" mean? (v. 18)

It was normal to have snakes and scorpions crawling on the floor in Near Eastern homes. Little children would pick them up and play with them. The snakes seldomly bit the children. The phrase "pick up snakes" should not be taken literally. Picking up snakes is not a test of one's loyalty to Yeshua. It means that a person will have faith in the LORD no matter the circumstance. The person should know that the LORD protects them.[216]

"Picking up snakes" is an Aramaic idiom that means overcoming one's enemies. The apostles had many enemies because of the teachings of Yeshua. Semitic people call their enemies snakes. They knew that the LORD would protect them.

6. What does it mean that poison would not hurt a follower? (v. 18)

If a person wanted to dispose of an enemy, a banquet would be held in honor of said person in the Near East. Poison would be added to the person's wine which usually killed the person. Suppose a person drinks poison and begins to fear it. The body's vitality and resistance to the poison are diminished, resulting in death. It is an expression of faith in the LORD that He would steer the follower away from dangers.

---

[215] IBID.
[216] IBID.

Thoughts

What is the message of this final narrative in Mark's Gospel? It offers a view of what baptism in Yeshua's name is all about. Today the church says that when a person is baptized, they die with Yeshua and rise with Yeshua into a new life. That fits with the original meaning. The baptism ritual uses flowery language to express the understanding that a person baptized in the name of Yeshua wants to live their life in a way that would please Yeshua. How do you do that? The answer is by reading the Gospels and acting in a way that follows how Yeshua lived. It sounds simple but is a difficult road.

Reflections

Why are there so many people in the church who claim to be followers of Yeshua but do not act like Him? Just sit in on a church leadership team meeting if you do not believe me. A different opinion is a great thing to have. It hopefully opens up ones thinking and expands ideas. Many times it causes arguments and pain. Why are there so many Christian denominations? Because people cannot learn to work with others through their differences of opinion. The "peace churches" have many denominations because when a disagreement occurs, they split the church. If the church intends to survive into the future, the membership needs to learn to work together.

BIBLIOGRAPHY

(Note that there are some additional references in the footnotes that do not appear in the bibliography)

"Abiathar." Encyclopædia Britannica. Encyclopædia Britannica, inc. Accessed April 27, 2022. https://www.britannica.com/biography/Abiathar.

Bible Map: Sidon. Accessed December 8, 2020. https://bibleatlas.org/full/sidon.htm.

Danker, Frederick W., William Arndt, and Walter Bauer. *A Greek-English Lexicon of the New Testament and Other Early Christian Literature*. Chicago: University of Chicago Press, 2000.

Davis, Anne Kimball. *The Synoptic Gospels - MP3*. Albuquerque, NM: Bibleinteract, 2012.

Errico, Rocco A., George M. Lamsa, and George M. Lamsa. *Aramaic Light on the Gospels of Mark and Luke: a Commentary on the Teachings of Jesus from the Aramaic and Unchanged Near Eastern Customs*. Smyrna, GA: Noohra Foundation, 2001.

Footalk. Sandals in Biblical Times, January 1, 1970. https://historyofsandals.blogspot.com/2010/11/biblical-sandals.html.

Funk, Robert Walter, and Roy W. Hoover. *The Five Gospels: the Search for the Authentic Words of Jesus: New Translation and Commentary*. San Francisco: HarperSanFrancisco, 2007.

"Galilee." Encyclopædia Britannica. Encyclopædia Britannica, inc. Accessed December 8, 2020. https://www.britannica.com/place/Galilee-region-Israel.

"Galilee." Wikipedia. Wikimedia Foundation, April 8, 2022. https://en.wikipedia.org/wiki/Galilee.

Gethsemane. Accessed March 22, 2022. https://2.bp.blogspot.com/-RFYxRW5VQh0/Wq5Q3VRAfsI/AAAAAAAAAg8/J8kD6Zp3rkokbxsfo_IMzSiNkr7Hpo OHQCLcBGAs/s1600/city%2Bof%2Bjerusalem%2Bmap.jpg.

Glenn, Mike, Laura Barringer; Scot McKnight, Scot McKnight, and Heather Hart. "Why Jesus Talked So Much about Agriculture." Jesus Creed | A Blog by Scot McKnight. Accessed February 3, 2021. https://www.christianitytoday.com/scot-mcknight/2020/january/why-jesus-talked-so-much-about-agriculture.html.

"God's Feminine Attributes." The Moody Church. Accessed October 7, 2020. https://www.moodychurch.org/gods-feminine-attributes/.

GotQuestions.org. "Home." GotQuestions.org, April 7, 2015. https://www.gotquestions.org/shake-dust-off-feet.html.

GotQuestions.org. "Home." GotQuestions.org, January 30, 2018. https://www.gotquestions.org/Moses-on-Mount-Sinai.html.

"Home." Bible Study. Accessed April 27, 2022. https://www.biblestudy.org/meaning-names/idumea.html.

"IdumeaMeaning of Bible Names." Bible Study. Accessed December 8, 2020. https://www.biblestudy.org/meaning-names/idumea.html.

"Institute for Historical Review." Mithraism: Formidable Rival to Early Christianity. Accessed April 27, 2022. http://www.ihr.org/jhr/v13/v13n2p34_weber.html.

Jakes, Michael, Meg Bucher, Frank Santora, Clarence L. Haynes Jr., and Bethany Pyle. "Dalmanutha Definition and Meaning - Bible Dictionary." biblestudytools.com. Accessed May 11, 2021. https://www.biblestudytools.com/dictionary/dalmanutha/.

"Judea." Ark of the Covenant - Bible History Online. Accessed December 8, 2020. https://www.bible-history.com/geography/ancient-israel/judea.html.

Koplitz, Michael Harvey. *Understanding Daniel.* York, PA: Independently Published, 2019.

"Literary Structure (Chiasm, Chiasmus) of Gospel of Mark." Literary structure (chiasm, chiasmus) of each pericopes of Gospel of Mark. Accessed March 2, 2021. http://www.bible.literarystructure.info/bible/41_Mark_pericope_e.html.

Lucey, Candice. "What Is THE APOLLYON?" Christianity.com. Salem Web Network, June 2, 2020. https://www.christianity.com/wiki/christian-terms/what-is-the-apollyon.html.

Mark, Joshua J. "Tyre." Ancient History Encyclopedia. Ancient History Encyclopedia, December 8, 2020. https://www.ancient.eu/Tyre/.

Moore, Sarah. "How Long Do Wheat Plants Take Before the Harvest?" Home Guides | SF Gate, November 17, 2020. https://homeguides.sfgate.com/long-wheat-plants-before-harvest-69823.html.

Murai, Hajime. "Literary Structure (Chiasm, Chiasmus) of Gospel of Mark." Literary structure (chiasm, chiasmus) of each pericopes of Gospel of Mark. Accessed October 12, 2021. http://www.bible.literarystructure.info/bible/41_Mark_pericope_e.html.

Myers, Ched. *Binding the Strong Man a Political Reading of Mark's Story of Jesus.* Maryknoll, NY: Orbis Books, 1988.

Nerushenko, Author Maria. "Get to Know the 12 Disciples of Jesus Christ: Apostle #9: Simon, the Zealot." The Talkative Man, August 31, 2017. https://www.talkativeman.com/apostle-simon-the-zealot/.

Nerushenko, Author Maria. "Get to Know the 12 Disciples of Jesus Christ: Apostle #9: Simon, the Zealot." The Talkative Man, August 31, 2017. https://www.talkativeman.com/apostle-simon-the-zealot/.

The New Interpreter's Bible: General Articles & Introduction, Commentary, & Reflections for Each Book of the Bible, Including the Apocryphal/Deuterocanonical Books. Nashville: Abingdon Press, 1994.

PastorStephenPugh, and Trevor Griffiths. "Salted with Fire." JerusalemPerspective.com Online. Accessed August 24, 2021. https://www.jerusalemperspective.com/2192/.

Richards, E. Randolph, and Brandon J. O'Brien. *Misreading Scripture with Western Eyes: Removing Cultural Blinders to Better Understand the Bible.* Downers Grove, IL: InterVarsity Press, 2012.

"Saint James." Encyclopædia Britannica. Encyclopædia Britannica, inc. Accessed October 20, 2020. https://www.britannica.com/biography/Saint-James-son-of-Zebedee.

Shell, Shellie Porter says: Victoria Moore says: Ciara says: Don Bennett says: Ralph Butcher says: and EP says: "God's Feminine Attributes." The Moody Church. Accessed April 7, 2020. https://www.moodychurch.org/gods-feminine-attributes/.

"Servant Songs." Wikipedia. Wikimedia Foundation, April 2, 2022. https://en.wikipedia.org/wiki/Servant_songs.

"Servant Songs." Wikipedia. Wikimedia Foundation, May 7, 2020. https://en.wikipedia.org/wiki/Servant_songs.

"St. James." Encyclopædia Britannica. Encyclopædia Britannica, inc. Accessed April 27, 2022. https://www.britannica.com/biography/Saint-James-son-of-Zebedee.

Steinsaltz, Adin. *The Soul.* New Milford, CT: Maggid Books, 2018.

Stern, David H. *Jewish New Testament Commentary: a Companion Volume to the Jewish New Testament.* Clarksville, MD: Jewish New Testament Publications, 1999.

Strugnell, John. "St. John the Baptist." Encyclopædia Britannica. Encyclopædia Britannica, inc., May 8, 2020. https://www.britannica.com/biography/Saint-John-the-Baptist.

Study.com. Accessed October 20, 2020. https://study.com/academy/lesson/andrew-the-apostle-biography-facts-death.html.

"Take Online Courses. Earn College Credit. Research Schools, Degrees & Careers." Study.com | Take Online Courses. Earn College Credit. Research Schools, Degrees & Careers. Accessed April 27, 2022. https://study.com/academy/lesson/andrew-the-apostle-biography-facts-death.html.

Toni. "History of John the Disciple of Jesus." AllAboutJesusChrist.org. All About Jesus Christ, June 20, 2005. https://www.allaboutjesuschrist.org/history-of-john-the-disciple-of-jesus-faq.htm.

Toni. "History of John the Disciple of Jesus." AllAboutJesusChrist.org. All About Jesus Christ, June 20, 2005. https://www.allaboutjesuschrist.org/history-of-john-the-disciple-of-jesus-faq.htm.

" ." The Ethiopian Orthodox Tewahedo Church. Accessed April 27, 2022. http://ethiopianorthodox.org/english/canonical/books.html.

www.ingramcontent.com/pod-product-compliance
Lightning Source LLC
Chambersburg PA
CBHW060557120726
48002CB00010B/2708